Thackray's 2014 Investor's Guide

THACKRAY'S 2014 INVESTOR'S GUIDE

Brooke Thackray MBA, CIM, CFP

Published in 2013 by: MountAlpha Media:
alphamountain.com

ISBN13: 978-0-9918735-0-0

Printed and Bound by Webcom Inc.
10 9 8 7 6 5 4 3 2 1

To my wife Jane

Acknowledgements

This book is the product of many years of research and could not have been written without the help of many people. I would like to thank my wife, Jane Steer-Thackray, and my children Justin, Megan, Carly and Madeleine, for the help they have given me and their patience during the many hours that I have devoted to writing this book. Thanks must be given to Wade Guenther for helping me source and filter a lot of the data in this book. I would also like to thank the proofreaders and editors, Amanda ODonnell and Jane Stiegler. Special mention goes to Jane for the countless hours she spent helping with writing, formatting and editing. This book could not have been written without her help.

INTRODUCTION

2014 THACKRAY'S INVESTOR'S GUIDE
Technical Commentary

The seasonal strategies that I have included in my previous books have proven to be very successful. The buy and sell dates are based upon iterative comparisons of different time periods measured by gain and frequency of success. Although the buy and sell dates are the optimal dates on which seasonal investors should focus on making their investment decisions, the markets have different dynamics from year to year, shifting the optimal buy and sell dates. Combining technical analysis with seasonal trends helps to adjust the decision process, allowing seasonal investors to enter and exit trades early or late, depending on market conditions.

The universe of technical indicators and techniques is huge. It is impossible to use all of the indicators. Only a small number of indicators and techniques that suit an investment style should be used. In the case of seasonal investing, a lot of long-term indicators provide very little benefit. For example, the standard Moving Average Convergence Divergence (MACD), is far too slow to be of any use. In this book I have chosen to illustrate the use of three technical indicators that have provided a lot of value in fine-tuning the dates for seasonal investing: Full Stochastic Oscillator (FSO), Relative Strength Index (RSI) and Relative Strength. The indicators are used in conjunction with the price pattern and moving averages of the security being considered. Investors must remember that technical analysis is not absolute and there will be exceptions when utilizing indicators and price patterns.

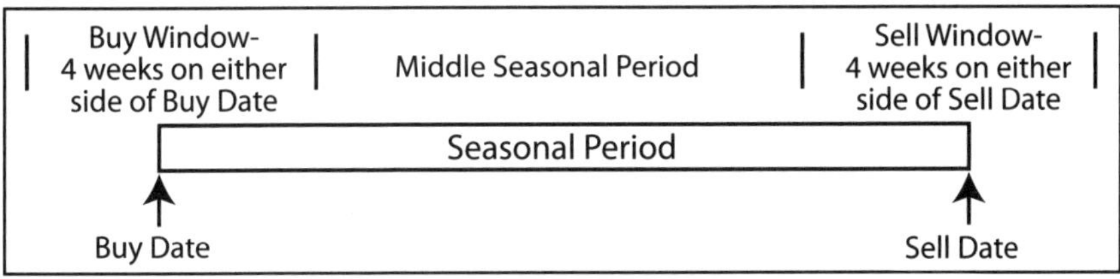

To combine technical indicators with seasonal trends, the indicators should only be used within the windows of the buy and sell dates. The indicators should be ignored outside the seasonal buy/sell windows. The only exception to this occurs when an indicator gives a signal during its seasonal middle period, which is in the seasonal period, but after the buy window and before the sell window. In this case a technical signal can support selling a full position based upon a fundamental breakdown in the price action of a security. By itself, a FSO or RSI indicator showing weakness in a security during its middle seasonal period, does not warrant action, it can only be used to support a decision being made in conjunction with underperformance relative to the broad market, or a major price action break.

Below are short descriptions of the three technical indicators that are used in this book and the metrics of how they are used with seasonal analysis. Full evaluation of the indicators and their uses with seasonal analysis is beyond the scope of this book.

Full Stochastic Oscillator (FSO)

A stochastic oscillator is a range bound momentum indicator that tracks the location of the close price relative to the high-low range, over a set number of periods. It tracks the momentum of price change and helps to indicate the strength and direction of price movement.

I have found that generally the best method to combine the FSO with seasonal trends is to buy an early partial position when the FSO turns up above 20 within four weeks of the seasonal buy date. Additionally, the best time to sell an early partial position occurs when the FSO turns below 80, within four weeks of the seasonal exit date.

For practical purposes in this book, %D, a 3 period smoothed %K, has been omitted. The standard variables are used in the FSO calculation (14 day look back period, and a 3 day simple moving average smoothing constant).

Relative Strength Index (RSI)

The RSI is a momentum oscillator that measures the speed and change of price movements. I have found that the best method to combine the RSI with seasonal trends is to buy an early partial position when the RSI turns up above 30 within four weeks of the seasonal buy date. The best time to sell an early partial position occurs when the RSI turns below 70, within four weeks of the seasonal exit date. Compared with the FSO, the RSI is less useful as it is slower and gives too few signals in the buy/sell windows.

Relative Strength

Relative strength calculates the performance of one security versus another security. When the relative strength is increasing, it indicates the seasonal security is outperforming. When the relative strength is declining, the seasonal security is underperforming. When a downward trend line is broken to the upside by the performance of the seasonal security, relative to the benchmark, this is a positive signal. This action carries a lot of weight and can justify a full early entry into a position if other technical evidence is positive. Likewise, if an upward trend line is broken to the downside, a negative technical signal is given and can justify a full early exit from a position if other technical evidence is negative.

THACKRAY'S 2014 INVESTOR'S GUIDE

You can choose great companies to invest in and still underperform the market. Unless you are in the market at the right time and in the best sectors, your investment expertise can be all for naught.

Successful investors know when they should be in the market. Very successful investors know when they should be in the market, and the best sectors in which to invest. *Thackray's 2014 Investor's Guide* is designed to provide investors with the knowledge of when and what to buy, and when to sell.

The goal of this book is to help investors capture extra profits by taking advantage of the seasonal trends in the markets. This book is straightforward. There are no complicated rules and there are no complex algorithms. The strategies put forward are intuitive and easy to understand.

It does not matter if you are a short-term or long-term investor, this book can be used to help establish entry and exit points. For the short-term investor, specific periods are identified that can provide profitable opportunities. For the long-term investor best buy dates are identified to launch new investments on a sound footing.

The stock market has its seasonal rhythms. Historically, the broad markets, such as the S&P 500, have a seasonal trend of outperforming during certain times of the year. Likewise, different sectors of the market have their own seasonal trends of outperformance. When oil stocks tend to do well in the springtime before "driving season," health care stocks tend to underperform the market. When utilities do well in the summertime, industrials do not. With different markets and different sectors having a tendency to outperform at different times of the year, there is always a place to invest.

Until recently, investors did not have access to the information necessary to analyse and create sector strategies. In recent years there have been a great number of sector Exchange Traded Funds (ETFs) and sector indexes introduced into the market. For the first time, investors are now able to easily implement a sector rotation strategy. This book provides a seasonal road map of what sectors tend to do well at different times of the year. It is a first of its kind, revealing new sector-based strategies that have never before been published.

In terms of market timing there are ample strategies in this book to help determine the times when equities should be over or underweight. During a favorable time for the market, investments can be purchased to overweight equities relative to their target weight in a portfolio (staying within risk tolerances). During an unfavorable time, investments can be sold to underweight equities relative to their target.

A large part of the book is devoted to sector seasonality – the underpinnings for a sector rotation strategy. The most practical rotation strategy is to create a core part of a portfolio that represents the broad market and then set aside an allocation to be rotated between favored sectors from one time period to the next.

It does not makes sense to apply any investment strategy only once with a large investment. Seasonal strategies are no exception. The best way to apply an investment strategy is to use a disciplined methodology that allows for diversification and a large enough number of investments to help remove the anomalies of the market. This reduces risk and increases the probability of a long term gain.

Following the specific buy and sell dates put forth in this book would have netted an investor large, above market returns. To "turbo-charge" gains, an investor can combine seasonality with technical analysis. As the seasonal periods are never exactly the same, technical analysis can help investors capture the extra gains when a sector turns up early, or momentum extends the trend.

IMPORTANT: Strategy Buy and Sell Dates
The beginning date of every strategy period in this book represents a full day in the market; therefore, investors should buy at the end of the preceding market day. For example the *Biotech Summer Solstice* seasonal period of strength is from June 23rd to September 13th. To be in the sector for the full seasonal period, an investor would enter the market before the closing bell on June 22nd. If the buy date landed on a weekend or holiday, then the buy would occur at the end of the preceding trading day.

The last day of a trading strategy is the sell date. For example, the Biotech sector investment would be sold at the end of the day on September 13th. If the sell date is a holiday or weekend, then the investment would be sold at the close on the preceding trading day.

What is Seasonal Investing?

In order to properly understand seasonal investing in the stock market, it is important to look briefly at its evolution. It may surprise investors to know that seasonal investing at the broad market level, i.e. Dow Jones or S&P 500, has been around for a long time. The initial seasonal strategies were written by Fields (1931, 1934) and Watchel (1942), who focused on the *January Effect*. Coincidentally, this strategy is still bantered about in the press every year.

Yale Yirsch Senior has been largely responsible for the next stage in the evolution, producing the *Stock Trader's Almanac* for more than forty years. This publication focuses on broad market trends such as the best six months of the year and tendencies of the market to do well depending on the political party in power and holiday trades.

In 1999, Brooke Thackray and Bruce Lindsay wrote, *Time In Time Out: Outsmart the Market Using Calendar Investment Strategies*. This work focused on a comprehensive analysis of the six month seasonal cycle and other shorter seasonal cycles in the broad markets such as the S&P 500.

Don Vialoux has written many articles on seasonal investing. His writings on this topic have developed a large following, via his free newsletter available at www.timingthemarket.ca.

Seasonal investing has changed over time. The focus has shifted from broad market strategies to taking advantage of sector rotation opportunities – investing in different sectors at different times of the year, depending on their seasonal strength. This has created a whole new set of investment opportunities. Rather than just being "in or out" of the market, investors can now always be invested by shifting between different sectors and asset classes, taking advantage of both up and down markets.

Definition – Seasonal investing is a method of investing in the market at the time of the year when it typically does well, or investing in a sector of the market when it typically outperforms the broad market such as the S&P 500.

The term seasonal investing is somewhat of a misnomer, and it is easy to see why some investors might believe that the discipline relates to investing based upon the seasons of the year – winter, spring, summer and autumn. Other than some agricultural commodities where the price is often correlated to growing seasons, generally seasonal investment strategies use the calendar as a reference for buy and sell dates. It is usually a specific event, i.e. Christmas sales, that occurs on a recurring annual basis that creates the seasonal opportunity.

The discipline of seasonal investing is not restricted to the stock market. It has been used successfully for a number of years in the commodities market. The opportunities in this market tend to be based upon changes in supply and/or demand that occur on a yearly basis. Most commodities, especially the agricultural commodities, tend to have cyclical supply cycles, i.e., crops are harvested only at certain times of the year. The supply bulge that occurs at the same time every year provides seasonal investors with profit opportunities. Recurring increased seasonal demand for commodities also plays a major part in providing opportunities for seasonal investors. This applies to most metals and many other commodities, whether the end-product is industrial or consumer based.

Seasonal investment strategies can be used with a lot of different types of investments. The premise is the same, outperformance during a certain period of the year based upon a repeating event in the markets or economy. In my past writings I have developed seasonal strategies that have been used successfully in the stock, commodity, bond and foreign exchange markets. Seasonal investing is still relatively new for most markets with a lot of new opportunities waiting to be discovered.

How Does Seasonal Investing Work?

Most stock market sector seasonal trends are the result of a recurring annual catalyst: an event that affects the sector positively. These events can range from a seasonal spike in demand, seasonal inventory lows, weather effects, conferences and other events. Mainstream investors very often anticipate a move in a sector and incorrectly try to take a position just before an event takes place that is supposed to drive a sector higher. A good example of this would be investors buying oil just before the cold weather sets in. Unfortunately, their efforts are usually unsuccessful as they are too late to the party and the opportunity has already passed.

By the time the anticipated event occurs, a substantial amount of investors have bought into the sector – fully pricing in the expected benefit. At this time there is little potential left in the short-term. Unless there is a strong positive surprise, the sector's outperformance tends to slowly roll over. If the event produces less than its desired result, the sector can be severely punished.

So how does the seasonal investor take advantage of this opportunity? "Be there" before the mainstream investors, and get out before they do. Seasonal investors usually enter a sector two or three months before an event is anticipated to have a positive effect on a sector and get out before the actual event takes place. In essence, seasonal investors are benefiting from the mainstream investor's tendency to "buy in" too late.

Seasonality in the markets occurs because of three major reasons: money flow, changing market analyst expectations and the *Anticipation-Realization Cycle*. First, money flows vary throughout the year and at different times of the month. Generally, money flows increase at the end of the year and into the start of the next year. This is a result of year end bonuses and tax related investments. In addition, money flows increase at month end from money managers "window dressing" their portfolios. As a result of these money flows, the months around the end of the year and the days around the end of the month, tend to have a stronger performance than the other times of the year.

Second, the analyst expectations cycle tends to push markets up at the end of the year and the beginning of the next year. Stock market analysts tend to be a positive bunch – the large investment houses pay them to be positive. They start the year with aggressive earnings for all of their favorite companies. As the year progresses, they generally back off their earnings forecast, which decreases their support for the market. After a lull in the summer and early autumn months, they start to focus on the next year with another rosy forecast. As a result, the stock market tends to rise once again at the end of the year.

Third, at the sector level, sectors of the market tend to be greatly influenced by the *Anticipation-Realization Cycle*. Although some investors may not be familiar with the term "anticipation-realization," they probably are familiar with the concept of "buy the rumor – sell the fact," or in the famous words of Lord Rothschild "Buy on the sound of the war-cannons; sell on the sound of the victory trumpets."

The *Anticipation-Realization Cycle* as it applies to human behavior has been much studied in psychology journals. In the investment world, the premise of this cycle rests on investors anticipating a positive event in the market to drive prices higher and buying in ahead of the event. When the event takes place, or is realized, upward pressure on prices decreases as there is very little impetus for further outperformance.

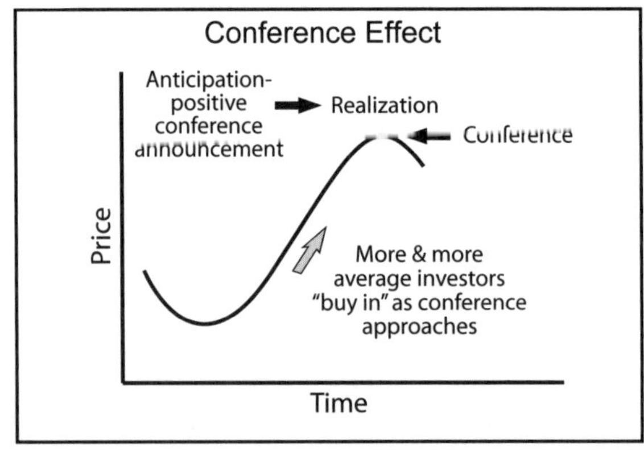

A good example of the *Anticipation-Realization Cycle* takes place with the "conference effect." Very often large industries have major conferences that occur at approximately the same time every year. Major companies in the industry often hold back positive announcements and product introductions to be released during the conference.

Two to three months prior to the conference, seasonal investors tend to buy into the sector. Shortly afterwards, the mainstream investors anticipate "good news" from the conference and start to buy in. As a result, prices are pushed up. Just before the conference starts, seasonal investors capture their profits by exiting their positions. As the conference unfolds, company announcements are made (realized), but as the potential good news has already been priced into the sector, there is little to push prices higher and the sector typically starts to rolls over.

The same *Anticipation-Realization Cycle* takes place with increased demand for oil to meet the "summer driving season", increased sales of goods at Christmas time, increased demand for gold jewellery to meet the autumn and winter demand, and many other events that tend to drive the outperformance of different sectors.

Does Seasonal Investing ALWAYS Work?

The simple answer to the above question is "No." There is not any investment system in the world that works all of the time. When following any investment system, it is probability of success that counts. It has often been said that "being correct in the markets 60% of the time will make you rich." Investors tend to forget this and become too emotionally attached to their losses. Just about every investment trading book states that investors typically fail to let their profits run and cut their losses quickly. I concur. In my many years in the investment industry, the biggest mistake that I have found with investors is not being able to cut their losses. Everyone wants to be right, that is how we have been raised. Investors feel that if they sell at a loss they have failed, and as a result, often suffer bigger losses by waiting for their position to trade at profit.

With any investment system, investors should let probability work for them. This means that investors should be able to enter and exit positions capturing both gains and losses without becoming emotionally attached to any positions. Emotional attachment clouds judgement, which leads to errors. When all of the trades are put together, the goal is for profits to be larger than losses in a way that minimizes risks and beats the market.

XOI vs S&P 500 1984 to 2013

Feb 25 to May 9	S&P 500	XOI	Diff
1984	1.7 %	5.6 %	3.9 %
1985	1.4	4.9	3.5
1986	6.0	7.7	1.7
1987	3.7	25.5	21.8
1988	-3.0	5.6	8.6
1989	6.3	8.1	1.8
1990	5.8	-0.6	-6.3
1991	4.8	6.8	2.0
1992	0.9	5.8	4.9
1993	0.3	6.3	6.0
1994	-4.7	3.2	7.9
1995	7.3	10.3	3.1
1996	-2.1	2.2	4.3
1997	1.8	4.7	2.9
1998	7.5	9.8	2.3
1999	7.3	35.4	28.1
2000	4.3	22.2	17.9
2001	0.8	10.2	9.4
2002	-1.5	5.3	6.9
2003	12.1	5.7	-6.4
2004	-3.5	4.0	7.5
2005	-1.8	-1.0	0.8
2006	2.8	9.4	6.6
2007	4.2	10.1	5.8
2008	2.6	7.6	5.0
2009	20.2	15.8	-4.4
2010	0.5	-2.3	-2.8
2011	3.1	-0.6	-3.7
2012	-0.8	-13.4	-12.5
2013	7.3	3.8	-3.5
Avg	3.2 %	7.3 %	4.1 %
Fq > 0	77 %	83 %	77 %

(Shaded cells = positive)

If we examine the winter oil stock trade, we can see how probability has worked in an investor's favor. This trade is based upon the premise that at the tail end of winter, the refineries drive up demand for oil in order to produce enough gas for the approaching "driving season" that starts in the spring. As a result, oil stocks tend to increase and outperform the market (from February 25th to May 9th). The oil stock sector, represented by the Amex Oil Index (XOI), has been very successful at this time of year, producing an average return of 7.3% and beating the S&P 500 by 4.1%, from 1984 to 2013. In addition it has been positive 25 out of 30 times. Investors should always evaluate the strength of seasonal trades before applying them to their own portfolios.

If an investor started using the seasonal investment discipline in 1984 and chose to invest in the winter-oil trade, they would have been very happy with the results. If they had chosen almost any other year, other than the last three years, to start the winter-oil trade in the last 30 years, they would have also been very pleased with the results. The years 1990, 2005, 2010, 2011 and 2012 produced losses of 0.6%, 1.0%, 2.3%, 0.6% and 13.5% respectively.

The fact that the trade did not produce a gain in 2010, 2011 and 2012, does not mean that the seasonal trade no longer works. All seasonal trades go through periods, sometimes multiple years where they do not work. An investor can start any methodology of trading at the "wrong time," and be unsuccessful in a particular trade. In fact, if an investor started the oil-winter trade in 1990 and had given up in the same year, they would have missed the following successful twelve years. Investors have to remember that it is the final score that counts, after all of the gains have been weighed against the losses.

In practical terms, investors should not put all of their investment strategies in one basket. If one or two large investments were made based upon seasonal strategies, it is possible that the seasonal methodology might be inappropriately evaluated and its use discontinued. A much more prudent strategy is to use a larger number of strategic seasonal investments with smaller investments. The end result will be to put the seasonal probability to work with a much greater chance of success.

Measuring Seasonal Performance

How do you determine if a seasonal strategy has been successful? Many people feel that ten years of data is a good sample size, others feel that fifteen years is better, and yet others feel that the more data the better. I tend to fall into the camp that, if possible, it is best to use fifteen or twenty years of data for sectors and more data for the broad markets, such as the S&P 500. Although the most recent data in almost any analytical framework is the most relevant, it is important to get enough data to reflect a sector's performance across different economic conditions. Given that historically the economy has performed on an eight year cycle, four years of expansion and then four years of contraction, using a short data set does not provide for enough exposure to different economic conditions.

A data set that is too long can run into the problem of older data having too much of an influence on the numbers when fundamental factors affecting a sector have changed. It is important to look at trends over time and assess if there has been a change that should be considered in determining the dates for a seasonal cycle. Each sector should be judged on its own merit. The analysis tables in this book illustrate the performance level for each year in order to provide the opportunity for readers to determine any relevant changes.

In order to determine if a seasonal strategy is effective there are two possible benchmarks, absolute and relative performance. Absolute performance measures if a profit is made and relative performance measures the performance of a sector in relationship to a major market. Both measurements have their merits and depending on your investment style, one measurement may be more valuable than another. This book provides both sets of measurement in tables and graphs.

It is not just the average percent gain of a sector over a certain time period that determines success. It is possible that one or two spectacular years of performance skew the results substantially (particularly with a small data set). The frequency of success is also very important: the higher the percentage of success the better. Also, the fewer large drawdowns the better. There is no magic number (percent success rate) per se of what constitutes a successful strategy. The success rate should be above fifty percent, otherwise it would be better to just invest in the broad market. Ideally speaking a strategy should have a high percentage success rate on both an absolute and relative basis. Some strategies are stronger than others, but that does not mean that the weaker strategies should not be used. Prudence should be used in determining the ideal portfolio allocation.

Illustrating the strength of a sector's seasonal performance can be accomplished through either an absolute yearly average performance graph, or a relative yearly average performance graph. The absolute graph shows the average yearly cumulative gain for a set number of years. It lets a reader visually identify the strong periods during the year. The relative graph shows the average yearly cumulative gain for the sector relative to the benchmark index.

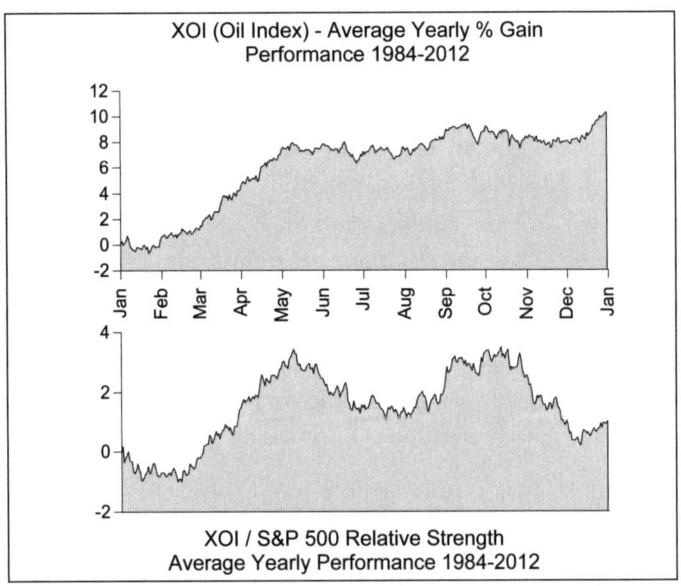

Both graphs are useful in determining the strength of a particular seasonal strategy. In the above diagram, the top graph illustrates the average year for the XOI (Oil Index) from 1984 to 2012. Essentially it illustrates the cumulative average gain if an investment were made in the index. The steep rising line starting in January/February shows the overall price rise that typically occurs in this sector at this time of year. In May the line flattens out and then rises very modestly starting in July.

The bottom graph is a ratio graph, illustrating the strength of the XOI Index relative to the S&P 500. It is derived by dividing the average year of the XOI by the average year of the S&P 500. When the line in the graph is rising, the XOI is outperforming the S&P 500, and vise versa when it is declining. This is an important graph and should be used in considering seasonal investments because the S&P 500 is a viable alternative to the energy sector. If both markets are increasing, but the S&P 500 is increasing at a faster rate, the S&P 500 represents a more attractive opportunity. This is particularly true when measuring the risk of a volatile sector relative to the broad market. If both investments were expected to produce the same rate of return, generally the broad market is a better investment because of its diversification.

Who Can Use Seasonal Investing?

Any investor from novice to expert, from short-term trader to long-term investor can benefit from using seasonal analysis. Seasonal investing is unique because it is an easy to understand system that can be used by itself or as a complement to another investment discipline. For the novice it provides an easy to follow strategy that makes intuitive sense. For the expert it can be used as a stand-alone system or as a complement to an existing system.

Seasonal investing is easily understood by all levels of investors, which allows investors to make rational decisions. This may seem obvious, but it is very common for investors to listen to a "guru of the market", be impressed and blindly follow his advice. When the advice works there is no problem. When the advice does not work investors wonder why they made the investment in the first place. When investors do not understand their investments it causes stress, bad decisions and a lack of "stick-to-it ness" with any investment discipline. Even expert investors realize the importance of understanding your investments. Peter Lynch of Fidelity Investments used to say "Never invest in any idea that you can't illustrate with a crayon." Investors do not need to go that far, but they should understand their investments.

Novice investors find seasonal strategies very easy to understand because they are intuitive. They do not have to be investing for years to understand why seasonal strategies work. They understand that an increase in demand for gold every year at the same time causes a ripple effect in the stock market pushing up gold stocks at the same time every year.

Most expert investors use information from a variety of sources in making their decisions. Even experts that primarily use fundamental analysis can benefit from using seasonal trends to get an edge in the market. Fundamental analysis is a very crude tool and provides very little in the way of timing an investment. Using seasonal trends can help with the timing of the buy and sell decisions and produce extra profit.

Seasonal investing can be used by both short-term and long-term investors, but in different ways. For short-term investors it provides a complete trade – buy and sell dates. For long-term investors it can provide a buy date for a sector of interest.

Combining Seasonal Analysis with other Investment Disciplines

Seasonal investing used by itself has historically produced above average market returns. Depending on an investor's particular style, it can be combined with one of the other three investment disciplines: fundamental, quantitative and technical analysis. There are two basic ways to combine seasonal analysis with other investment methodologies – as the primary or secondary method. If it is used as a primary method, seasonally strong time periods are established for a number of sectors and then appropriate sectors are chosen based upon fundamental, quantitative or technical screens. If it is used as a secondary method, sector selections are first made based upon one of three methods and then final sectors are chosen based upon which ones are in their seasonally strong period.

Technical analysis is an ideal mate for seasonal analysis. Unlike fundamental and quantitative analysis, which are very blunt timing tools at best, seasonal and technical analysis can provide specific trigger points to buy and sell. The combination can turbo-charge investment strategies, adding extra profits by fine-tuning entry and exit dates.

Seasonal analysis provides both buy and sell dates. Although a sector in the market can sometimes bottom on the exact seasonal buy date, it more often bottoms a bit early or a bit late. After all, the seasonal buy date is based upon an average of historical performance. Depending on the sector, buying opportunities start to develop approximately one month before and after the seasonal buy date. Using technical analysis gives an investor the advantage of buying into a sector when it turns up early or waiting when it turns up late. Likewise, technical analysis can be used to trigger a sell signal when the market turns down before or after the sell date.

The sell decision can be extended with the help of a trailing stop-loss order. If a sector has strong momentum and the technical tools do not provide a sell signal, it is possible to let the sector "run." When a trailing stop-loss is used, a profitable sell point is established. If the price continues to run, then the selling point is raised. If, on the other hand, the price falls through the stop-loss point, the position is sold.

Sectors of the Market

Standard & Poor's has done an excellent job in categorizing the U.S. stock market into its different parts. Although the demand for this service initially came from institutional investors, many individual investors now seek the same information. Knowing the sector breakdown in the market allows investors to see how different their portfolio is relative to the market. As a result, they are able to make conscious decisions on what parts of the stock market to overweight based upon their beliefs of which sectors will outperform. It also helps control the amount of desired risk.

Standard & Poor's uses four levels of detail in its Global Industry Classification Standard (GICS©) to categorize stock markets around the world. From the most specific, it classifies companies into sub-industries, industries, industry groups and finally economic sectors. All companies in the Standard & Poor's global family of indices are classified according to the GICS structure.

This book focuses on the U.S. market, analysing the trends of the venerable S&P 500 index and its economic sectors and industry groups. The following diagram illustrates the index classified according to its economic sectors.

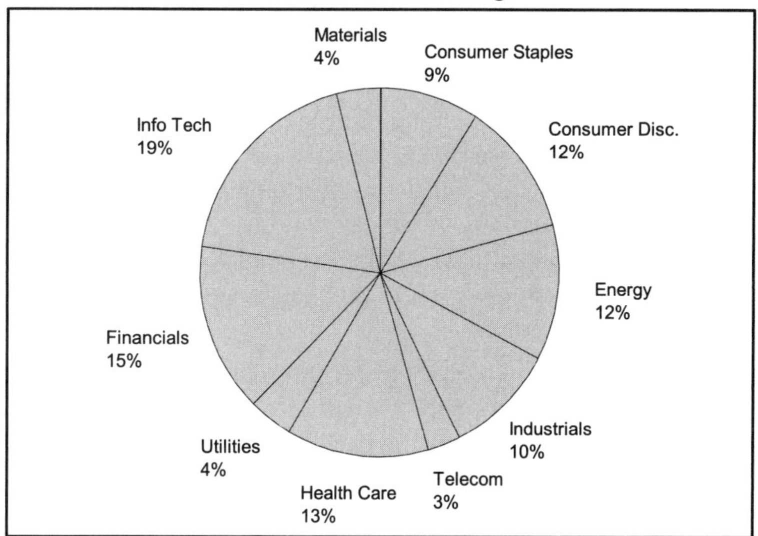

Standard and Poor's, Understanding Sectors, June 30, 2010

For more information on Standard and Poor's Global Industry Classification Standard (GICS©), refer to www.standardandpoors.com

Investment Products – Which One Is The Right One?

There are many ways to take advantage of the seasonal trends at the broad stock market and sector levels. Regardless of the investment products that you currently use, whether exchange traded funds, mutual funds, stocks or options, all can be used with the strategies in this book. Different investments offer different risk-reward relationships and return potential.

Exchange Traded Funds (ETFs)

Exchange Traded Funds (ETFs) offer the purest method of seasonal investment. The broad market ETFs are designed to track the major indices and the sector ETFs are designed to track specific sectors without using active management. Relatively new, ETFs are a great way to capture both market and sector trends. They were originally introduced into the Canadian market in 1993 to represent the Toronto stock market index. Shortly afterward they were introduced to the U.S. market and there are now hundreds of ETFs to represent almost every market, sector, style of investing and company capitalization. Originally ETFs were mainly of interest to institutional investors, but individual investors have fast realized the merits of ETF investing and have made some of the broad market ETFs the most heavily traded securities in the world.

An ETF is a single security that represents a market, such as the S&P 500; a sector of the market, such as the financial sector; or a commodity, such as gold. In the case of the S&P 500, an investor buying one security is buying all 500 stocks in the index. By investing into a financial ETF, an investor is buying the companies that make up the financial sector of the market. By investing into a gold commodity ETF, an investor is buying a security that represents the price of gold.

ETFs trade on the open market just like stocks. They have a bid and an ask, can be shorted and many are option eligible. They are a very low cost, tax efficient method of targeting specific parts of the market.

Mutual Funds

Mutual funds are a good way to combine market or sector investing with active management. In recent years, many mutual fund companies have added sector funds to accommodate an increasing appetite in this area.

As the seasonal strategies put forward in this book have a short-term nature, it is important to make sure that there are no fees (or a nominal charge) for getting into and out of a position in the market.

Stocks

Stocks provide an opportunity to make better returns than the market or sector. If the market increases during its seasonal period, some stocks will increase dramatically more than the index. Choosing one of the outperforming stocks will greatly enhance returns; choosing one of the underperforming stocks can create substantial loses. Using stocks requires increased attention to diversification and security selection.

Options

> Disclaimer: Options involve risk and are not suitable for every investor. Because they are cash-settled, investors should be aware of the special risks associated with index options and should consult a tax advisor. Prior to buying or selling options, a person must receive a copy of Characteristics and Risks of Standardized Options and should thoroughly understand the risks involved in any use of options. Copies may be obtained from The Options Clearing Corporation, 440 S. LaSalle Street, Chicago, IL 60605.

Options, for more sophisticated investors, are a good tool to take advantage of both market and sector opportunities. An option position can be established with either stocks or ETFs. There are many different ways to use options for seasonal trends: establish a long position on the market during its seasonally strong period, establish a short position during its seasonally weak period, or create a spread trade to capture the superior gains of a sector over the market.

THACKRAY'S 2014 INVESTOR'S GUIDE

CONTENTS

JANUARY

	MONDAY	TUESDAY	WEDNESDAY
WEEK 01	30	31	1 30 CAN Closed - New Year's Day USA Market Closed - New Year's Day
WEEK 02	6 25	7 24	8 23
WEEK 03	13 18	14 17	15 16
WEEK 04	20 11 USA Market Closed- Martin Luther King Jr. Day	21 10	22 9
WEEK 05	27 4	28 3	29 2

THURSDAY		FRIDAY	
2	29	**3**	28
9	22	**10**	21
16	15	**17**	14
23	8	**24**	7
30	1	**31**	

FEBRUARY

M	T	W	T	F	S	S
					1	2
3	4	5	6	7	8	9
10	11	12	13	14	15	16
17	18	19	20	21	22	23
24	25	26	27	28		

MARCH

M	T	W	T	F	S	S
					1	2
3	4	5	6	7	8	9
10	11	12	13	14	15	16
17	18	19	20	21	22	23
24	25	26	27	28	29	30
31						

APRIL

M	T	W	T	F	S	S
	1	2	3	4	5	6
7	8	9	10	11	12	13
14	15	16	17	18	19	20
21	22	23	24	25	26	27
28	29	30				

MAY

M	T	W	T	F	S	S
			1	2	3	4
5	6	7	8	9	10	11
12	13	14	15	16	17	18
19	20	21	22	23	24	25
26	27	28	29	30	31	

JANUARY
SUMMARY

	Dow Jones	S&P 500	Nasdaq	TSX Comp
Month Rank	6	5	1	4
# Up	41	39	27	17
# Down	22	24	14	11
% Pos	65	61	66	61
% Avg. Gain	1.1	1.1	2.8	1.2

Dow & S&P 1950-2012, Nasdaq 1972-2012, TSX 1985-2012

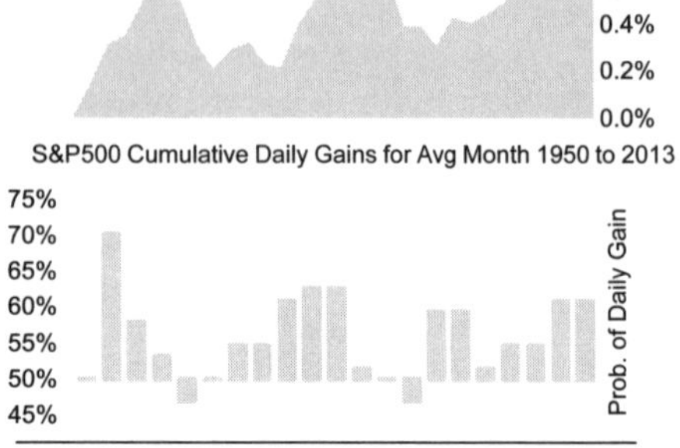

♦ January has a reputation of being a positive month and after three years in a row (2008, 2009, 2010) of negative performance, January is once again living up to its reputation as a positive month with positive performances in 2011, 2012 and 2013. ♦ January tends to behave in a schizophrenic manner as most of the cyclical sectors tend to perform well and the defensive sectors poorly. ♦ The retail sector starts its seasonal trade later in January. The trade has been successful in the last six years and once again performed strongly in 2013.

BEST / WORST JANUARY BROAD MKTS. 2004-2013

BEST JANUARY MARKETS

- Russell 2000 (2006) 8.9%
- Nasdaq (2012) 8.0%
- Nikkei 225 (2013) 7.2%

WORST JANUARY MARKETS

- Nikkei (2008) -11.2%
- Russell 2000 (2009) -11.2%
- Nasdaq (2008) -9.9%

Index Values End of Month

	2004	2005	2006	2007	2008	2009	2010	2011	2012	2013
Dow	10,488	10,490	10,865	12,622	12,650	8,001	10,067	11,892	12,633	13,861
S&P 500	1,131	1,181	1,280	1,438	1,379	826	1,074	1,286	1,312	1,498
Nasdaq	2,066	2,062	2,306	2,464	2,390	1,476	2,147	2,700	2,814	3,142
TSX Comp.	8,521	9,204	11,946	13,034	13,155	8,695	11,094	13,552	12,452	12,685
Russell 1000	1,163	1,219	1,341	1,507	1,444	860	1,133	1,371	1,396	1,599
Russell 2000	1,443	1,551	1,822	1,989	1,773	1,102	1,496	1,942	1,970	2,242
FTSE 100	4,391	4,852	5,760	6,203	5,880	4,150	5,189	5,863	5,682	6,277
Nikkei 225	10,784	11,388	16,650	17,383	13,592	7,994	10,198	10,238	8,803	11,139

Percent Gain for January

	2004	2005	2006	2007	2008	2009	2010	2011	2012	2013
Dow	0.3	-2.7	1.4	1.3	-4.6	-8.8	-3.5	2.7	3.4	5.8
S&P 500	1.7	-2.5	2.5	1.4	-6.1	-8.6	-3.7	2.3	4.4	5.0
Nasdaq	3.1	-5.2	4.6	2.0	-9.9	-6.4	-5.4	1.8	8.0	4.1
TSX Comp.	3.7	-0.5	6.0	1.0	-4.9	-3.3	-5.5	0.8	4.2	2.0
Russell 1000	1.8	-2.6	2.7	1.8	-6.1	-8.3	-3.7	2.3	4.8	5.3
Russell 2000	4.3	-4.2	8.9	1.6	-6.9	-11.2	-3.7	-0.3	7.0	6.2
FTSE 100	-1.9	0.8	2.5	-0.3	-8.9	-6.4	-4.1	-0.6	2.0	6.4
Nikkei 225	1.0	-0.9	3.3	0.9	-11.2	-9.8	-3.3	0.1	4.1	7.2

January Market Avg. Performance 2004 to 2013(1)

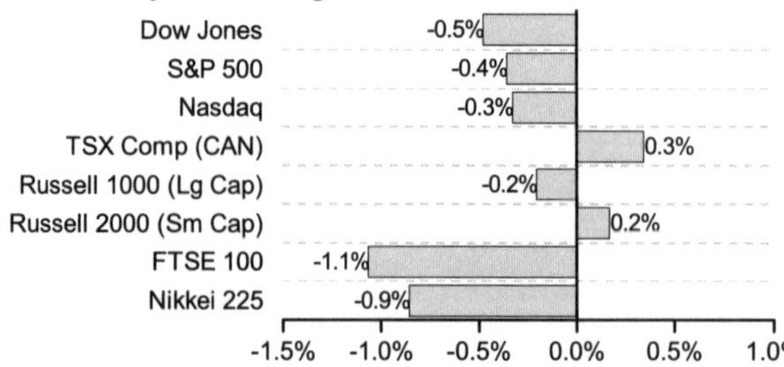

Interest Corner Jan(2)

	Fed Funds % (3)	3 Mo. T-Bill %(4)	10 Yr %(5)	20 Yr %(6)
2013	0.25	0.07	2.02	2.79
2012	0.25	0.06	1.83	2.59
2011	0.25	0.15	3.42	4.33
2010	0.25	0.08	3.63	4.38
2009	0.25	0.24	2.87	3.86

(1) Russell Data provided by Russell (2) Federal Reserve Bank of St. Louis- end of month values (3) Target rate set by FOMC (4)(5)(6) Constant yield maturities.

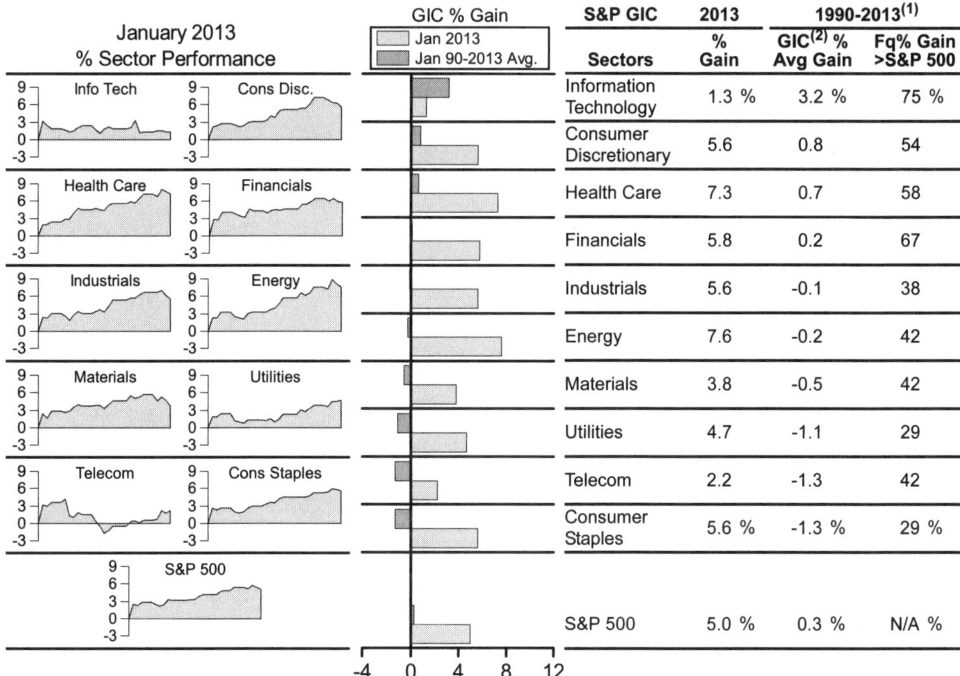

S&P GIC Sectors	2013 % Gain	1990-2013[1] GIC[2] % Avg Gain	1990-2013[1] Fq% Gain >S&P 500
Information Technology	1.3 %	3.2 %	75 %
Consumer Discretionary	5.6	0.8	54
Health Care	7.3	0.7	58
Financials	5.8	0.2	67
Industrials	5.6	-0.1	38
Energy	7.6	-0.2	42
Materials	3.8	-0.5	42
Utilities	4.7	-1.1	29
Telecom	2.2	-1.3	42
Consumer Staples	5.6 %	-1.3 %	29 %
S&P 500	5.0 %	0.3 %	N/A %

Sector Commentary

♦ January 2013 was a very strong month for the S&P 500, producing a gain of 5.0%. All of the major sectors in the market were positive. ♦ The consumer discretionary sector outperformed the S&P 500.♦ The energy sector was the strongest performer, producing a gain of 7.6%. This is not typical for the sector, but occasionally the sector does start its seasonal run early.♦ The health care sector is on average one of the strongest performing sectors in January and in 2013 it produced a gain of 7.3%.

Sub-Sector Commentary

♦ The top performing sub-sector was homebuilders, as it produced a very strong 13.5%. January is the last full month for its seasonally strong period.♦ The worst performing sub-sector was the metal and mining. It is usually best to avoid this sub-sector for most of January and 2013 was no different.♦ The transportation sub-sector produced a gain of 7.9%. It typically starts one of its seasonal periods on January 23rd, but this year it started its seasonal run a bit earlier.♦ The biotech sub-sector often puts in a good performance at the end of the year which can carry over into the New Year, as it did in 2013.

SELECTED SUB-SECTORS[3]

Sub-Sector	2013 % Gain	GIC % Avg Gain	Fq% Gain >S&P 500
SOX (1995-2013)	7.5 %	4.5 %	58 %
Home-builders	13.5	3.3	58
Silver	6.9	3.1	67
Software & Services	5.5	2.5	71
Biotech (1993-2013)	6.9	2.2	52
Steel	2.5	1.6	54
Railroads	7.4	1.5	58
Gold (London PM)	0.4	1.2	54
Banks	3.7	0.3	50
Agriculture (1994-2013)	4.2	0.3	40
Transporta-tion	7.9	0.3	50
Retail	6.9	0.2	54
Pharma	7.2	0.1	54
Metals & Mining	0.1	-0.5	46
Chemicals	4.7	-0.5	42

(1) Sector data provided by Standard and Poors (2) GIC is short form for Global Industry Classification (3) Sub Sector data provided by Standard and Poors, except where marked by symbol.

CAT CATERPILLAR
January 23rd to May 5th

The performance of Caterpillar's stock is very much related to the outlook for the worldwide economy. When the outlook for the economy is strong, Caterpillar tends to perform well.

Generally, expectations for economic growth tend to be stronger during the first part of the year compared with the rest of the year. As a result, companies that are more dependent on the economic cycle tend to perform better during the first part of the year. This includes companies in the industrial sector such as Caterpillar.

14.0% gain & positive 83% of the time

From January 23rd to May 5th, during the period of 1990 to 2013, Caterpillar has produced an average rate of return of 14.0% and has been positive 83% of the time. During this period it has also outperformed the S&P 500, 71% of the time.

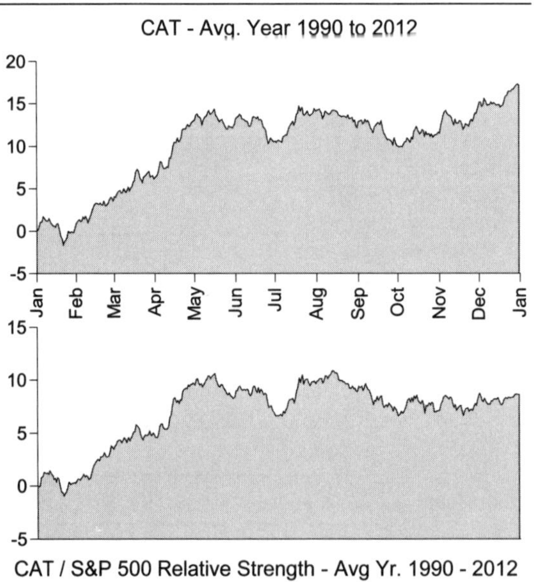

CAT / S&P 500 Relative Strength - Avg Yr. 1990 - 2012

CAT* vs. S&P 500
1990 to 2013

(Shaded = Positive)

Jan 23 to May 5	S&P 500	CAT	Diff
1990	2.4%	15.4%	13.0%
1991	16.0	17.2	1.2
1992	-0.3	14.2	14.5
1993	1.9	24.3	22.4
1994	-4.9	14.0	19.0
1995	11.9	5.9	-6.0
1996	4.6	1.6	-3.0
1997	5.6	26.0	20.4
1998	15.8	22.8	7.0
1999	10.0	48.2	38.2
2000	-0.6	-17.6	-17.0
2001	-5.7	23.7	29.4
2002	-4.1	12.1	16.2
2003	5.5	18.5	13.1
2004	-2.0	-6.2	-4.2
2005	0.4	0.7	0.3
2006	5.1	31.6	26.5
2007	5.8	25.7	19.9
2008	7.4	29.7	22.3
2009	9.2	5.9	-3.4
2010	6.8	21.6	14.8
2011	4.0	17.9	13.9
2012	4.1	-6.8	-10.9
2013	8.2	-11.0	-19.2
Avg	4.5%	14.0%	9.5%
Fq > 0	75%	83%	71%

Although the seasonal Caterpillar strategy has had solid results, there have been years where the strategy has not worked, including the last two years.

In the year 2000, cyclical stocks including Caterpillar underperformed during the first part of the year as the technology bubble broke and investors were concerned about the impact on world economic growth. Caterpillar's negative performance in 2004 was largely the result of "consolidating" after producing an 86% gain in 2003.

In 2012 and 2013, Caterpillar started off the year with strong outperformance, but started to underperform the S&P 500 in February as investors shunned cyclical stocks in favor of defensive stocks. Favouring defensive stocks at this time of the year is not typical and often points to a market pull back later in the springtime. From a strategic standpoint, investors should consider exiting the Caterpillar strategy early if it shows continued underperformance relative to the S&P 500 during its seasonal period.

Despite the drawdown exceptions, the overall positive results of the Caterpillar strategy make it a trade worthy of a seasonal portfolio.

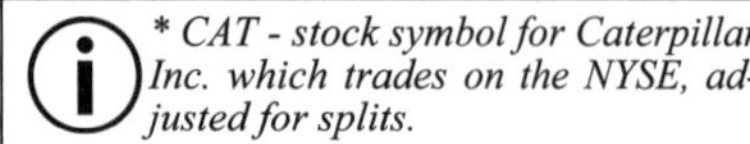
** CAT - stock symbol for Caterpillar Inc. which trades on the NYSE, adjusted for splits.*

2012-13 Strategy Performance

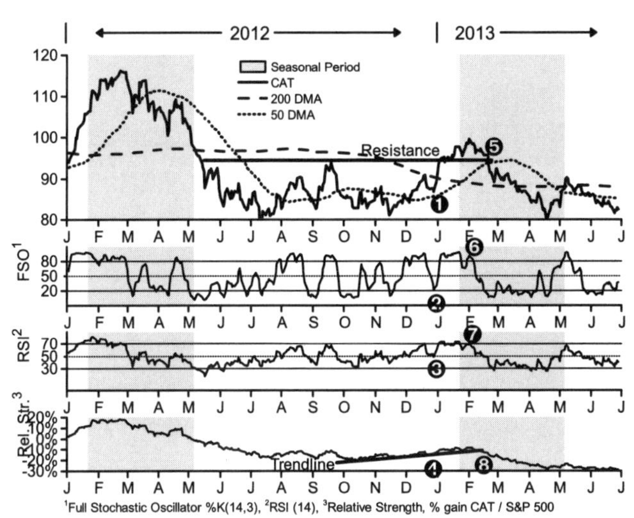

¹Full Stochastic Oscillator %K(14,3), ²RSI (14), ³Relative Strength, % gain CAT / S&P 500

Caterpillar Performance

Concerns over a "European relapse" led many industrial stocks, including Caterpillar, to underperform the S&P 500 for the first half of 2012. In the summer months, Caterpillar entered into a consolidation pattern and then started to outperform in the fourth quarter.

Early in 2013, once again, investors decided to seek the safety of the defensive sectors and as a result, industrial stocks, including Caterpillar underperformed the S&P 500.

Technical Conditions– January 23rd to May 5th, 2013

Entry Strategy* – *Bullish – Buy Position Early–

In 2012, Caterpillar had been outperforming the S&P 500 since early October. In late December, less than a month before the official seasonal start date, Caterpillar was trading above its 50 day moving average❶ and the FSO triggered a buy signal by rising above 20❷, validating an early entry. At the same time the RSI bounced higher off 50❸, and the relative strength compared to the S&P 500 maintained its upward trajectory❹. Positive performance at the start of the seasonal period justified a full position.

Exit Strategy*– *Bearish – Sell Position Early–

The FSO turned below 80❻ and the RSI turned below 70❼ in early February indicating that possible poor performance could be ahead. The trade became a broken trade later in February when CAT broke its resistance level❺ and started to underperform the S&P 500❽. At this time exiting the position early was justified.

WEEK 01

Market Indices & Rates
Weekly Values**

Stock Markets	2012	2013
Dow	12,398	13,336
S&P500	1,278	1,454
Nasdaq	2,660	3,084
TSX	12,215	12,496
FTSE	5,661	6,016
DAX	6,102	7,771
Nikkei	8,480	10,688
Hang Seng	18,753	23,175

Commodities	2012	2013
Oil	102.39	92.74
Gold	1,606.6	1,673.8

Bond Yields	2012	2013
USA 5 Yr Treasury	0.88	0.78
USA 10 Yr T	1.99	1.87
USA 20 Yr T	2.71	2.64
Moody's Aaa	3.87	3.77
Moody's Baa	5.28	4.71
CAN 5 Yr T	1.29	1.43
CAN 10 Yr T	1.97	1.87

Money Market	2012	2013
USA Fed Funds	0.25	0.25
USA 3 Mo T-B	0.02	0.07
CAN tgt overnight rate	1.00	1.00
CAN 3 Mo T-B	0.78	0.92

Foreign Exchange	2012	2013
EUR/USD	1.29	1.31
GBP/USD	1.55	1.62
USD/CAD	1.02	0.99
USD/JPY	76.89	87.24

JANUARY

M	T	W	T	F	S	S
		1	2	3	4	5
6	7	8	9	10	11	12
13	14	15	16	17	18	19
20	21	22	23	24	25	26
27	28	29	30	31		

FEBRUARY

M	T	W	T	F	S	S
					1	2
3	4	5	6	7	8	9
10	11	12	13	14	15	16
17	18	19	20	21	22	23
24	25	26	27	28		

MARCH

M	T	W	T	F	S	S
					1	2
3	4	5	6	7	8	9
10	11	12	13	14	15	16
17	18	19	20	21	22	23
24	25	26	27	28	29	30
31						

SILVER — THREE BEST PERIODS
JAN to MAR, & SEP, & NOV

If there is only one time of the year that investors should look at investing in silver, it is the period from January to March. That is not to say that September and November cannot be fruitful, but greater emphasis should be given to the beginning of the year.

The three periods of strength are the result of silver being both a precious metal and an industrial metal. With two strong influences affecting silver, opportunities are produced in its yearly trends. The rise from January 1st to March 31st is mainly the result of increased economic activity at the start of the new year. Generally, this is the time of the year when positive expectations are formed for the economy over the upcoming year and as a result investors focus on the industrial aspect of silver, pushing up its price.

11.6% gain and positive 69% of the time

Silver often performs well in September because of its relationship with gold as a precious metal. Gold often rises at this time of year as the result of the large quantities of gold jewellery that is consumed in the fourth quarter of the year (see *Gold Shines* strategy). As gold often has a weak month in October, so does silver. Both silver and gold tend to turnaround in November.

As investors adjust their year-end portfolios in December, both gold and silver generally put in mediocre performances and underperform the S&P 500.

It is important to note that when silver is in a bull run with a lot of momentum, it will bridge the gaps, performing well in both October and December. Investors can benefit from using technical analysis to fine tune strategies in choosing buy and sell dates.

> *Source: Bank of England*
> *London pricing is recognized as the world benchmark for silver prices.*

Silver Performance
Jan-Mar, Sep & Nov 1984-2012

Positive [shaded]

	Jan1 to Mar31	Sep1 to Sep30	Nov1 to Nov30	Compound Growth
1984	8.3 %	-0.1 %	-2.0 %	6.0 %
1985	5.9	-3.1	0.1	2.7
1986	-3.2	6.8	-4.0	-0.7
1987	19.4	1.3	5.4	27.5
1988	0.8	-4.5	-3.8	-7.4
1989	-4.7	4.2	6.4	5.6
1990	-4.8	-0.7	-3.2	-8.5
1991	-8.5	8.4	-0.6	-1.4
1992	6.7	1.3	-0.8	7.2
1993	6.0	-16.8	1.5	-10.5
1994	12.1	4.9	-5.1	11.7
1995	6.4	3.9	-3.4	6.8
1996	7.3	-6.0	-1.7	-0.9
1997	6.9	9.4	10.0	28.7
1998	5.8	12.5	-2.6	16.1
1999	0.4	9.8	-2.1	7.9
2000	-7.4	-0.5	-2.3	-10.0
2001	-5.4	9.2	-3.2	0.1
2002	3.4	-0.7	-1.0	1.7
2003	-4.4	0.2	4.2	-0.2
2004	31.2	-1.1	8.3	40.5
2005	5.5	11.7	5.7	24.6
2006	33.1	-8.3	13.3	38.2
2007	3.5	14.2	-0.6	17.5
2008	21.9	-5.8	9.1	25.2
2009	21.5	13.1	9.5	50.5
2010	3.0	17.0	13.2	36.4
2011	23.6	-26.4	-8.4	-16.6
2012	15.1	13.5	6.2	38.8
Avg	7.2 %	2.3 %	1.7 %	11.6 %
Fq>0	76 %	59 %	45 %	69 %

Silver (London) - Avg. Year 1984 to 2012

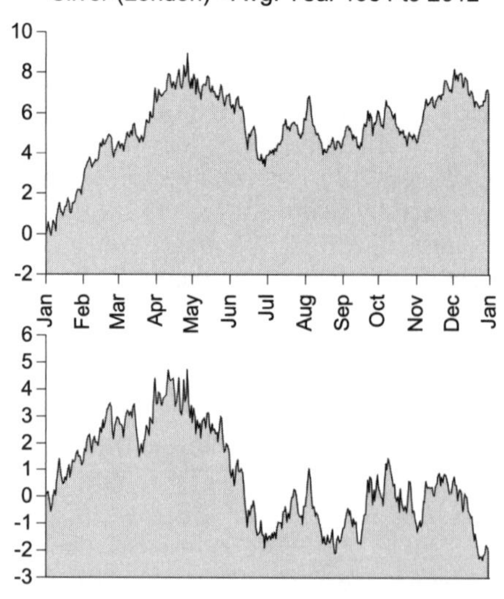

Silver / S&P 500 Rel. Strength- Avg Yr. 1984-2012

2012-13 Strategy Performance

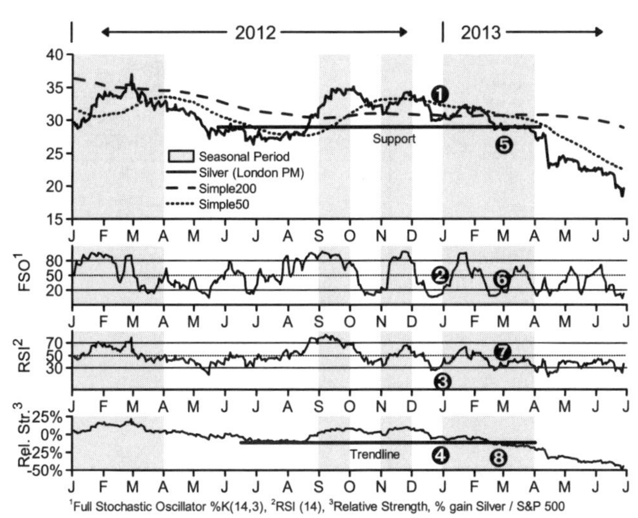

[1]Full Stochastic Oscillator %K(14,3), [2]RSI (14), [3]Relative Strength, % gain Silver / S&P 500

Silver (CME Spot Price) Performance

Silver performed well in September of 2012, a seasonally strong period. It then corrected in October, and rose in November, another seasonally strong period. It then corrected in December, setting up well for its seasonally strong period starting in January.

Technical Conditions– January to March 2013

Entry Strategy –Buy Position on Entry Date–

At the start of the seasonal period in January, silver started to tick upwards and crossed above its 200 day moving average❶. Confirming this move was the FSO crossing above 20❷ and the RSI crossing above 30❸. Silver also bounced off its relative performance line to the S&P 500❹. Overall, the trade was setup well at the start of its seasonal period. The only concerning factor was that the high established in November was lower than the September high, leading to the possibility of a bearish pattern of lower highs going forward.

Exit Strategy– Sell Position Early–

The trade started off well, performing positively and outperforming the S&P 500 for most of January. In February, the sector started to roll over, crossed below the December low and then broke through its support level later in March❺. At the same time, the FSO was below 20❻ and the RSI was below 30❼. Most importantly, silver broke its trendline to the downside and continued to underperform❽, warranting an early exit.

Market Indices & Rates
Weekly Values**

Stock Markets	2012	2013
Dow	12,440	13,413
S&P500	1,290	1,465
Nasdaq	2,705	3,109
TSX	12,247	12,546
FTSE	5,656	6,088
DAX	6,131	7,715
Nikkei	8,439	10,628
Hang Seng	19,064	23,256

Commodities	2012	2013
Oil	100.44	93.36
Gold	1,636.6	1,658.3

Bond Yields	2012	2013
USA 5 Yr Treasury	0.83	0.79
USA 10 Yr T	1.95	1.90
USA 20 Yr T	2.66	2.67
Moody's Aaa	3.85	3.77
Moody's Baa	5.21	4.70
CAN 5 Yr T	1.28	1.47
CAN 10 Yr T	1.96	1.93

Money Market	2012	2013
USA Fed Funds	0.25	0.25
USA 3 Mo T-B	0.03	0.07
CAN tgt overnight rate	1.00	1.00
CAN 3 Mo T-B	0.78	0.92

Foreign Exchange	2012	2013
EUR/USD	1.27	1.32
GBP/USD	1.54	1.61
USD/CAD	1.02	0.99
USD/JPY	76.86	88.14

JANUARY

M	T	W	T	F	S	S
		1	2	3	4	5
6	7	8	9	10	11	12
13	14	15	16	17	18	19
20	21	22	23	24	25	26
27	28	29	30	31		

FEBRUARY

M	T	W	T	F	S	S
					1	2
3	4	5	6	7	8	9
10	11	12	13	14	15	16
17	18	19	20	21	22	23
24	25	26	27	28		

MARCH

M	T	W	T	F	S	S
					1	2
3	4	5	6	7	8	9
10	11	12	13	14	15	16
17	18	19	20	21	22	23
24	25	26	27	28	29	30
31						

RETAIL – POST HOLIDAY BARGAIN

Ist of **II** Retail Strategies for the Year
SHOP Jan 21st and RETURN Your Investment Apr 12th

Once again the retail sector outperformed the S&P 500 in 2013 during its seasonally strong period. This was the sixth straight year of outperformance and positive returns. The combination of strong returns and minimal drawdowns over the long-term make this one of the stronger seasonal trades.

A few weeks after the Christmas holidays, retail stocks go on sale, representing a good buying opportunity in mid to late January. The opportunity coincides with the earnings season.

Historically, the retail sector has outperformed from January 21st until April 12th - the start of the next earnings season. From 1990 to 2013, during its seasonally strong period, the retail sector has averaged 8.8%, compared with the S&P 500 which has averaged 2.4%. Not only has the retail sector had greater gains than the broad market, but it has also outperformed it on a fairly regular basis: 83% of the time.

6.4% extra & 83% of the time better than the S&P 500

Retail Sector vs.
S&P 500 1990 to 2013

Jan 21 to Apr 12	S&P 500	Retail	Diff
1990	1.5 %	9.7 %	8.1 %
1991	14.5	29.9	15.4
1992	-2.9	-2.7	0.2
1993	3.5	-0.6	-4.0
1994	-5.8	2.0	7.8
1995	9.1	7.4	-1.8
1996	4.1	19.7	15.7
1997	-5.0	6.0	11.0
1998	13.5	20.1	6.6
1999	8.1	23.4	15.2
2000	1.5	5.8	4.3
2001	-11.8	-0.5	11.3
2002	-1.5	6.7	8.2
2003	-3.7	6.5	10.3
2004	0.6	6.7	6.1
2005	1.1	-1.6	-2.7
2006	2.1	3.4	1.3
2007	1.2	-0.7	-1.9
2008	0.6	3.5	3.0
2009	0.4	25.1	18.7
2010	5.1	15.5	10.4
2011	2.7	4.4	1.7
2012	5.5	12.1	6.6
2013	6.9	10.1	3.2
Avg.	2.4 %	8.8 %	6.4 %
Fq > 0	75 %	79 %	83 %

Positive (shaded)

Retail Sector - Avg. Year 1990 to 2012

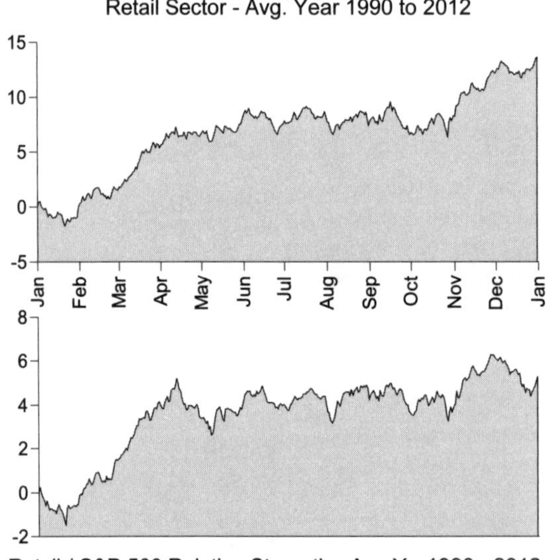

Retail / S&P 500 Relative Strength - Avg Yr. 1990 - 2012

Most investors think the best time to invest in retail stocks is before Black Friday in November. Yes, there is a positive seasonal cycle at this time, but it is not nearly as strong as the cycle from January to April.

The January retail bounce coincides with the "rosy" stock market analysts' forecasts that tend to occur at the beginning of the year. These forecasts generally rely on healthy consumer spending as it makes up approximately 2/3 of the GDP. The retail sector benefits from the optimistic forecasts and tends to outperform the S&P 500.

From a seasonal basis, investors have been best served by exiting the retail sector in April and then returning to it later at the end of October (see *Retail Shop Early* strategy).

Retail SP GIC Sector # 2550:
An index designed to represent a cross section of retail companies

For more information on the retail sector, see www.standardandpoors.com.

2012-13 Strategy Performance

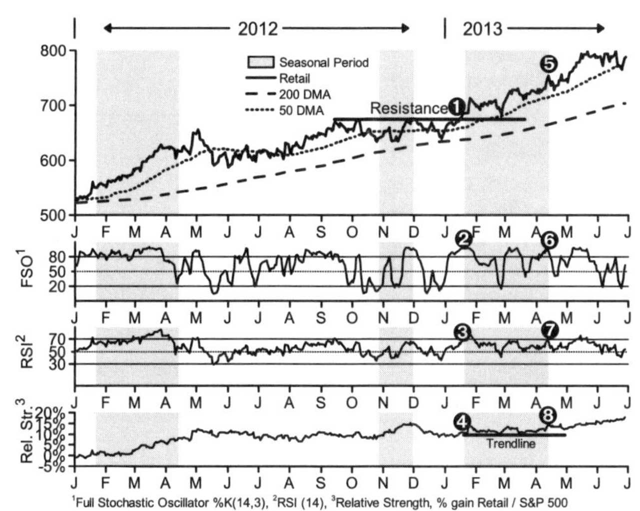

[1]Full Stochastic Oscillator %K(14,3), [2]RSI (14), [3]Relative Strength, % gain Retail / S&P 500

Retail Sector Performance

After outperforming the S&P 500 in its autumn seasonal period from October 28th to November 29th in 2012, the retail sector corrected for two weeks and then performed at "market," up until the second half of January, setting up for the start of the strongest seasonal period for the retail sector.

Technical Conditions – January 21st to April 12th, 2013

Entry Strategy – Buy Position on Entry Date–
From a price pattern perspective, the retail sector set up very well at the start of its seasonal period, as it had just broken above a key resistance level❶. At the same time the FSO was over 80❷ and the RSI was just under 70❸ and rising, indicating an overbought condition. An overbought condition by itself, at the start of a seasonal, does not negate the entry into a seasonal trade. Just after the entry date for the trade, the retail sector outperformed the S&P 500❹ briefly and then returned to market performance.

Exit Strategy – Sell Position on Exit Date–
Although in mid-March the FSO turned below 80❻ and the RSI❼ was trending lower after bouncing off 70, the retail sector was still outperforming the S&P 500 and had not crossed below its 50 day moving average❺. After a slight relapse, the retail sector started to outperform the S&P 500, putting in a strong finishing kick❽ to produce a 10.1% return during its seasonal performance, which was 3.2% better than the S&P 500 over the same time period.

WEEK 03

Market Indices & Rates Weekly Values**

Stock Markets	2012	2013
Dow	12,601	13,560
S&P500	1,308	1,477
Nasdaq	2,768	3,123
TSX	12,319	12,651
FTSE	5,705	6,123
DAX	6,346	7,707
Nikkei	8,560	10,751
Hang Seng	19,676	23,419

Commodities	2012	2013
Oil	100.04	94.58
Gold	1650.4	1677.4

Bond Yields	2012	2013
USA 5 Yr Treasury	0.85	0.77
USA 10 Yr T	1.96	1.87
USA 20 Yr T	2.68	2.63
Moody's Aaa	3.83	3.76
Moody's Baa	5.20	4.69
CAN 5 Yr T	1.32	1.46
CAN 10 Yr T	1.98	1.92

Money Market	2012	2013
USA Fed Funds	0.25	0.25
USA 3 Mo T-B	0.05	0.08
CAN tgt overnight rate	1.00	1.00
CAN 3 Mo T-B	0.84	0.90

Foreign Exchange	2012	2013
EUR/USD	1.28	1.33
GBP/USD	1.54	1.60
USD/CAD	1.01	0.99
USD/JPY	76.91	89.33

JANUARY

M	T	W	T	F	S	S
		1	2	3	4	5
6	7	8	9	10	11	12
13	14	15	16	17	18	19
20	21	22	23	24	25	26
27	28	29	30	31		

FEBRUARY

M	T	W	T	F	S	S
					1	2
3	4	5	6	7	8	9
10	11	12	13	14	15	16
17	18	19	20	21	22	23
24	25	26	27	28		

MARCH

M	T	W	T	F	S	S
					1	2
3	4	5	6	7	8	9
10	11	12	13	14	15	16
17	18	19	20	21	22	23
24	25	26	27	28	29	30
31						

TJX TJX COMPANIES INC.
January 22nd to March 30th

In 2013, for the sixth straight year in a row, TJX during its seasonally strong period, performed positively. Over the long-term, TJX stock has typically outperformed the retail sector when the sector has been positive, making it an excellent complement to a retail sector investment at this time of the year.

TJX is an off-price apparel and home fashions retailer that typically reports its fourth quarter earnings in approximately the third week of February. The company, like the retail sector, benefits from investors expecting positive results from the Christmas season.

TJX's period of seasonal strength is similar to the seasonal period for the retail sector. The best time to invest in TJX has been from January 22nd to March 30th. From 1990 to 2013, investing in this period has produced an average gain of 13.0%, which is substantially better than the 1.8% performance of the S&P 500. It is also important to note that the stock has been positive 75% of the time during this period.

13.0% gain & positive 75% of the time

Equally impressive is the amount of times TJX has produced a large gain, versus a large loss. In the last twenty-four years, TJX has only had one loss of 10% or greater. This compares to twelve times where the company had gains of 10% or greater.

TJX* vs. Retail vs. S&P 500
1990 to 2013

(Shaded = Positive)

Jan 22 to Mar 30	S&P 500	Retail	TJX
1990	0.2%	6.3%	6.5%
1991	13.3	21.7	60.6
1992	-2.3	1.7	17.1
1993	3.8	3.0	19.1
1994	-6.1	-0.1	-3.0
1995	8.1	9.7	-7.7
1996	5.5	19.7	44.0
1997	-1.1	10.4	-0.4
1998	12.6	19.7	25.6
1999	5.3	16.5	19.0
2000	3.2	5.1	33.0
2001	-13.6	1.7	16.3
2002	1.8	4.7	2.9
2003	-2.7	6.6	-6.7
2004	-1.8	5.4	3.4
2005	1.2	-0.6	-1.5
2006	3.1	4.5	3.7
2007	-0.7	-2.7	-10.3
2008	-0.8	1.4	13.2
2009	-6.3	8.1	29.0
2010	5.1	12.5	17.3
2011	3.5	3.5	6.0
2012	7.1	12.9	19.3
2013	5.6	6.2	4.5
Avg	1.8%	7.4%	13.0%
Fq > 0	63%	88%	75%

It is interesting to note that the seasonally strong period for TJX ends before one of the strongest months of the year, April. It is possible that by the end of March, after a typically strong run for TJX, that the full value of TJX's first quarter earnings report has already been priced into the stock and investors look to other companies in which to invest. This is particularly true if the economy and the stock market are in good shape.

On the other hand, in a soft economy, consumers favor off-price apparel companies such as TJX. In this scenario, TJX is more likely to perform strongly past the end of its seasonal period in March, allowing seasonal investors to continue to hold TJX until it shows signs of weakness.

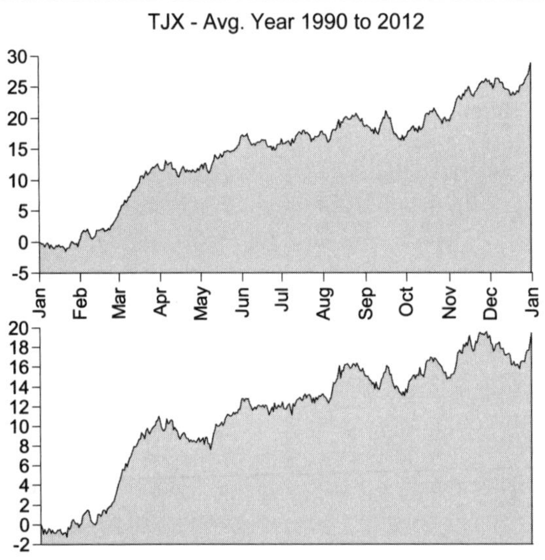

TJX / S&P 500 Relative Strength - Avg Yr. 1990 - 2012

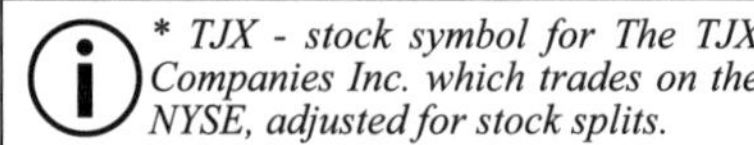
* *TJX - stock symbol for The TJX Companies Inc. which trades on the NYSE, adjusted for stock splits.*

2012-13 Strategy Performance

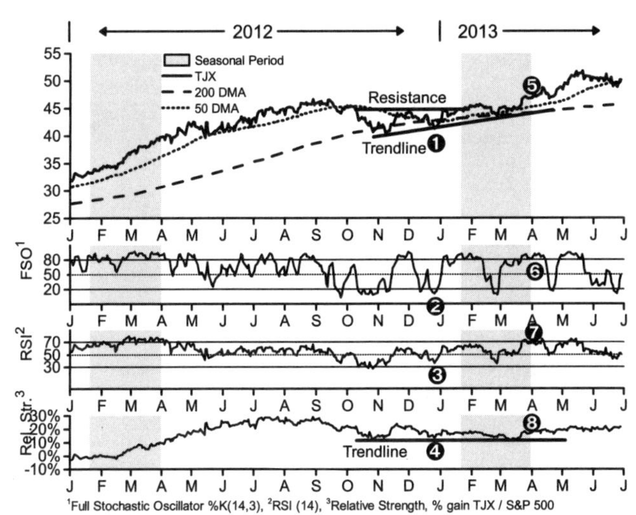

¹Full Stochastic Oscillator %K(14,3), ²RSI (14), ³Relative Strength, % gain TJX / S&P 500

TJX Performance

After a positive 2012 seasonal trade, TJX kept outperforming the S&P 500 into the summer, at which point it started to underperform the S&P 500. Towards the end of 2012, TJX was performing at market.

Technical Conditions– January 22nd to March 30th, 2013

Entry Strategy – Buy Position Early–

In late December TJX turned up above its 50 day moving average❶ and at the same time the FSO crossed above 20❷, triggering an early buy signal. At the same time, the RSI crossed above 50❸ and relative strength to the market was just starting to increase❹. In the end, establishing an early position provided slightly better returns than just entering on the seasonal start date. On the seasonal start date, TJX was performing at market.

Exit Strategy– Sell Position on Exit Date–

Although TJX had been slightly underperfoming the S&P 500 for the first two months of its seasonal strategy, it did not break down below a key level. Just before the end of the seasonal trade TJX spiked in price❺ placing it into overbought territory for the FSO❻ and the RSI❼. After the end of the seasonal trade, TJX returned to market performance❽.

WEEK 04

Market Indices & Rates
Weekly Values**

Stock Markets	**2012**	**2013**
Dow	12,707	13,803
S&P500	1,318	1,496
Nasdaq	2,802	3,144
TSX	12,477	12,811
FTSE	5,757	6,221
DAX	6,466	7,752
Nikkei	8,825	10,698
Hang Seng	20,470	23,613
Commodities	**2012**	**2013**
Oil	99.31	95.34
Gold	1688.8	1679.9
Bond Yields	**2012**	**2013**
USA 5 Yr Treasury	0.84	0.79
USA 10 Yr T	2.01	1.90
USA 20 Yr T	2.77	2.66
Moody's Aaa	3.90	3.78
Moody's Baa	5.29	4.72
CAN 5 Yr T	1.37	1.45
CAN 10 Yr T	2.04	1.91
Money Market	**2012**	**2013**
USA Fed Funds	0.25	0.25
USA 3 Mo T-B	0.06	0.08
CAN tgt overnight rate	1.00	1.00
CAN 3 Mo T-B	0.86	0.92
Foreign Exchange	**2012**	**2013**
EUR/USD	1.31	1.34
GBP/USD	1.57	1.58
USD/CAD	1.01	1.00
USD/JPY	77.32	89.63

JANUARY

M	T	W	T	F	S	S
		1	2	3	4	5
6	7	8	9	10	11	12
13	14	15	16	17	18	19
20	21	22	23	24	25	26
27	28	29	30	31		

FEBRUARY

M	T	W	T	F	S	S
					1	2
3	4	5	6	7	8	9
10	11	12	13	14	15	16
17	18	19	20	21	22	23
24	25	26	27	28		

MARCH

M	T	W	T	F	S	S
					1	2
3	4	5	6	7	8	9
10	11	12	13	14	15	16
17	18	19	20	21	22	23
24	25	26	27	28	29	30
31						

** Weekly avg closing values- except Fed Funds & CAN overnight tgt rate weekly closing values.

UNPLUG THE CHRISTMAS TREE SHORT UTILITIES – Jan 1st to Mar 13th

At the beginning of the year, investors are more interested in growth investments rather than dividend investments. As a result, the utilities sector tends to underperform the S&P 500 up until mid-March.

If investors are looking for a strategy to reduce their portfolio risk at the beginning of the year, shorting the utilities sector should be a consideration.

2.6% gain and successful 58% of the time

Pairing up a short position in the utilities sector (during its seasonal short period) with a long position in the S&P 500 has performed well, regardless of the market direction. From 1990 to 2013, the utilities sector has only managed to beat the S&P 500 approximately one-quarter of the time. The two largest losses (shorting) the utilities sector were 8.2% in 2013 and 7.9% in 1993. The next largest loss was 4.0% in 2005. Overall, shorting the utilities sector has produced low drawdowns with a fairly strong positive upside.

S&P Utilities Sector vs. S&P 500 1990 to 2013

Jan 1 to Mar 13	S&P 500	Utilities	Diff
		Negative	
1990	-4.9 %	-7.6 %	-2.7 %
1991	13.4	0.8	-12.6
1992	-2.7	-9.1	-6.4
1993	3.2	7.9	4.6
1994	0.0	-7.6	-7.5
1995	6.7	3.2	-3.6
1996	3.7	-5.5	-9.2
1997	6.6	-3.3	-9.9
1998	10.1	0.3	-9.8
1999	5.3	-5.8	-11.1
2000	-5.8	-0.7	5.1
2001	-9.3	-9.1	0.2
2002	0.5	-1.8	-2.3
2003	-5.5	-8.4	-2.9
2004	0.8	2.4	1.6
2005	-1.0	4.0	5.0
2006	2.9	0.5	-2.3
2007	-2.8	3.0	5.9
2008	-10.4	-10.7	-0.3
2009	-16.2	-19.4	-3.2
2010	3.1	-4.8	-7.9
2011	3.7	2.9	-0.8
2012	11	-1.7	-12.7
2013	9.0	8.2	-0.8
Avg.	0.9 %	-2.6 %	-3.5 %
Fq > 0	58 %	42 %	25 %

Utilities Sector - Avg. Year 1990 to 2012

Utilities / S&P 500 Relative Strength - Avg Yr. 1990 - 2012

The average loss for the utilities sector has been 2.6% (gain for a short position) during its seasonal short period. This compares to a gain of 0.9% for the S&P 500. The real value for this trade is how often the utilities sector underperforms the S&P 500 during its seasonal period. Since 1990, the sector has underperformed the S&P 500, 25% of the time. In other words, a pair trade with a long position in the S&P 500 and a short position in the utilities would have worked 75% of the time.

Very often the utilities sector puts in a strong run at the end of the year as investors sell their small-cap higher beta stocks for tax loss reasons and rotate into the more conservative utilities sector. When this phenomenon occurs and the utilities sector becomes overbought, this provides a very good opportunity to short the sector at the beginning of the year when the sector often corrects.

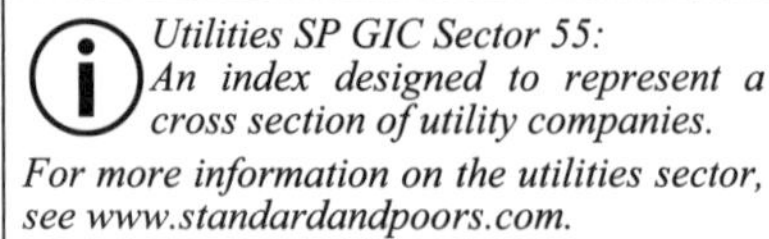

Utilities SP GIC Sector 55: An index designed to represent a cross section of utility companies.

For more information on the utilities sector, see www.standardandpoors.com.

2012-13 Strategy Performance

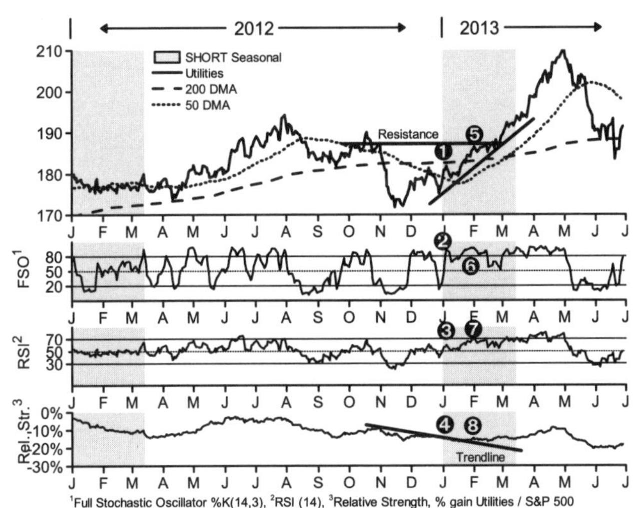

¹Full Stochastic Oscillator %K(14,3), ²RSI (14), ³Relative Strength, % gain Utilities / S&P 500

Utilities Sector (SHORT) Performance

The utilities sector started to underperform the S&P 500 in August 2012. Coming into the seasonal time to short the utilities sector, the utilities sector was starting to pick up on an absolute basis, but still underperforming the S&P 500.

Technical Conditions– January 1st to March 13th, 2013

Entry Strategy– (Short)– Buy Position on Entry Date– Although the FSO fell below 80 a few weeks before the end of the year, presenting an early entry opportunity, the last part of December can be very positive for the utilities sector and in most cases when this abrupt seasonal change occurs, it is best to wait until the start of the seasonal period. At the start of the seasonal period, the utilities sector was increasing, but below its 200 day moving average❶. Shortly after the start of the seasonal period the FSO was registering an overbought condition at 80❷, and the RSI was trading above 50❸. The sector was continuing its trend of underperforming the S&P 500❹.

Exit Strategy– (Short) – Sell Position Early– During the seasonal period, the sector remained in a pattern of positive performance❺ with the FSO❻ and RSI❼ remaining in their upper bands. At the beginning of February, the utilities sector had broken above its 200 day moving average and had broken its trend of underperforming the S&P 500❽ (moving to a trend of market performance). At the beginning of March, the utilities sector broke above a key resistance level, justifying an early exit.

WEEK 05

Market Indices & Rates Weekly Values**

Stock Markets	2012	2013
Dow	12,714	13,923
S&P500	1,324	1,504
Nasdaq	2,848	3,154
TSX	12,507	12,779
FTSE	5,768	6,316
DAX	6,588	7,820
Nikkei	8,823	11,027
Hang Seng	20,476	23,720

Commodities	2012	2013
Oil	97.81	97.44
Gold	1739.6	1666.3

Bond Yields	2012	2013
USA 5 Yr Treasury	0.73	0.89
USA 10 Yr T	1.88	2.02
USA 20 Yr T	2.66	2.79
Moody's Aaa	3.80	3.91
Moody's Baa	5.13	4.85
CAN 5 Yr T	1.29	1.50
CAN 10 Yr T	1.94	2.00

Money Market	2012	2013
USA Fed Funds	0.25	0.25
USA 3 Mo T-B	0.08	0.06
CAN tgt overnight rate	1.00	1.00
CAN 3 Mo T-B	0.88	0.93

Foreign Exchange	2012	2013
EUR/USD	1.31	1.35
GBP/USD	1.58	1.58
USD/CAD	1.00	1.00
USD/JPY	76.33	91.43

JANUARY

M	T	W	T	F	S	S
		1	2	3	4	5
6	7	8	9	10	11	12
13	14	15	16	17	18	19
20	21	22	23	24	25	26
27	28	29	30	31		

FEBRUARY

M	T	W	T	F	S	S
					1	2
3	4	5	6	7	8	9
10	11	12	13	14	15	16
17	18	19	20	21	22	23
24	25	26	27	28		

MARCH

M	T	W	T	F	S	S
					1	2
3	4	5	6	7	8	9
10	11	12	13	14	15	16
17	18	19	20	21	22	23
24	25	26	27	28	29	30
31						

** Weekly avg closing values- except Fed Funds & CAN overnight tgt rate weekly closing values.

FEBRUARY

	MONDAY	TUESDAY	WEDNESDAY
WEEK 06	3 25	4 24	5 23
WEEK 07	10 18	11 17	12 16
WEEK 08	17 11 CAN Market Closed - Family Day USA Market Closed - Presidents' Day	18 10	19 9
WEEK 09	24 4	25 3	26 2
WEEK 10	3	4	5

FEBRUARY

THURSDAY		FRIDAY	
6	22	**7**	21
13	15	**14**	14
20	8	**21**	7
27	1	**28**	
6		7	

MARCH

M	T	W	T	F	S	S
					1	2
3	4	5	6	7	8	9
10	11	12	13	14	15	16
17	18	19	20	21	22	23
24	25	26	27	28	29	30
31						

APRIL

M	T	W	T	F	S	S
	1	2	3	4	5	6
7	8	9	10	11	12	13
14	15	16	17	18	19	20
21	22	23	24	25	26	27
28	29	30				

MAY

M	T	W	T	F	S	S
			1	2	3	4
5	6	7	8	9	10	11
12	13	14	15	16	17	18
19	20	21	22	23	24	25
26	27	28	29	30	31	

JUNE

M	T	W	T	F	S	S
						1
2	3	4	5	6	7	8
9	10	11	12	13	14	15
16	17	18	19	20	21	22
23	24	25	26	27	28	29
30						

FEBRUARY
S U M M A R Y

0.4%
0.2%
0.0%
-0.2%

S&P500 Cumulative Daily Gains for Avg Month 1950 to 2013

	Dow Jones	S&P 500	Nasdaq	TSX Comp
Month Rank	8	11	9	5
# Up	36	34	21	16
# Down	27	29	20	12
% Pos	57	54	51	57
% Avg. Gain	0.1	-0.1	0.4	0.9

Dow & S&P 1950-2012, Nasdaq 1972-2012, TSX 1985-2012

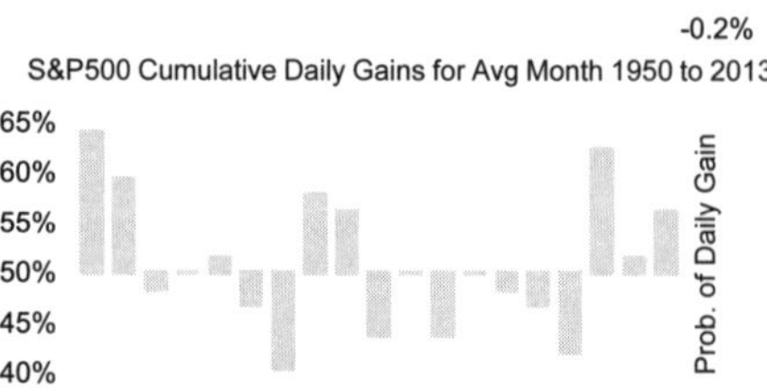

♦ Historically, February has been the second weakest month of the year. From 1950 to 2012, the S&P 500 has produced an average loss of 0.1% and has been positive 53% of the time. ♦ In the last three years (2011 to 2013), February has produced strong gains. ♦ The energy, materials and consumer discretionary sectors tend to perform well, while the defensive sectors, health care, utilities and telecom, have on average produced losses since 1990. ♦ When the defensive sectors perform well in February, it often indicates a conservative market ahead.

BEST / WORST FEBRUARY BROAD MKTS. 2004-2013

BEST FEBRUARY MARKETS

- Nikkei 225 (2012) 10.5%
- Nasdaq (2012) 5.4%
- Russell 2000 (2011) 5.4%

WORST FEBRUARY MARKETS

- Russell 2000 (2009) -12.3%
- Dow (2009) -11.7%
- S&P 500 (2009) -11.0%

Index Values End of Month

	2004	2005	2006	2007	2008	2009	2010	2011	2012	2013
Dow	10,584	10,766	10,993	12,269	12,266	7,063	10,325	12,226	12,952	14,054
S&P 500	1,145	1,204	1,281	1,407	1,331	735	1,104	1,327	1,366	1,515
Nasdaq	2,030	2,052	2,281	2,416	2,271	1,378	2,238	2,782	2,967	3,160
TSX Comp.	8,788	9,668	11,688	13,045	13,583	8,123	11,630	14,137	12,644	12,822
Russell 1000	1,178	1,244	1,341	1,478	1,396	768	1,168	1,415	1,454	1,617
Russell 2000	1,455	1,576	1,816	1,972	1,705	967	1,562	2,046	2,015	2,264
FTSE 100	4,492	4,969	5,792	6,172	5,884	3,830	5,355	5,994	5,872	6,361
Nikkei 225	11,042	11,741	16,205	17,604	13,603	7,568	10,126	10,624	9,723	11,559

Percent Gain for February

	2004	2005	2006	2007	2008	2009	2010	2011	2012	2013
Dow	0.9	2.6	1.2	-2.8	-3.0	-11.7	2.6	2.8	2.5	1.4
S&P 500	1.2	1.9	0.0	-2.2	-3.5	-11.0	2.9	3.2	4.1	1.1
Nasdaq	-1.8	-0.5	-1.1	-1.9	-5.0	-6.7	4.2	3.0	5.4	0.6
TSX Comp.	3.1	5.0	-2.2	0.1	3.3	-6.6	4.8	4.3	1.5	1.1
Russell 1000	1.2	2.0	0.0	-1.9	-3.3	-10.7	3.1	3.3	4.1	1.1
Russell 2000	0.8	1.6	-0.3	-0.9	-3.8	-12.3	4.4	5.4	2.3	1.0
FTSE 100	2.3	2.4	0.5	-0.5	0.1	-7.7	3.2	2.2	3.3	1.3
Nikkei 225	2.4	3.1	-2.7	1.3	0.1	-5.3	-0.7	3.8	10.5	3.8

February Market Avg. Performance 2004 to 2013(1)

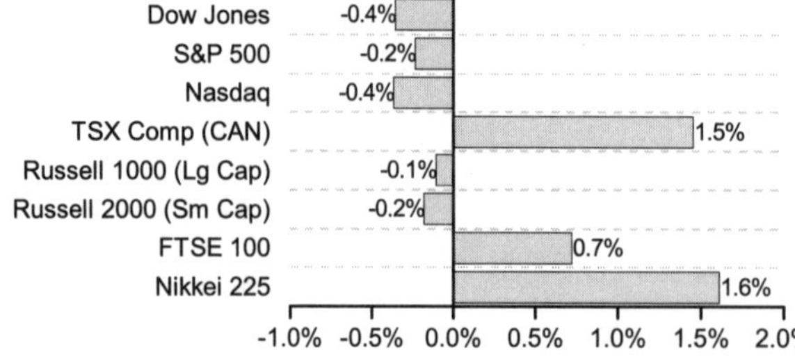

Interest Corner Feb2)

	Fed Funds % (3)	3 Mo. T-Bill %(4)	10 Yr %(5)	20 Yr %(6)
2013	0.25	0.11	1.89	2.71
2012	0.25	0.08	1.98	2.73
2011	0.25	0.15	3.42	4.25
2010	0.25	0.13	3.61	4.40
2009	0.25	0.26	3.02	3.98

(1) Russell Data provided by Russell (2) Federal Reserve Bank of St. Louis- end of month values (3) Target rate set by FOMC (4)(5)(6) Constant yield maturities.

FEBRUARY SECTOR PERFORMANCE

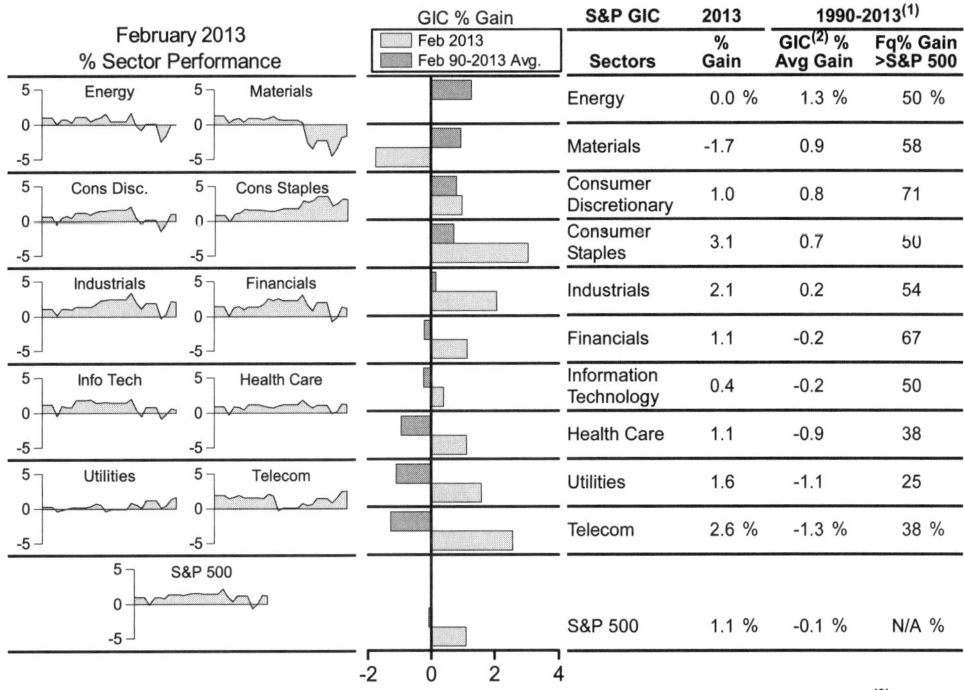

S&P GIC	2013	1990-2013[1]	
Sectors	% Gain	GIC[2] % Avg Gain	Fq% Gain >S&P 500
Energy	0.0 %	1.3 %	50 %
Materials	-1.7	0.9	58
Consumer Discretionary	1.0	0.8	71
Consumer Staples	3.1	0.7	50
Industrials	2.1	0.2	54
Financials	1.1	-0.2	67
Information Technology	0.4	-0.2	50
Health Care	1.1	-0.9	38
Utilities	1.6	-1.1	25
Telecom	2.6 %	-1.3 %	38 %
S&P 500	1.1 %	-0.1 %	N/A %

SELECTED SUB-SECTORS[3]

SOX (1995-2013)	3.4 %	2.5 %	58 %
Silver	-9.6	2.4	50
Retail	1.0	1.6	67
Chemicals	-1.0	1.2	71
Metals & Mining	-7.9	1.0	54
Gold (London PM)	-4.6	0.8	46
Agriculture (1994-2013)	11.7	0.6	55
Transportation	2.9	0.3	58
Steel	-8.8	0.3	50
Railroads	4.6	0.0	50
Banks	0.7	0.0	58
Software & Services	0.8	-0.3	46
Homebuilders	-6.8	-0.5	58
Pharma	1.2	-1.1	38
Biotech (1993-2013)	5.5	-1.4	52

Sector Commentary

♦ February is considered to be a weaker month of the year, but in February 2013 the S&P 500 produced a respectable gain of 1.1%. ♦ What is interesting are the sectors that outperformed and underperformed. ♦ The materials sector was the worst performer. Typically, at this time of the year the materials sector is a strong performer, but it faded towards the end of the month, indicating that the cyclicals may have trouble in the near future. ♦ The three defensive sectors, health care, utilities and health care all performed at market or better. This is not typical for this time of the year and was indicating a shift of investors becoming more cautious with their investments.

Sub-Sector Commentary

♦ The top performing sub-sector was agriculture as it continued its strong run that started in mid-November. ♦ The homebuilders sub-sector ended its successful seasonal period with a big drop just after its seasonal period ended. The result was a loss of 6.8% for the month. ♦ The steel sub-sector underperformed along with materials. ♦ Silver can often perform well in February, but if both gold and the industrial metals are decreasing, silver will decrease, as it did in February.

DUPONT
January 28th to May 5th

Dupont has been positive for the last twelve years during its seasonally strong period, extending a record of being positive twenty-three times over the last twenty-four years. In 2013 and for the sixth year in a row, Dupont outperformed the S&P 500. The Dupont trade is considered to be a strong consistent performer at this time of the year.

DuPont is a diversified chemicals company that operates in seven segments: Agriculture & Nutrition, Electronics & Communications, Performance Chemicals, Performance Coatings, Performance Materials, Safety & Protection, and Pharmaceuticals.

The chemicals sector is a large part of the U.S. materials sector, which has a seasonally strong period from January 23rd to May 5th. DuPont has a similar seasonal trend that starts a few days later on January 28th. Investors can use technical analysis to determine if an earlier position in DuPont should be taken.

10.9% gain & positive 96% of the time

The DuPont seasonal trade has worked very well since 1990, producing an average gain of 10.9% with a very high 96% frequency rate of being positive.

DuPont vs. S&P 500
1990 to 2013

Jan 28 to May 5	S&P 500	DD	Diff
		(shaded)	Positive
1990	3.9%	0.3%	-3.5%
1991	13.3	19.6	6.3
1992	0.5	11.2	10.7
1993	1.5	15.2	13.8
1994	-5.4	6.6	12.0
1995	10.6	21.8	11.2
1996	3.2	6.1	2.9
1997	8.5	4.4	-4.2
1998	15.1	35.2	20.0
1999	8.4	33.6	25.2
2000	2.4	-16.7	-19.1
2001	-6.5	12.8	19.3
2002	-5.3	3.2	8.4
2003	9.3	11.3	2.0
2004	-2.0	2.5	4.5
2005	-0.2	2.6	2.8
2006	3.3	13.4	10.1
2007	5.9	4.2	-1.7
2008	5.8	11.1	5.4
2009	6.9	24.9	18.1
2010	6.2	15.3	9.0
2011	2.7	7.2	4.4
2012	4.0	4.3	0.3
2013	7.4	11.6	4.2
Avg	4.2%	10.9%	6.7%
Fq > 0	79%	96%	83%

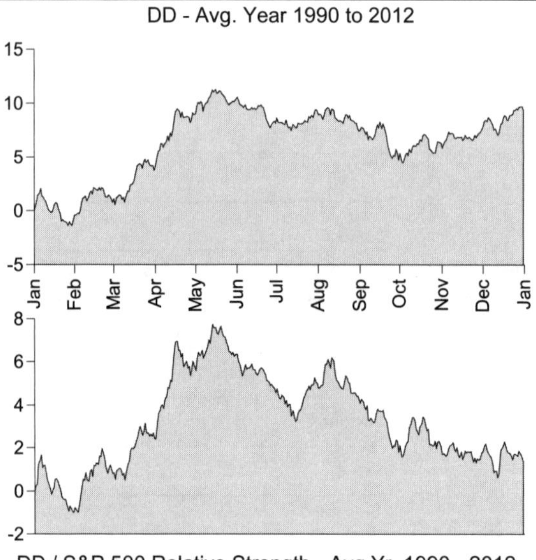

Investors should be aware that DuPont does not perform as well as the broad market from May 6th to the end of the year. In fact, during this period, from 1990 to 2012, Dupont has generated an average loss of 3.0% and has only been positive 39% of the time.

This compares to the S&P 500, which has produced an average gain of 3.7% and has been positive 70% of the time, during the same time period.

If investors are interested in purchasing DuPont on a seasonal basis, it is clear that they should concentrate their efforts from the end of January to the beginning of May.

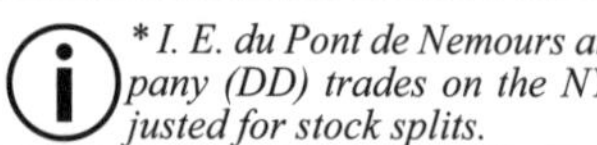

** I. E. du Pont de Nemours and Company (DD) trades on the NYSE, adjusted for stock splits.*

2012-13 Strategy Performance

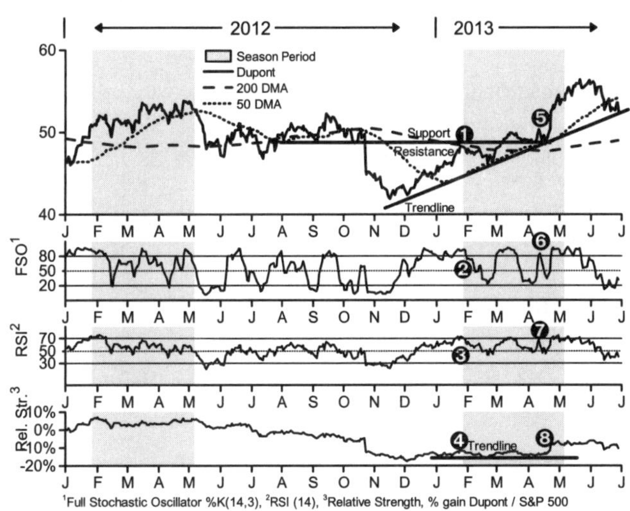

¹Full Stochastic Oscillator %K(14,3), ²RSI (14), ³Relative Strength, % gain Dupont / S&P 500

Dupont Performance

Dupont started to outperform the S&P 500 at the beginning of December 2012 and continued its outperformance up until the end of January, which is the start of its seasonally strong period.

Technical Conditions– January 28th to May 5th, 2013

Entry Strategy –Buy Position on Entry Date–

As a clear entry signal had not been given before the seasonal entry date, the first allocation to Dupont should have taken place at the start of the seasonally strong period. On the entry date, Dupont was touching its 50 day moving average❶, had overbought levels with both the FSO❷ and RSI❸ and was mildly underperforming the S&P 500❹. Dupont performed at market until mid-April, at which time it strongly outperformed the S&P 500.

Exit Strategy – Sell Position on Exit Date–

In mid-April, the FSO turned down below 80❻ and the RSI turned down from 70❼, but Dupont remained solidly above its 50 day moving average❺ and its support level. In addition, Dupont continued to perform at market. On April 23rd, Dupont announced solid earnings, beating analyst expectations, and driving the stock price to outperform the S&P 500❽.

WEEK 06

Market Indices & Rates Weekly Values**

Stock Markets	**2012**	**2013**
Dow	12,860	13,957
S&P500	1,347	1,509
Nasdaq	2,911	3,166
TSX	12,496	12,756
FTSE	5,881	6,263
DAX	6,750	7,625
Nikkei	8,962	11,256
Hang Seng	20,844	23,297
Commodities	**2012**	**2013**
Oil	98.51	96.20
Gold	1729.7	1670.0
Bond Yields	**2012**	**2013**
USA 5 Yr Treasury	0.81	0.85
USA 10 Yr T	1.99	2.00
USA 20 Yr T	2.77	2.80
Moody's Aaa	3.89	3.90
Moody's Baa	5.17	4.86
CAN 5 Yr T	1.40	1.48
CAN 10 Yr T	2.04	1.99
Money Market	**2012**	**2013**
USA Fed Funds	0.25	0.25
USA 3 Mo T-B	0.09	0.07
CAN tgt overnight rate	1.00	1.00
CAN 3 Mo T-B	0.89	0.94
Foreign Exchange	**2012**	**2013**
EUR/USD	1.32	1.35
GBP/USD	1.58	1.57
USD/CAD	1.00	1.00
USD/JPY	77.13	93.19

FEBRUARY

M	T	W	T	F	S	S
					1	2
3	4	5	6	7	8	9
10	11	12	13	14	15	16
17	18	19	20	21	22	23
24	25	26	27	28		

MARCH

M	T	W	T	F	S	S
					1	2
3	4	5	6	7	8	9
10	11	12	13	14	15	16
17	18	19	20	21	22	23
24	25	26	27	28	29	30
31						

APRIL

M	T	W	T	F	S	S
	1	2	3	4	5	6
7	8	9	10	11	12	13
14	15	16	17	18	19	20
21	22	23	24	25	26	27
28	29	30				

** Weekly avg closing values- except Fed Funds & CAN overnight tgt rate weekly closing values.

DON'T WASTE THIS OPPORTUNITY
February 24th to May 14th

Waste Management Inc. tends to perform well just prior to the peak of the waste disposal season in the summer time.

This is mainly the result of increased construction and demolition at this time of the year. In addition the company undergoes increased maintenance on its equipment in the winter time during slower times, which raises expenses. Overall, investors are attracted to the stock as revenue and profits increase in the summer months.

From February 24th to May 14th, during the period from 1992 to 2013, Waste Management Inc. produced an average return of 9.2% and has been positive 68% of the time.

9.2% gain & better than the S&P 500 73% of the time

Although the frequency of positive performance is less than the S&P 500, it has beaten the S&P 500, 73% of the time. In other words, when Waste Management Inc. has produced positive performances, it has typically outperformed the S&P 500.

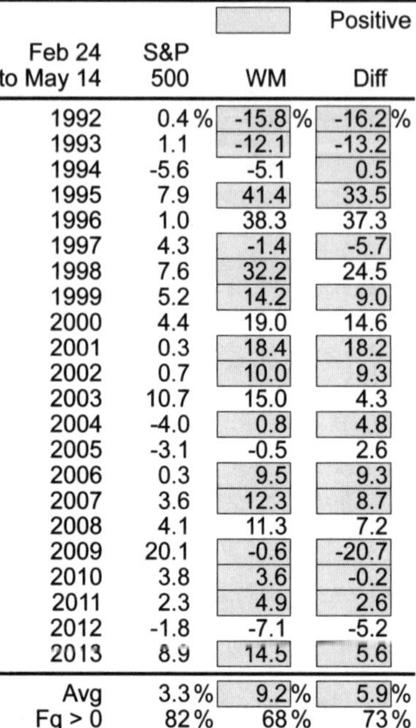

WM* vs. S&P 500
1992 to 2013

Feb 24 to May 14	S&P 500	WM	Diff
1992	0.4 %	-15.8 %	-16.2 %
1993	1.1	-12.1	-13.2
1994	-5.6	-5.1	0.5
1995	7.9	41.4	33.5
1996	1.0	38.3	37.3
1997	4.3	-1.4	-5.7
1998	7.6	32.2	24.5
1999	5.2	14.2	9.0
2000	4.4	19.0	14.6
2001	0.3	18.4	18.2
2002	0.7	10.0	9.3
2003	10.7	15.0	4.3
2004	-4.0	0.8	4.8
2005	-3.1	-0.5	2.6
2006	0.3	9.5	9.3
2007	3.6	12.3	8.7
2008	4.1	11.3	7.2
2009	20.1	-0.6	-20.7
2010	3.8	3.6	-0.2
2011	2.3	4.9	2.6
2012	-1.8	-7.1	-5.2
2013	8.9	14.5	5.6
Avg	3.3 %	9.2 %	5.9 %
Fq > 0	82 %	68 %	73 %

Positive (shaded)

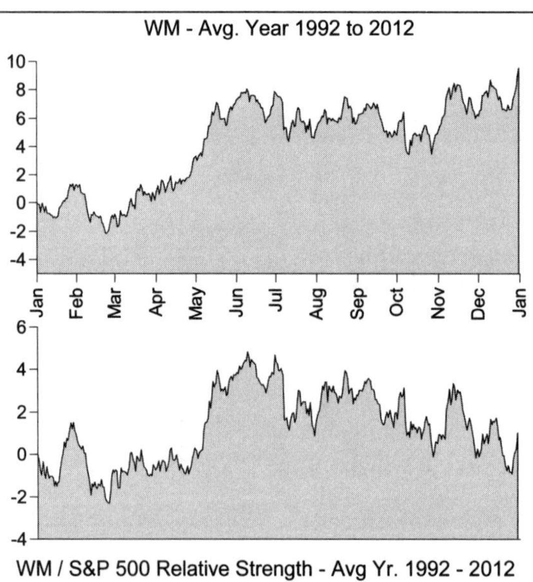

WM / S&P 500 Relative Strength - Avg Yr. 1992 - 2012

The frequency of positive performance of Waste Management Inc. during its seasonal period is skewed downwards by the first three years as a public company.

From 1990 to 2012, outside of its seasonal period (unfavourable period), Waste Management Inc. has produced an average gain of 1.2% and has been positive 52% of the time.

This compares to the S&P 500 which produced an average gain of 5.2% and was positive 76% of the time.

Although historically Waste Management Inc. has produced a gain during its unfavorable period, its performance is substantially less than the S&P 500 and investors should be looking to invest in other areas during this unfavorable season.

** WM - stock symbol for Waste Management Inc. which trades on the NYSE exchange. Prices adjusted for stock splits and dividends.*

2012-13 Strategy Performance

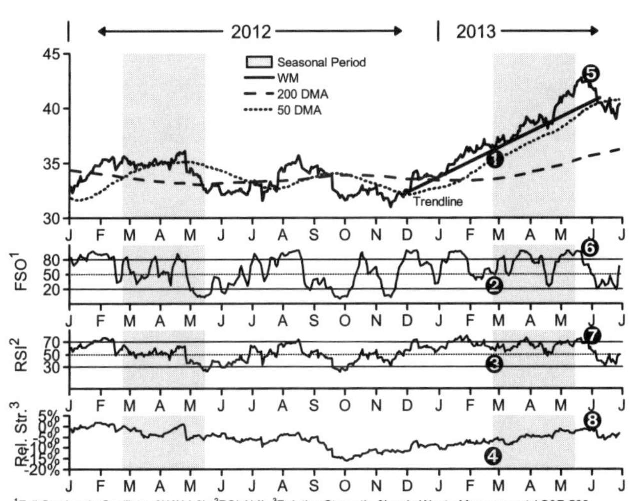

¹Full Stochastic Oscillator %K(14,3), ²RSI (14), ³Relative Strength, % gain Waste Management / S&P 500

Waste Management Performance

After underperforming the S&P 500 for eight months in 2012, Waste Management Inc. started to outperform the S&P 500 in October 2012. On an absolute basis, it started to increase from mid-November. After establishing a positive trendline, Waste Management Inc. was well setup entering its seasonal period.

Technical Conditions– February 24th to May 14th, 2013

Entry Strategy –Buy Position on Entry Date–
An early buy date was not triggered as the FSO did not drop below 20 and then cross above, within a month of the buy date. On the entry date Waste Management Inc. was in an uptrend and trading above its 50 and 200 day moving averages❶. The FSO was approximately 50❷ and the RSI 60❸. Although the stock had been performing well, it was not in an overbought condition and was still outperforming the S&P 500❹.

Exit Strategy – Sell Position after Exit Date–
The FSO turned down below 80 just outside of the four week window before the seasonal exit date. Shortly afterwards, Waste Management Inc. continued its outperformance. On the exit date, Waste Management Inc. was performing well, with the FSO still above 80, allowing a position to be maintained past the exit date. Waste Management Inc. peaked in mid-May❺, and then the FSO crossed below 80❻, later in May, generating a late sell signal. At the same time the FSO triggered a sell signal, the RSI crossed back just below 70❼ and Waste Management Inc. started to perform at market❽. Overall, exiting a bit later than the typical sell date created extra performance with a trade that was already successful.

** Weekly avg closing values- except Fed Funds & CAN overnight tgt rate weekly closing values.

WEEK 07

Market Indices & Rates Weekly Values**

Stock Markets	2012	2013
Dow	12,877	13,986
S&P500	1,353	1,520
Nasdaq	2,938	3,193
TSX	12,412	12,744
FTSE	5,898	6,326
DAX	6,765	7,646
Nikkei	9,187	11,275
Hang Seng	21,188	23,429

Commodities	2012	2013
Oil	101.80	96.94
Gold	1722.2	1640.6

Bond Yields	2012	2013
USA 5 Yr Treasury	0.84	0.88
USA 10 Yr T	1.97	2.01
USA 20 Yr T	2.76	2.81
Moody's Aaa	3.84	3.91
Moody's Baa	5.15	4.86
CAN 5 Yr T	1.41	1.47
CAN 10 Yr T	2.04	2.00

Money Market	2012	2013
USA Fed Funds	0.25	0.25
USA 3 Mo T-B	0.09	0.10
CAN tgt overnight rate	1.00	1.00
CAN 3 Mo T-B	0.93	0.95

Foreign Exchange	2012	2013
EUR/USD	1.31	1.34
GBP/USD	1.58	1.56
USD/CAD	1.00	1.00
USD/JPY	78.59	93.51

FEBRUARY

M	T	W	T	F	S	S
					1	2
3	4	5	6	7	8	9
10	11	12	13	14	15	16
17	18	19	20	21	22	23
24	25	26	27	28		

MARCH

M	T	W	T	F	S	S
					1	2
3	4	5	6	7	8	9
10	11	12	13	14	15	16
17	18	19	20	21	22	23
24	25	26	27	28	29	30
31						

APRIL

M	T	W	T	F	S	S
	1	2	3	4	5	6
7	8	9	10	11	12	13
14	15	16	17	18	19	20
21	22	23	24	25	26	27
28	29	30				

ROYAL BANK— A TRADE TO BANK ON

①Oct 10 - Nov 28 ②Jan 23 - Apr 13

Canadians love their banks and tend to hold large amounts of the banking sector in their portfolios. Their love for the sector has remained strong, as international accolades have supported a positive viewpoint of Canadian banks. In a 2012 Bloomberg report, the Canadian banks dominated the top ten strongest banks in the world, with four banks in the top ten.

For years, Royal Bank was considered one of the most conservative banks and often attracted investors during tough times. After a few mis-steps in their expansion into the U.S., Royal Bank seems to be getting back on track.

Through its ups and downs, Royal Bank has followed the same general pattern as the banking sector: rising in autumn and then once again in the new year.

12.2% gain & positive 75% of the time

In the period from October 10th to November 28th, from 1989 to 2012, Royal Bank has produced an average gain of 5.1% and has been positive 88% of the time. The bank tends to perform well at this time, as Canadians tend to increase their bank holdings before the year-end earnings reports are released in late November. It is not a coincidence that Royal Bank's seasonally strong period ends at approximately the same time as their year-end earnings announcements. Seasonal investors benefit from buying Royal Bank before the "masses," whom are also trying to take advantage of the possibility of positive earnings.

The second seasonal period from January 23rd to April 13 is also very positive. In this time period, Canadian banks in general tend to outperform the TSX Composite, as they benefit from the typically strong economic forecasts at the beginning of the year. In addition, they "echo," or get a boost from the strong seasonal performance of the U.S banks at this time.

Royal Bank* vs. TSX Comp 1989/90 to 2011/12 Positive

Year	Oct 10 to Nov 28 TSX Comp	Oct 10 to Nov 28 RY	Jan 23 to Apr 13 TSX Comp	Jan 23 to Apr 13 RY	Compound Growth TSX Comp	Compound Growth RY
1989/90	-2.8 %	2.4 %	-6.3 %	-10.0 %	-8.9 %	-7.8 %
1990/91	0.2	3.5	9.8	11.6	10.0	15.5
1991/92	2.9	3.3	-6.8	-14.5	-4.1	-11.6
1992/93	1.8	5.0	10.7	17.6	12.6	23.4
1993/94	3.8	0.0	-5.6	-13.1	-2.1	-13.1
1994/95	-4.7	2.2	5.0	13.2	0.0	15.7
1995/96	4.0	3.3	3.6	0.0	7.7	3.3
1996/97	10.7	23.3	-6.2	1.3	3.9	24.9
1997/98	-8.7	7.6	19.9	24.0	9.4	33.4
1998/99	18.0	20.9	4.8	0.6	23.7	21.6
1999/00	10.9	8.6	3.8	34.5	15.1	46.0
2000/01	-14.5	5.1	-14.1	-12.0	-26.5	-7.5
2001/02	7.1	3.2	2.3	11.8	9.6	15.4
2002/03	16.4	18.1	-4.3	1.8	11.4	20.2
2003/04	3.4	0.3	2.0	1.8	5.4	2.1
2004/05	2.8	4.0	4.5	17.6	7.3	22.3
2005/06	3.1	7.3	5.5	7.0	8.8	14.8
2006/07	7.2	8.5	6.9	7.1	14.5	16.2
2007/08	-4.4	-5.1	8.2	-4.9	3.5	-9.8
2008/09	-3.4	4.3	9.4	35.0	5.7	40.8
2009/10	0.2	1.3	6.7	12.6	6.9	14.1
2010/11	2.9	0.4	4.3	12.4	7.3	12.0
2011/12	0.5	-6.3	-2.9	3.8	-2.4	-2.8
2012/13	-1.1	2.1	-3.8	-0.3	-4.8	1.9
Avg.	2.3 %	5.1 %	2.4 %	6.6 %	4.8 %	12.2 %
Fq > 0	71 %	88 %	67 %	71 %	75 %	75 %

Royal Bank* Avg. Year 1990 to 2012

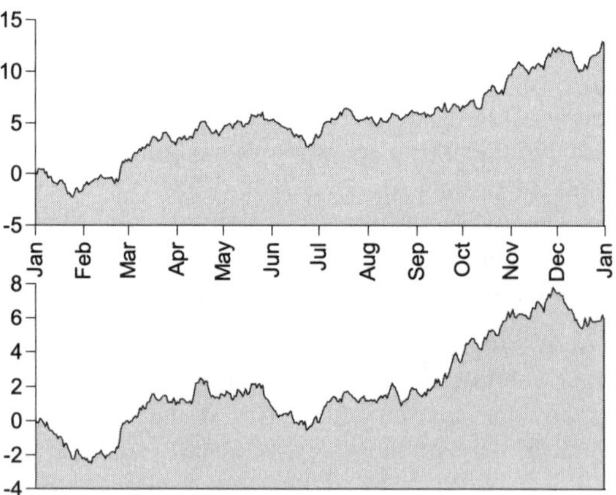

Royal Bank / TSX Comp. Rel. Str. - Avg Yr. 1990 - 2012

Alternate Strategy—
Investors can bridge the gap between the two positive seasonal trends for the bank sector by holding from October 10th to April 13th. Longer term investors may prefer this strategy, shorter term investors can use technical tools to determine the appropriate strategy.

** Royal Bank of Canada (RBC) is a diversified financial services company that trades on both the Toronto and NYSE exchanges under the symbol RY. Data from TSX Exchange, includes stock splits only.*

2012-13 Strategy Performance

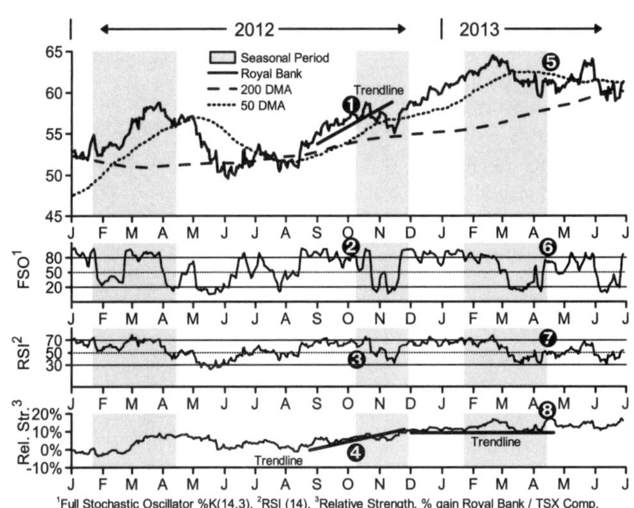

[1]Full Stochastic Oscillator %K(14,3), [2]RSI (14), [3]Relative Strength, % gain Royal Bank / TSX Comp.

Royal Bank Performance

After a successful seasonal strategy in the spring of 2012, Royal Bank, on a relative basis compared to the TSX Composite, corrected into August and then once again started to outperform. It continued to outperform into the start of its seasonal period in October.

Technical Conditions– October 10, 2012 to April 13, 2013

Entry Strategy –Buy Position on Entry Date–

As Royal Bank was outperforming coming into the start of its seasonal period, the shorter-term momentum indicators did not trigger an early buy signal. At the start of the seasonal period, Royal Bank was in an uptrend❶ and was outperforming the TSX Composite❹. Its FSO had just touched 80❷ and turned down, and the RSI had just touched 70❸ and turned down. Despite the FSO and RSI being in overbought territory, this condition does not negate entering into the seasonal trade.

Exit Strategy – Sell Position on Exit Date–

After outperforming the market in November, Royal Bank started the second leg of its seasonal trade in January on a positive note. At the beginning of March, Royal Bank started to turn down, but only returned to its market performance line. Towards the end of its seasonal period, Royal Bank increased both on an absolute basis and a relative basis to the TSX Composite. At the end of the seasonal period, Royal Bank was still below its 50 day moving average❺ and the FSO was just below 80❻ and the RSI was at 50❼. Royal Bank was just starting to perform at market❽.

WEEK 08

Market Indices & Rates
Weekly Values**

Stock Markets	2012	2013
Dow	12,968	13,961
S&P500	1,362	1,515
Nasdaq	2,951	3,168
TSX	12,695	12,716
FTSE	5,933	6,344
DAX	6,875	7,671
Nikkei	9,549	11,389
Hang Seng	21,448	23,104
Commodities	**2012**	**2013**
Oil	107.19	94.08
Gold	1757.5	1592.1
Bond Yields	**2012**	**2013**
USA 5 Yr Treasury	0.89	0.87
USA 10 Yr T	2.01	2.00
USA 20 Yr T	2.79	2.80
Moody's Aaa	3.85	3.93
Moody's Baa	5.15	4.87
CAN 5 Yr T	1.47	1.45
CAN 10 Yr T	2.05	2.00
Money Market	**2012**	**2013**
USA Fed Funds	0.25	0.25
USA 3 Mo T-B	0.10	0.13
CAN tgt overnight rate	1.00	1.00
CAN 3 Mo T-B	0.94	0.96
Foreign Exchange	**2012**	**2013**
EUR/USD	1.33	1.33
GBP/USD	1.58	1.53
USD/CAD	1.00	1.02
USD/JPY	80.17	93.53

FEBRUARY

M	T	W	T	F	S	S
					1	2
3	4	5	6	7	8	9
10	11	12	13	14	15	16
17	18	19	20	21	22	23
24	25	26	27	28		

MARCH

M	T	W	T	F	S	S
					1	2
3	4	5	6	7	8	9
10	11	12	13	14	15	16
17	18	19	20	21	22	23
24	25	26	27	28	29	30
31						

APRIL

M	T	W	T	F	S	S
	1	2	3	4	5	6
7	8	9	10	11	12	13
14	15	16	17	18	19	20
21	22	23	24	25	26	27
28	29	30				

OIL – WINTER/SPRING STRATEGY
Ist of **II** Oil Stock Strategies for the Year
February 25th to May 9th

In 2013, the energy sector produced a gain, but underperformed the S&P 500 during its winter-spring seasonal period. In 2012, the energy sector produced a loss of 13.4%. Nevertheless, the *Energy- Winter/ Spring Strategy* is still a strong seasonal performer over the long-term. From 1984 to 2013, for the two and half months starting on February 25th and ending May 9th, the energy sector (XOI) has outperformed the S&P 500 by an average 4.1%.

What is even more impressive are the positive returns 25 out of 30 times, and the outperformance of the S&P 500, 23 out of 30 times.

4.1% extra and 25 out of 30 times positive, in just over two months

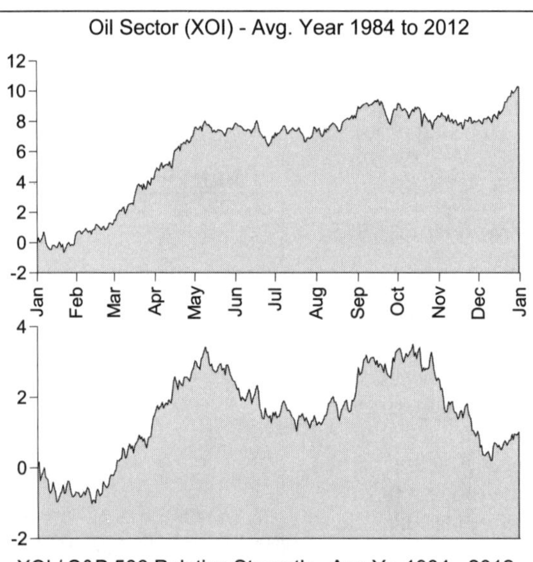

A lot of investors assume that the time to buy oil stocks is just before the winter cold sets in. The rationale is that oil will climb in price as the temperature drops.

The results in the market have not supported this assumption. The price for a barrel of oil has more to do with oil inventory. Refineries have a choice: they can produce either gasoline or heating oil. As the winter progresses, refineries start to convert their operations from heating oil to gasoline.

XOI vs S&P 500 1984 to 2013

Feb 25 to May 9	S&P 500	XOI	Diff
(shaded = positive)			
1984	1.7 %	5.6 %	3.9 %
1985	1.4	4.9	3.5
1986	6.0	7.7	1.7
1987	3.7	25.5	21.8
1988	-3.0	5.6	8.6
1989	6.3	8.1	1.8
1990	5.8	-0.6	-6.3
1991	4.8	6.8	2.0
1992	0.9	5.8	4.9
1993	0.3	6.3	6.0
1994	-4.7	3.2	7.9
1995	7.3	10.3	3.1
1996	-2.1	2.2	4.3
1997	1.8	4.7	2.9
1998	7.5	9.8	2.3
1999	7.3	35.4	28.1
2000	4.3	22.2	17.9
2001	0.8	10.2	9.4
2002	-1.5	5.3	6.9
2003	12.1	5.7	-6.4
2004	-3.5	4.0	7.5
2005	-1.8	-1.0	0.8
2006	2.8	9.4	6.6
2007	4.2	10.1	5.8
2008	2.6	7.6	5.0
2009	20.2	15.8	-4.4
2010	0.5	-2.3	-2.8
2011	3.1	-0.6	-3.7
2012	-0.8	-13.4	-12.5
2013	7.3	3.8	-3.5
Avg	3.2 %	7.3 %	4.1 %
Fq > 0	77 %	83 %	77 %

During this switch-over time, low inventory levels of both heating oil and gasoline can drive up the price of a barrel of oil and oil stocks. In early May, before the kick-off of the driving season (Memorial Day in May), the refineries have finished their conversion to gasoline. The price of oil and oil stocks tend to decline.

> **i** *Amex Oil Index (XOI):*
> *An index designed to represent a cross section of widely held oil corporations involved in various phases of the oil industry.*
>
> *For more information on the XOI index, see www.cboe.com*

2012-13 Strategy Performance

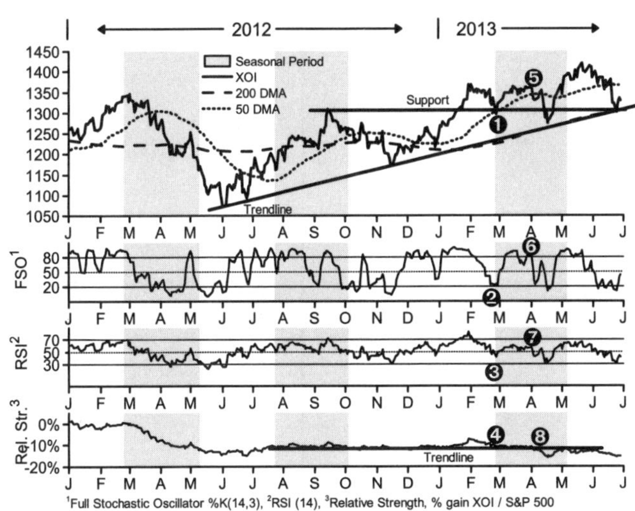

¹Full Stochastic Oscillator %K(14,3), ²RSI (14), ³Relative Strength, % gain XOI / S&P 500

Amex Oil Index (XOI) Performance

From October 2012, the energy sector was performing at market, although initially it was correcting with the rest of the market. It bottomed in mid-November and rose with the rest of the market. At the end of January, it spiked higher and then started to underperform the S&P 500 in February.

Technical Conditions– February 25th to May 9th, 2013

Entry Strategy –Buy Position on Entry Date–
Coming into its winter seasonal period, energy stocks were correcting and underperforming the S&P 500. From a momentum standpoint, at the start of its seasonal period, XOI bounced off its 50 day moving average❶, the FSO bounced off a level close to 20❷ and the RSI❸ turned higher. Overall, the trade had a positive technical picture. Nevertheless, XOI continued to underperform the S&P 500❹.

Exit Strategy –Sell Position Early–
XOI performed at market up until the beginning of April. At that time, it started to turn down, crossing its 50 day moving average❺ and concurrently the FSO turning below 80❻ and the RSI❼ turning down, and most importantly the sector started to underperform the S&P 500❽. Selling the position early was justified when the sector started to underperform the S&P 500. This action was confirmed when XOI broke its support level in April.

WEEK 09

Market Indices & Rates
Weekly Values**

Stock Markets	2012	2013
Dow	12,979	13,981
S&P500	1,370	1,507
Nasdaq	2,977	3,148
TSX	12,690	12,728
FTSE	5,911	6,338
DAX	6,891	7,699
Nikkei	9,713	11,496
Hang Seng	21,483	22,763

Commodities	2012	2013
Oil	107.54	92.18
Gold	1748.8	1590.4

Bond Yields	2012	2013
USA 5 Yr Treasury	0.86	0.77
USA 10 Yr T	1.97	1.88
USA 20 Yr T	2.74	2.70
Moody's Aaa	3.82	3.84
Moody's Baa	5.08	4.78
CAN 5 Yr T	1.43	1.32
CAN 10 Yr T	1.99	1.85

Money Market	2012	2013
USA Fed Funds	0.25	0.25
USA 3 Mo T-B	0.07	0.11
CAN tgt overnight rate	1.00	1.00
CAN 3 Mo T-B	0.92	0.96

Foreign Exchange	2012	2013
EUR/USD	1.33	1.31
GBP/USD	1.59	1.51
USD/CAD	0.99	1.03
USD/JPY	81.03	92.44

FEBRUARY

M	T	W	T	F	S	S
					1	2
3	4	5	6	7	8	9
10	11	12	13	14	15	16
17	18	19	20	21	22	23
24	25	26	27	28		

MARCH

M	T	W	T	F	S	S
					1	2
3	4	5	6	7	8	9
10	11	12	13	14	15	16
17	18	19	20	21	22	23
24	25	26	27	28	29	30
31						

APRIL

M	T	W	T	F	S	S
	1	2	3	4	5	6
7	8	9	10	11	12	13
14	15	16	17	18	19	20
21	22	23	24	25	26	27
28	29	30				

** Weekly avg closing values- except Fed Funds & CAN overnight tgt rate weekly closing values.

MARCH

	MONDAY	TUESDAY	WEDNESDAY
WEEK 10	3 28	4 27	5 26
WEEK 11	10 21	11 20	12 19
WEEK 12	17 14	18 13	19 12
WEEK 13	24 7	25 6	26 5
WEEK 14	31	1	2

THURSDAY		FRIDAY	
6	25	7	24
13	18	14	17
20	11	21	10
27	4	28	3
3		4	

APRIL

M	T	W	T	F	S	S
	1	2	3	4	5	6
7	8	9	10	11	12	13
14	15	16	17	18	19	20
21	22	23	24	25	26	27
28	29	30				

MAY

M	T	W	T	F	S	S
			1	2	3	4
5	6	7	8	9	10	11
12	13	14	15	16	17	18
19	20	21	22	23	24	25
26	27	28	29	30	31	

JUNE

M	T	W	T	F	S	S
						1
2	3	4	5	6	7	8
9	10	11	12	13	14	15
16	17	18	19	20	21	22
23	24	25	26	27	28	29
30						

JULY

M	T	W	T	F	S	S
	1	2	3	4	5	6
7	8	9	10	11	12	13
14	15	16	17	18	19	20
21	22	23	24	25	26	27
28	29	30	31			

MARCH
SUMMARY

	Dow Jones	S&P 500	Nasdaq	TSX Comp
Month Rank	5	4	7	3
# Up	41	41	26	17
# Down	22	22	15	11
% Pos	65	65	63	61
% Avg. Gain	1.1	1.2	0.7	1.2

Dow & S&P 1950-2012, Nasdaq 1972-2012, TSX 1985-2012

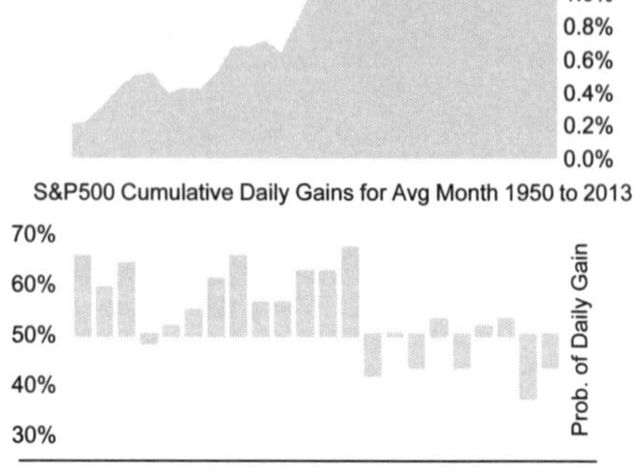

♦ March tends to be a strong month for stocks. From 1990 to 2013, the S&P 500 has produced an average gain of 1.2%.♦ Typically, it is the cyclicals that perform well and the defensive sectors that underperform.♦ The retail sector tends to perform well and since 1990 has produced an average gain of 3.8% in-March.♦ Silver can perform well in March given its industrial uses, but its success is not reflected in gold, which since 1990 has produced an average loss of 0.8% and has only beaten the S&P 500, 41% of the time.

BEST / WORST MARCH BROAD MKTS. 2004-2013

BEST MARCH MARKETS

- Nasdaq (2009) 10.9%
- Nikkei 225 (2010) 9.5%
- Russell 2000 (2009) 8.7%

WORST MARCH MARKETS

- Nikkei 225 (2011) -8.2%
- Nikkei 225 (2008) -7.9%
- FTSE 100 (2008) -3.1%

Index Values End of Month

	2004	2005	2006	2007	2008	2009	2010	2011	2012	2013
Dow	10,358	10,504	11,109	12,354	12,263	7,609	10,857	12,320	13,212	14,579
S&P 500	1,126	1,181	1,295	1,421	1,323	798	1,169	1,326	1,408	1,569
Nasdaq	1,994	1,999	2,340	2,422	2,279	1,529	2,398	2,781	3,092	3,268
TSX	8,586	9,612	12,111	13,166	13,350	8,720	12,038	14,116	12,392	12,750
Russell 1000	1,160	1,222	1,359	1,492	1,385	834	1,238	1,417	1,497	1,676
Russell 2000	1,467	1,529	1,902	1,990	1,710	1,051	1,687	2,096	2,064	2,365
FTSE 100	4,386	4,894	5,965	6,308	5,702	3,926	5,680	5,909	5,768	6,412
Nikkei 225	11,715	11,669	17,060	17,288	12,526	8,110	11,090	9,755	10,084	12,398

Percent Gain for March

	2004	2005	2006	2007	2008	2009	2010	2011	2012	2013
Dow	-2.1	-2.4	1.1	0.7	0.0	7.7	5.1	0.8	2.0	3.7
S&P 500	-1.6	-1.9	1.1	1.0	-0.6	8.5	5.9	-0.1	3.1	3.6
Nasdaq	-1.8	-2.6	2.6	0.2	0.3	10.9	7.1	0.0	4.2	3.4
TSX	-2.3	-0.6	3.6	0.9	-1.7	7.4	3.5	-0.1	-2.0	-0.6
Russell 1000	-1.5	-1.7	1.3	0.9	-0.8	8.5	6.0	0.1	3.0	3.7
Russell 2000	0.8	-3.0	4.7	0.9	0.3	8.7	8.0	2.4	2.4	4.4
FTSE 100	-2.4	-1.5	3.0	2.2	-3.1	2.5	6.1	-1.4	-1.8	0.8
Nikkei 225	6.1	-0.6	5.3	-1.8	-7.9	7.1	9.5	-8.2	3.7	7.3

March Market Avg. Performance 2004 to 2013(1)

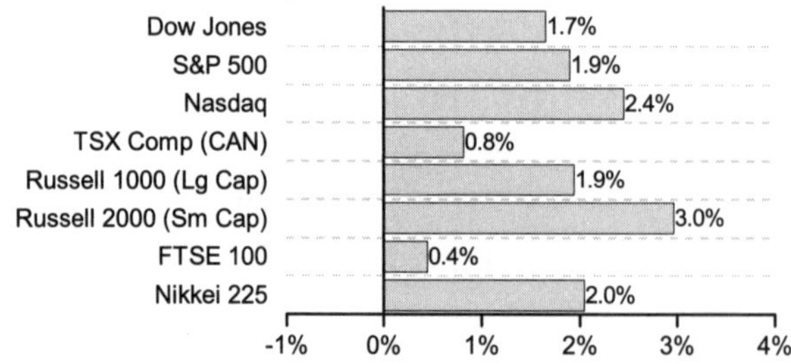

Interest Corner Mar(2)

	Fed Funds % (3)	3 Mo. T-Bill %(4)	10 Yr %(5)	20 Yr %(6)
2013	0.25	0.00	1.87	2.71
2012	0.25	0.07	2.23	3.00
2011	0.25	0.09	3.47	4.29
2010	0.25	0.16	3.84	4.55
2009	0.25	0.21	2.71	3.61

(1) Russell Data provided by Russell (2) Federal Reserve Bank of St. Louis- end of month values (3) Target rate set by FOMC (4)(5)(6) Constant yield maturities.

MARCH SECTOR PERFORMANCE

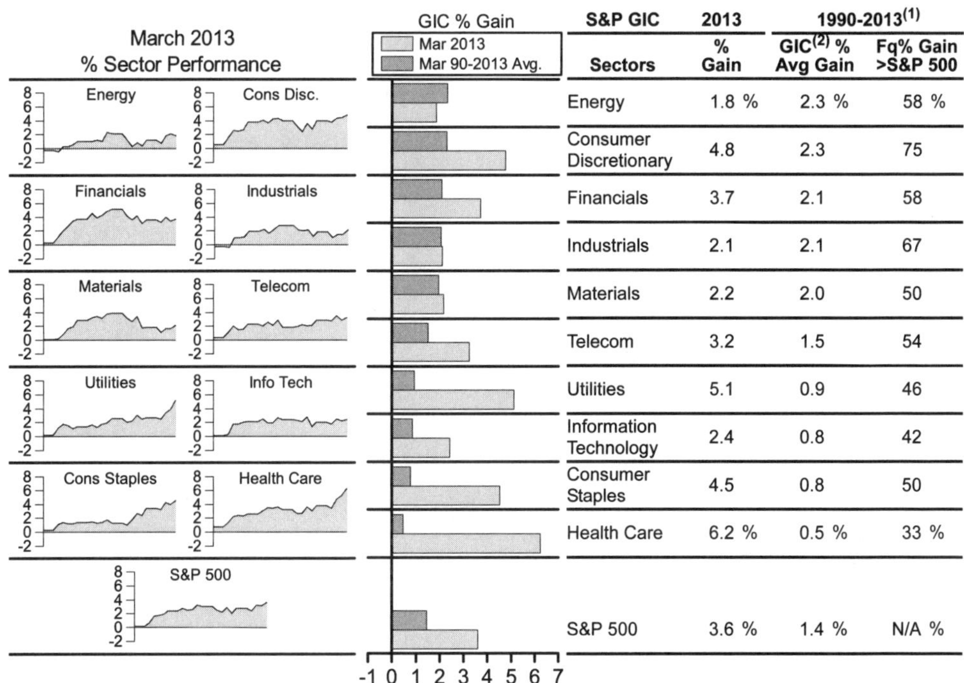

S&P GIC Sectors	2013 % Gain	1990-2013[(1)] GIC[(2)] % Avg Gain	1990-2013[(1)] Fq% Gain >S&P 500
Energy	1.8 %	2.3 %	58 %
Consumer Discretionary	4.8	2.3	75
Financials	3.7	2.1	58
Industrials	2.1	2.1	67
Materials	2.2	2.0	50
Telecom	3.2	1.5	54
Utilities	5.1	0.9	46
Information Technology	2.4	0.8	42
Consumer Staples	4.5	0.8	50
Health Care	6.2 %	0.5 %	33 %
S&P 500	3.6 %	1.4 %	N/A %

Sector Commentary

♦ In 2013, the S&P 500 produced a much stronger performance than it typically does in the month of March.♦ The outperforming sectors were the defensive sectors, which is uncharacteristic for this time of the year.♦ Health care continued its strong run that took flight at the beginning of January.♦ The utilities and consumer staples sectors also outperformed the S&P 500.♦ The strong performance of the defensive sectors was indicating that the market was getting "nervous."

Sub-Sector Commentary

♦ Biotech benefited from the health care sector's performance and as a result produced a gain of 13.0%.♦ The cyclical sub-sectors performed poorly, with steel producing a loss of 2.8%.♦ Railroads, which typically perform well at this time of the year, produced a gain of 5%.♦ The transportation sub-sector produced a respectable 3.0% gain, slightly underperforming the S&P 500.♦ After a sharp drop in March, the homebuilders sub-sector bounced to produce a gain of 7.3%. This is not entirely unexpected. When a sector has a substantial correction out of its seasonal period, it can have a reflexive bounce, but it does not necessarily mean that a new trend has started.

SELECTED SUB-SECTORS[(3)]

Sub-Sector	2013 % Gain	GIC % Avg Gain	Fq% Gain >S&P 500
Retail	3.0 %	3.8 %	79 %
Chemicals	1.9	2.4	58
Steel	-2.8	2.4	58
Transportation	3.0	2.3	67
Railroads	5.0	2.2	50
Silver	-1.1	2.0	50
Software & Services	2.6	1.7	58
Banks	4.1	1.6	50
SOX (1995-2013)	2.4	1.4	42
Metals & Mining	1.5	1.1	42
Homebuilders	7.3	1.0	46
Pharma	6.1	0.5	33
Agriculture (1994-2013)	5.9	0.4	30
Biotech (1993-2013)	13.0	0.3	38
Gold (London PM)	0.6	-1.0	38

RIDE A HARLEY SPRING & SUMMER EARNINGS SEASON

①Mar9 to Apr18 ②Jun22 to Jul18

Very few people want to ride a Harley in the winter and neither should seasonal investors ride the stock at that time.

Active investors do not like dead money; money that sits around waiting for some distant catalyst to move the stock. They need to know there is a good possibility that an event could move the stock higher; otherwise, they will invest somewhere else. In the case of Harley Davidson, it is the spring and summer earnings season that provides the catalyst for the stock to move higher– the two big earnings seasons for the company.

Seasonal investors take a position in the stock, approximately one month before the company releases its earnings, and sell approximately when their earnings are set to be released.

17.3% gain & positive 83% of the time

Harley Davidson vs. S&P 500 1990 to 2013 — Positive (shaded)

Year	Mar 9 to Apr 18 S&P 500	Mar 9 to Apr 18 HOG	Jun 22 to Jul 18 S&P 500	Jun 22 to Jul 18 HOG	Compound Growth S&P 500	Compound Growth HOG
1990	0.1	13.0 %	1.0	20.6 %	1.2	37.4 %
1991	3.6	14.8	2.0	0.6	5.7	15.4
1992	2.9	2.9	3.0	5.2	5.9	8.2
1993	-1.3	2.1	-0.1	7.5	-1.4	9.8
1994	-5.0	-5.2	0.9	6.1	-4.2	0.6
1995	4.6	0.0	2.7	9.1	7.4	9.1
1996	1.6	23.0	-3.5	-4.2	-1.9	17.9
1997	-4.8	8.8	1.9	7.5	-3.0	17.0
1998	6.4	27.1	7.8	13.9	14.7	44.8
1999	2.8	5.4	5.2	6.4	8.1	12.1
2000	5.5	14.3	1.0	25.6	6.5	43.5
2001	-2.1	2.3	-2.4	7.2	-4.4	9.7
2002	-3.4	1.9	-10.9	-6.2	-13.9	-4.5
2003	7.8	10.2	-0.2	8.2	7.5	19.2
2004	-1.1	8.9	-2.6	1.9	-3.6	11.0
2005	-6.0	-23.4	0.6	6.4	-5.4	-18.4
2006	2.3	1.1	-1.2	-1.0	1.0	0.1
2007	5.0	-3.6	1.6	1.7	6.7	-1.9
2008	7.5	7.7	-4.3	0.6	2.8	8.3
2009	27.3	127.0	2.1	14.2	29.9	159.3
2010	4.7	24.2	-4.3	-10.6	0.2	11.1
2011	-1.3	-4.6	0.8	9.2	-0.5	4.2
2012	1.4	8.0	3.6	-9.6	5.0	-2.3
2013	-0.6	-6.9	6.1	11.3	5.4	3.7
Avg.	2.4 %	10.8 %	0.4 %	5.5 %	2.9 %	17.3 %
Fq>0	63 %	75 %	63 %	79 %	63 %	83 %

Over the period from 1990 to 2013, from March 9th to April 18th, Harley Davidson has produced an average rate of return of 10.8% and has been positive 75% of the time. In the same yearly period, from June 22nd to July 18th, Harley Davidson has produced an average rate of return of 5.5% and has been positive 79% of the time.

Interestingly, Harley Davidson also produces a spike of outperformance compared with the S&P 500 just before its October earnings announcement.

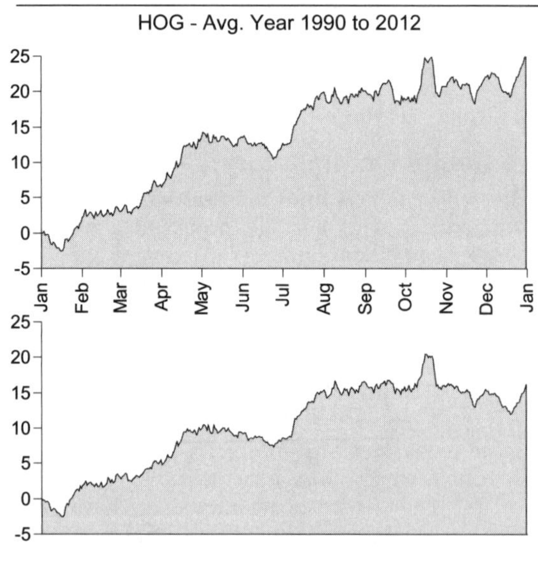

> *HOG - stock symbol for Harley Davidson which trades on the NYSE. HOG data includes dividends and stock splits.*

2012-13 Strategy Performance

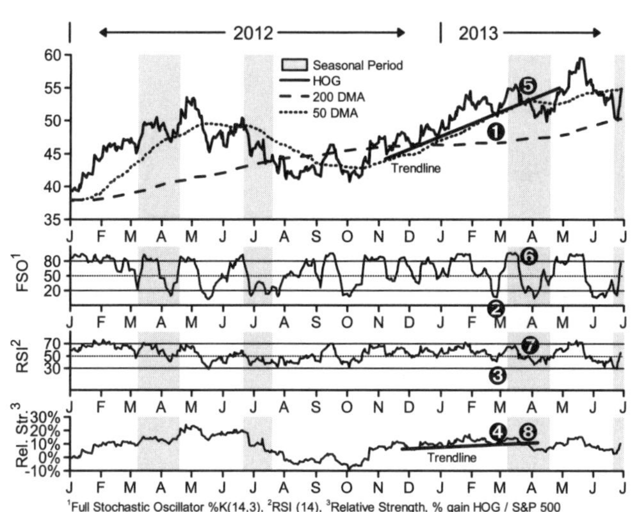

HOG Performance

As the stock market started to perform favorably at the start of its six month seasonal period in October 2012, Harley Davidson responded by outperforming. After a spike in outperformance in October, HOG consistently outperformed the markets by a small amount heading into its seasonal period.

Technical Conditions– March 9th to April 18th, 2013

Entry Strategy –Buy Position Early–

In late February 2013, HOG corrected down to its 50 day moving average❶ and bounced upwards. An early buy signal was triggered when the FSO crossed above 20❷. At the same time, the RSI rose above 50❸ and HOG started to outperform the S&P 500❹.

Exit Strategy – Sell Position Early–

The success of the early entry was short lived as HOG started to underperform the S&P 500 at the beginning of its seasonally strong period. In mid-March, HOG turned down, crossed below its upward trendline❺, with the FSO going below 80❻ and the RSI crossing below 50❼. Most importantly, HOG crossed below its relative trendline of performance❽, signalling a breakdown and justifying an early exit.

WEEK 10

Market Indices & Rates Weekly Values**

Stock Markets	2012	2013
Dow	12,878	14,281
S&P500	1,359	1,540
Nasdaq	2,951	3,221
TSX	12,428	12,788
FTSE	5,836	6,426
DAX	6,777	7,882
Nikkei	9,722	11,904
Hang Seng	20,937	22,748
Commodities	**2012**	**2013**
Oil	106.31	90.98
Gold	1685.8	1577.9
Bond Yields	**2012**	**2013**
USA 5 Yr Treasury	0.87	0.82
USA 10 Yr T	2.00	1.96
USA 20 Yr T	2.78	2.78
Moody's Aaa	3.88	3.92
Moody's Baa	5.11	4.85
CAN 5 Yr T	1.45	1.33
CAN 10 Yr T	1.98	1.86
Money Market	**2012**	**2013**
USA Fed Funds	0.25	0.25
USA 3 Mo T-B	0.09	0.10
CAN tgt overnight rate	1.00	1.00
CAN 3 Mo T-B	0.91	0.96
Foreign Exchange	**2012**	**2013**
EUR/USD	1.32	1.30
GBP/USD	1.58	1.50
USD/CAD	1.00	1.03
USD/JPY	81.51	94.33

MARCH

M	T	W	T	F	S	S
					1	2
3	4	5	6	7	8	9
10	11	12	13	14	15	16
17	18	19	20	21	22	23
24	25	26	27	28	29	30
31						

APRIL

M	T	W	T	F	S	S
	1	2	3	4	5	6
7	8	9	10	11	12	13
14	15	16	17	18	19	20
21	22	23	24	25	26	27
28	29	30				

MAY

M	T	W	T	F	S	S
			1	2	3	4
5	6	7	8	9	10	11
12	13	14	15	16	17	18
19	20	21	22	23	24	25
26	27	28	29	30	31	

** Weekly avg closing values- except Fed Funds & CAN overnight tgt rate weekly closing values.

BOEING– LET YOUR PORTFOLIO FLY
March 13th to June 15th

Boeing has just completed a production cycle and released its 787 Dreamliner. The plane was much anticipated and after battery and fire problems were fixed, the plane was reapproved by the FAA in late April 2013.

11.6% gain & positive 79% of the time

Many investors avoid investing in airplane manufacturers when they are in the design stage of a new plane. They do this to avoid any detrimental effects from costs overruns and delays. There is an increased interest once the plane is in production, as sales and profits are more predictable.

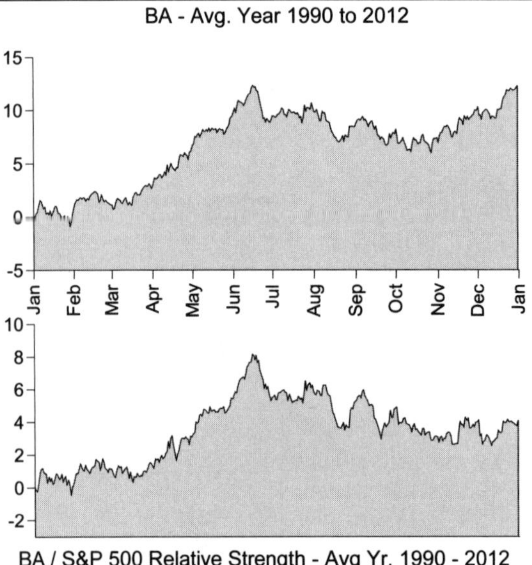

BA / S&P 500 Relative Strength - Avg Yr. 1990 - 2012

Boeing starts to outperform the S&P 500 in mid-March and then peaks three months later in mid-June. The driver for the seasonal trend is the annual Paris Air Show that takes place in mid-June.

This is the time of year when the major players from the airline industry get together to sign contracts for new plane orders.

Investors tend to take a position in Boeing before the Paris Air Show to take advantage of any positive announcements. Seasonal investors start to take positions earlier to benefit from the run-up to the air show and exit when the air show starts in mid-June.

Boeing has a distinct seasonal pattern and on average has produced a loss of 4.9% from June 16th to October 27th, during the period 1990 to 2013. Essentially, once the major impetus for the seasonal trend finishes, the stock tends to underperform.

BA* vs. S&P 500
1990 to 2013

Mar 13 to Jun15	S&P 500	BA	Positive Diff
1990	7.2%	34.6%	27.4%
1991	3.3	3.4	0.1
1992	1.6	-1.7	-3.3
1993	-0.8	11.4	12.1
1994	-1.3	3.2	4.4
1995	9.7	36.3	26.6
1996	4.5	2.0	-2.5
1997	11.1	7.3	-3.8
1998	0.7	-15.5	-16.2
1999	0.5	21.2	20.7
2000	6.0	20.7	14.7
2001	2.9	5.3	2.4
2002	-13.9	-15.4	-1.8
2003	22.9	40.5	17.6
2004	1.0	22.2	21.2
2005	0.5	12.0	11.5
2006	-2.0	13.4	15.4
2007	9.0	7.6	-1.4
2008	3.9	3.7	-0.2
2009	23.0	47.3	24.2
2010	-3.0	-3.4	-0.3
2011	-3.0	3.1	6.1
2012	-2.1	-2.2	-0.1
2013	4.8	21.0	16.2
Avg	3.6%	11.6%	8%
Fq > 0	71%	79%	63%

There will be years when the June to October time period will be positive, but they are few and far between. Not only has Boeing produced an average loss since 1990 in this time period, but it has only been positive 33% of the time and outperformed the S&P 500, 25% of the time.

Seasonal investors should look to take a position in Boeing from March 13th to June 15th. In this time period, from 1990 to 2013, Boeing has produced an average 11.6% gain and has been positive 79% of the time.

** BA- stock symbol for The Boeing Company which trades on the NYSE exchange. Prices adjusted for stock splits.*

2012-13 Strategy Performance

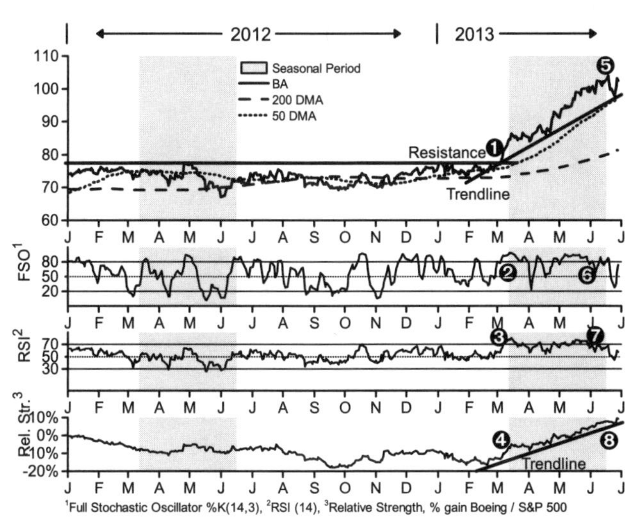

¹Full Stochastic Oscillator %K(14,3), ²RSI (14), ³Relative Strength, % gain Boeing / S&P 500

Boeing Performance

Boeing had its fair share of problems with fires on their new Dreamliner in 2012 and 2013. In 2012 its share price traded in a range between $70 and $78, but generally underperformed the S&P 500.

Technical Conditions– March 13th to June 15th, 2013

Entry Strategy –Buy Position on Entry Date–

In late February 2013, Boeing finally broke above $78❶ (just before the start of its seasonal period). At the same time, the FSO was in the 40's❷, but had not dropped below 20 and turned back up, and the RSI was above 50❸. In other words, an early short-term momentum buy was not triggered. Also, confirming Boeing's upward trend was its outperformance compared to the S&P 500❹ that started in late February.

Exit Strategy –Sell Partial Position Early–

In the beginning of June, the FSO turned below 80❻ and the RSI turned below 70❼, triggering a partial early exit. A full exit was not justified as the share price of Boeing was still in an uptrend❺ and it was still outperforming the S&P 500❽. In the end, small additional gains were made by holding the position to the seasonal exit date.

WEEK 11

Market Indices & Rates
Weekly Values**

Stock Markets	2012	2013
Dow	13,163	14,481
S&P500	1,394	1,557
Nasdaq	3,035	3,250
TSX	12,459	12,822
FTSE	5,940	6,503
DAX	7,056	8,005
Nikkei	10,019	12,369
Hang Seng	21,291	22,738

Commodities	2012	2013
Oil	106.13	92.72
Gold	1667.6	1588.8

Bond Yields	2012	2013
USA 5 Yr Treasury	1.06	0.88
USA 10 Yr T	2.21	2.04
USA 20 Yr T	3.00	2.86
Moody's Aaa	4.05	4.00
Moody's Baa	5.28	4.91
CAN 5 Yr T	1.61	1.38
CAN 10 Yr T	2.13	1.92

Money Market	2012	2013
USA Fed Funds	0.25	0.25
USA 3 Mo T-B	0.09	0.09
CAN tgt overnight rate	1.00	1.00
CAN 3 Mo T-B	0.91	0.97

Foreign Exchange	2012	2013
EUR/USD	1.31	1.30
GBP/USD	1.57	1.50
USD/CAD	0.99	1.03
USD/JPY	83.18	95.98

MARCH

M	T	W	T	F	S	S
					1	2
3	4	5	6	7	8	9
10	11	12	13	14	15	16
17	18	19	20	21	22	23
24	25	26	27	28	29	30
31						

APRIL

M	T	W	T	F	S	S
	1	2	3	4	5	6
7	8	9	10	11	12	13
14	15	16	17	18	19	20
21	22	23	24	25	26	27
28	29	30				

MAY

M	T	W	T	F	S	S
			1	2	3	4
5	6	7	8	9	10	11
12	13	14	15	16	17	18
19	20	21	22	23	24	25
26	27	28	29	30	31	

SYSCO– "THE FOOD COMPANY"

①Apr23 to May30 ②Oct11 to Nov21

The other "Sysco," the one in the food marketing and distribution business, tends to outperform the S&P 500 in the spring and autumn.

11.2% gain & positive 83% of the time

Why does Sysco outperform at these two times of the year? There are two parts to this answer. First, Sysco is part of the consumer staples sector, which tends to be one of the top performing sectors during the transition times, to and from the favorable six month period in late October and early May. The consumer staples sector performs well at these times because investors are looking for stable earnings.

Second, Sysco tends to release its earnings in the first week in November and the first week in May. Investors are attracted to the stock before the earnings are released to benefit from any positive announcements.

Usually, the best time to exit a stock position that has a seasonal period driven by earnings, is just before the earnings release date. In Sysco's case, it is typically best to hold onto the stock after the earnings announcements for another two to three weeks.

It is possible that the strategy of holding past Sysco's earnings release date, is the result of Sysco's strong seasonal performance occurring during the transition times for the stock market, when the unfavourable season transitions to the favorable season, and vice versa.

Sysco vs. S&P 500 1990 to 2012 Positive

	Apr 23 to May 30		Oct 11 to Nov 21		Compound Growth	
Year	S&P 500	SYY	S&P 500	SYY	S&P 500	SYY
1990	7.7	14.8 %	5.2	0.3 %	13.3	15.1 %
1991	1.6	16.6	-0.1	3.8	1.4	21.0
1992	1.4	2.6	6.0	8.6	7.4	11.4
1993	2.4	14.5	0.5	-1.1	3.0	13.2
1994	2.2	0.0	-0.2	5.4	2.0	5.4
1995	3.0	-4.6	3.9	15.7	7.0	10.4
1996	3.7	7.4	6.9	3.0	10.9	10.6
1997	9.5	-0.3	-0.4	16.5	9.1	16.1
1998	-3.5	-1.3	18.2	11.3	14.1	9.9
1999	-4.2	3.5	6.4	16.3	2.0	20.4
2000	-0.8	20.5	-2.9	23.8	-3.7	49.2
2001	0.4	9.0	5.2	-1.2	5.6	7.6
2002	-3.9	-6.3	16.2	10.2	11.6	3.3
2003	5.7	11.3	-0.3	5.8	5.4	17.7
2004	-1.7	-3.6	4.3	18.4	2.5	14.2
2005	4.1	7.6	5.7	3.6	10.0	11.5
2006	-3.9	-0.6	3.7	6.1	-0.4	5.4
2007	3.1	-1.6	-9.3	-6.8	-6.5	-8.3
2008	1.8	9.4	-11.0	-9.5	-9.4	-1.0
2009	9.0	8.3	1.9	8.0	11.0	16.9
2010	0.0	-0.4	0.0	1.1	-7.2	-2.4
2011	-0.5	10.3	-0.2	4.1	-0.6	14.8
2012	-4.7	-3.5	-2.9	-2.2	-7.5	-5.6
Avg.	1.0 %	4.8 %	2.6 %	6.1 %	3.5 %	11.2 %
Fq>0	61 %	57 %	61 %	78 %	70 %	83 %

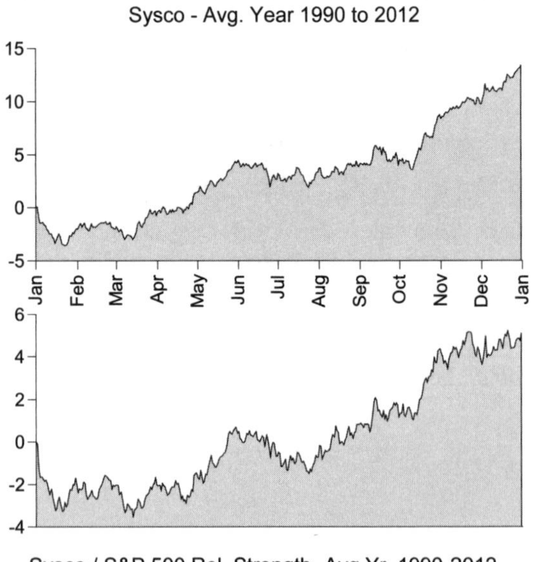

Sysco / S&P 500 Rel. Strength- Avg Yr. 1990-2012

SYY - stock symbol for Sysco which trades on the NYSE exchange. Prices adjusted for stock splits.

2012-13 Strategy Performance

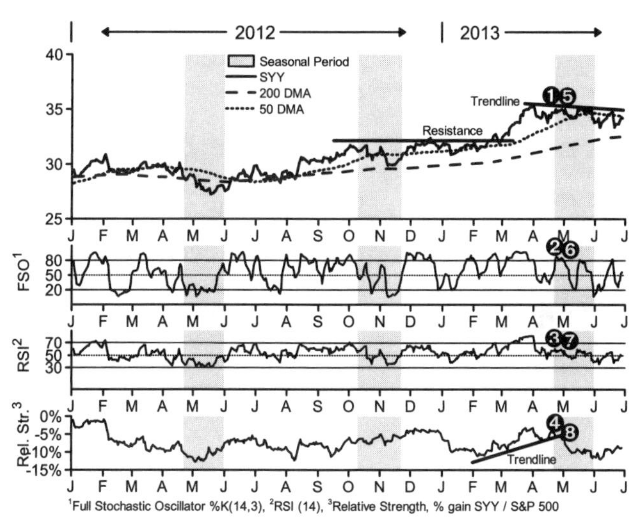

¹Full Stochastic Oscillator %K(14,3), ²RSI (14), ³Relative Strength, % gain SYY / S&P 500

Sysco Performance

Starting in March 2012, Sysco broke through a resistance level that had existed for six months and started to outperform the S&P 500. By the end of March, Sysco had turned down and started to underperform the S&P 500.

Technical Conditions– April 23rd to May 30th, 2013

Entry Strategy –Buy Position on Entry Date–

Coming into the start of the seasonal trade in April 2013, Sysco was in a downtrend❶ and underperforming the S&P 500❹. The FSO was above 80❷, registering an overbought condition and the RSI was in its upper band❸. In other words, it was not a favorable trend. Nevertheless, Sysco was above its 50 day moving average and had not "broken down" relative to the S&P 500.

Exit Strategy –Sell Position Early–

Sysco started to perform poorly shortly after the trade was initiated as it started to turn down in early May❺, causing the FSO to drop below 80❻, triggering an early sell signal. At the same time, the RSI started to drop and shortly afterwards crossed below 50❼. As a result, Sysco started to underperform the S&P 500❽. Exiting the trade early, proved to be the correct decision as Sysco continued its decline.

WEEK 12

Market Indices & Rates Weekly Values**

Stock Markets	2012	2013
Dow	13,132	14,471
S&P500	1,402	1,552
Nasdaq	3,072	3,238
TSX	12,435	12,777
FTSE	5,889	6,423
DAX	7,051	7,961
Nikkei	10,092	12,416
Hang Seng	20,886	22,145
Commodities	**2012**	**2013**
Oil	106.40	92.88
Gold	1653.4	1608.7
Bond Yields	**2012**	**2013**
USA 5 Yr Treasury	1.16	0.80
USA 10 Yr T	2.32	1.94
USA 20 Yr T	3.07	2.77
Moody's Aaa	4.09	3.93
Moody's Baa	5.34	4.85
CAN 5 Yr T	1.70	1.33
CAN 10 Yr T	2.24	1.84
Money Market	**2012**	**2013**
USA Fed Funds	0.25	0.25
USA 3 Mo T-B	0.08	0.07
CAN tgt overnight rate	1.00	1.00
CAN 3 Mo T-B	0.90	0.98
Foreign Exchange	**2012**	**2013**
EUR/USD	1.32	1.29
GBP/USD	1.59	1.51
USD/CAD	0.99	1.02
USD/JPY	83.07	95.15

MARCH

M	T	W	T	F	S	S
					1	2
3	4	5	6	7	8	9
10	11	12	13	14	15	16
17	18	19	20	21	22	23
24	25	26	27	28	29	30
31						

APRIL

M	T	W	T	F	S	S
	1	2	3	4	5	6
7	8	9	10	11	12	13
14	15	16	17	18	19	20
21	22	23	24	25	26	27
28	29	30				

MAY

M	T	W	T	F	S	S
			1	2	3	4
5	6	7	8	9	10	11
12	13	14	15	16	17	18
19	20	21	22	23	24	25
26	27	28	29	30	31	

** Weekly avg closing values- except Fed Funds & CAN overnight tgt rate weekly closing values.

CANADIANS GIVE 3 CHEERS FOR AMERICAN HOLIDAYS

When I used to work on the retail side of the investment business, I was always amazed at how often the Canadian market increased on American holidays, when the Canadian stock market was open and the American market was closed.

The holidays always had light volume, tended not to have large increases or decreases, but nevertheless usually ended the day with a gain.

1% average gain from 1977 to 2012 and 94% of the time positive

How the trade works

For the three big holidays in the United States that do not exist in Canada (Memorial, Independence and U.S. Thanksgiving Days), buy at the end of the market day before the holiday (TSX Composite) and sell at the end of the U.S. holiday when the U.S markets are closed.

For U.S. investors to take advantage of this trade, they must have access to the TSX Composite. Unfortunately, as of the current time SEC regulations do not allow Americans to purchase foreign ETFs.

Generally, markets perform well around most major American holidays, hence the trading strategies for American holidays included in this book. The typical U.S. holiday trade is to get into the stock market the day before the holiday and then exit the day after the holiday.

The main reason for the strong performance around these holidays is a lack of institutional involvement in the markets, allowing bullish retail investors to push up the markets.

On the actual holidays, there are no economic news releases in America and very seldom is there anything released in Canada of significance. During market hours without any influences, the market tends to float, preferring to wait until the next day before making any significant moves.

Despite this laxidasical action during the day, the TSX Composite tends to end the day on a gain. This is true for the three major holidays that are covered in this book: Memorial, Independence and U.S. Thanksgiving Day.

From a theoretical perspective, a lot of the gain that is captured on the U.S. holiday is realized on the next day when the markets are open in the United States. This does not invalidate the *Canadians Give 3 Cheers* trade – it presents more alternatives for the astute investor.

For example, an investor can allocate a portion of money to a standard American holiday trade and another portion to the *Canadian Give 3 Cheers* version. By spreading out the exit days, the overall risk in the trade is reduced.

S&P/TSX Comp Gain 1977-2012 — Positive (shaded)

	Memorial	Independence	Thanksgiving	Compound Growth
1977	0.10 %	-0.08 %	0.61 %	0.63 %
1978	-0.05	-0.16	0.57	0.36
1979	1.11	0.23	0.58	1.93
1980	1.64	0.76	0.89	3.32
1981	0.51	-0.15	1.03	1.40
1982	-0.18	-0.01	0.35	0.17
1983	0.29	0.53	0.15	0.97
1984	0.86	-0.11	0.73	1.48
1985	0.61	0.31	0.31	1.24
1986	0.23	-0.02	0.22	0.44
1987	-0.11	1.08	1.57	2.55
1988	0.44	0.08	0.58	1.11
1989	0.10	-0.12	-0.11	-0.13
1990	0.11	0.43	0.02	0.57
1991	0.02	0.18	-0.09	0.11
1992	-0.06	0.35	0.36	0.65
1993	0.42	-0.18	0.14	0.38
1994	-0.19	0.70	0.91	1.43
1995	0.14	0.25	0.29	0.68
1996	0.11	0.25	0.54	0.90
1997	1.08	-0.04	-0.85	0.18
1998	0.56	0.18	0.51	1.25
1999	0.57	1.63	1.14	3.39
2000	0.43	1.04	0.91	2.40
2001	-0.02	-0.23	0.70	0.45
2002	-0.01	0.08	0.38	0.45
2003	0.03	0.03	0.26	0.31
2004	0.84	-0.02	0.55	1.39
2005	0.56	0.39	1.48	2.45
2006	0.70	1.04	0.70	2.46
2007	0.35	-0.03	0.76	1.08
2008	0.24	-0.94	1.28	0.56
2009	0.76	0.36	-1.29	-0.18
2010	0.78	-0.92	0.34	0.19
2011	0.23	0.64	-0.75	0.12
2012	-0.09	0.55	0.44	0.90
Avg	0.37 %	0.22 %	0.45 %	1.04 %
Fq > 0	78 %	62 %	86 %	94 %

2012-13 Strategy Performance

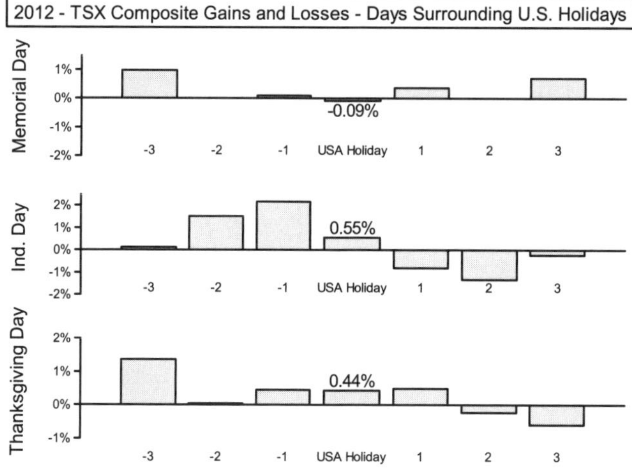

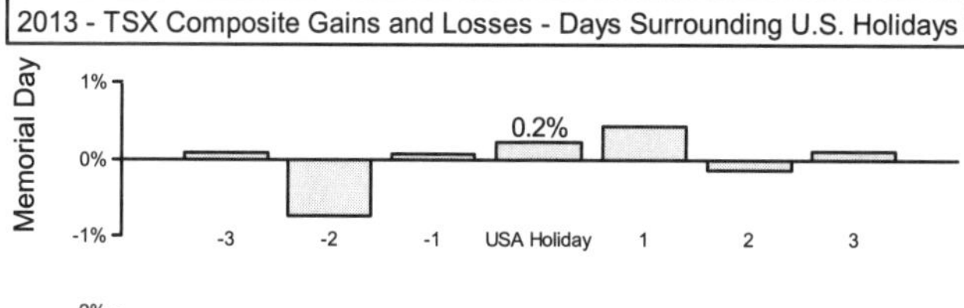

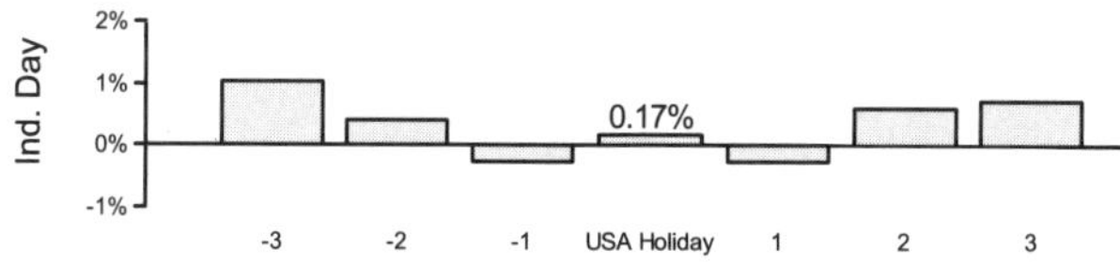

Canadians Give 3 Cheers Performance

Overall, the *Canadians Give 3 Cheers for American Holidays* strategy proved to be successful in 2012 and so far in 2013. The only loss suffered was the small loss during the Memorial Day trade in 2012, which occurred when both the S&P 500 and the TSX Composite were declining sharply in the month of May.

In 2012, the two days on either side of Thanksgiving were both strongly positive, supporting the Thanksgiving trade in the American markets (see *Thanksgiving– Give Thanks and Take Returns* strategy).

WEEK 13

Market Indices & Rates Weekly Values**

Stock Markets	2012	2013
Dow	13,185	14,528
S&P500	1,409	1,562
Nasdaq	3,107	3,253
TSX	12,446	12,709
FTSE	5,818	6,394
DAX	6,996	7,834
Nikkei	10,131	12,449
Hang Seng	20,753	22,332

Commodities	2012	2013
Oil	105.11	96.18
Gold	1673.7	1279.7

Bond Yields	2012	2013
USA 5 Yr Treasury	1.05	0.78
USA 10 Yr T	2.22	1.90
USA 20 Yr T	2.97	2.73
Moody's Aaa	4.00	3.90
Moody's Baa	5.25	4.83
CAN 5 Yr T	1.59	1.31
CAN 10 Yr T	2.13	1.83

Money Market	2012	2013
USA Fed Funds	0.25	0.25
USA 3 Mo T-B	0.07	0.07
CAN tgt overnight rate	1.00	1.00
CAN 3 Mo T-B	0.91	0.98

Foreign Exchange	2012	2013
EUR/USD	1.33	1.28
GBP/USD	1.60	1.52
USD/CAD	1.00	1.02
USD/JPY	82.84	94.29

MARCH

M	T	W	T	F	S	S
					1	2
3	4	5	6	7	8	9
10	11	12	13	14	15	16
17	18	19	20	21	22	23
24	25	26	27	28	29	30
31						

APRIL

M	T	W	T	F	S	S
	1	2	3	4	5	6
7	8	9	10	11	12	13
14	15	16	17	18	19	20
21	22	23	24	25	26	27
28	29	30				

MAY

M	T	W	T	F	S	S
			1	2	3	4
5	6	7	8	9	10	11
12	13	14	15	16	17	18
19	20	21	22	23	24	25
26	27	28	29	30	31	

** Weekly avg closing values- except Fed Funds & CAN overnight tgt rate weekly closing values.

APRIL

	MONDAY	TUESDAY	WEDNESDAY
WEEK 14	31	1 29	2 28
WEEK 15	7 23	8 22	9 21
WEEK 16	14 16	15 15	16 14
WEEK 17	21 9	22 8	23 7
WEEK 18	28 2	29 1	30

APRIL

THURSDAY		FRIDAY	
3	27	**4**	26
10	20	**11**	19
17	13	**18**	12
		USA Market Closed- Good Friday CAN Market Closed- Good Friday	
24	6	**25**	5
1		2	

MAY

M	T	W	T	F	S	S
			1	2	3	4
5	6	7	8	9	10	11
12	13	14	15	16	17	18
19	20	21	22	23	24	25
26	27	28	29	30	31	

JUNE

M	T	W	T	F	S	S
						1
2	3	4	5	6	7	8
9	10	11	12	13	14	15
16	17	18	19	20	21	22
23	24	25	26	27	28	29
30						

JULY

M	T	W	T	F	S	S
	1	2	3	4	5	6
7	8	9	10	11	12	13
14	15	16	17	18	19	20
21	22	23	24	25	26	27
28	29	30	31			

AUGUST

M	T	W	T	F	S	S
				1	2	3
4	5	6	7	8	9	10
11	12	13	14	15	16	17
18	19	20	21	22	23	24
25	26	27	28	29	30	31

APRIL SUMMARY

	Dow Jones	S&P 500	Nasdaq	TSX Comp
Month Rank	1	2	4	7
# Up	41	43	26	16
# Down	22	20	15	12
% Pos	65	68	63	57
% Avg. Gain	2.0	1.5	1.4	0.7

Dow & S&P 1950-2012, Nasdaq 1972-2012, TSX 1985-2012

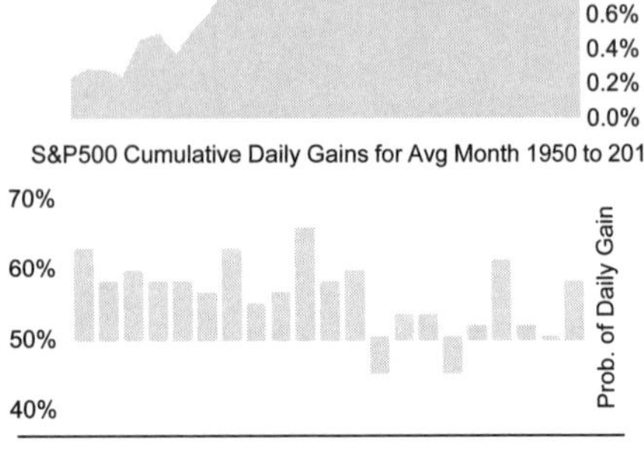

♦ April, on average, has been the second strongest month for the S&P 500. From 1950 to 2012, April has produced an average gain of 1.5% and been positive 68% of the time. ♦ The first part of April tends to be the strongest (see *18 Day Earnings Month Effect strategy*). ♦ The last part of April tends to be "flat." ♦ Overall, April tends to be a volatile month with the cyclical sectors outperforming. When the defensive sectors outperform in April, it often indicates market weakness ahead.

BEST / WORST APRIL BROAD MKTS. 2004-2013

BEST APRIL MARKETS

- Russell 2000 (2009) 15.3%
- Nasdaq (2009) 12.3%
- Nikkei 225 (2013) 11.8%

WORST APRIL MARKETS

- Russell 2000 (2005) -5.8%
- Nikkei 225 (2005) -5.7%
- Nikkei 225 (2012) -5.6%

Index Values End of Month

	2004	2005	2006	2007	2008	2009	2010	2011	2012	2013
Dow	10,226	10,193	11,367	13,063	12,820	8,168	11,009	12,811	13,214	14,840
S&P 500	1,107	1,157	1,311	1,482	1,386	873	1,187	1,364	1,398	1,598
Nasdaq	1,920	1,922	2,323	2,525	2,413	1,717	2,461	2,874	3,046	3,329
TSX	8,244	9,369	12,204	13,417	13,937	9,325	12,211	13,945	12,293	12,457
Russell 1000	1,138	1,198	1,373	1,553	1,453	917	1,259	1,458	1,487	1,705
Russell 2000	1,391	1,440	1,900	2,024	1,780	1,212	1,781	2,150	2,030	2,355
FTSE 100	4,490	4,802	6,023	6,449	6,087	4,244	5,553	6,070	5,738	6,430
Nikkei 225	11,762	11,009	16,906	17,400	13,850	8,828	11,057	9,850	9,521	13,861

Percent Gain for April

	2004	2005	2006	2007	2008	2009	2010	2011	2012	2013
Dow	-1.3	-3.0	2.3	5.7	4.5	7.3	1.4	4.0	0.0	1.8
S&P 500	-1.7	-2.0	1.2	4.3	4.8	9.4	1.5	2.8	-0.7	1.8
Nasdaq	-3.7	-3.9	-0.7	4.3	5.9	12.3	2.6	3.3	-1.5	1.9
TSX	-4.0	-2.5	0.8	1.9	4.4	6.9	1.4	-1.2	-0.8	-2.3
Russell 1000	-1.9	-2.0	1.1	4.1	5.0	10.0	1.8	2.9	-0.7	1.7
Russell 2000	-5.2	-5.8	-0.1	1.7	4.1	15.3	5.6	2.6	-1.6	-0.4
FTSE 100	2.4	-1.9	1.0	2.2	6.8	8.1	-2.2	2.7	-0.5	0.3
Nikkei 225	0.4	-5.7	-0.9	0.7	10.6	8.9	-0.3	1.0	-5.6	11.8

April Market Avg. Performance 2004 to 2013[(1)]

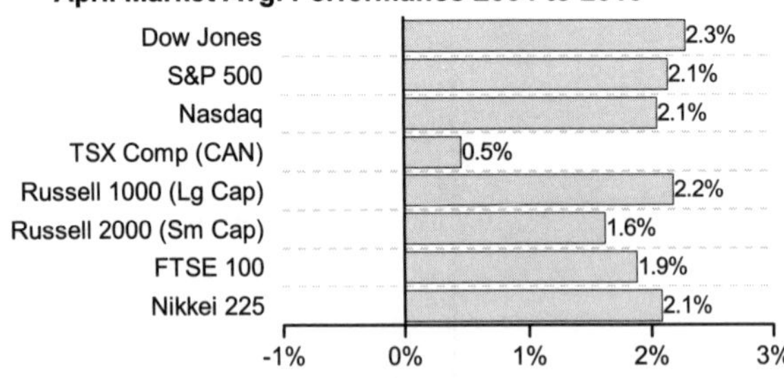

Interest Corner Apr[(2)]

	Fed Funds % [(3)]	3 Mo. T-Bill %[(4)]	10 Yr %[(5)]	20 Yr %[(6)]
2013	0.25	0.05	1.70	2.49
2012	0.25	0.10	1.95	2.73
2011	0.25	0.04	3.32	4.15
2010	0.25	0.16	3.69	4.36
2009	0.25	0.14	3.16	4.10

(1) Russell Data provided by Russell (2) Federal Reserve Bank of St. Louis- end of month values (3) Target rate set by FOMC (4)(5)(6) Constant yield maturities.

APRIL SECTOR PERFORMANCE

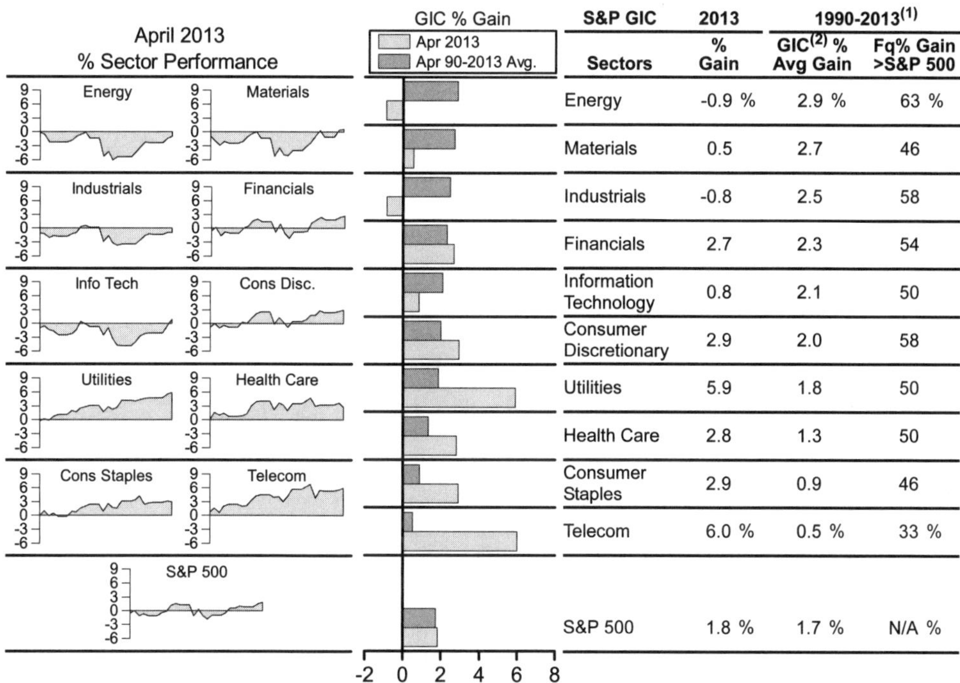

S&P GIC Sectors	2013 % Gain	1990-2013[1] GIC[2] % Avg Gain	1990-2013[1] Fq% Gain >S&P 500
Energy	-0.9 %	2.9 %	63 %
Materials	0.5	2.7	46
Industrials	-0.8	2.5	58
Financials	2.7	2.3	54
Information Technology	0.8	2.1	50
Consumer Discretionary	2.9	2.0	58
Utilities	5.9	1.8	50
Health Care	2.8	1.3	50
Consumer Staples	2.9	0.9	46
Telecom	6.0 %	0.5 %	33 %
S&P 500	1.8 %	1.7 %	N/A %

SELECTED SUB-SECTORS[3]

Sub-Sector	2013 % Gain	GIC % Avg Gain	Fq% Gain >S&P 500
SOX (1995-2013)	1.8 %	4.2 %	58 %
Railroads	2.3	3.5	63
Chemicals	3.7	3.3	71
Banks	1.1	2.8	54
Transportation	0.6	2.5	58
Homebuilders	3.5	2.1	50
Pharma	3.2	1.8	54
Software & Services	2.2	1.6	50
Steel	-5.1	1.3	42
Metals & Mining	-10.0	1.0	38
Retail	3.0	1.0	63
Gold (London PM)	-8.1	0.3	46
Biotech (1993-2013)	4.6	0.2	43
Agriculture (1994-2013)	0.6	-0.2	50
Silver	-14.7	-0.2	42

Sector Commentary

♦ In April 2013, the energy sector underperformed the S&P 500. Typically, April is one of the best months for the energy sector.♦ Overall, in the spring of 2013 the cyclical sectors underperformed. Very often when this happens in the late spring, it is a sign that the market is weakening and is prone to a correction.

Sub-Sector Commentary

♦ The worst performing sub-sector in April 2013 was silver, with the metals and mining, and gold, close behind.♦ Gold had been correcting for a number of months and many investors could not resist entering at lower prices, only to find out that gold was still heading lower.♦ The biotech sub-sector was the strongest sub-sector, producing a gain of 4.6% in April. Biotech typically performs well starting in June, but it had been outperforming the S&P 500 since the end of February.

(1) Sector data provided by Standard and Poors (2) GIC is short form for Global Industry Classification (3) Sub Sector data provided by Standard and Poors, except where marked by symbol.

18 DAY EARNINGS MONTH EFFECT

Markets Outperform 1st 18 Calendar Days of Earnings Months

Earnings season occurs the first month of every quarter. At this time, public companies report their financials for the previous quarter and often give guidance on future expectations. As a result investors tend to bid up stocks, anticipating good earnings. Earnings are a major driver of stock market prices as investors generally like to get in the stock market early in anticipation of favorable results, which helps to run up stock prices in the first half of the month.

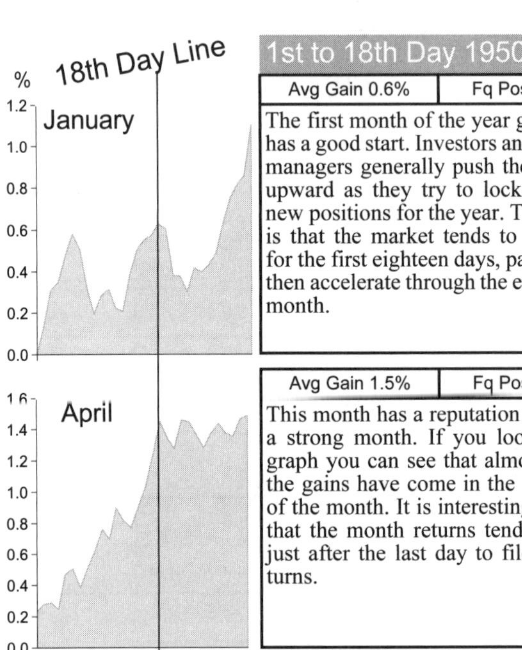

1st to 18th Day 1950-2012

Avg Gain 0.6%	Fq Pos 63%

The first month of the year generally has a good start. Investors and money managers generally push the market upward as they try to lock in their new positions for the year. The result is that the market tends to increase for the first eighteen days, pause, and then accelerate through the end of the month.

Avg Gain 1.5%	Fq Pos 70%

This month has a reputation of being a strong month. If you look at the graph you can see that almost all of the gains have come in the first half of the month. It is interesting to note that the month returns tend to peak just after the last day to file tax returns.

July

Avg Gain 0.8%	Fq Pos 63%

This is the month in which the market can peak in strong bull markets. The returns in the first half of the month can be positive, but investors should be cautious, as the time period following in August and September has a tendency towards negative returns.

October

Avg Gain 0.8%	Fq Pos 65%

This is the month with a bad reputation. Once again, the first part of the month tends to do well. It is the middle segment, centered around the notorious Black Monday, that brings down the results. Toward the end of the month investors realize that the world has not ended and start to buy stocks again, providing a strong finish to the month.

1st to 18th Day Gain S&P500

	JAN	APR	JUL	OCT
1950	0.54 %	4.28 %	-3.56 %	2.88 %
1951	4.85	3.41	4.39	1.76
1952	2.02	-3.57	-0.44	-1.39
1953	-2.07	-2.65	0.87	3.38
1954	2.50	3.71	2.91	-1.49
1955	-3.28	4.62	3.24	-4.63
1956	-2.88	-1.53	4.96	2.18
1957	-4.35	2.95	2.45	-4.93
1958	2.78	1.45	1.17	2.80
1959	1.09	4.47	1.23	0.79
1960	-3.34	2.26	-2.14	1.55
1961	2.70	1.75	-0.36	2.22
1962	-4.42	-1.84	2.65	0.12
1963	3.30	3.49	-1.27	2.26
1964	2.05	1.99	2.84	0.77
1965	2.05	2.31	1.87	1.91
1966	1.64	2.63	2.66	2.77
1967	6.80	1.84	3.16	-1.51
1968	-0.94	7.63	1.87	2.09
1969	-1.76	-0.27	-2.82	3.37
1970	-1.24	-4.42	6.83	-0.02
1971	1.37	3.17	0.42	-1.01
1972	1.92	2.40	-1.22	-2.13
1973	0.68	0.02	2.00	1.46
1974	-2.04	0.85	-2.58	13.76
1975	3.50	3.53	-2.09	5.95
1976	7.55	-2.04	0.38	-3.58
1977	-3.85	2.15	0.47	-3.18
1978	-4.77	4.73	1.40	-2.00
1979	3.76	0.11	-1.19	-5.22
1980	2.90	-1.51	6.83	4.83
1981	-0.73	-0.96	-0.34	2.59
1982	-4.35	4.33	1.33	13.54
1983	4.10	4.43	-2.20	1.05
1984	1.59	-0.80	-1.16	1.20
1985	2.44	0.10	1.32	2.72
1986	-1.35	1.46	-5.77	3.25
1987	9.96	-1.64	3.48	-12.16
1988	1.94	0.12	-1.09	2.75
1989	3.17	3.78	4.20	-2.12
1990	-4.30	0.23	1.73	-0.10
1991	0.61	3.53	3.83	1.20
1992	0.42	3.06	1.83	-1.45
1993	0.26	-0.60	-1.06	2.07
1994	1.67	-0.74	2.46	1.07
1995	2.27	0.93	2.52	0.52
1996	-1.25	-0.29	-4.04	3.42
1997	4.78	1.22	3.41	-0.33
1998	-0.92	1.90	4.67	3.88
1999	1.14	2.54	3.36	-2.23
2000	-0.96	-3.80	2.69	-6.57
2001	2.10	6.71	-1.36	2.66
2002	-1.79	-2.00	-10.94	8.48
2003	2.50	5.35	1.93	4.35
2004	2.51	0.75	-3.46	-0.05
2005	-1.32	-2.93	2.50	-4.12
2006	2.55	1.22	0.51	3.15
2007	1.41	4.33	-3.20	1.48
2008	-9.75	5.11	-1.51	-19.36
2009	-5.88	8.99	2.29	2.89
2010	1.88	1.94	3.32	3.81
2011	2.97	-1.56	-1.15	8.30
2012	4.01	-1.66	0.78	1.16
Avg	0.65 %	1.45 %	0.76 %	0.82 %

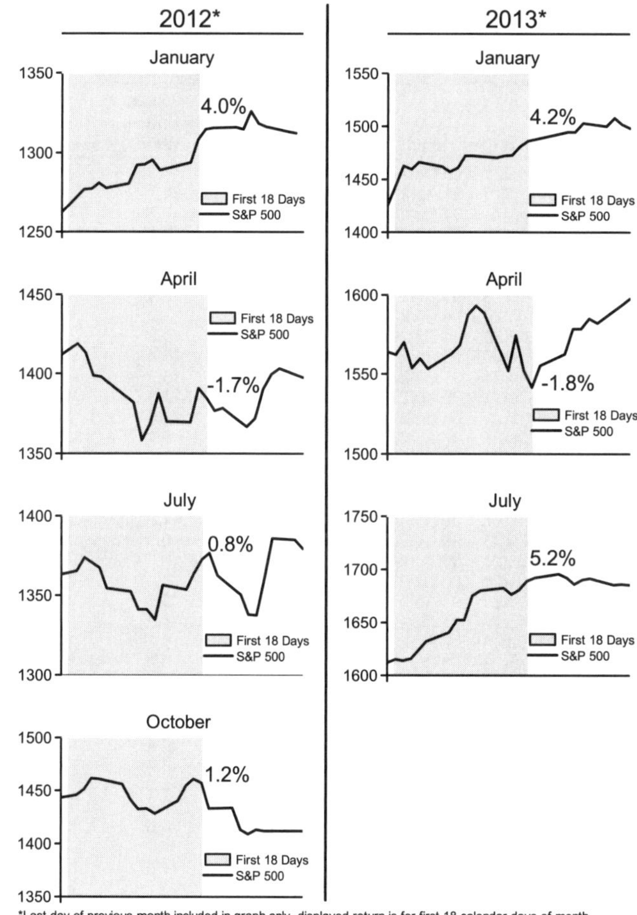

*Last day of previous month included in graph only, displayed return is for first 18 calendar days of month

WEEK 14

Market Indices & Rates Weekly Values**

Stock Markets	2012	2013
Dow	13,150	14,591
S&P500	1,407	1,560
Nasdaq	3,095	3,228
TSX	12,278	12,499
FTSE	5,785	6,376
DAX	6,900	7,824
Nikkei	9,887	12,394
Hang Seng	20,635	22,144

Commodities	2012	2013
Oil	103.51	94.93
Gold	1651.4	1254.6

Bond Yields	2012	2013
USA 5 Yr Treasury	1.02	0.73
USA 10 Yr T	2.21	1.81
USA 20 Yr T	2.98	2.64
Moody's Aaa	4.03	3.82
Moody's Baa	5.29	4.70
CAN 5 Yr T	1.63	1.26
CAN 10 Yr T	2.14	1.82

Money Market	2012	2013
USA Fed Funds	0.25	0.25
USA 3 Mo T-B	0.07	0.07
CAN tgt overnight rate	1.00	1.00
CAN 3 Mo T-B	0.93	0.97

Foreign Exchange	2012	2013
EUR/USD	1.32	1.29
GBP/USD	1.59	1.52
USD/CAD	0.99	1.02
USD/JPY	82.27	94.72

APRIL

M	T	W	T	F	S	S
	1	2	3	4	5	6
7	8	9	10	11	12	13
14	15	16	17	18	19	20
21	22	23	24	25	26	27
28	29	30				

MAY

M	T	W	T	F	S	S
			1	2	3	4
5	6	7	8	9	10	11
12	13	14	15	16	17	18
19	20	21	22	23	24	25
26	27	28	29	30	31	

JUNE

M	T	W	T	F	S	S
						1
2	3	4	5	6	7	8
9	10	11	12	13	14	15
16	17	18	19	20	21	22
23	24	25	26	27	28	29
30						

Earnings Month Effect Performance

Investing during the *Earnings Month Effect* in 2012 and for the first three earnings months of 2013, has provided large net returns. The first eighteen calendar days in January in both years, produced gains over 4% and April in both years produced a loss just over 1.5%.

Although the *Earnings Month Effect* for July 2012 was positive, it was not nearly as strong as the same period of 2013. After a mild correction in June 2013, the market was anticipating strong earnings from reporting companies. At the same time, the economic numbers being reported were positive, helping to push the market even higher. The net result in July 2013 for the *Earnings Month Effect* period was 5.2%, the largest return over the last sixty-three years.

** Weekly avg closing values- except Fed Funds & CAN overnight tgt rate weekly closing values.

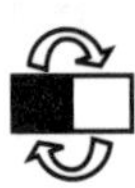

CONSUMER SWITCH
SELL CONSUMER DISCRETIONARY
BUY CONSUMER STAPLES

Consumer Staples Outperform Apr 23 to Oct 27

The *Consumer Switch* strategy has allowed investors to use a set portion of their account to switch between the two related consumer sectors. To use this strategy, investors invest in the consumer discretionary sector from October 28th to April 22nd, and then use the proceeds to invest in the consumer staples sector from April 23rd to October 27th, and then repeat the cycle.

The end result has been outperformance compared with buying and holding both consumer sectors, or buying and holding the broad market.

2938% total aggregate gain compared with 377% for the S&P 500

The basic premise of the strategy is that the consumer discretionary sector tends to outperform during the favorable six months when more money flows into the market, pushing up stock prices. On the other hand, the consumer staples sector tends to outperform when investors are looking for safety and stability of earnings in the six months when the market tends to move into a defensive mode.

Consumer Staples & Discretionary Switch Strategy*

Investment Period	Buy @ Beginning of Period	% Gain @ End of Period	% Gain Cumulative
90 Apr23 - 90 Oct29	Staples	7.7%	8%
90 Oct29 - 91 Apr23	Discretionary	41.7	53
91 Apr23 - 91 Oct28	Staples	2.1	56
91 Oct28 - 92 Apr23	Discretionary	15.9	81
92 Apr23 - 92 Oct27	Staples	6.3	92
92 Oct27 - 93 Apr23	Discretionary	6.3	104
93 Apr23 - 93 Oct27	Staples	5.8	116
93 Oct27 - 94 Apr25	Discretionary	-3.7	108
94 Apr25 - 94 Oct27	Staples	10.2	129
94 Oct27 - 95 Apr24	Discretionary	4.4	139
95 Apr24 - 95 Oct27	Staples	15.3	176
95 Oct27 - 96 Apr23	Discretionary	17.3	227
96 Apr23 - 96 Oct27	Staples	12.6	265
96 Oct27 - 97 Apr23	Discretionary	5.1	283
97 Apr23 - 97 Oct27	Staples	2.5	293
97 Oct27 - 98 Apr23	Discretionary	35.9	434
98 Apr23 - 98 Oct27	Staples	-0.7	423
98 Oct27 - 99 Apr23	Discretionary	41.8	651
99 Apr23 - 99 Oct27	Staples	-9.7	578
99 Oct27 - 00 Apr24	Discretionary	11.9	659
00 Apr24 - 00 Oct27	Staples	16.5	785
00 Oct27 - 01 Apr23	Discretionary	9.8	872
01 Apr23 - 01 Oct29	Staples	4.0	910
01 Oct29 - 02 Apr23	Discretionary	16.1	1073
02 Apr23 - 02 Oct28	Staples	-13.9	910
02 Oct28 - 03 Apr23	Discretionary	3.0	941
03 Apr23 - 03 Oct27	Staples	8.4	1028
03 Oct27 - 04 Apr23	Discretionary	9.6	1137
04 Apr23 - 04 Oct27	Staples	-7.4	1045
04 Oct27 - 05 Apr25	Discretionary	-2.0	1021
05 Apr25 - 05 Oct27	Staples	-0.5	1016
05 Oct27 - 06 Apr24	Discretionary	9.2	1119
06 Apr24 - 06 Oct27	Staples	10.6	1249
06 Oct27 - 07 Apr23	Discretionary	6.3	1334
07 Apr23 - 07 Oct29	Staples	4.6	1400
07 Oct29 - 08 Apr23	Discretionary	-13.7	1194
08 Apr23 - 08 Oct27	Staples	-21.5	916
08 Oct27 - 09 Apr23	Discretionary	17.7	1096
09 Apr23 - 09 Oct27	Staples	20.6	1342
09 Oct27 - 10 Apr23	Discretionary	29.7	1770
10 Apr23 - 10 Oct27	Staples	2.4	1815
10 Oct27 - 11 Apr25	Discretionary	13.7	2079
11 Apr25 - 11 Oct27	Staples	2.2	2126
11 Oct27 - 12 Apr23	Discretionary	10.9	2368
12 Apr23 - 12 Oct31	Staples	4.7	2485
12 Oct31 13 Apr23	Discretionary	17.5	2938

* If buy date lands on weekend or holiday, then date used is next trading date

Total Gains From Apr 1990 to Apr 2013

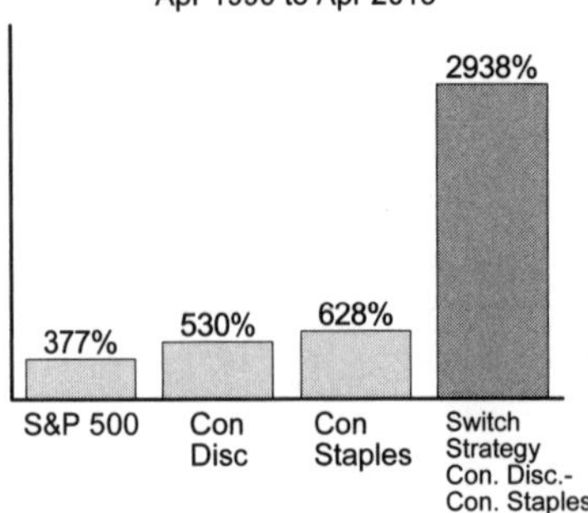

Consumer Discretionary / Consumer Staples Relative Strength Avg. Year 1990 - 2012

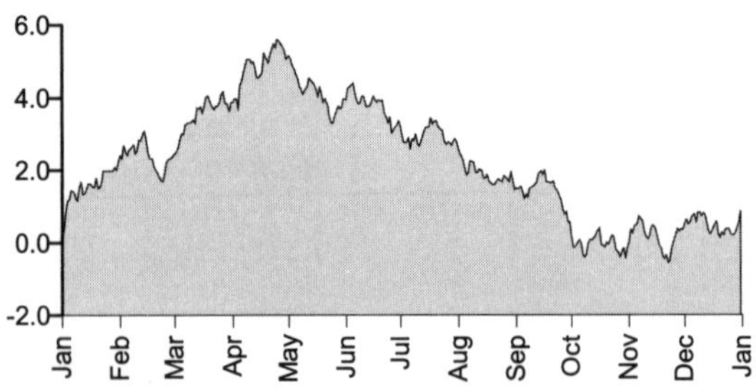

2012-13 Strategy Performance

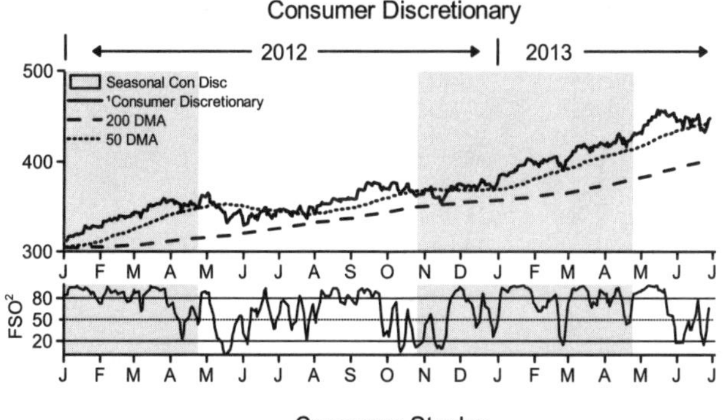

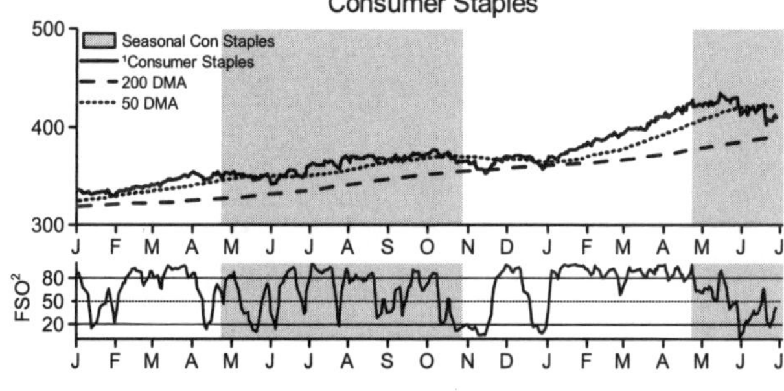

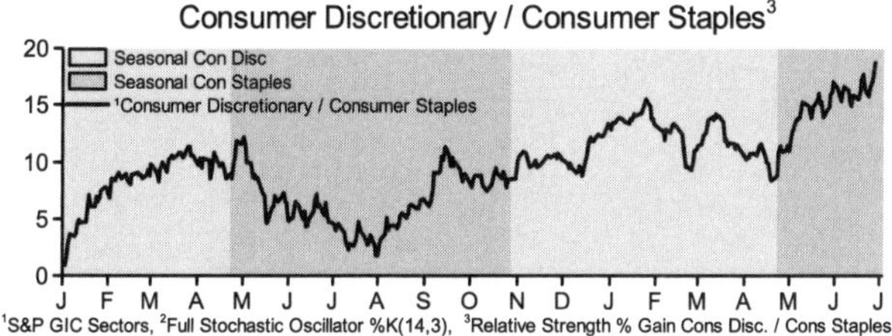

¹S&P GIC Sectors, ²Full Stochastic Oscillator %K(14,3), ³Relative Strength % Gain Cons Disc. / Cons Staples

Consumer Switch Strategy Performance

As can be seen from the above graphs, both the consumer discretionary sector and the consumer staples sector generally increased and decreased together in both 2012 and 2013. The success of the strategy has been in the relative performance of the two sectors. In 2012, the consumer discretionary sector outperformed during the January to April time period and the consumer staples sector outperformed from the May to October time period. From October 2012 to April 2013, the consumer discretionary sector mildly outperformed the staples sector. As the talk of the Federal Reserve tapering its quantitative stimulus program increased in May 2013, investors shied away from higher dividend paying stocks such as the consumer staples sector, as a result, the consumer discretionary stocks outperformed.

** Weekly avg closing values- except Fed Funds & CAN overnight tgt rate weekly closing values.

WEEK 15

Market Indices & Rates
Weekly Values**

Stock Markets	2012	2013
Dow	12,857	14,764
S&P500	1,373	1,580
Nasdaq	3,024	3,270
TSX	12,047	12,436
FTSE	5,648	6,356
DAX	6,652	7,745
Nikkei	9,541	13,341
Hang Seng	20,381	21,963
Commodities	**2012**	**2013**
Oil	102.53	93.40
Gold	1659.3	1565.6
Bond Yields	**2012**	**2013**
USA 5 Yr Treasury	0.88	0.72
USA 10 Yr T	2.04	1.79
USA 20 Yr T	2.81	2.58
Moody's Aaa	3.94	3.75
Moody's Baa	5.19	4.62
CAN 5 Yr T	1.54	1.24
CAN 10 Yr T	2.02	1.77
Money Market	**2012**	**2013**
USA Fed Funds	0.25	0.25
USA 3 Mo T-B	0.09	0.06
CAN tgt overnight rate	1.00	1.00
CAN 3 Mo T-B	0.96	0.97
Foreign Exchange	**2012**	**2013**
EUR/USD	1.31	1.31
GBP/USD	1.59	1.53
USD/CAD	1.00	1.02
USD/JPY	80.97	99.24

APRIL

M	T	W	T	F	S	S
	1	2	3	4	5	6
7	8	9	10	11	12	13
14	15	16	17	18	19	20
21	22	23	24	25	26	27
28	29	30				

MAY

M	T	W	T	F	S	S
			1	2	3	4
5	6	7	8	9	10	11
12	13	14	15	16	17	18
19	20	21	22	23	24	25
26	27	28	29	30	31	

JUNE

M	T	W	T	F	S	S
						1
2	3	4	5	6	7	8
9	10	11	12	13	14	15
16	17	18	19	20	21	22
23	24	25	26	27	28	29
30						

BIG BLUE – MAKES GREEN

IBM

Positive Action During Earnings Season ①Apr14-May19 ②Jul7-Jul30 ③Oct28-Nov26

What do April, July and October have in common? They are all earnings months and IBM tends to perform well at some time in all of these earnings months. January is also an earnings month, and IBM also outperforms the S&P 500 at this time, but the results are not as strong as the other three earnings months.

17.8% gain & positive 87% of the time

In April, starting on the 14th, IBM tends to outperform the S&P 500 just after the earnings season gets underway.

In July, starting on July 7th, IBM tends to outperform the S&P 500 at the same time as the earnings seasons gets underway.

In October, starting on October 28th, IBM tends to outperform the S&P 500 after the earnings season is underway.

In all three strategy periods, IBM tends to outperform even after the earnings season has gotten underway.

It is possible that investors rotate into IBM, a blue chip company with a lower beta than the market, as the market starts to fade the earnings season.

IBM* vs. S&P 500 1990 to 2012 — Positive (shaded)

	Apr 14 to May 19		Jul 7 to Jul 30		Oct 28 to Nov 26		Compound Growth	
Year	S&P 500	IBM	S&P 500	IBM	S&P 500	IBM	S&P 500	IBM
1990	3.0 %	7.7 %	-0.8 %	-5.0 %	3.9	6.8 %	6.1 %	9.3 %
1991	-2.1	-4.4	3.4	3.0	-1.6	-0.1	-0.5	-1.6
1992	2.5	5.7	2.4	-2.8	2.6	-0.6	7.7	2.1
1993	-0.4	0.6	1.5	-5.1	-0.3	21.2	0.8	15.7
1994	2.3	17.2	2.7	8.6	-2.9	-4.5	2.0	21.5
1995	2.0	8.1	1.6	11.9	3.5	-0.6	7.2	20.2
1996	5.1	-0.6	-3.4	9.7	7.9	24.9	9.5	36.2
1997	13.0	26.5	3.9	11.8	8.5	22.0	27.3	72.5
1998	0.0	20.0	-1.2	17.5	11.4	15.5	10.0	62.9
1999	-0.4	31.5	-4.3	-4.1	9.3	12.4	4.1	41.3
2000	-2.3	-3.6	-2.5	10.1	-2.7	6.4	-7.4	12.9
2001	9.2	22.1	1.2	-0.6	4.8	4.7	15.7	27.0
2002	-0.4	0.1	-8.7	-2.3	1.7	14.1	-7.5	11.5
2003	6.0	9.8	0.2	-3.6	2.7	1.6	9.0	7.5
2004	-3.6	-6.4	-1.3	1.6	5.1	5.2	0.0	0.0
2005	1.5	-8.8	3.3	10.1	7.6	7.9	12.7	8.4
2006	-1.7	-2.1	0.4	-1.5	1.7	2.9	0.3	-0.7
2007	4.8	13.8	-3.7	5.0	-8.3	-10.3	-7.5	7.1
2008	7.0	9.0	1.7	7.8	4.6	2.5	13.8	20.5
2009	5.8	5.6	9.8	16.0	4.4	5.5	21.3	29.1
2010	-6.9	-0.1	7.2	4.0	0.6	1.8	0.4	5.7
2011	2.2	4.1	-3.5	2.3	-9.8	-5.0	-11.0	1.2
2012	-5.5	-3.4	2.3	2.8	-0.4	-0.2	-3.7	-1.0
Avg.	1.8 %	7.0 %	0.5 %	4.2 %	2.3 %	6.1 %	4.8 %	17.8 %
Fq>0	57 %	65 %	61	65 %	70 %	70 %	70 %	87 %

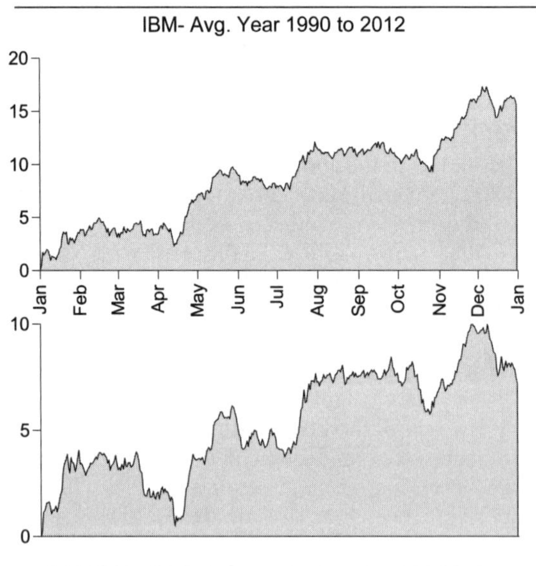

**International Business Machines Corporation (IBM) is an information technology (IT) company that trades on NYSE. Data adjusted for dividends and stock splits.*

2012-13 Strategy Performance

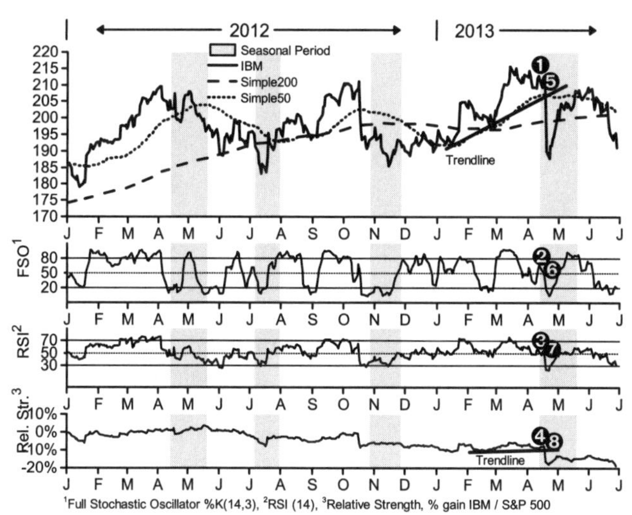

¹Full Stochastic Oscillator %K(14,3), ²RSI (14), ³Relative Strength, % gain IBM / S&P 500

IBM Performance

After disappointing earnings results in October 2012, IBM corrected sharply. After a brief period of underperformance relative to the S&P 500, IBM mildly underperformed the S&P 500 for the next two months and then started to perform at market. Investors seemed to be giving IBM another chance.

Technical Conditions– April 14th to May 19th, 2013

Entry Strategy –Buy on Entry Date–

In April 2013, IBM started the month with a negative performance. At the beginning of its seasonal period, IBM was above its 50 day moving average❶ with both the FSO and the RSI above 50❷❸. IBM was still performing at market❹. As a result, buying on the entry date was appropriate.

Exit Strategy –Sell Position Early–

On April 18th 2013, IBM announced poor earnings once again and the stock corrected sharply. The stock went through its 50 day moving average❺, dropped below 50❻❼ for both the FSO and the RSI, and most importantly, it broke its market performance trend❽. An early sell signal was triggered because IBM started to undeperform the S&P 500. In this case, it would have been better to hold onto the position until the exit date, as IBM bounced sharply upwards, once all of the bad news had been digested.

WEEK 16

Market Indices & Rates
Weekly Values**

Stock Markets	2012	2013
Dow	13,013	14,612
S&P500	1,380	1,555
Nasdaq	3,014	3,212
TSX	12,121	12,027
FTSE	5,739	6,285
DAX	6,716	7,566
Nikkei	9,550	13,283
Hang Seng	20,792	21,708

Commodities	2012	2013
Oil	103.02	87.97
Gold	1644.8	1393.3

Bond Yields	2012	2013
USA 5 Yr Treasury	0.86	0.71
USA 10 Yr T	2.00	1.73
USA 20 Yr T	2.76	2.51
Moody's Aaa	3.93	3.68
Moody's Baa	5.15	4.54
CAN 5 Yr T	1.61	1.18
CAN 10 Yr T	2.05	1.71

Money Market	2012	2013
USA Fed Funds	0.25	0.25
USA 3 Mo T-B	0.08	0.05
CAN tgt overnight rate	1.00	0.80
CAN 3 Mo T-B	1.00	0.98

Foreign Exchange	2012	2013
EUR/USD	1.31	1.31
GBP/USD	1.60	1.53
USD/CAD	0.99	1.02
USD/JPY	81.13	98.02

APRIL

M	T	W	T	F	S	S
	1	2	3	4	5	6
7	8	9	10	11	12	13
14	15	16	17	18	19	20
21	22	23	24	25	26	27
28	29	30				

MAY

M	T	W	T	F	S	S
			1	2	3	4
5	6	7	8	9	10	11
12	13	14	15	16	17	18
19	20	21	22	23	24	25
26	27	28	29	30	31	

JUNE

M	T	W	T	F	S	S
						1
2	3	4	5	6	7	8
9	10	11	12	13	14	15
16	17	18	19	20	21	22
23	24	25	26	27	28	29
30						

CANADIAN DOLLAR STRONG APRIL

Since the year 2000 when the price of oil started its ascent, the Canadian dollar has been labelled as a "petro" currency by foreign investors.

All other things being equal, if oil increases in price, investors favor the Canadian dollar over the U.S. dollar. They do so with good reason, as Canada is a net exporter of oil and benefits from its rising price.

Oil tends to do well in the month of April as this is the heart of one of the strongest seasonal strategies – oil and oil stocks outperform from February 25th to May 9th (see *Oil Winter/Spring Strategy*). With the rising price of oil in April, the Canadian dollar gets a free ride upwards.

April has been a strong month for the Canadian dollar relative to the U.S. dollar. The largest losses have had a tendency to occur in years when the Fed Reserve has been aggressively hiking their target rate.

At some point during the years 1987, 2000, 2004 and 2005, the Fed increased their target rate by a total of at least 1% in each year. Since 1971, three of these years (1987, 2004 and 2005) were three of the biggest losers for the Canadian dollar in the month of April.

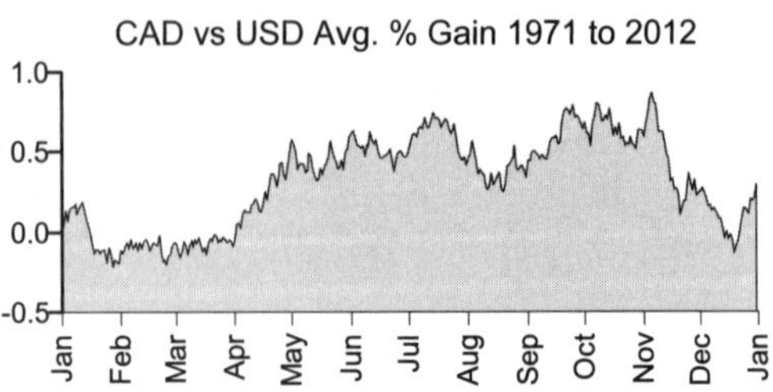

The Canadian dollar has been strong in April regardless of the long-term trend of the dollar moving either up or down. The Canadian dollar started at approximately par in 1971 and reached a low in 2002 of \$0.62 and then reached a recent high of \$1.09 in 2007.

In both the ups and downs of the economy, the Canadian dollar has outperformed the U.S. dollar in

CAD vs USD Apr % Gain 1971-2013 — Positive (shaded)

Year	%	Year	%	Year	%	Year	%	Year	%
		1980	0.44%	1990	0.44%	2000	-2.09%	2010	-0.26%
1971	-0.10%	1981	-0.74	1991	0.65	2001	2.65	2011	2.70
1972	0.53	1982	0.89	1992	-0.48	2002	1.74	2012	1.16
1973	-0.41	1983	0.36	1993	-1.02	2003	2.60	2013	1.01
1974	1.08	1984	-0.62	1994	0.09	2004	-4.58		
1975	-1.56	1985	0.04	1995	3.17	2005	-3.81		
1976	0.55	1986	1.69	1996	-0.15	2006	4.62		
1977	0.91	1987	-2.38	1997	-0.97	2007	3.99		
1978	0.09	1988	0.41	1998	-0.78	2008	1.73		
1979	1.61	1989	0.60	1999	3.42	2009	5.68		
Avg.	0.30%		-0.02%		0.44%		1.25%		1.18%

CAD vs. USD Avg. Year By Month By Decade (1971 to 2012)

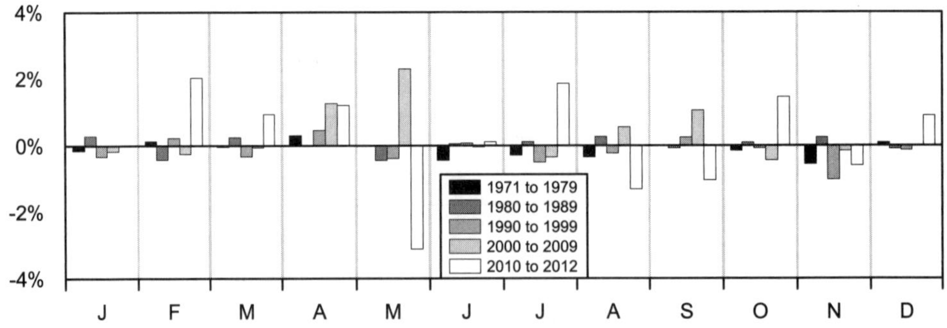

2012-13 Strategy Performance

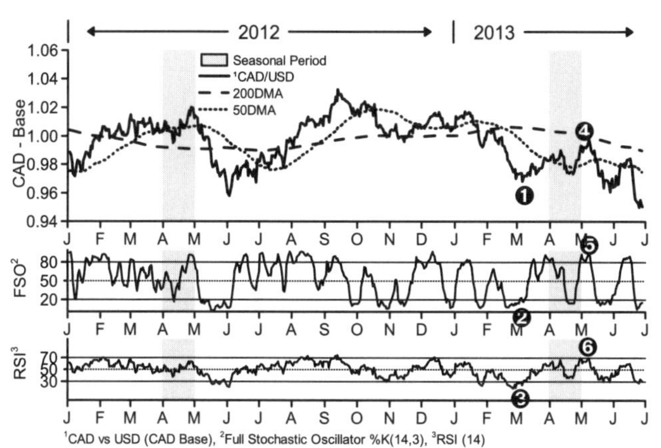

¹CAD vs USD (CAD Base), ²Full Stochastic Oscillator %K(14,3), ³RSI (14)

Canadian Dollar Performance

From the start of 2013, the Canadian dollar had been dropping relative to the US dollar. This was mainly the result of commodities decreasing in price, which in turn caused the Canadian dollar to lose value. In January, the Canadian dollar broke below its 50 day moving average and in February, it fell sharply. The drop stabilized in late February, setting up for an early entry into the trade.

Technical Conditions– April 1st to April 30th, 2013

Entry Strategy –Buy Position Early–

After falling in February, the Canadian dollar stabilized at the beginning of March and then started to turn upwards❶. As a result, the FSO crossed above 20❷, triggering an early buy signal. In support the RSI crossed above 30❸.

Exit Strategy –Sell Position on Exit Date–

After correcting in the middle part of April, the Canadian dollar rose sharply into the end of the month and ended up just short of its 200 day moving average❹. The FSO was above 80❺ but was starting to turn down and the RSI bounced downwards from 70❻. Overall, the trade proved to be a success and shortly after the trade finished, the Canadian dollar started to decrease in value.

WEEK 17

Market Indices & Rates Weekly Values**

Stock Markets	2012	2013
Dow	13,090	14,675
S&P500	1,387	1,577
Nasdaq	3,016	3,268
TSX	12,093	12,200
FTSE	5,724	6,398
DAX	6,672	7,709
Nikkei	9,531	13,750
Hang Seng	20,700	22,197

Commodities	2012	2013
Oil	103.80	90.99
Gold	1646.7	1436.7

Bond Yields	2012	2013
USA 5 Yr Treasury	0.84	0.70
USA 10 Yr T	1.98	1.73
USA 20 Yr T	2.74	2.50
Moody's Aaa	3.95	3.70
Moody's Baa	5.15	4.53
CAN 5 Yr T	1.66	1.19
CAN 10 Yr T	2.07	1.72

Money Market	2012	2013
USA Fed Funds	0.25	0.25
USA 3 Mo T-B	0.09	0.05
CAN tgt overnight rate	1.00	1.00
CAN 3 Mo T-B	1.06	0.99

Foreign Exchange	2012	2013
EUR/USD	1.32	1.30
GBP/USD	1.62	1.53
USD/CAD	0.99	1.02
USD/JPY	81.02	99.11

APRIL

M	T	W	T	F	S	S
	1	2	3	4	5	6
7	8	9	10	11	12	13
14	15	16	17	18	19	20
21	22	23	24	25	26	27
28	29	30				

MAY

M	T	W	T	F	S	S
			1	2	3	4
5	6	7	8	9	10	11
12	13	14	15	16	17	18
19	20	21	22	23	24	25
26	27	28	29	30	31	

JUNE

M	T	W	T	F	S	S
						1
2	3	4	5	6	7	8
9	10	11	12	13	14	15
16	17	18	19	20	21	22
23	24	25	26	27	28	29
30						

** Weekly avg closing values- except Fed Funds & CAN overnight tgt rate weekly closing values.

MAY

	MONDAY	TUESDAY	WEDNESDAY
WEEK 18	28	29	30
WEEK 19	5 26	6 25	7 24
WEEK 20	12 19	13 18	14 17
WEEK 21	19 12 CAN Market Closed- Victoria Day	20 11	21 10
WEEK 22	26 5 USA Market Closed- Memorial Day	27 4	28 3

MAY

THURSDAY		FRIDAY	
1	30	**2**	29
8	23	**9**	22
15	16	**16**	15
22	9	**23**	8
29	2	**30**	

JUNE

M	T	W	T	F	S	S
						1
2	3	4	5	6	7	8
9	10	11	12	13	14	15
16	17	18	19	20	21	22
23	24	25	26	27	28	29
30						

JULY

M	T	W	T	F	S	S
	1	2	3	4	5	6
7	8	9	10	11	12	13
14	15	16	17	18	19	20
21	22	23	24	25	26	27
28	29	30	31			

AUGUST

M	T	W	T	F	S	S
				1	2	3
4	5	6	7	8	9	10
11	12	13	14	15	16	17
18	19	20	21	22	23	24
25	26	27	28	29	30	31

SEPTEMBER

M	T	W	T	F	S	S
1	2	3	4	5	6	7
8	9	10	11	12	13	14
15	16	17	18	19	20	21
22	23	24	25	26	27	28
29	30					

MAY SUMMARY

	Dow Jones	S&P 500	Nasdaq	TSX Comp
Month Rank	8	8	5	2
# Up	31	35	24	18
# Down	32	28	17	20
% Pos	49	56	59	64
% Avg. Gain	-0.1	0.1	0.8	1.6

Dow & S&P 1950-2012, Nasdaq 1972-2012, TSX 1985-2012

0.6%
0.4%
0.2%
0.0%
-0.2%
-0.4%

S&P500 Cumulative Daily Gains for Avg Month 1950 to 2013

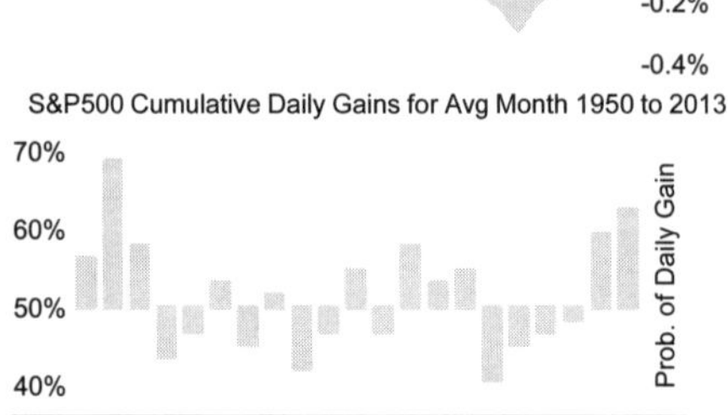

♦ The S&P 500 often peaks in May and as a result seasonal investors should start to be more cautious with their investments. ♦ After producing a loss for three years in a row from 2010 to 2012, the S&P 500 produced a gain of 2.1% in May 2013. ♦ The first few days and the last few days in May, tend to be strong. The period in between tends to negative. ♦ A lot of the cyclical sectors finish their seasonal periods at the beginning of May.

BEST / WORST MAY BROAD MKTS. 2004-2013

BEST MAY MARKETS

- TSX Comp. (2009) 11.2%
- Nikkei 225 (2009) 7.9%
- Nasdaq (2005) 7.6%

WORST MAY MARKETS

- Nikkei 225 (2010) -11.7%
- Nikkei 225 (2012) -10.3%
- Nikkei 225 (2006) -8.5%

Index Values End of Month

	2004	2005	2006	2007	2008	2009	2010	2011	2012	2013
Dow	10,188	10,467	11,168	13,628	12,638	8,500	10,137	12,570	12,393	15,116
S&P 500	1,121	1,192	1,270	1,531	1,400	919	1,089	1,345	1,310	1,631
Nasdaq	1,987	2,068	2,179	2,605	2,523	1,774	2,257	2,835	2,827	3,456
TSX Comp.	8,417	9,607	11,745	14,057	14,715	10,370	11,763	13,803	11,513	12,650
Russell 1000	1,152	1,239	1,330	1,605	1,477	965	1,157	1,439	1,392	1,739
Russell 2000	1,412	1,533	1,792	2,105	1,860	1,247	1,644	2,108	1,893	2,446
FTSE 100	4,431	4,964	5,724	6,621	6,054	4,418	5,188	5,990	5,321	6,583
Nikkei 225	11,236	11,277	15,467	17,876	14,339	9,523	9,769	9,694	8,543	13,775

Percent Gain for May

	2004	2005	2006	2007	2008	2009	2010	2011	2012	2013
Dow	-0.4	2.7	-1.7	4.3	-1.4	4.1	-7.9	-1.9	-6.2	1.9
S&P 500	1.2	3.0	-3.1	3.3	1.1	5.3	-8.2	-1.4	-6.3	2.1
Nasdaq	3.5	7.6	-6.2	3.1	4.6	3.3	-8.3	-1.3	-7.2	3.8
TSX Comp.	2.1	2.5	-3.8	4.8	5.6	11.2	-3.7	-1.0	-6.3	1.6
Russell 1000	1.3	3.4	-3.2	3.4	1.6	5.3	-8.1	-1.3	-6.4	2.0
Russell 2000	1.5	6.4	-5.7	4.0	4.5	2.9	-7.7	-2.0	-6.7	3.9
FTSE 100	-1.3	3.4	-5.0	2.7	-0.6	4.1	-6.6	-1.3	-7.3	2.4
Nikkei 225	-4.5	2.4	-8.5	2.7	3.5	7.9	-11.7	-1.6	-10.3	-0.6

May Market Avg. Performance 2004 to 2013(1)

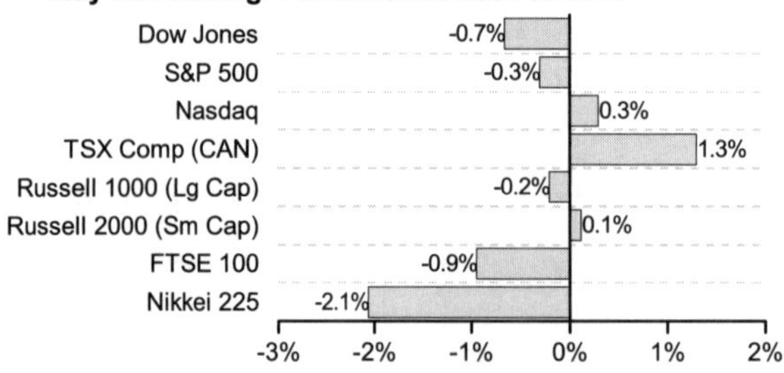

Interest Corner May(2)

	Fed Funds % (3)	3 Mo. T-Bill %(4)	10 Yr %(5)	20 Yr %(6)
2013	0.25	0.04	2.16	2.95
2012	0.25	0.07	1.59	2.27
2011	0.25	0.06	3.05	3.91
2010	0.25	0.16	3.31	4.05
2009	0.25	0.14	3.47	4.34

(1) Russell Data provided by Russell (2) Federal Reserve Bank of St. Louis- end of month values (3) Target rate set by FOMC (4)(5)(6) Constant yield maturities.

MAY SECTOR PERFORMANCE

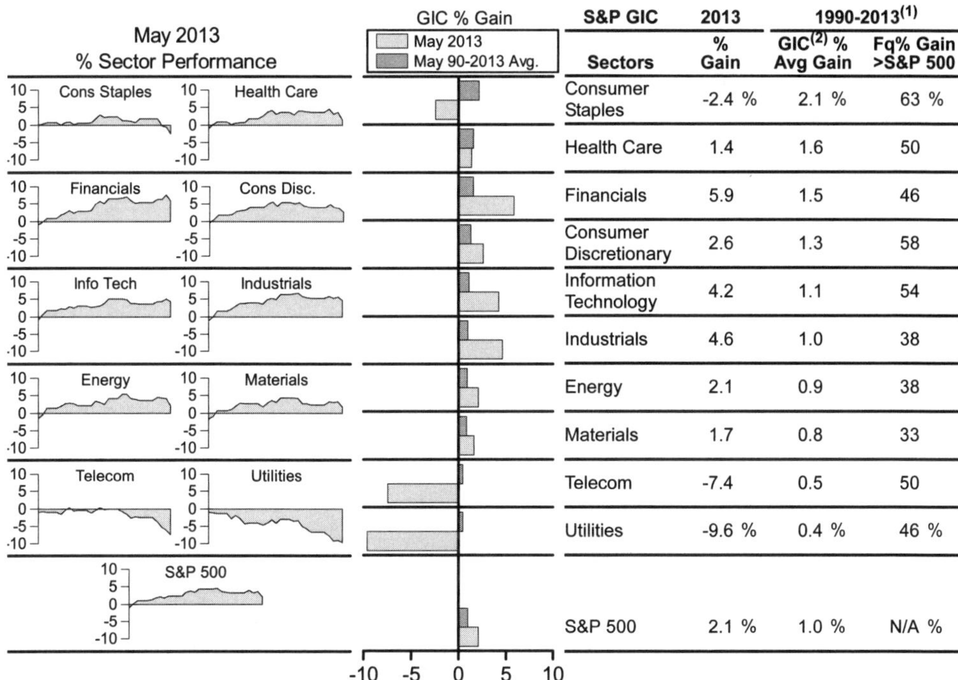

S&P GIC Sectors	2013 % Gain	1990-2013[1] GIC[2] % Avg Gain	1990-2013[1] Fq% Gain >S&P 500
Consumer Staples	-2.4 %	2.1 %	63 %
Health Care	1.4	1.6	50
Financials	5.9	1.5	46
Consumer Discretionary	2.6	1.3	58
Information Technology	4.2	1.1	54
Industrials	4.6	1.0	38
Energy	2.1	0.9	38
Materials	1.7	0.8	33
Telecom	-7.4	0.5	50
Utilities	-9.6 %	0.4 %	46 %
S&P 500	2.1 %	1.0 %	N/A %

Sector Commentary

♦ In May 2013, a month when the S&P 500 produced a gain of 2.1%, the performance ranking of the major sectors, flipped upside down. Previously, the defensive sectors had been outperforming the S&P 500, but in May they started to underperform and produce large losses. This was particularly true for the utilities sector which lost 9.6% and the telecom sector which lost 7.4%.♦ The defensive sectors had performed well in the spring and once talk of tapering the Fed's quantitative easing program started, the higher yielding defensive sectors were hit hard.♦ On a positive note, some of the non-defensive sectors that had not been performing well, started to outperform.♦ The financial sector continued its strong performance with a gain of 5.9%.

Sub-Sector Commentary

♦ Gold continued its correction and lost a total of 5.1% in May. Silver lost even more (7.6%). Precious metals were out of their seasonally strong periods and their prices were still falling.♦ Retail was performing well past the end of its seasonal period. ♦Biotech continued to strongly outperform the market.♦ As money left the defensive sectors, it went into some of the higher beta sectors. Investors were trying to ride the wave for higher returns.

SELECTED SUB-SECTORS[3]

Sub-Sector	2013 % Gain	GIC % Avg Gain	Fq% Gain >S&P 500
Banks	6.6 %	2.2 %	50 %
Agriculture (1994-2013)	-5.0	2.1	50
Biotech (1993-2013)	4.0	2.0	67
Retail	5.2	1.8	58
Railroads	2.9	1.6	58
Metals & Mining	1.7	1.4	50
Pharma	-1.8	1.3	46
Steel	-0.8	1.1	54
Chemicals	1.7	0.8	46
Software & Services	3.6	0.6	33
Transportation	2.1	0.6	50
Gold (London PM)	-5.1	0.4	58
SOX (1995-2013)	5.5	-0.2	47
Silver	-7.6	-0.2	50
Homebuilders	-2.8	-1.4	46

1/2 'N' 1/2

First 1/2 of April – Financial Stocks
Second 1/2 of April – Information Technology Stocks

The *1/2 'N' 1/2* strategy is a short-term switch combination that takes advantage of the superior performance of financial stocks in the first part of April and information technology stocks in the second half.

The opportunity exists because technology stocks tend to start increasing at the same time financial stocks tend to start decreasing, in mid-April. This creates an ideal switch opportunity between the two sectors.

2.9% extra & 18 times out of 24 better than the S&P 500

Why do financial stocks tend to start their decline relative to the broad market in mid-April? Is it a coincidence that the rate on the three month T-Bill tends to bottom out at the same time?

Liquidity is the common denominator that affects both the financial stocks and the money market. Basically, investors sell-off their money market positions in the beginning of April to cover their taxes that are due to the IRS in mid-April. As a result, short-term money market rates decrease.

Decreasing short-term yields are good for financial stocks, particularly banks. Banks tend to make more money with a steeper yield curve. They borrow short-term money (your savings account) and lend out long-term (mortgages). The steeper the curve, the more money banks make.

The end result is that financial stocks benefit from this trend in the first half of April.

On the flip side, investors stop selling their money market positions to cover taxes by mid-month. At this time, short-term yields tend to increase and financial stocks decrease.

Financials & Info Tech & 1/2 & 1/2 > S&P 500 [shaded]

	April 1st to April 15th		April 16th to April 30		April Compound Growth	
Year	S&P 500	Financials	S&P 500	Info Tech	S&P 500	1/2 & 1/2
1990	1.3 %	1.3 %	-3.9 %	-1.9 %	-2.7 %	-0.6 %
1991	1.6	2.3	-1.5	-3.1	0.0	-0.9
1992	3.1	1.0	-0.3	-1.3	2.8	-0.3
1993	-0.7	3.5	-1.8	-2.2	-2.5	1.3
1994	0.1	4.9	1.1	3.5	1.2	8.6
1995	1.7	2.9	1.1	5.8	2.8	8.8
1996	-0.5	-2.3	1.8	8.2	1.3	5.8
1997	-0.3	0.3	6.2	11.3	5.8	11.6
1998	1.6	5.5	-0.7	4.3	0.9	10.0
1999	2.8	5.0	0.9	1.3	3.8	6.4
2000	-9.5	-7.0	7.1	14.8	-3.1	6.8
2001	2.0	0.2	5.6	8.3	7.7	8.5
2002	-3.9	-1.6	-2.3	-3.5	-6.1	-5.1
2003	5.0	9.3	2.9	5.3	8.1	15.1
2004	0.2	-3.0	-1.9	-5.0	-1.7	-7.8
2005	-3.2	-2.6	1.2	2.3	-2.0	-0.4
2006	-0.4	-0.3	1.7	1.3	1.2	-1.0
2007	2.3	0.5	2.0	2.7	4.3	3.2
2008	0.9	-0.6	3.8	6.8	4.8	6.2
2009	6.8	23.0	2.4	5.8	9.4	30.1
2010	3.6	6.5	-2.1	-2.9	1.5	3.4
2011	-0.5	-1.6	3.3	4.6	2.9	2.9
2012	-2.7	-4.4	2.0	0.0	-0.7	-4.4
2013	-1.1	-0.8	2.9	3.4	1.8	2.6
Avg.	0.4 %	1.7 %	1.3 %	2.8 %	1.7 %	4.6 %

Fortunately, information technology stocks tend to present a good opportunity in mid-April, just when financials stocks are starting to underperform. Very often at this time of the year, technology stocks have corrected after their seasonal period finished in January and have become oversold and setup for a bounce.

Alternate Strategy—
The first few days in May tend to produce gains. An alternate strategy is to hold the information technology position for the first three trading days in May.

The SP GICS Financial Sector # 40 encompasses a wide range financial based companies.
The SP GICS Information Technology Sector # 45 encompasses a wide range technology based companies. For more information on the information technology sector, see www.standardandpoors.com

2013 Strategy Performance

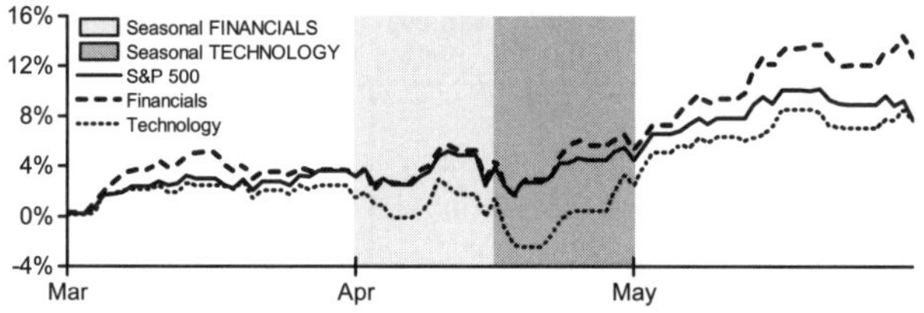

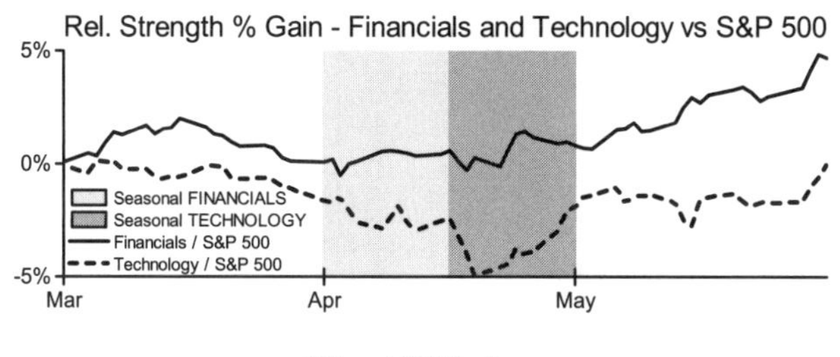

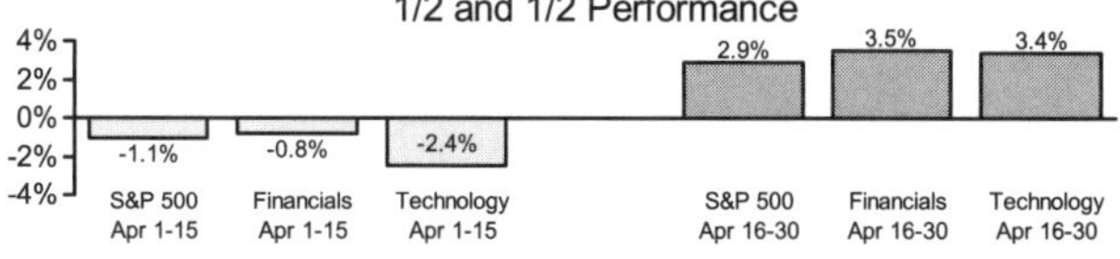

1/2 and 1/2 Performance

In the first half of March 2013, the S&P 500 as well as the financial sector and the technology sector were all rising. The financial sector was outperforming the technology sector and the S&P 500. The last half of March was relatively flat for the S&P 500 and the financial and the technology sectors were in turn underperforming the S&P 500. Overall, the setup for the half and half trade was neither positive nor negative.

Technical Conditions–
Entry Date Financial Sector April 1st, 2013 –

At the beginning of April, the market started to trend down, bringing down with it the financial and technology sectors. At the start of the second week in April, the S&P 500 started to increase and both the technology sector and the financial sectors started to outperform. At the end of the first half of the month, the financial sector slightly outperformed the S&P 500 and the first part of the *1/2 and 1/2* trade was successful.

Entry Date Technology Sector April 16th, 2013 –

Starting in the second half of April, the S&P 500 started to decrease and the technology sector responded sharply downwards. In a matter of days, the S&P 500 started to rebound and the technology sector strongly outperformed the S&P 500 for the rest of the month. In the end, the technology sector outperformed the S&P 500 by 0.5%.

WEEK 18

Market Indices & Rates
Weekly Values**

Stock Markets	2012	2013
Dow	13,201	14,833
S&P500	1,393	1,597
Nasdaq	3,027	3,331
TSX	12,148	12,382
FTSE	5,746	6,464
DAX	6,682	7,968
Nikkei	9,366	13,785
Hang Seng	21,185	22,669
Commodities	**2012**	**2013**
Oil	103.46	93.72
Gold	1649.0	1466.0
Bond Yields	**2012**	**2013**
USA 5 Yr Treasury	0.82	0.68
USA 10 Yr T	1.95	1.70
USA 20 Yr T	2.72	2.49
Moody's Aaa	3.95	3.69
Moody's Baa	5.15	4.52
CAN 5 Yr T	1.57	1.18
CAN 10 Yr T	2.02	1.70
Money Market	**2012**	**2013**
USA Fed Funds	0.25	0.25
USA 3 Mo T-B	0.07	0.05
CAN tgt overnight rate	1.00	1.00
CAN 3 Mo T-B	1.01	0.99
Foreign Exchange	**2012**	**2013**
EUR/USD	1.32	1.31
GBP/USD	1.62	1.55
USD/CAD	0.99	1.01
USD/JPY	80.02	97.91

MAY

M	T	W	T	F	S	S
			1	2	3	4
5	6	7	8	9	10	11
12	13	14	15	16	17	18
19	20	21	22	23	24	25
26	27	28	29	30	31	

JUNE

M	T	W	T	F	S	S
						1
2	3	4	5	6	7	8
9	10	11	12	13	14	15
16	17	18	19	20	21	22
23	24	25	26	27	28	29
30						

JULY

M	T	W	T	F	S	S
	1	2	3	4	5	6
7	8	9	10	11	12	13
14	15	16	17	18	19	20
21	22	23	24	25	26	27
28	29	30	31			

SIX 'N' SIX
Take a Break for Six Months - May 6th to October 27th

In the last three, years the stock market has corrected sharply in the spring, which has prompted many pundits to release reports in the media on "Sell in May and Go Away." But most do not grasp the full value of the favorable six month period from October 28th to May 5th, compared to the other six months: the unfavorable six month period.

Not only does the favorable period, on average have bigger gains more frequently and smaller losses, but the period, also on a yearly basis outperforms the unfavorable period 71% of the time (last column in the table with YES values). There is no question which six month period seasonal investors should favor.

$1,291,313 gain on $10,000

The accompanying table uses the S&P 500 to compare the returns made from Oct 28th to May 5th, to the returns made during the remainder of the year.

Starting with $10,000 and investing from October 28th to May 5th every year (October 28th, 1950, to May 5th, 2013) has produced a gain of $1,291,313. On the flip side, being invested from May 6th to October 27th, has actually lost money. An initial investment of $10,000 has lost $3,191 over the same time period.

S&P 500 Unfavorable 6 Month Avg. Gain vs Favorable 6 Month Avg. Gain (1950-2013)

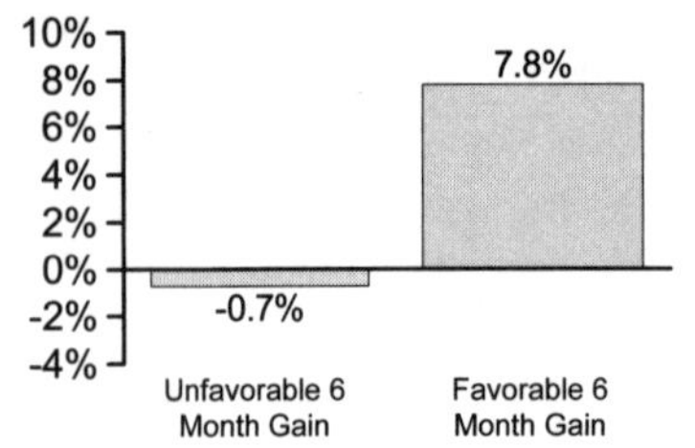

The above growth rates are geometric averages in order to represent the cumulative growth of a dollar investment over time. These figures differ from the arithmetic mean calculations used in the Six 'N' Six Take a Break Strategy, which are used to represent an average year.

	S&P 500 % May 6 to Oct 27	$10,000 Start	S&P 500 % Oct 28 to May 5	$10,000 Start	Oct28-May5 > May6-Oct27
1950/51	8.5%	10,851	15.2%	11,517	YES
1951/52	0.2	10,870	3.7	11,947	YES
1952/53	1.8	11,067	3.9	12,413	YES
1953/54	-3.1	10,727	16.6	14,475	YES
1954/55	13.2	12,141	18.1	17,097	YES
1955/56	11.4	13,528	15.1	19,681	YES
1956/57	-4.6	12,903	0.2	19,711	YES
1957/58	-12.4	11,302	7.9	21,265	YES
1958/59	15.1	13,013	14.5	24,356	
1959/60	-0.6	12,939	-4.5	23,270	
1960/61	-2.3	12,647	24.1	28,869	YES
1961/62	2.7	12,993	-3.1	27,982	
1962/63	-17.7	10,698	28.4	35,929	YES
1963/64	5.7	11,306	9.3	39,264	YES
1964/65	5.1	11,882	5.5	41,440	YES
1965/66	3.1	12,253	-5.0	39,388	
1966/67	-8.8	11,180	17.7	46,364	YES
1967/68	0.6	11,241	3.9	48,171	YES
1968/69	5.6	11,872	0.2	48,249	
1969/70	-6.2	11,141	-19.7	38,722	
1970/71	5.8	11,782	24.9	48,346	YES
1971/72	-9.6	10,647	13.7	54,965	YES
1972/73	3.7	11,046	0.3	55,154	
1973/74	0.3	11,084	-18.0	45,205	
1974/75	-23.2	8,513	28.5	58,073	YES
1975/76	-0.4	8,480	12.4	65,290	YES
1976/77	0.9	8,554	-1.6	64,231	
1977/78	-7.8	7,890	4.5	67,146	YES
1978/79	-2.0	7,732	6.4	71,476	YES
1979/80	-0.1	7,723	5.8	75,605	YES
1980/81	20.2	9,283	1.9	77,047	
1981/82	-8.5	8,498	-1.4	76,001	YES
1982/83	15.0	9,769	21.4	92,293	YES
1983/84	0.3	9,803	-3.5	89,085	
1984/85	3.9	10,183	8.9	97,057	YES
1985/86	4.1	10,604	26.8	123,044	YES
1986/87	0.4	10,651	23.7	152,196	YES
1987/88	-21.0	8,409	11.0	168,904	YES
1988/89	7.1	9,010	10.9	187,380	YES
1989/90	8.9	9,814	1.0	189,242	
1990/91	-10.0	8,837	25.0	236,498	YES
1991/92	0.9	8,916	8.5	256,590	YES
1992/93	0.4	8,952	6.2	272,550	YES
1993/94	4.5	9,356	-2.8	264,789	
1994/95	3.2	9,656	11.6	295,636	YES
1995/96	11.5	10,762	10.7	327,219	
1996/97	9.2	11,757	18.5	387,591	YES
1997/98	5.6	12,419	27.2	493,003	YES
1998/99	-4.5	11,860	26.5	623,489	YES
1999/00	-3.8	11,415	10.5	688,842	YES
2000/01	-3.7	10,992	-8.2	632,435	
2001/02	-12.8	9,586	-2.8	614,583	YES
2002/03	-16.4	8,016	3.2	634,369	YES
2003/04	11.3	8,921	8.8	689,985	
2004/05	0.3	8,952	4.2	718,942	YES
2005/06	0.5	9,000	12.5	808,503	YES
2006/07	3.9	9,350	9.3	883,804	YES
2007/08	2.0	9,534	-8.3	810,240	
2008/09	-39.7	5,750	6.5	862,619	YES
2009/10	17.7	6,766	9.6	934,470	
2010/11	1.4	6,862	12.9	1,067,851	YES
2011/12	-3.8	6,602	6.6	1,138,103	YES
2012/13	3.1	6,809	14.3	1,301,313	YES
Total Gain (Loss)		**($3,191)**		**$1,291,313**	

2012-13 Strategy Performance

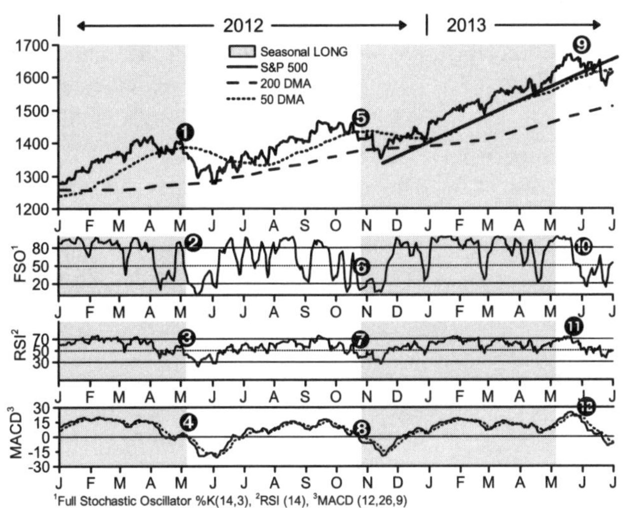

[1]Full Stochastic Oscillator %K(14,3), [2]RSI (14), [3]MACD (12,26,9)

Favorable vs. Unfavorable Seasons 2011-2013 (S&P 500)

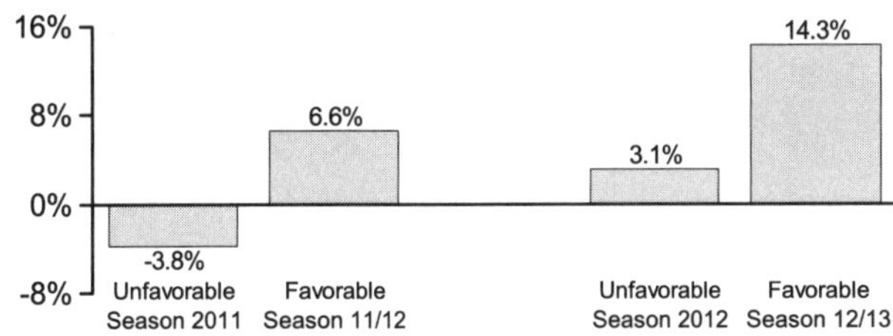

Technical Conditions– May 6th to October 27th, 2012

In 2012, the S&P 500 started to turn down right on seasonal cue at the beginning of May, as it crossed below its 50 day moving average❶. There was an early sell signal from the FSO that crossed below 80❷ and both the RSI and MACD turned down from neutral positions❸❹.

Technical Conditions– October 28th to May 5th, 2013

Entry Strategy – Buy Position On Entry Date– On October 28th 2012, the S&P 500 had just crossed below its 50 day moving average❺ and the trend was still down. Out of the three technical indicators❻❼❽, only the FSO was poised to present a buy signal, being below 20 and turning upwards. Despite not having all of the technical signals indicating a buy condition, entering at the start of the six month seasonal period is still prudent.

Exit Strategy – Sell Position Late– The S&P 500 still had strong momentum on the exit date and did not turn down until later in May❾. A full exit was warranted when the FSO turned below 80❿. Shortly afterwards, the RSI confirmed exiting the trade by turning below 70⓫. At the same time, the MACD also turned down⓬.

WEEK 19

Market Indices & Rates Weekly Values**

Stock Markets	2012	2013
Dow	12,890	15,066
S&P500	1,360	1,627
Nasdaq	2,941	3,410
TSX	11,734	12,527
FTSE	5,551	5,272
DAX	6,517	8,217
Nikkei	9,062	14,316
Hang Seng	20,309	23,148
Commodities	**2012**	**2013**
Oil	96.99	96.17
Gold	1591.6	1160.9
Bond Yields	**2012**	**2013**
USA 5 Yr Treasury	0.77	0.76
USA 10 Yr T	1.88	1.83
USA 20 Yr T	2.63	2.63
Moody's Aaa	3.87	3.81
Moody's Baa	5.08	4.65
CAN 5 Yr T	1.49	1.28
CAN 10 Yr T	1.99	1.82
Money Market	**2012**	**2013**
USA Fed Funds	0.25	0.25
USA 3 Mo T-B	0.10	0.04
CAN tgt overnight rate	1.00	1.00
CAN 3 Mo T-B	1.01	1.00
Foreign Exchange	**2012**	**2013**
EUR/USD	1.30	1.31
GBP/USD	1.61	1.55
USD/CAD	1.00	1.01
USD/JPY	79.86	99.91

MAY

M	T	W	T	F	S	S
			1	2	3	4
5	6	7	8	9	10	11
12	13	14	15	16	17	18
19	20	21	22	23	24	25
26	27	28	29	30	31	

JUNE

M	T	W	T	F	S	S
						1
2	3	4	5	6	7	8
9	10	11	12	13	14	15
16	17	18	19	20	21	22
23	24	25	26	27	28	29
30						

JULY

M	T	W	T	F	S	S
	1	2	3	4	5	6
7	8	9	10	11	12	13
14	15	16	17	18	19	20
21	22	23	24	25	26	27
28	29	30	31			

CANADIAN SIX 'N' SIX
Take a Break for Six Months - May 6th to October 27th

In analysing long-term trends for the broad markets such as the S&P 500 or the TSX Composite, a large data set is preferable because it incorporates various economic cycles. The daily data set for the TSX Composite starts in 1977.

Over this time period, investors have been rewarded for following the six month cycle of investing from October 28th to May 5th, versus the other unfavorable six months, May 6th to October 27th.

Starting with an investment of $10,000 in 1977, investing in the unfavorable six months has produced a loss of $3,593, versus investing in the favorable six months which has produced a gain of $183,348.

$183,348 gain on $10,000 since 1977

The TSX Composite Average Year 1977 to 2012 (graph below) indicates that the market tended to peak in mid-July or the end of August. In our book *Time In Time Out, Outsmart the Stock Market Using Calendar Investment Strategies*, Bruce Lindsay and I analysed a number of market trends and peaks over different decades.

What we found was that the markets tend to peak at the beginning of May or mid-July. The mid-July peak was usually the result of a strong bull market in place that had a lot of momentum.

The main reason that the TSX Composite data shows a peak occurring in July-August is that the data is primarily from the biggest bull market in history, starting in 1982.

TSX Composite % Gain Avg. Year 1977 to 2012

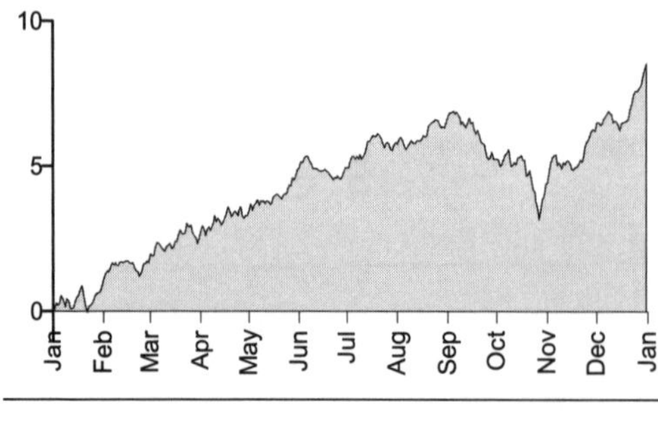

Does a later average peak in the stock market mean that the best six month cycle does not work? No. Dividing the year up into six month intervals, the period from October to May is far superior compared with the other half of the year.

The table below illustrates the superiority of the best six months over the worst six months. Going down the table year by year, the period from October 28 to May 5th outperforms the period from May 6th to October 27.

In a strong bull market, investors always have the choice of using a stop loss or technical indicators to help extend the exit point past the May date.

	TSX Comp May 6 to Oct 27	$10,000 Start	TSX Comp Oct 28 to May 5	$10,000 Start
1977/78	-3.9 %	9,608	13.1 %	11,313
1978/79	12.1	10,775	21.3	13,728
1979/80	2.9	11,084	23.0	16,883
1980/81	22.5	13,579	-2.4	16,479
1981/82	-17.0	11,272	-18.2	13,488
1982/83	16.6	13,138	34.6	18,150
1983/84	-0.9	13,015	-1.9	17,811
1984/85	1.6	13,226	10.7	19,718
1985/86	0.5	13,299	16.5	22,978
1986/87	-1.9	13,045	24.8	28,666
1987/88	-23.4	9,992	15.3	33,050
1988/89	2.7	10,260	5.7	34,939
1989/90	7.9	11,072	-13.3	30,294
1990/91	-8.4	10,148	13.1	34,266
1991/92	-1.6	9,982	-2.0	33,571
1992/93	-2.3	9,750	15.3	38,704
1993/94	10.8	10,801	1.7	39,365
1994/95	-0.1	10,792	0.3	39,483
1995/96	1.3	10,936	18.2	46,671
1996/97	8.3	11,843	10.8	51,725
1997/98	7.3	12,707	17.0	60,510
1998/99	-22.3	9,870	17.1	70,871
1999/00	-0.2	9,853	36.9	97,009
2000/01	-2.9	9,570	-14.4	83,062
2001/02	-12.2	8,399	9.4	90,875
2002/03	-16.4	7,020	4.0	94,476
2003/04	15.1	8,079	10.3	104,252
2004/05	3.9	8,398	7.8	112,379
2005/06	8.1	9,080	19.8	134,587
2006/07	0.0	9,079	12.2	151,053
2007/08	3.8	9,426	-0.2	150,820
2008/09	-40.2	5,638	15.7	174,551
2009/10	11.9	6,307	7.4	187,526
2010/11	5.8	6,674	7.1	200,778
2011/12	-7.4	6,183	-4.8	191,207
2012/13	3.6	6,407	1.1	193,348
Total Gain (Loss)		**($-3,593)**		**$183,348**

2012-13 Strategy Performance

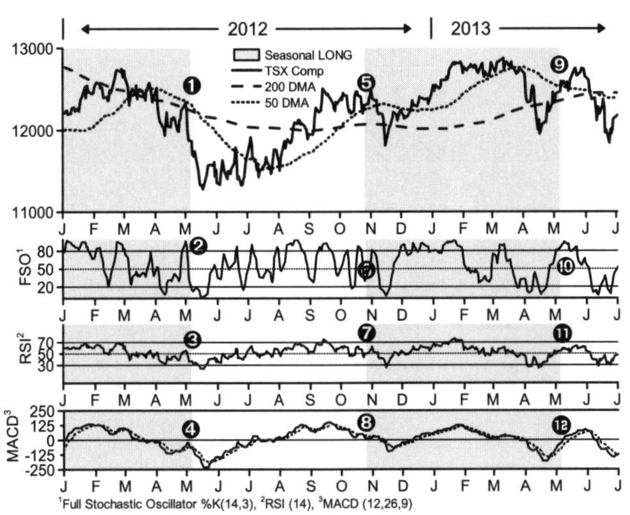

Favorable vs. Unfavorable Seasons 2011-2013 (TSX Composite)

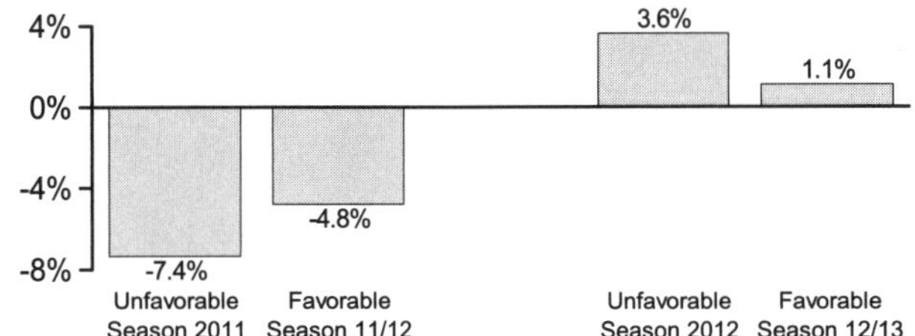

TSX Composite Performance– May 6th to October 27, 2012

At the beginning of the unfavorable season, bearish conditions existed. The TSX Composite started to erode in late April 2012, crossing below its 200 day moving average❶ and the FSO turned below 80❷. Both the RSI and the MACD, turned down from neutral positions❸❹.

October 28th to May 5th, 2013

Entry Strategy – Buy Position On Entry Date– Since September 2012, the TSX Composite had been trading sideways, but was positively above its 50 and 200 day moving averages❺. The FSO, RSI and MACD were all neutral❻❼❽.

Exit Strategy –Sell Partial Position On Exit Date– The TSX Composite was trending upwards and was above its 50 and 200 day moving averages❾. The FSO had not started turning down from above 80❿. The RSI and MACD were rising, but in neutral territory⓫⓬. A full exit was warranted when the FSO turned below 80 in mid-May.

WEEK 20

Market Indices & Rates Weekly Values**

Stock Markets	2012	2013
Dow	12,548	15,234
S&P500	1,319	1,652
Nasdaq	2,853	3,467
TSX	11,354	12,540
FTSE	5,383	6,684
DAX	6,363	8,350
Nikkei	8,833	14,962
Hang Seng	19,408	23,012
Commodities	**2012**	**2013**
Oil	93.12	94.97
Gold	1561.4	1404.9
Bond Yields	**2012**	**2013**
USA 5 Yr Treasury	0.74	0.83
USA 10 Yr T	1.74	1.93
USA 20 Yr T	2.46	2.74
Moody's Aaa	3.72	3.91
Moody's Baa	4.98	4.74
CAN 5 Yr T	1.44	1.36
CAN 10 Yr T	1.91	1.92
Money Market	**2012**	**2013**
USA Fed Funds	0.25	0.25
USA 3 Mo T-B	0.08	0.04
CAN tgt overnight rate	1.00	1.00
CAN 3 Mo T-B	0.98	1.00
Foreign Exchange	**2012**	**2013**
EUR/USD	1.27	1.29
GBP/USD	1.59	1.52
USD/CAD	1.01	1.02
USD/JPY	79.73	102.39

MAY

M	T	W	T	F	S	S
			1	2	3	4
5	6	7	8	9	10	11
12	13	14	15	16	17	18
19	20	21	22	23	24	25
26	27	28	29	30	31	

JUNE

M	T	W	T	F	S	S
						1
2	3	4	5	6	7	8
9	10	11	12	13	14	15
16	17	18	19	20	21	22
23	24	25	26	27	28	29
30						

JULY

M	T	W	T	F	S	S
	1	2	3	4	5	6
7	8	9	10	11	12	13
14	15	16	17	18	19	20
21	22	23	24	25	26	27
28	29	30	31			

COST COSTCO– BUY AT A DISCOUNT

①May26 to Jun30 ②Oct4 to Dec1

Shoppers are attracted to Costco because of their consistently low prices. They take comfort in the fact that although the prices may not always be the lowest, they are consistently in the lower range.

Costco performs well in the late spring and early summer, and in the autumn and early winter. These two periods are considered to be transition periods where the stock market is moving to and from its unfavorable and favorable seasons. Companies such as Costco that have stable earnings are desirable at these times.

Many investors see Costco as a bargain stock, but there are two times when it is a seasonal bargain: May 26th to June 30th and October 4th to December 1st. From 1990 to 2012, during the period of May 26th to June 30th, Costco has averaged a gain of 6.2% and has been positive 70% of the time. From October 4th to December 1st, Costco has averaged a gain of 9.9% and has been positive 78% of the time.

Costco vs. S&P 500 1990 to 2012 Positive [shaded]

Year	May 26 to Jun 30 S&P 500	May 26 to Jun 30 COST	Oct 4 to Dec 1 S&P 500	Oct 4 to Dec 1 COST	Compound Growth S&P 500	Compound Growth COST
1990	1.0	16.5 %	3.5	26.5 %	4.5	47.4 %
1991	-1.7	-2.1	-2.4	-3.7	-4.0	-5.7
1992	-1.4	-2.2	5.0	22.7	3.5	20.1
1993	0.4	17.2	0.1	13.4	0.5	32.9
1994	-2.6	10.7	-2.8	-6.3	-5.3	3.7
1995	3.1	19.2	4.2	-2.1	7.4	16.7
1996	-1.2	9.4	9.3	15.5	8.0	26.4
1997	4.5	3.1	1.0	16.6	5.6	20.2
1998	2.1	17.6	17.2	41.1	19.7	65.9
1999	6.9	8.1	9.0	30.7	16.5	41.2
2000	5.3	10.0	-7.8	-3.6	-2.9	6.1
2001	-4.2	9.3	6.3	12.3	1.8	22.6
2002	-8.7	-0.8	14.3	4.6	4.4	3.8
2003	4.4	5.3	3.9	13.5	8.5	19.4
2004	2.5	10.3	5.3	17.3	7.9	29.4
2005	0.1	-1.5	3.1	13.9	3.2	12.2
2006	-0.2	5.0	4.7	6.0	4.5	11.3
2007	-0.8	3.8	-3.8	8.9	-4.6	12.9
2008	-7.0	-1.7	-25.8	-23.5	-30.9	-24.7
2009	3.6	-5.2	8.2	7.5	12.1	1.9
2010	-4.0	-3.0	5.2	5.0	1.0	1.9
2011	0.0	1.2	13.2	6.7	13.2	7.9
2012	3.4	12.5	-2.4	4.3	0.9	17.6
Avg.	0.2 %	6.2 %	3.0 %	9.9 %	3.3 %	17.0 %
Fq>0	57 %	70 %	74 %	78 %	78 %	91 %

17.0% gain

Putting both seasonal periods together has produced a 91% positive success rate and an average gain of 17.0%. Although the earlier strong years in the 1990's skews that data to the high-side, Costco has still maintained its strong seasonal performances in both the May to June and the October to December time frames. When investors go shopping for stocks, Costco is one consumer staples company that should be on their list. They should also remember not to bulk up with too much, even if it is selling at a discount.

COST - stock symbol for Costco which trades on the Nasdaq exchange. Stock data adjusted for stock splits.

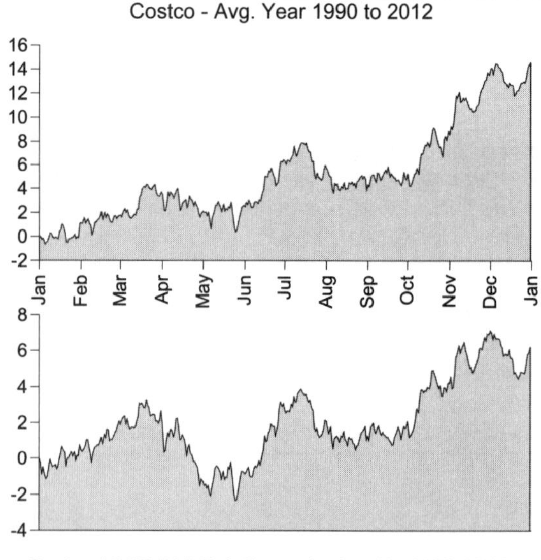

Costco / S&P 500 Rel. Strength- Avg Yr. 1990-2012

2012-13 Strategy Performance

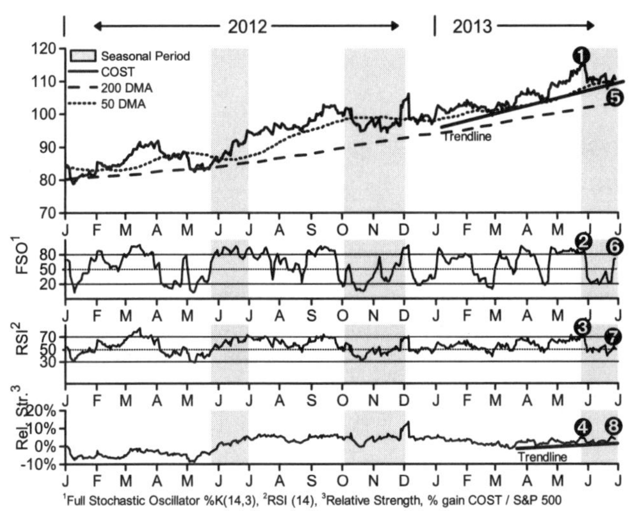

[1]Full Stochastic Oscillator %K(14,3), [2]RSI (14), [3]Relative Strength, % gain COST / S&P 500

Costco Performance

After outperforming the S&P 500 in its October to November 2012 time period, Costco produced a steady rate of ascent, but underperformed the market up until mid-March. In mid-March, Costco started to slowly outperform the S&P 500 once again.

Technical Conditions– May 26th to June 30th, 2013

Entry Strategy – Buy Position On Entry Date– A week before the start of its seasonal period, Costco's price spiked❶ and it outperformed the S&P 500❹, putting it into overbought territory with its FSO above 80❷ and the RSI above 70❸. Despite being overbought, Costco's price was rising and above its 50 day moving average, making the start date a reasonable entry point.

Exit Strategy –Sell Position On Exit Date–
After the entry date for the seasonal period, Costco's price fell❺ and it underperformed the market for the next week. As a result, there was not an early exit date triggered within the four week window of the exit date. Costco did manage to produce a price spurt at the end of its seasonal period, helping it to outperform the S&P 500❽ briefly, but not enough to outperform over the whole seasonal period. At the end of the trade, both the FSO and the RSI were above 50❻❼ and rising.

WEEK 21

Market Indices & Rates Weekly Values**

Stock Markets	2012	2013
Dow	12,498	15,326
S&P500	1,318	1,658
Nasdaq	2,843	3,476
TSX	11,540	12,705
FTSE	5,335	6,750
DAX	6,342	8,423
Nikkei	8,613	15,093
Hang Seng	18,825	23,082

Commodities	2012	2013
Oil	90.98	94.93
Gold	1572.4	1379.0

Bond Yields	2012	2013
USA 5 Yr Treasury	0.76	0.88
USA 10 Yr T	1.76	1.99
USA 20 Yr T	2.44	2.80
Moody's Aaa	3.76	3.95
Moody's Baa	5.09	4.78
CAN 5 Yr T	1.39	1.37
CAN 10 Yr T	1.87	1.94

Money Market	2012	2013
USA Fed Funds	0.25	0.25
USA 3 Mo T-B	0.09	0.04
CAN tgt overnight rate	1.00	1.00
CAN 3 Mo T-B	0.94	1.00

Foreign Exchange	2012	2013
EUR/USD	1.26	1.29
GBP/USD	1.57	1.51
USD/CAD	1.02	1.03
USD/JPY	79.60	102.25

MAY

M	T	W	T	F	S	S
			1	2	3	4
5	6	7	8	9	10	11
12	13	14	15	16	17	18
19	20	21	22	23	24	25
26	27	28	29	30	31	

JUNE

M	T	W	T	F	S	S
						1
2	3	4	5	6	7	8
9	10	11	12	13	14	15
16	17	18	19	20	21	22
23	24	25	26	27	28	29
30						

JULY

M	T	W	T	F	S	S
	1	2	3	4	5	6
7	8	9	10	11	12	13
14	15	16	17	18	19	20
21	22	23	24	25	26	27
28	29	30	31			

** Weekly avg closing values- except Fed Funds & CAN overnight tgt rate weekly closing values.

MEMORIAL DAY – BE EARLY & STAY LATE

Positive 2 Market Days Before Memorial Day to 5 Market Days into June

A lot of strategies that focus on investing around holidays concentrate on the market performance the day before and the day after a holiday.

1% average gain and positive 63% of the time

Not all holidays were created equal. The typical Memorial Day trade is to invest the day before the holiday and sell the day after. If you invested in the stock market for just these two days, you would be missing out on a lot of gains.

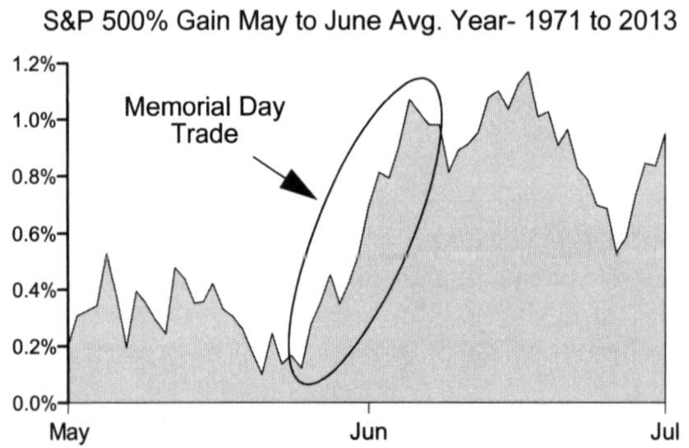

Historically, the best strategy has been to invest two market days before Memorial Day and hold until five market days into June.

Extending the investment into June makes sense. The first few days in June tend to be positive– so why sell early?

The graph shows the average performance of the S&P 500 on a calendar basis for the months of May and June from 1971 to 2013.

The increase from the end of May into June represents the opportunity with the "*Memorial Day - Be Early & Stay Late*" trade.

The graph clearly shows a spike in the market that occurs at the end of the month and carries on into June.

Investors using the typical Memorial Day trade, miss out on the majority of the gain. The *Memorial Day - Be Early & Stay Late* strategy has produced an average gain of 1.0% and has been positive 63% of the time (S&P 500, 1971 to 2013). Not a bad gain for being invested an average of ten market days.

The *Memorial Day - Be Early & Stay Late* trade can be extended into June primarily because the first market days of the month tend to be positive. These days are part of the end of the month effect. (see *Super Seven* strategy).

2 Market Days Before Memorial Day to 5 Market Days Into June - S&P 500   Positive (shaded)

		1980	5.1 %	1990	1.1 %	2000	5.2 %	2010	-1.6 %
1971	1.5 %	1981	0.2	1991	0.9	2001	-0.9	2011	-2.7
1972	-2.4	1982	-2.6	1992	-0.5	2002	-5.4	2012	-0.3
1973	1.7	1983	-2.1	1993	-1.3	2003	7.0	2013	-0.7
1974	6.3	1984	1.2	1994	0.4	2004	2.3		
1975	3.8	1985	4.3	1995	0.9	2005	0.6		
1976	-0.7	1986	4.3	1996	0.0	2006	-0.2		
1977	1.0	1987	5.5	1997	2.2	2007	-2.1		
1978	3.1	1988	4.5	1998	-0.5	2008	-2.2		
1979	1.9	1989	2.4	1999	2.3	2009	4.1		
Avg.	1.8 %		2.3 %		0.6 %		0.8 %		-1.3 %

History of Memorial Day:

Originally called Decoration Day in remembrance of those who died in the nation's service. Memorial Day was first observed on May 30th 1868 when flowers were placed on the graves of Union and Confederate soldiers at Arlington National Cemetery. The South acknowledged the day after World War I, when the holiday changed from honoring just those who died fighting in the Civil War to honoring Americans who died fighting in any war. In 1971 Congress passed the National Holiday Act recognizing Memorial Day as the last Monday in May.

2013 Strategy Performance

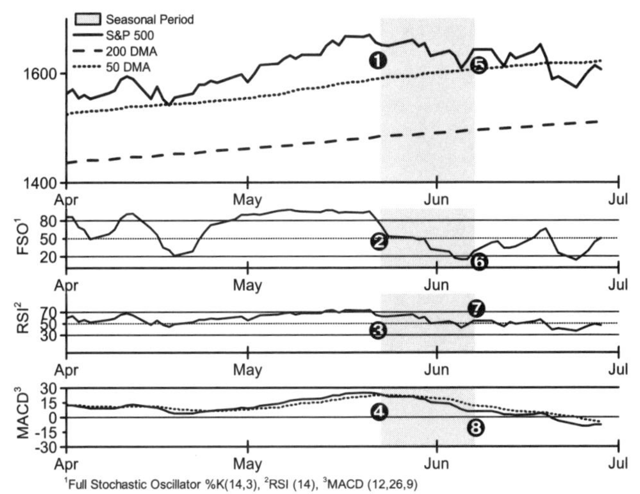

¹Full Stochastic Oscillator %K(14,3), ²RSI (14), ³MACD (12,26,9)

Memorial Day Performance

Starting in mid-April 2013, the S&P 500 started to rise after touching its 50 day moving average. It continued its strong performance until mid-May and then started to turn down.

Technical Conditions– 2 Market Days Before Memorial Day to 5 Market Days into June, 2013

Entry Strategy –Buy Position on Entry Date–

The Memorial Day trade started on a negative footing with a negative trend❶, the FSO crossing below 80❷, the RSI dropping below 70❸ and the MACD crossing❹ on a downtrend. In other words, the technical picture could not be much worse. In this case, there could be a strong argument to have not entered the trade.

Exit Strategy –Sell Position on Exit Date–

Despite bouncing off its 50 day moving average and providing a bit of a spurt at the end of its seasonal trade, the S&P 500 still ended up lower than where it started❺, with the FSO just above 20❻, the RSI at 50❼ and the MACD still in a downtrend❽.

WEEK 22

Market Indices & Rates Weekly Values**

Stock Markets	**2012**	**2013**
Dow	12,378	15,288
S&P500	1,309	1,648
Nasdaq	2,821	3,476
TSX	11,497	12,715
FTSE	5,325	5,326
DAX	6,263	8,390
Nikkei	8,573	14,029
Hang Seng	18,747	22,608

Commodities	**2012**	**2013**
Oil	87.09	93.43
Gold	1571.6	1113.4

Bond Yields	**2012**	**2013**
USA 5 Yr Treasury	0.69	1.03
USA 10 Yr T	1.61	2.14
USA 20 Yr T	2.29	2.93
Moody's Aaa	3.65	4.06
Moody's Baa	5.01	4.90
CAN 5 Yr T	1.27	1.46
CAN 10 Yr T	1.78	2.05

Money Market	**2012**	**2013**
USA Fed Funds	0.25	0.25
USA 3 Mo T-B	0.07	0.04
CAN tgt overnight rate	1.00	1.00
CAN 3 Mo T-B	0.88	1.02

Foreign Exchange	**2012**	**2013**
EUR/USD	1.24	1.30
GBP/USD	1.55	1.51
USD/CAD	1.03	1.03
USD/JPY	78.87	101.13

MAY

M	T	W	T	F	S	S
			1	2	3	4
5	6	7	8	9	10	11
12	13	14	15	16	17	18
19	20	21	22	23	24	25
26	27	28	29	30	31	

JUNE

M	T	W	T	F	S	S
						1
2	3	4	5	6	7	8
9	10	11	12	13	14	15
16	17	18	19	20	21	22
23	24	25	26	27	28	29
30						

JULY

M	T	W	T	F	S	S
	1	2	3	4	5	6
7	8	9	10	11	12	13
14	15	16	17	18	19	20
21	22	23	24	25	26	27
28	29	30	31			

** Weekly avg closing values- except Fed Funds & CAN overnight tgt rate weekly closing values.

JUNE

	MONDAY		TUESDAY		WEDNESDAY	
	2	28	3	27	4	26
WEEK 23						
	9	21	10	20	11	19
WEEK 24						
	16	14	17	13	18	12
WEEK 25						
	23	7	24	6	25	5
WEEK 26						
	30		1		2	
WEEK 27						

THURSDAY		FRIDAY	
5	25	6	24
12	18	13	17
19	11	20	10
26	4	27	3
3		4	

JULY

M	T	W	T	F	S	S
	1	2	3	4	5	6
7	8	9	10	11	12	13
14	15	16	17	18	19	20
21	22	23	24	25	26	27
28	29	30	31			

AUGUST

M	T	W	T	F	S	S
				1	2	3
4	5	6	7	8	9	10
11	12	13	14	15	16	17
18	19	20	21	22	23	24
25	26	27	28	29	30	31

SEPTEMBER

M	T	W	T	F	S	S
1	2	3	4	5	6	7
8	9	10	11	12	13	14
15	16	17	18	19	20	21
22	23	24	25	26	27	28
29	30					

OCTOBER

M	T	W	T	F	S	S
		1	2	3	4	5
6	7	8	9	10	11	12
13	14	15	16	17	18	19
20	21	22	23	24	25	26
27	28	29	30	31		

JUNE
SUMMARY

	Dow Jones	S&P 500	Nasdaq	TSX Comp
Month Rank	11	10	6	11
# Up	29	32	24	13
# Down	34	31	17	15
% Pos	46	51	59	46
% Avg. Gain	-0.3	0.0	0.8	-0.3

Dow & S&P 1950-2012, Nasdaq 1972-2012, TSX 1985-2012

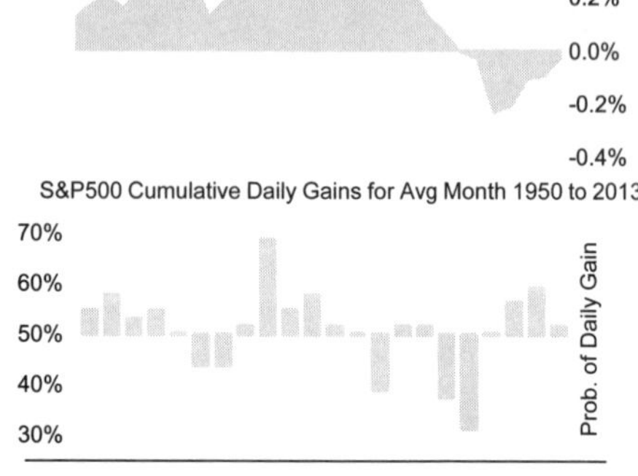

♦ On average, June is not a strong month. From 1950 to 2012, it was the third worst month for the S&P 500, producing a flat return of 0.0%. ♦ From year to year, different sectors of the market tend to lead in June and there is not a strong consistent outperforming major sector. ♦ On average, the biotech sector starts its seasonal run in late June. ♦ The last few days of June tend to be positive, and start the successful *Independence Day Trade*.

BEST / WORST JUNE BROAD MKTS. 2004-2013

BEST JUNE MARKETS

- Nikkei 225 (2004) 5.5%
- Nikkei 225 (2012) 5.4%
- Russell 2000 (2012) 4.8%

WORST JUNE MARKETS

- Dow (2008) -10.2%
- Nasdaq (2008) -9.1%
- S&P 500 (2008) -8.6%

Index Values End of Month

	2004	2005	2006	2007	2008	2009	2010	2011	2012	2013
Dow	10,435	10,275	11,150	13,409	11,350	8,447	9,774	12,414	12,880	14,910
S&P 500	1,141	1,191	1,270	1,503	1,280	919	1,031	1,321	1,362	1,606
Nasdaq	2,048	2,057	2,172	2,603	2,293	1,835	2,109	2,774	2,935	3,403
TSX Comp.	8,546	9,903	11,613	13,907	14,467	10,375	11,294	13,301	11,597	12,129
Russell 1000	1,171	1,242	1,330	1,573	1,352	966	1,091	1,412	1,443	1,712
Russell 2000	1,470	1,590	1,801	2,072	1,714	1,263	1,515	2,056	1,984	2,429
FTSE 100	4,464	5,113	5,833	6,608	5,626	4,249	4,917	5,946	5,571	6,215
Nikkei 225	11,859	11,584	15,505	18,138	13,481	9,958	9,383	9,816	9,007	13,677

Percent Gain for June

	2004	2005	2006	2007	2008	2009	2010	2011	2012	2013
Dow	2.4	-1.8	-0.2	-1.6	-10.2	-0.6	-3.6	-1.2	3.9	-1.4
S&P 500	1.8	0.0	0.0	-1.8	-8.6	0.0	-5.4	-1.8	4.0	-1.5
Nasdaq	3.1	-0.5	-0.3	0.0	-9.1	3.4	-6.5	-2.2	3.8	-1.5
TSX Comp.	1.5	3.1	-1.1	-1.1	-1.7	0.0	-4.0	-3.6	0.7	-4.1
Russell 1000	1.7	0.3	0.0	-2.0	-8.5	0.1	-5.7	-1.9	3.7	-1.5
Russell 2000	4.1	3.7	0.5	-1.6	-7.8	1.3	-7.9	-2.5	4.8	-0.7
FTSE 100	0.8	3.0	1.9	-0.2	-7.1	-3.8	-5.2	-0.7	4.7	-5.6
Nikkei 225	5.5	2.7	0.2	1.5	-6.0	4.6	-4.0	1.3	5.4	-0.7

June Market Avg. Performance 2004 to 2013[1]

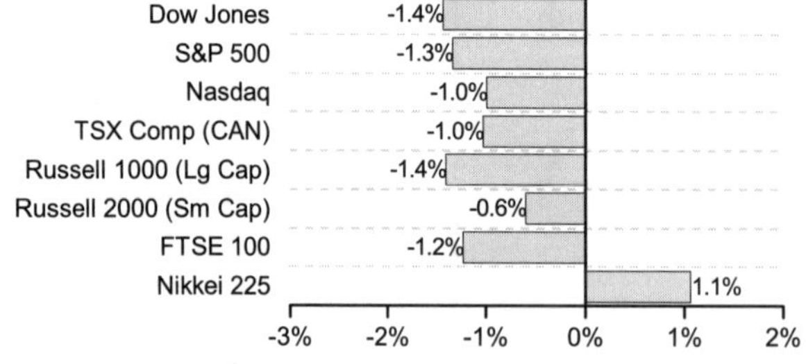

Interest Corner Jun[2]

	Fed Funds % [3]	3 Mo. T-Bill %[4]	10 Yr %[5]	20 Yr %[6]
2013	0.25	0.04	2.52	3.22
2012	0.25	0.09	1.67	2.38
2011	0.25	0.03	3.18	4.09
2010	0.25	0.18	2.97	3.74
2009	0.25	0.19	3.53	4.30

(1) Russell Data provided by Russell (2) Federal Reserve Bank of St. Louis- end of month values (3) Target rate set by FOMC (4)(5)(6) Constant yield maturities.

JUNE SECTOR PERFORMANCE

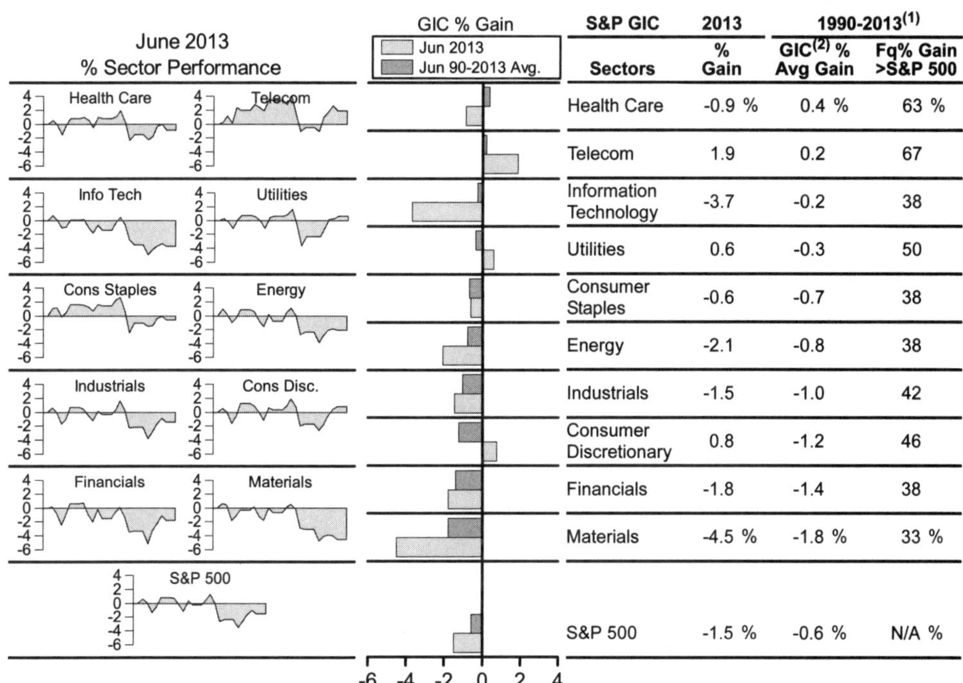

S&P GIC Sectors	2013 % Gain	1990-2013(1) GIC(2) % Avg Gain	1990-2013(1) Fq% Gain >S&P 500
Health Care	-0.9 %	0.4 %	63 %
Telecom	1.9	0.2	67
Information Technology	-3.7	-0.2	38
Utilities	0.6	-0.3	50
Consumer Staples	-0.6	-0.7	38
Energy	-2.1	-0.8	38
Industrials	-1.5	-1.0	42
Consumer Discretionary	0.8	-1.2	46
Financials	-1.8	-1.4	38
Materials	-4.5 %	-1.8 %	33 %
S&P 500	-1.5 %	-0.6 %	N/A %

Sector Commentary

♦ After a strong run over many months, the S&P 500 finally had a small correction of 1.5% in June 2013. The materials sector decreased the most, with a loss of 4.5%. ♦ The cyclical sectors were generally hit, as investors worried that the potential tapering of the Fed's quantitative easing program would impact the economy. ♦ After correcting sharply in May, the defensive sectors were due for a bounce. As the stock market corrected, the sectors of choice in June were the defensive sectors.

Sub-Sector Commentary

♦ Gold continued to lose ground, falling 14.5% for the month. ♦ Silver fared even worse, producing a loss of 16.4%. The good news was that the strong seasonal period for gold was just around the corner in July. ♦ The homebuilders sub-sector corrected sharply after a strong preceding month. The strong performance in May, out of season, was too good to be true. ♦ After a strong rise in the previous months, biotech corrected. ♦ The metals and mining sub-sector underperformed once again, as investors continued to avoid the deep cyclical stocks.

SELECTED SUB-SECTORS(3)

Sub-Sector	2013 % Gain	GIC % Avg Gain	Fq% Gain >S&P 500
Software & Services	-2.9 %	2.3 %	75 %
Pharma	-0.1	0.6	67
Retail	0.2	-0.6	42
Gold (London PM)	-14.5	-0.6	46
SOX (1995-2013)	0.0	-0.9	37
Railroads	-3.0	-1.1	42
Biotech (1993-2013)	-5.5	-1.1	43
Metals & Mining	-7.8	-1.1	54
Steel	-3.6	-1.2	46
Transportation	-1.7	-1.3	33
Agriculture (1994-2013)	5.2	-1.4	35
Chemicals	-3.9	-1.8	33
Homebuilders	-11.1	-1.9	38
Banks	2.1	-2.5	25
Silver	-16.4	-2.7	38

(1) Sector data provided by Standard and Poors (2) GIC is short form for Global Industry Classification (3) Sub Sector data provided by Standard and Poors, except where marked by symbol.

BIOTECH SUMMER SOLSTICE
June 23rd to September 13th

The *Biotech Summer Solstice* trade starts on June 23rd and lasts until September 13th. The trade is aptly named as its outperformance starts approximately on the day summer solstice starts– the longest day of the year.

There are two main drivers of the trade: biotech is a good substitute for technology stocks in the summer, and investors want to take a position in the biotech sector before the autumn conferences.

11.1% extra & 86% of the time better than the S&P 500

Biotech vs. S&P 500 1992 to 2012

Positive (shaded)

Jun 23 to Sep 13	S&P 500	Biotech	Diff
1992	4.0 %	17.9 %	13.8 %
1993	3.6	3.6	0.0
1994	3.2	24.2	21.0
1995	5.0	31.5	26.5
1996	2.1	7.0	4.9
1997	2.8	-18.9	-21.7
1998	-8.5	20.6	29.1
1999	0.6	64.3	63.7
2000	2.3	7.6	5.4
2001	-10.8	-3.6	7.2
2002	-10.0	8.1	18.2
2003	2.3	6.4	4.1
2004	-0.8	8.9	9.6
2005	1.4	26.0	24.5
2006	5.8	7.4	1.6
2007	-1.2	6.0	7.2
2008	-5.0	11.4	16.5
2009	16.8	7.7	-9.1
2010	2.4	2.8	0.4
2011	-8.9	-3.7	5.2
2012	0.4	15.8	6.2
Avg	0.8 %	11.9 %	11.1 %
Fq>0	67 %	86 %	86 %

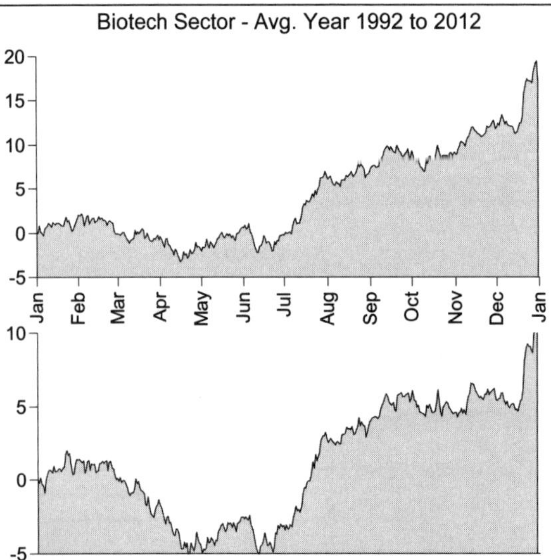

Biotech / S&P 500 Relative Strength - Avg Yr. 1992 - 2012

The biotechnology sector is often considered the cousin of the technology sector, a good place for speculative investments. The sectors are similar as both include concept companies (companies without a product but with good potential).

Despite their similarity, investors view the sectors differently. The technology sector is viewed as being largely dependent on the economy and conversely the biotech sector as being much less dependent on the economy. The end product of biotechnology companies is mainly medicine, which is not economically sensitive.

As a result, in the summer months when investors tend to be more cautious, they are more willing to commit speculative money into the biotech sector, compared with the technology sector.

The biotech sector is one of the few sectors that starts its outperformance in June. This is in part because of the biotech conferences that occur in autumn. With positive announcements in autumn, the price of biotech companies on the stock market can increase dramatically. As a result, investors try to lock in positions early.

Biotech SP GIC Sector # 352010: Companies primarily engaged in the research, development, manufacturing and/or marketing of products based on genetic analysis and genetic engineering. This includes companies specializing in protein-based therapeutics to treat human diseases.

2012-13 Strategy Performance

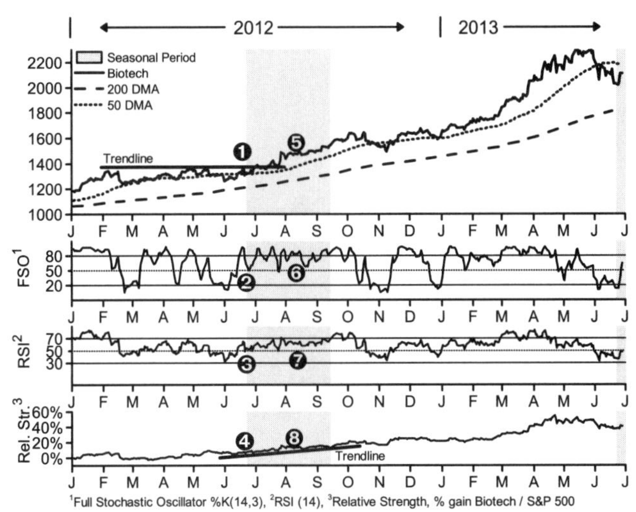

[1]Full Stochastic Oscillator %K(14,3), [2]RSI (14), [3]Relative Strength, % gain Biotech / S&P 500

Biotech Sector Performance

From February 2012 to just before the beginning of its seasonal period, the biotech sector had its ups and downs, but was generally "flat." This created a very strong setup for the biotech sector.

Technical Conditions– June 23rd to September 13th, 2012

Entry Strategy – Buy Partial Position Early–

At the beginning of June, the biotech sector was trading just below its 50 day moving average❶, but an early buy signal was triggered when the FSO rose above 20❷ and the RSI rose above 30❸. The sector started to outperform the S&P 500. At this time, the S&P 500 was struggling and biotech was rising slightly. In late July, the sector spiked in price which helped it to continue its outperformance relative to the S&P 500❹.

Exit Strategy –Sell Partial Position Early–

In its seasonal period, the biotech sector was outperforming the S&P 500❺. Nevertheless, in the second week in August, the FSO turned down below 80❻, triggering an early sell signal. At the same time, the RSI was in its upper band but had just turned down❼, and the sector was performing at market❽. After the sell signal was triggered, the biotech sector continued to rise, but performed at market.

WEEK 23

Market Indices & Rates Weekly Values**

Stock Markets	**2012**	**2013**
Dow	12,332	15,136
S&P500	1,304	1,629
Nasdaq	2,814	3,441
TSX	11,514	12,486
FTSE	5,422	6,450
DAX	6,063	8,226
Nikkei	8,462	13,118
Hang Seng	18,429	22,010
Commodities	**2012**	**2013**
Oil	84.44	94.26
Gold	1605.8	1398.4
Bond Yields	**2012**	**2013**
USA 5 Yr Treasury	0.70	1.04
USA 10 Yr T	1.61	2.12
USA 20 Yr T	2.29	2.93
Moody's Aaa	3.67	4.10
Moody's Baa	5.03	4.99
CAN 5 Yr T	1.24	1.48
CAN 10 Yr T	1.77	2.07
Money Market	**2012**	**2013**
USA Fed Funds	0.25	0.25
USA 3 Mo T-B	0.09	0.04
CAN tgt overnight rate	1.00	1.00
CAN 3 Mo T-B	0.88	1.02
Foreign Exchange	**2012**	**2013**
EUR/USD	1.25	1.31
GBP/USD	1.55	1.54
USD/CAD	1.03	1.03
USD/JPY	79.08	98.63

JUNE

M	T	W	T	F	S	S
						1
2	3	4	5	6	7	8
9	10	11	12	13	14	15
16	17	18	19	20	21	22
23	24	25	26	27	28	29
30						

JULY

M	T	W	T	F	S	S
	1	2	3	4	5	6
7	8	9	10	11	12	13
14	15	16	17	18	19	20
21	22	23	24	25	26	27
28	29	30	31			

AUGUST

M	T	W	T	F	S	S
				1	2	3
4	5	6	7	8	9	10
11	12	13	14	15	16	17
18	19	20	21	22	23	24
25	26	27	28	29	30	31

SUPER SEVEN DAYS
7 Best Days of the Month

The end of the month tends to be an excellent time to invest: portfolio managers "window dress" (adjust their portfolios to look good for month end reports), investors stop procrastinating and invest their extra cash, and brokers try to increase their commissions by investing their client's extra cash.

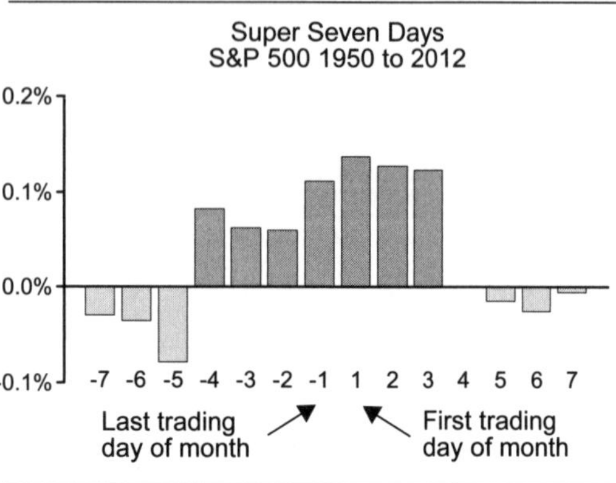

From 1950 to 2012 All 7 days better than market average

All of these factors tend to produce above average returns in the market during the days around month end.

The above graph illustrates the strength of the *Super Seven* days. The *Super Seven* days are the last four trading days of the month and the first three trading days of the next month represented by the dark columns from day -4 to day 3. All of the *Super Seven* days have daily average gains above the daily market average gain of 0.03% (since 1950).

% Gain Super Seven Day Period From 2003 to 2012

	2003	2004	2005	2006	2007	2008	2009	2010	2011	2012	Avg.
Jan	-1.1 %	-2.5 %	1.8 %	-0.1 %	1.6 %	-4.5 %	-0.5 %	0.0 %	1.2 %	1.4 %	-0.5 %
Feb	-0.3	0.9	2.2	-0.4	-5.6	-2.8	4.1	1.0	1.2	0.1	-0.9
Mar	0.2	3.7	0.9	0.8	0.1	1.2	3.5	2.0	1.4	-1.2	1.2
Apr	1.7	-1.2	1.2	0.0	1.5	1.3	4.3	-3.8	0.9	1.4	0.5
May	5.7	1.9	0.2	0.5	1.6	0.1	5.0	2.7	-1.2	-2.7	1.8
Jun	0.2	-2.1	0.3	1.9	1.8	-3.9	-0.2	-4.2	5.6	4.1	-0.6
Jul	-3.3	1.3	1.3	0.9	-5.6	2.2	2.1	1.1	-5.8	4.0	0.0
Aug	3.4	0.8	1.7	0.4	0.8	-2.4	-2.4	4.7	0.5	1.5	0.7
Sep	2.0	2.9	-1.6	1.8	1.4	-7.3	-1.0	1.1	-1.6	-0.4	-0.1
Oct	2.0	4.4	2.0	-1.3	-0.8	12.2	-1.9	1.0	2.6	0.3	1.8
Nov	2.8	1.2	-0.3	1.0	5.5	8.8	-0.6	3.7	8.2	0.2	2.2
Dec	2.7	-1.8	0.4	-0.1	-5.7	7.7	0.9	1.5	1.2	2.8	0.6
Avg.	1.3 %	0.8 %	0.8 %	0.0 %	0.0 %	1.1 %	0.4 %	0.9 %	1.2 %	1.0 %	0.5 %

Over the last ten years, the super seven strategy has worked very well and has produced an average gain of 0.5% per month. On an annualized basis, this return is greater than 6% per year. Given that the average month has twenty-two trading days, the Super Seven strategy has investors in the market for less than one third of the time. On a time-adjusted basis, adjusting returns for the amount of time in the market, the strategy has produced much greater gains than a buy and hold discipline.

Historically it has been best not to use the Super Seven for July and August. Both of these months have negative average performances and have been negative more often than positive over the last ten years.

If there is one time of the month that investors should be concentrating on investing, it is the last four trading days of the current month and the first three of the next month.

2012-13 Strategy Performance

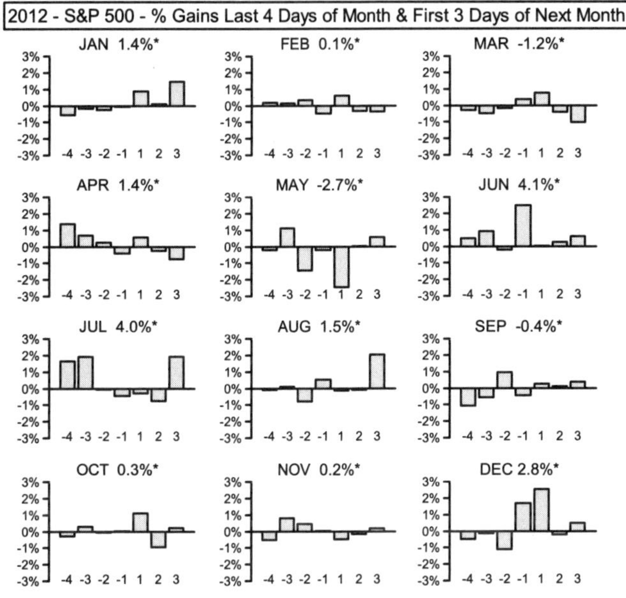

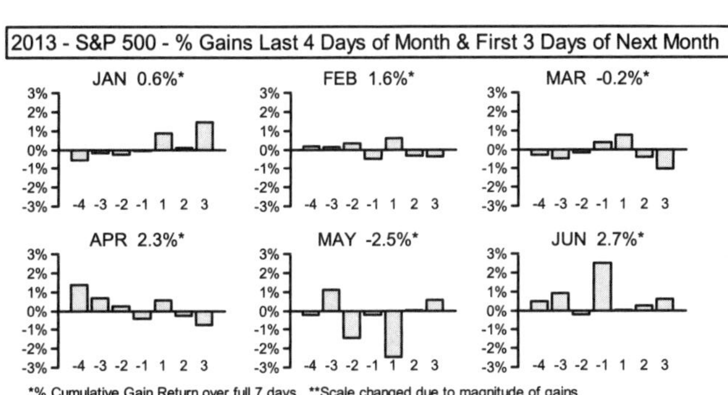

*% Cumulative Gain Return over full 7 days, **Scale changed due to magnitude of gains

Super Seven Performance

The *Super Seven* strategy continued to provide superior returns in both 2012 and 2013. There were only three losses in 2012: March produced a loss as the S&P 500 peaked towards the end of the month, May produced a loss as the S&P 500 continued on with a negative trend that started at the beginning of the month and September produced a loss as the market started to consolidate at the end of the month.

So far there has only been two losses in the first six months of 2013: March produced a loss as the S&P 500 started to consolidate and May produced a loss as the negative trend that started mid-month continued at month end.

WEEK 24

Market Indices & Rates Weekly Values**

Stock Markets	**2012**	**2013**
Dow	12,580	15,120
S&P500	1,324	1,629
Nasdaq	2,836	3,436
TSX	11,478	12,236
FTSE	5,467	6,331
DAX	6,165	8,179
Nikkei	8,578	13,051
Hang Seng	18,979	21,206
Commodities	**2012**	**2013**
Oil	83.32	96.31
Gold	1609.6	1383.3
Bond Yields	**2012**	**2013**
USA 5 Yr Treasury	0.71	1.11
USA 10 Yr T	1.62	2.20
USA 20 Yr T	2.32	3.00
Moody's Aaa	3.67	4.24
Moody's Baa	5.05	5.11
CAN 5 Yr T	1.25	1.59
CAN 10 Yr T	1.77	2.17
Money Market	**2012**	**2013**
USA Fed Funds	0.25	0.25
USA 3 Mo T-B	0.09	0.05
CAN tgt overnight rate	1.00	1.00
CAN 3 Mo T-B	0.88	1.02
Foreign Exchange	**2012**	**2013**
EUR/USD	1.26	1.33
GBP/USD	1.56	1.57
USD/CAD	1.03	1.02
USD/JPY	79.31	96.10

JUNE

M	T	W	T	F	S	S
						1
2	3	4	5	6	7	8
9	10	11	12	13	14	15
16	17	18	19	20	21	22
23	24	25	26	27	28	29
30						

JULY

M	T	W	T	F	S	S
	1	2	3	4	5	6
7	8	9	10	11	12	13
14	15	16	17	18	19	20
21	22	23	24	25	26	27
28	29	30	31			

AUGUST

M	T	W	T	F	S	S
				1	2	3
4	5	6	7	8	9	10
11	12	13	14	15	16	17
18	19	20	21	22	23	24
25	26	27	28	29	30	31

** Weekly avg closing values- except Fed Funds & CAN overnight tgt rate weekly closing values.

INDEPENDENCE DAY – THE FULL TRADE PROFIT BEFORE & AFTER FIREWORKS

Two Market Days Before June Month End To 5 Market Days After Independence Day

The beginning of July is a time for celebration and the markets tend to agree.

Based on previous market data, the best way to take advantage of this trend is to be invested for the two market days prior to the June month end and hold until five market days after Independence Day. This time period has produced above average returns on a fairly consistent basis.

0.9% avg. gain &
72% of the time positive

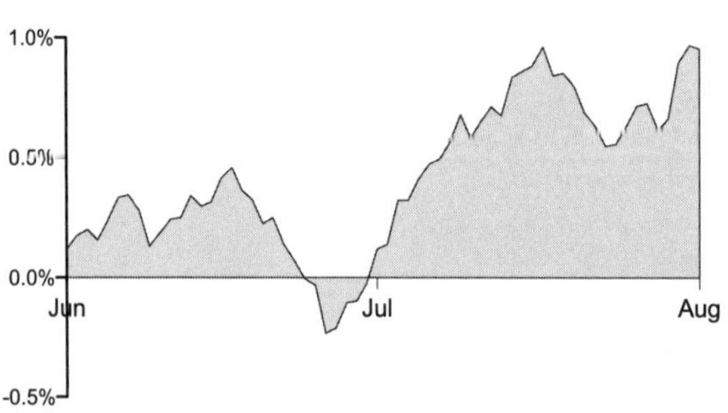

The typical Independence Day trade put forward by quite a few pundits has been to invest one or two days before the holiday and take profits one or two days after the holiday.

Although this strategy has produced profits, it has left a lot of money on the table. This strategy misses out on the positive days at the end of June and on the full slate of positive days after Independence Day.

The beginning part of the *Independence Day* positive trend is driven by two combining factors.

First, portfolio managers "window dress" (buying stocks that have a favorable perception in the market); thereby pushing stock prices up at the end of the month.

Second, investors have become "wise" to the *Independence Day Trade* and try to jump in before everyone else.

Depending on market conditions at the time, investors should consider extending the exit date until eighteen calendar days in July. With July being an earnings month, the market can continue to rally until mid-month (see *18 Day Earnings Month Strategy*).

History of Independence Day: Independence Day is celebrated on July 4th because that is the day when the Continental Congress adopted the final draft of the Declaration of Independence in 1776. Independence Day was made an official holiday at the end of the War of Independence in 1783. In 1941 Congress declared the 4th of July a federal holiday.

S&P 500, 2 Market Days Before June Month End To 5 Market Days after Independence Day % Gain 1950 to 2013 (Positive shaded)

Year	%	Year	%	Year	%	Year	%	Year	%	Year	%	Year	%
1950	-4.4 %	1960	-0.1 %	1970	1.5 %	1980	1.4 %	1990	1.7 %	2000	1.8 %	2010	0.4 %
1951	1.5	1961	1.7	1971	3.2	1981	-2.4	1991	1.4	2001	-2.6	2011	1.8
1952	0.9	1962	9.8	1972	0.3	1982	-0.6	1992	2.8	2002	-4.7	2012	0.7
1953	0.8	1963	0.5	1973	2.1	1983	1.5	1993	-0.6	2003	1.2	2013	4.5
1954	2.9	1964	2.3	1974	-8.8	1984	-0.7	1994	0.4	2004	-1.7		
1955	4.9	1965	5.0	1975	-0.2	1985	1.5	1995	1.8	2005	1.5		
1956	3.4	1966	2.1	1976	2.4	1986	-2.6	1996	-2.8	2006	2.1		
1957	3.8	1967	1.3	1977	-0.6	1987	0.4	1997	3.7	2007	0.8		
1958	2.0	1968	2.3	1978	0.6	1988	-0.6	1998	2.7	2008	-3.4		
1959	3.3	1969	-1.5	1979	1.3	1989	0.9	1999	5.1	2009	-4.3		
Avg.	1.9 %		2.3 %		0.2 %		-0.1 %		1.8 %		-0.9 %		1.8 %

2013 Strategy Performance

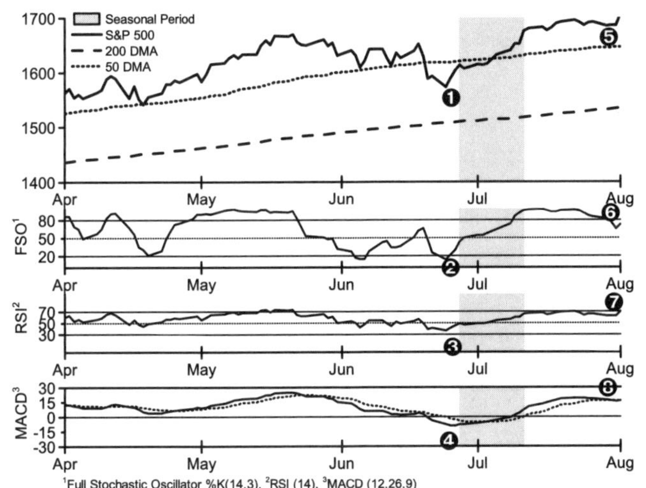

¹Full Stochastic Oscillator %K(14,3), ²RSI (14), ³MACD (12,26,9)

Independence Day Performance

The S&P 500 started to turn down mid-May. It fell below its 50 day moving average in mid-June. In late June, two days before the start of the Independence Day trade, the S&P 500 reversed its downtrend, setting up well for the *Independence Day* trade.

Technical Conditions– Two Market Days Before June Month End to Five Market Days After Independence Day, 2013

Entry Strategy –Buy Position Early–

The S&P 500 turned up❶ two days before the start of the Independence Day trade, and was supported by an early buy signal being triggered by the FSO crossing above 20❷. At the same time, the RSI was already above 30❸. The MACD was just starting to turn positive❹ when an early buy signal was triggered.

Exit Strategy– Sell Position Late–

After a very strong performance during its seasonal holiday trade, the S&P 500 still had strong upwards momentum, with the FSO above 80 and the RSI trending upwards just below 70. The MACD was also moving upwards. The FSO did not cross below 80❻ until late in July when the performance of the S&P 500 was starting to trend down❺. The RSI was below 70❼ and the MACD was crossing on a downwards trend❽. The extra benefit of staying in the trade past its exit date provided a small benefit in a very successful trade.

WEEK 25

Market Indices & Rates
Weekly Values**

Stock Markets	**2012**	**2013**
Dow	12,724	15,034
S&P500	1,344	1,620
Nasdaq	2,901	3,420
TSX	11,599	12,178
FTSE	5,556	6,266
DAX	6,322	8,072
Nikkei	8,750	13,106
Hang Seng	19,325	20,817
Commodities	**2012**	**2013**
Oil	81.26	96.69
Gold	1597.9	1342.4
Bond Yields	**2012**	**2013**
USA 5 Yr Treasury	0.73	1.22
USA 10 Yr T	1.64	2.33
USA 20 Yr T	2.32	3.11
Moody's Aaa	3.64	4.33
Moody's Baa	5.02	5.23
CAN 5 Yr T	1.26	1.65
CAN 10 Yr T	1.76	2.27
Money Market	**2012**	**2013**
USA Fed Funds	0.25	0.25
USA 3 Mo T-B	0.09	0.05
CAN tgt overnight rate	1.00	1.00
CAN 3 Mo T-B	0.87	1.03
Foreign Exchange	**2012**	**2013**
EUR/USD	1.26	1.33
GBP/USD	1.57	1.56
USD/CAD	1.02	1.03
USD/JPY	79.66	96.29

JUNE

M	T	W	T	F	S	S
						1
2	3	4	5	6	7	8
9	10	11	12	13	14	15
16	17	18	19	20	21	22
23	24	25	26	27	28	29
30						

JULY

M	T	W	T	F	S	S
	1	2	3	4	5	6
7	8	9	10	11	12	13
14	15	16	17	18	19	20
21	22	23	24	25	26	27
28	29	30	31			

AUGUST

M	T	W	T	F	S	S
				1	2	3
4	5	6	7	8	9	10
11	12	13	14	15	16	17
18	19	20	21	22	23	24
25	26	27	28	29	30	31

** Weekly avg closing values- except Fed Funds & CAN overnight tgt rate weekly closing values.

DISNEY— TIME TO STAY AWAY & TIME TO VISIT

NEW

①SELL SHORT (Jun5-Sep30) ②LONG(Oct1-Feb15)

Although some children receive Disney stock as a gift to hold onto for life, using a seasonal investment approach to owning the stock has proven to be a better strategy. Disney's stock price has performed like a seasonal roller coaster: up strongly in the late autumn, into the winter; and down in the summer.

23.4% extra &
positive 20 times out of 24 times

Disney vs. S&P 500 1990 to 2012

Negative Short (boxed) / Positive Long (shaded)

Year	SHORT Jun 5 to Sep 30 S&P 500	SHORT Jun 5 to Sep 30 Disney	LONG Oct 1 to Feb 15 S&P 500	LONG Oct 1 to Feb 15 Disney	Compound Growth S&P 500	Compound Growth Disney
1990/91	-16.7 %	-29.4 %	20.6 %	30.1 %	40.7 %	68.4 %
1991/92	0.0	-3.0	6.4	25.4	6.3	29.1
1992/93	1.1	-2.7	6.4	29.7	5.2	33.1
1993/94	2.0	-14.7	3.0	23.9	0.9	42.1
1994/95	0.6	-13.2	4.7	38.5	4.1	56.7
1995/96	9.8	2.7	11.5	11.3	0.6	8.3
1996/97	2.2	5.2	17.6	23.6	15.1	17.1
1997/98	12.8	0.9	7.7	38.2	-6.1	36.9
1998/99	-7.1	-30.4	21.0	39.6	29.6	82.1
1999/00	-3.4	-15.1	9.3	41.9	13.0	63.3
2001/01	-2.8	-5.4	-7.7	-15.3	-5.1	-10.7
2001/02	-17.9	-41.1	6.1	28.4	25.0	81.1
2002/03	-21.7	-31.9	2.4	10.5	24.6	45.8
2003/04	1.0	-2.7	15.0	33.5	13.9	37.1
2004/05	-0.7	-6.3	8.6	31.2	9.3	39.4
2005/06	2.7	-11.7	4.2	11.4	1.3	24.4
2006/07	3.7	1.0	9.1	12.2	5.0	11.1
2007/08	-0.8	-3.7	-11.6	-5.5	-10.9	-2.1
2008/09	-15.3	-10.7	-29.1	-39.7	-18.3	-33.2
2009/10	12.2	9.2	1.7	9.5	-10.6	0.6
2010/11	7.2	-1.0	16.4	30.2	8.0	32.5
2011/12	-13.0	-23.4	18.7	36.8	34.1	68.8
2012/13	12.7	17.7	5.5	6.4	-7.9	-12.5
Avg.	-1.4 %	-9.0 %	6.4 %	19.6 %	7.7 %	31.2 %
Fq>0	57	26	8.7	87	74	78

Disney's year-end occurs at the end of September and they typically report their results in the first week of November. Investors start to increase their positions at the beginning of October in anticipation of positive year-end news.

Investors are particularly attracted to Disney at this time of the year as Q4 tends to be a big revenue reporting quarter.

According to their Form 10-K filed with the Securities and Exchange Commission for the year ended September 29, 2012: "Revenues in our Media Networks segment are subject to seasonal advertising patterns... these commitments are typically satisfied during the second half of the Company's fiscal year." The media segment is the biggest driver of revenue for Disney. In addition, their other business segments are skewed towards revenue generation in the summer.

Do not visit the Disney stock from June 5th to September 30th. For the period from 1990 to 2012, Disney produced an average loss of 9% and only beat the S&P 500, 13% of the time.

DIS - stock symbol for Walt Disney Company which trades on the NYSE. is a diversified worldwide entertainment company. Price is adjusted for stock splits.

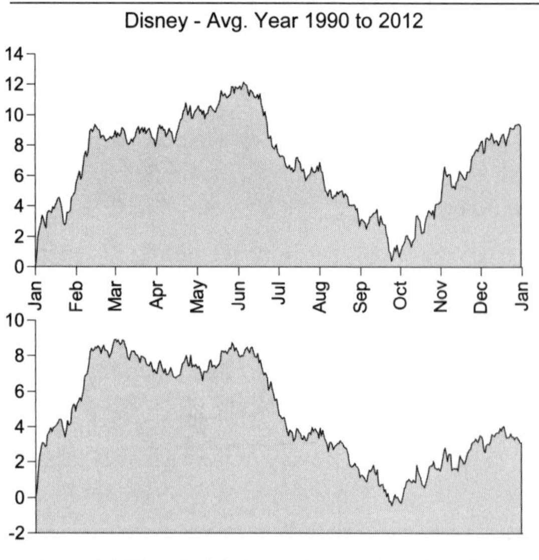

Disney / S&P 500 Rel. Strength- Avg Yr. 1990-2012

2012-13 Strategy Performance

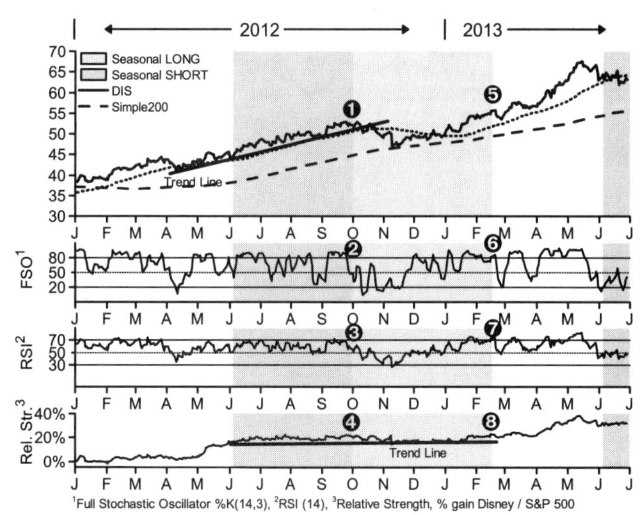

[1]Full Stochastic Oscillator %K(14,3), [2]RSI (14), [3]Relative Strength, % gain Disney / S&P 500

Disney Performance

After producing a positive performance during the time period in which Disney usually underperforms the S&P 500, Disney entered into its seasonally strong period, starting October 1st, 2012. Unfortunately, Disney started to underperform the S&P 500 just as the seasonally strong period started.

Technical Conditions– October 1st to February 15th, 2013

Entry Strategy –Buy Position on Entry Date–

The short seasonal period for Disney occurs right before a positive seasonal period. In this particular circumstance, it is generally best to wait until the start of the strong period before entering the long position. The exception to this would occur if a very strong buy signal was triggered close to the entry date. In Disney's case, a buy signal was not triggered early. At the start of the long seasonal date, Disney was trading above its 50 day moving average❶ and performing at market❹. The FSO had already fallen from above 80❷ and the RSI had fallen below 70❸.

Exit Strategy – Sell Partial Position Early–

After underperforming the S&P 500 at the beginning of the trade, Disney performed at market from November to January, at which time it started to outperform the S&P 500 briefly in January. At the start of February, the FSO turned below 80❺ and the RSI turned below 70❻, triggering an early sell signal. After the early sell signal, Disney continued to perform positively and performed at market until the end of the trade❼. In the end, Disney outperformed the S&P 500❽ at the early exit date and at the end of the seasonal period.

** Weekly avg closing values- except Fed Funds & CAN overnight tgt rate weekly closing values.

WEEK 26

Market Indices & Rates Weekly Values**

Stock Markets	2012	2013
Dow	12,629	14,853
S&P500	1,331	1,597
Nasdaq	2,870	3,370
TSX	11,419	11,986
FTSE	5,497	6,151
DAX	6,213	7,879
Nikkei	8,802	13,151
Hang Seng	19,105	20,250

Commodities	2012	2013
Oil	80.25	95.90
Gold	1575.3	1245.4

Bond Yields	2012	2013
USA 5 Yr Treasury	0.72	1.44
USA 10 Yr T	1.64	2.55
USA 20 Yr T	2.33	3.26
Moody's Aaa	3.60	4.41
Moody's Baa	5.00	5.42
CAN 5 Yr T	1.22	1.83
CAN 10 Yr T	1.72	2.48

Money Market	2012	2013
USA Fed Funds	0.25	0.25
USA 3 Mo T-B	0.09	0.04
CAN tgt overnight rate	1.00	1.00
CAN 3 Mo T-B	0.87	1.02

Foreign Exchange	2012	2013
EUR/USD	1.25	1.31
GBP/USD	1.56	1.53
USD/CAD	1.03	1.05
USD/JPY	79.63	98.15

JUNE

M	T	W	T	F	S	S
						1
2	3	4	5	6	7	8
9	10	11	12	13	14	15
16	17	18	19	20	21	22
23	24	25	26	27	28	29
30						

JULY

M	T	W	T	F	S	S
	1	2	3	4	5	6
7	8	9	10	11	12	13
14	15	16	17	18	19	20
21	22	23	24	25	26	27
28	29	30	31			

AUGUST

M	T	W	T	F	S	S
				1	2	3
4	5	6	7	8	9	10
11	12	13	14	15	16	17
18	19	20	21	22	23	24
25	26	27	27	29	30	31

JULY

	MONDAY	TUESDAY	WEDNESDAY
WEEK 27	30	1 30 CAN Market Closed- Canada Day	2 29
WEEK 28	7 24	8 23	9 22
WEEK 29	14 17	15 16	16 15
WEEK 30	21 10	22 9	23 8
WEEK 31	28 3	29 2	30 1

THURSDAY		FRIDAY	
3	28	**4**	27
		USA Market Closed - Independence Day	
10	21	**11**	20
17	14	**18**	13
24	7	**25**	6
31		1	

AUGUST

M	T	W	T	F	S	S
				1	2	3
4	5	6	7	8	9	10
11	12	13	14	15	16	17
18	19	20	21	22	23	24
25	26	27	28	29	30	31

SEPTEMBER

M	T	W	T	F	S	S
1	2	3	4	5	6	7
8	9	10	11	12	13	14
15	16	17	18	19	20	21
22	23	24	25	26	27	28
29	30					

OCTOBER

M	T	W	T	F	S	S
		1	2	3	4	5
6	7	8	9	10	11	12
13	14	15	16	17	18	19
20	21	22	23	24	25	26
27	28	29	30	31		

NOVEMBER

M	T	W	T	F	S	S
					1	2
3	4	5	6	7	8	9
10	11	12	13	14	15	16
17	18	19	20	21	22	23
24	25	26	27	28	29	30

JULY SUMMARY

	Dow Jones	S&P 500	Nasdaq	TSX Comp
Month Rank	4	6	11	6
# Up	39	34	21	18
# Down	24	29	20	10
% Pos	62	54	51	64
% Avg. Gain	1.2	1.0	0.1	0.8

Dow & S&P 1950-2012, Nasdaq 1972-2012, TSX 1985-2012

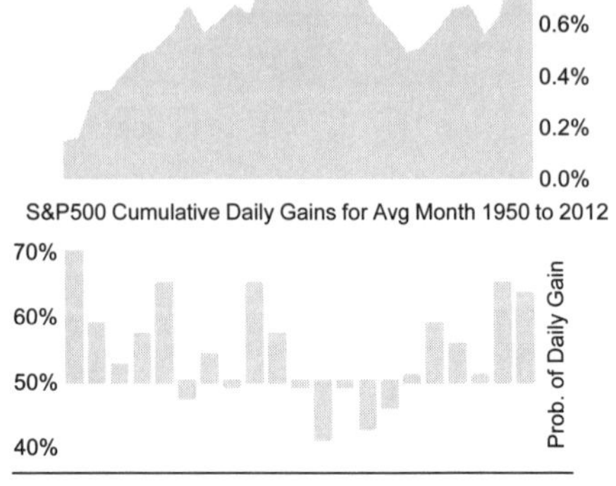

♦ When a summer rally occurs, the gains are usually made in July. ♦ Typically, it is the first part of July that produces the gains as the market rallies for Independence Day and into the first eighteen calendar days (see the 18 *Days Earning Month Effect*). In 2013, July produced a very strong gain of 5.2% during its first eighteen calendar days. ♦ Two major sector opportunities in July are gold and energy. In July 2013, both sectors started their seasonal periods with positive performances.

BEST / WORST JULY BROAD MKTS. 2003-2012

BEST JULY MARKETS

- Russell 2000 (2009) 9.5%
- Dow (2009) 8.6%
- FTSE 100 (2009) 8.5%

WORST JULY MARKETS

- Nasdaq (2004) -7.8%
- Russell 2000 (2007) -6.9%
- Russell 2000 (2004) -6.8%

Index Values End of Month

	2003	2004	2005	2006	2007	2008	2009	2010	2011	2012
Dow	9,234	10,140	10,641	11,186	13,212	11,378	9,172	10,466	12,143	13,009
S&P 500	990	1,102	1,234	1,277	1,455	1,267	987	1,102	1,292	1,379
Nasdaq	1,735	1,887	2,185	2,091	2,546	2,326	1,979	2,255	2,756	2,940
TSX Comp.	7,258	8,458	10,423	11,831	13,869	13,593	10,787	11,713	12,946	11,665
Russell 1000	1,016	1,129	1,288	1,331	1,523	1,334	1,038	1,165	1,380	1,458
Russell 2000	1,183	1,370	1,689	1,741	1,929	1,776	1,384	1,618	1,981	1,956
FTSE 100	4,157	4,413	5,282	5,928	6,360	5,412	4,608	5,258	5,815	5,635
Nikkei 225	9,563	11,326	11,900	15,457	17,249	13,377	10,357	9,537	9,833	8,695

Percent Gain for July

	2003	2004	2005	2006	2007	2008	2009	2010	2011	2012
Dow	2.8	-2.8	3.6	0.3	-1.5	0.2	8.6	7.1	-2.2	1.0
S&P 500	1.6	-3.4	3.6	0.5	-3.2	-1.0	7.4	6.9	-2.1	1.3
Nasdaq	6.9	-7.8	6.2	-3.7	-2.2	1.4	7.8	6.9	-0.6	0.2
TSX Comp.	3.9	-1.0	5.3	1.9	-0.3	-6.0	4.0	3.7	-2.7	0.6
Russell 1000	1.8	-3.6	3.8	0.1	-3.2	-1.3	7.5	6.8	-2.3	1.1
Russell 2000	6.2	-6.8	6.3	-3.3	-6.9	3.6	9.5	6.8	-3.7	-1.4
FTSE 100	3.1	-1.1	3.3	1.6	-3.8	-3.8	8.5	6.9	-2.2	1.2
Nikkei 225	5.3	-4.5	2.7	-0.3	-4.9	-0.8	4.0	1.6	0.2	-3.5

July Market Avg. Performance 2003 to 2012(1)

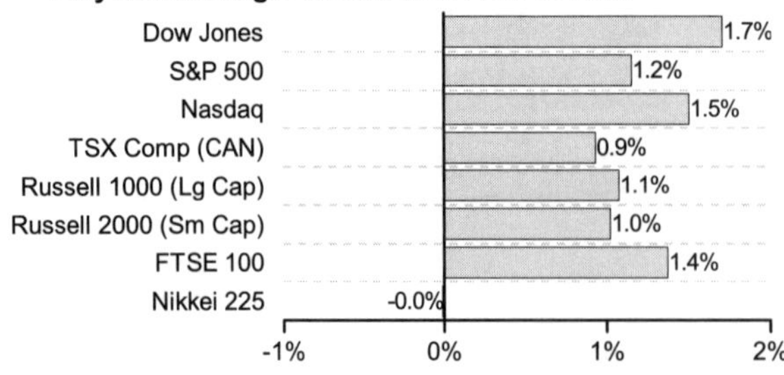

Interest Corner Jul(2)

	Fed Funds % (3)	3 Mo. T-Bill %(4)	10 Yr %(5)	20 Yr %(6)
2012	0.25	0.11	1.51	2.21
2011	0.25	0.10	2.82	3.77
2010	0.25	0.15	2.94	3.74
2009	0.25	0.18	3.52	4.29
2008	2.00	1.68	3.99	4.63

(1) Russell Data provided by Russell (2) Federal Reserve Bank of St. Louis- end of month values (3) Target rate set by FOMC (4)(5)(6) Constant yield maturities.

JULY SECTOR PERFORMANCE

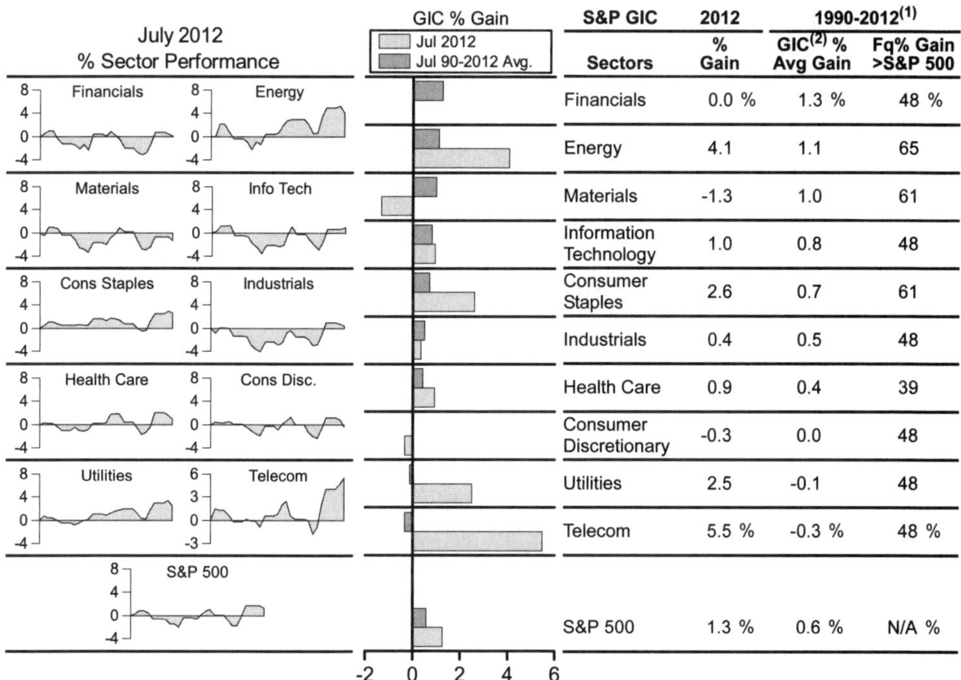

S&P GIC Sectors	2012 % Gain	1990-2012[1] GIC[2] % Avg Gain	1990-2012[1] Fq% Gain >S&P 500
Financials	0.0 %	1.3 %	48 %
Energy	4.1	1.1	65
Materials	-1.3	1.0	61
Information Technology	1.0	0.8	48
Consumer Staples	2.6	0.7	61
Industrials	0.4	0.5	48
Health Care	0.9	0.4	39
Consumer Discretionary	-0.3	0.0	48
Utilities	2.5	-0.1	48
Telecom	5.5 %	-0.3 %	48 %
S&P 500	1.3 %	0.6 %	N/A %

Sector Commentary

♦ July is earnings months and in 2012, the S&P 500 performed very well, producing a gain of 1.3%.♦ The energy sector for most of July performed at market, but right at the start of its seasonal period, the energy sector started to outperform. By the end of the month, it produced a gain of 4.1%.♦ The other big winner of the month was the telecom sector, producing a gain of 5.5%.♦ Utilities also produced a strong gain of 2.5%, as investors favored the defensive sectors.♦ The biggest losing sector was materials, as investors avoided the deep cyclicals.

Sub-Sector Commentary

♦ The best performing sub-sector was biotech, with a gain of 7.4%. July is the sweet spot for the biotech seasonal trade and biotech was responding accordingly.♦ The biggest loser was the agriculture sub-sector with a loss of 11.6%. This was partly the result of snapping back after a large 5.2% gain in June.♦ The other losers were steel with a loss of 3.8% and metals and mining with a loss of 3.9%.

SELECTED SUB-SECTORS[3]

Sub-Sector	2012 % Gain	GIC % Avg Gain	Fq% Gain >S&P 500
Biotech (1993-2012)	7.4 %	6.4 %	80 %
Railroads	2.8	2.5	65
Silver	4.1	1.6	61
Home-builders	-2.1	1.5	48
Chemicals	-1.2	1.4	57
Banks	1.1	1.3	61
Transportation	-0.8	1.1	48
Retail	0.7	0.5	52
SOX (1995-2012)	-0.5	0.4	44
Metals & Mining	-3.9	0.2	48
Gold (London PM)	1.5	0.2	52
Pharma	2.7	0.0	48
Steel	-3.8	-0.8	48
Agriculture (1994-2012)	-11.6	-1.9	42
Software & Services	0.5	-1.9	26

(1) Sector data provided by Standard and Poors (2) GIC is short form for Global Industry Classification (3) Sub Sector data provided by Standard and Poors, except where marked by symbol.

ALTRIA– 'BUYEM' WHILE THEY R' SMOKIN

July 19th to December 19th

Altria Group, Inc., through its subsidiaries, engages in the manufacture and sale of cigarettes, smokeless products, and wine in the United States and internationally.

You may not think that smoking is good for you, but investing in tobacco stocks has been good for profits, especially from July 19th to December 19th of each year.

It makes sense that Altria starts to outperform in mid-July, as this is when the broad stock market often peaks. At this time, investors still wanting to invest, rotate some of their available capital into defensive stocks, such as Altria.

12.6% gain & positive 78% of the time

Although the sweet spot of the seasonal trade is from mid-July into the beginning of September, Altria still manages to outperform until mid-December. The value of this trade is not just the superior gains, but also the diversification that is added to the portfolio.

Altria* vs. S&P 500
1990 to 2012

Jul 19 to Dec 19	S&P 500	MO	Diff
1990	-9.3%	2.0%	11.3%
1991	-0.7	8.6	9.3
1992	6.2	-2.4	-8.6
1993	4.6	15.4	10.8
1994	0.6	5.5	4.9
1995	9.6	19.0	9.5
1996	15.9	12.6	-3.3
1997	3.4	9.3	5.9
1998	0.1	31.6	31.4
1999	0.2	-40.6	-40.8
2000	-12.6	79.2	91.8
2001	-4.8	2.4	7.2
2002	0.3	-4.0	-4.3
2003	9.6	36.4	26.8
2004	8.4	23.2	14.8
2005	3.2	16.2	13.0
2006	15.3	10.8	-4.5
2007	-6.0	9.1	15.1
2008	-29.6	-25.3	4.3
2009	17.2	13.3	-3.9
2010	16.8	17.5	0.7
2011	-7.7	10.3	18.0
2012	4.6	-8.7	-13.2
Avg	2.0%	12.6%	10.7%
Fq > 0	70%	78%	70%

(Shaded cells: Positive)

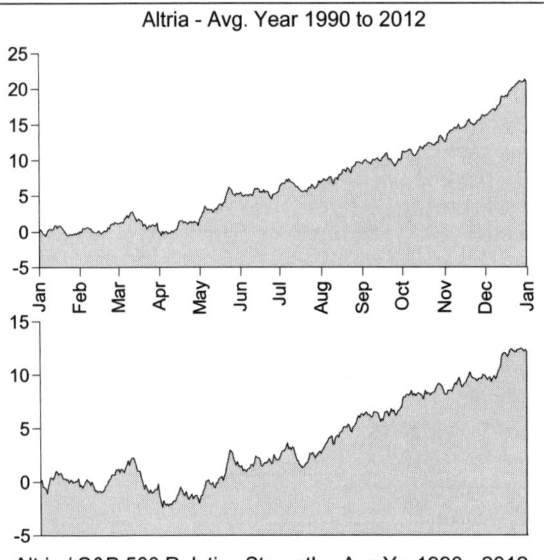

Altria - Avg. Year 1990 to 2012

Altria / S&P 500 Relative Strength - Avg Yr. 1990 - 2012

During the period of July 19th to December 19th, from 1990 to 2012, Altria has produced an average gain of 12.6% and has been positive 78% of the time. This compares to the S&P 500 which has produced an average gain of 2.0% and has only been positive 70% of the time.

Investors should start to follow the performance of Altria in March, well before the start of its strong seasonal period. Very often, if Altria starts to outperform much earlier in the spring, this is an indication that investors are concerned about the "health" of the market and as a result are starting to favor defensive stocks. If Altria starts to send up this "smoke" signal in the spring, investors should invest cautiously in the market.

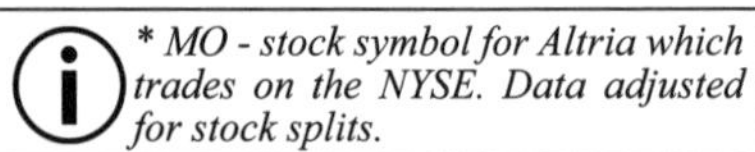

** MO - stock symbol for Altria which trades on the NYSE. Data adjusted for stock splits.*

2012-13 Strategy Performance

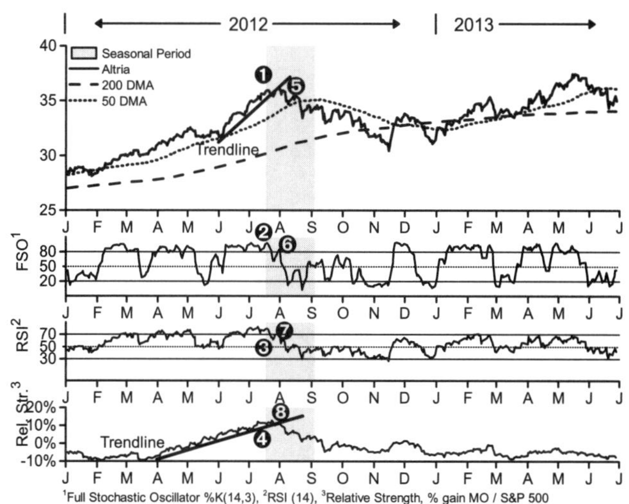

[1]Full Stochastic Oscillator %K(14,3), [2]RSI (14), [3]Relative Strength, % gain MO / S&P 500

Altria Performance

Altria performed very well in the late spring of 2012 and in April, started to strongly outperform the S&P 500. It continued its strong outperformance all the way to mid-July, the start of the strong seasonal period for Altria.

Technical Conditions July 19th to December 19th, 2012

Entry Strategy –Buy Position on Entry Date–

On the seasonal entry date, Altria was rising and above its 50 and 200 day moving averages❶. Both the FSO and RSI were overbought, with readings above 80❷ and 70❸ respectively. Altria was still trending positively in its outperformance of the S&P 500❹.

Exit Strategy –Sell Position Early–

Right after the entry date for the seasonal period, Altria started to perform negatively❺ and the FSO and RSI both turned down from their overbought positions❻❼. As a result, Altria started to underperform the S&P 500❽, creating a broken trade and triggering an early exit. Altria's underperformance was largely a result of how strongly Altria outperformed the S&P 500 before the start of its seasonal period. Essentially, Altria exhausted itself with continued strong outperformance before its seasonal period started.

WEEK 27

Market Indices & Rates
Weekly Values**

Stock Markets	**2011**	**2012**
Dow	12,643	12,871
S&P500	1,344	1,365
Nasdaq	2,848	2,960
TSX	13,399	11,810
FTSE	6,018	5,674
DAX	7,438	6,517
Nikkei	10,046	9,055
Hang Seng	22,659	19,764
Commodities	**2011**	**2012**
Oil	97.10	85.77
Gold	1520.3	1602.8
Bond Yields	**2011**	**2012**
USA 5 Yr Treasury	1.67	0.67
USA 10 Yr T	3.12	1.61
USA 20 Yr T	4.05	2.32
Moody's Aaa	5.07	3.60
Moody's Baa	5.84	5.03
CAN 5 Yr T	2.29	1.24
CAN 10 Yr T	3.04	1.72
Money Market	**2011**	**2012**
USA Fed Funds	0.25	0.25
USA 3 Mo T-B	0.03	0.08
CAN tgt overnight rate	1.00	1.00
CAN 3 Mo T-B	0.93	0.85
Foreign Exchange	**2011**	**2012**
EUR/USD	1.44	1.25
GBP/USD	1.60	1.56
USD/CAD	0.96	1.02
USD/JPY	80.93	79.75

JULY

M	T	W	T	F	S	S
	1	2	3	4	5	6
7	8	9	10	11	12	13
14	15	16	17	18	19	20
21	22	23	24	25	26	27
28	29	30	31			

AUGUST

M	T	W	T	F	S	S
				1	2	3
4	5	6	7	8	9	10
11	12	13	14	15	16	17
18	19	20	21	22	23	24
25	26	27	27	29	30	31

SEPTEMBER

M	T	W	T	F	S	S
1	2	3	4	5	6	7
8	9	10	11	12	13	14
15	16	17	18	19	20	21
22	23	24	25	26	27	28
29	30					

** Weekly avg closing values- except Fed Funds & CAN overnight tgt rate weekly closing values.

(Metal)

GOLD SHINES

Gold (Metal) Outperforms – July 12th to October 9th

"Foul cankering rust the hidden treasure frets, but gold that's put to use more gold begets."

(William Shakespeare, *Venus and Adonis*)

For many years, gold was thought to be a dead investment. It was only the "gold bugs" that espoused the virtues of investing in the precious metal. Investors were mesmerized with technology stocks and central bankers, confident of their currencies, were selling gold, "left, right and center."

4.3% gain & positive 69% of the time

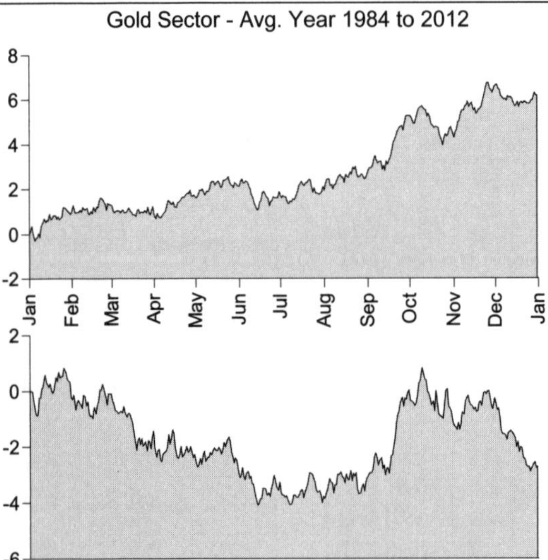

Gold / S&P 500 Relative Strength - Avg Yr. 1984 - 2012

Times have changed and investors have taken a shine to gold. In the last few years, gold has substantially outperformed the stock market. On a seasonal basis, on average from 1984 to 2012, gold has done well relative to the stock market from July 12th to October 9th. The reasons for gold's seasonal changes in price, are related to jewellery production and European Central banks selling cycles (see *Golden Times* strategy page).

The movement of gold stock prices, represented by the index (XAU) on the Philadelphia Exchange, coincides closely with the price of gold. Although there is a strong correlation between gold and gold stocks, there are other factors, such as company operations and hedging policies which determine each company's price in the market. Gold has typically started its seasonal strong period a few weeks earlier than gold stocks and finished just after gold stocks have turned down.

Gold (Metal) London PM vs S&P 500
1984 to 2012

Jul 12 to Oct 9th	S&P 500	Gold	Diff
1984	7.4 %	0.5 %	-6.9 %
1985	-5.4	4.1	9.5
1986	-2.6	25.2	27.8
1987	0.9	3.9	3.0
1988	2.8	-7.5	-10.3
1989	9.4	-4.2	-13.6
1990	-15.5	12.1	27.6
1991	0.0	-2.9	-2.8
1992	-2.9	0.4	3.3
1993	2.7	-8.8	-11.5
1994	1.6	1.6	0.0
1995	4.3	-0.1	-4.3
1996	7.9	-0.4	-8.3
1997	5.9	4.4	-1.5
1998	-15.5	2.8	18.2
1999	-4.8	25.6	30.4
2000	-5.3	-4.5	0.8
2001	-10.5	8.4	18.8
2002	-16.2	1.7	17.9
2003	4.1	7.8	3.8
2004	0.8	3.8	2.9
2005	-1.9	11.4	13.4
2006	6.1	-8.8	-14.9
2007	3.1	11.0	8.0
2008	-26.6	-8.2	18.4
2009	21.9	15.2	- 6.7
2010	8.1	11.0	2.9
2011	-12.4	6.2	18.6
2012	7.5	12.5	5.0
Avg.	-0.9 %	4.3 %	5.2 %
Fq > 0	55 %	69 %	66 %

Positive (shaded)

Investors should know that gold can have a run in the month of November. Although this is a positive time for gold, producing an average gain of 2.0% and being positive 69% of the time (1984 to 2012), the trouble is in the following month. December has a history of being negative for gold, producing an average loss of 0.4% and only being positive 45% of the time, which is a lot less than the 2.0% average return of the S&P 500. The S&P 500 also has a record of being positive 83% of the time, in the same yearly period.

Source: Bank of England
London PM is recognized as the world benchmark for gold prices. London PM represents the close value of gold in afternoon trading in London.

2012-13 Strategy Performance

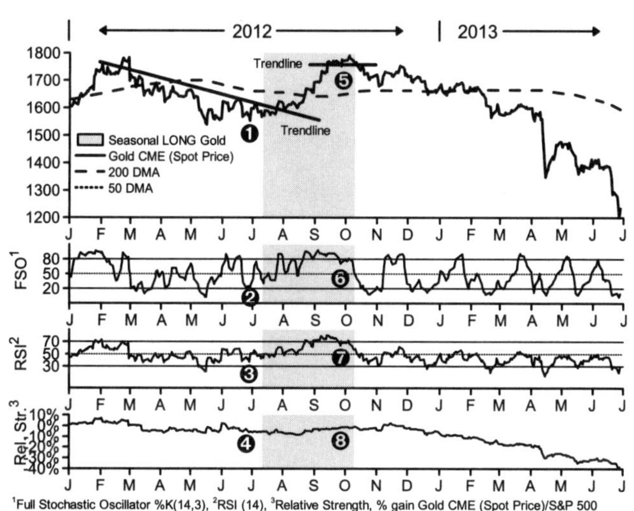

¹Full Stochastic Oscillator %K(14,3), ²RSI (14), ³Relative Strength, % gain Gold CME (Spot Price)/S&P 500

Gold Bullion Performance

In 2012, gold started to correct at the end of February. In March, gold started to consolidate, but did not manage to break through its down trendline.

Technical Conditions– July 12th to October 9th, 2012

Entry Strategy –Buy Position Early–

Towards the end of June, gold started to increase just above its May low❶. The FSO crossed above 20❷, triggering an early buy signal. At the same time, the RSI crossed above 50❸, and gold was underperforming the S&P 500❹. The one concerning factor was that gold had not broken above its downtrend line, which was rectified just after the seasonal start date.

Exit Strategy – Sell Position Early–

Gold performed very well until mid-September, at which time it started to consolidate. It still managed to outperform the S&P 500. Towards the end of September, gold had a very small correction❺ and as a result the FSO dipped below 80❻, triggering an early sell signal. At the same time, the RSI dropped below 70❼ and gold was still outperforming the S&P 500❽. Although the early sell date produced a very profitable trade, it ended up producing the same results as selling at the end of the seasonal period.

WEEK 28

Market Indices & Rates
Weekly Values**

Stock Markets	**2011**	**2012**
Dow	12,472	12,669
S&P500	1,315	1,345
Nasdaq	2,787	2,899
TSX	13,258	11,526
FTSE	5,879	5,646
DAX	7,221	6,451
Nikkei	9,974	8,810
Hang Seng	21,951	19,272
Commodities	**2011**	**2012**
Oil	96.71	85.78
Gold	1572.5	1581.8
Bond Yields	**2011**	**2012**
USA 5 Yr Treasury	1.48	0.63
USA 10 Yr T	2.94	1.52
USA 20 Yr T	3.89	2.21
Moody's Aaa	4.89	3.44
Moody's Baa	5.71	4.90
CAN 5 Yr T	2.16	1.18
CAN 10 Yr T	2.91	1.65
Money Market	**2011**	**2012**
USA Fed Funds	0.25	0.25
USA 3 Mo T-B	0.02	0.10
CAN tgt overnight rate	1.00	1.00
CAN 3 Mo T-B	0.92	0.87
Foreign Exchange	**2011**	**2012**
EUR/USD	1.41	1.23
GBP/USD	1.60	1.55
USD/CAD	0.96	1.02
USD/JPY	79.35	79.45

JULY

M	T	W	T	F	S	S
	1	2	3	4	5	6
7	8	9	10	11	12	13
14	15	16	17	18	19	20
21	22	23	24	25	26	27
28	29	30	31			

AUGUST

M	T	W	T	F	S	S
				1	2	3
4	5	6	7	8	9	10
11	12	13	14	15	16	17
18	19	20	21	22	23	24
25	26	27	27	29	30	31

SEPTEMBER

M	T	W	T	F	S	S
1	2	3	4	5	6	7
8	9	10	11	12	13	14
15	16	17	18	19	20	21
22	23	24	25	26	27	28
29	30					

(Stocks)

GOLDEN TIMES

Gold Stocks Outperform – July 27th to September 25th

Gold stocks were shunned for many years. It is only recently that interest in the sector has again increased. What few investors know is that even during the twenty year bear market in gold that started in 1981, it was possible to make money in gold stocks.

7.0% gain when the S&P 500 has been negative

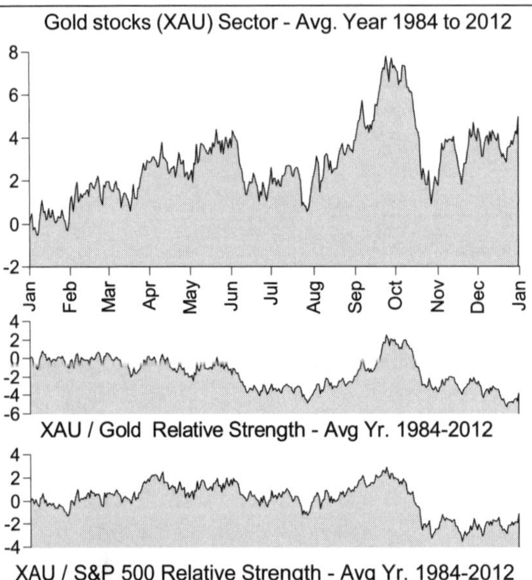

XAU (Gold Stocks) vs S&P 500 and Gold (1984 to 2012)

XAU>S&P 500 (shaded box)
XAU>Gold (outlined box)

Jul 27 to Sep 25	S&P 500	Gold	XAU
1984	10.4 %	0.3 %	20.8 %
1985	-6.1	3.6	-5.5
1986	-3.5	23.0	36.9
1987	3.5	1.9	23.0
1988	1.7	-7.2	-11.9
1989	1.8	-1.3	10.5
1990	-13.4	9.5	3.8
1991	1.6	-3.1	-11.9
1992	0.7	-2.2	-3.8
1993	1.9	-8.7	-7.3
1994	1.4	2.5	18.2
1995	3.6	-0.8	-1.0
1996	7.9	-0.7	-1.0
1997	-0.1	0.2	8.7
1998	-8.4	1.2	12.0
1999	-5.2	6.5	16.9
2000	-0.9	-2.3	-2.8
2001	-15.8	7.7	3.2
2002	-1.5	6.6	29.8
2003	0.5	7.6	11.0
2004	2.4	4.4	16.5
2005	-1.3	9.3	20.5
2006	4.6	-4.8	-11.9
2007	2.3	8.7	14.0
2008	-3.9	-3.5	-18.5
2009	6.7	4.2	6.0
2010	3.0	9.6	14.7
2011	-14.7	4.7	-13.7
2012	6.0	9.5	23.4
Avg.	-0.5 %	3.0 %	7.0 %
Fq > 0	59 %	66 %	62 %

On average from 1984 (start of the XAU index) to 2012, gold stocks as represented by the XAU index, have outperformed the S&P 500 from July 27th to September 25th. One factor that has led to a rise in the price of gold stocks in August and September is the Indian festival and wedding season that starts in October and finishes in November during Diwali. The Asian culture places a great emphasis on gold as a store of value and a lot of it is "consumed" as jewellery during the festival and wedding season. The price of gold tends to increase in the months preceding this season as the jewellery fabricators purchase gold to make their final product.

The August-September increase in gold stocks coincides with the time that a lot of investors are pulling their money out of the broad market and are looking for a place to invest. This makes gold a very attractive investment at this time of the year.

Be careful. Just as the gold stocks tend to go up in August-September, they also tend to go down in October. Historically, this negative trend has been caused by European Central banks selling some of their gold holdings in autumn when their annual allotment of possible sales is renewed yearly. In recent years, European Central banks have reduced gold sales. This has muted gold's negative trend in October.

Nevertheless, gold stocks have still underperformed in October. From October 1st to October 27th, for the period 1984 to 2012, XAU has produced an average loss of 5.6% and has only been positive 34% of the time.

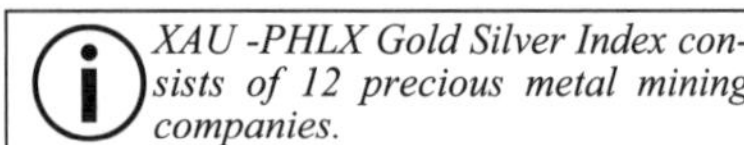

XAU -PHLX Gold Silver Index consists of 12 precious metal mining companies.

2012-13 Strategy Performance

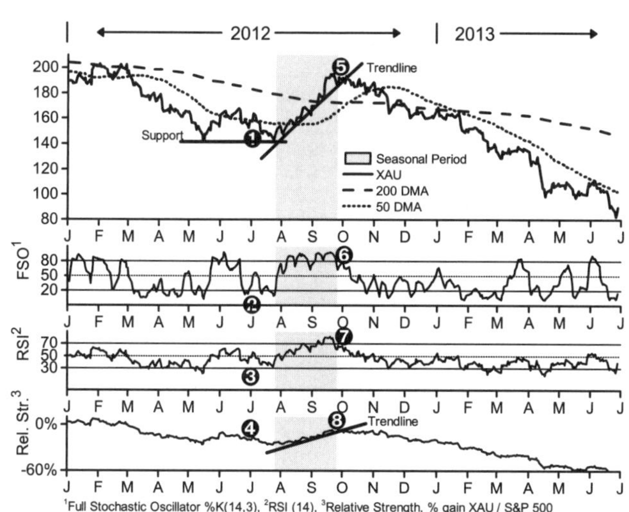

[1]Full Stochastic Oscillator %K(14,3), [2]RSI (14), [3]Relative Strength, % gain XAU / S&P 500

PHLX Gold Silver Index (XAU) Performance

Gold stocks in 2012 bottomed in early May and then increased in price, only to bottom once again in June. This set gold stocks up for an early start to their seasonal period.

Technical Conditions July 27th to September 25th, 2012

Entry Strategy –Buy Position Early–

In late June, XAU crossed above its 50 day moving average❶ and at the same time, the FSO crossed above 20❷, triggering an early buy signal. The RSI crossed above 50❸ and it looked as if XAU was going to start to outperform the S&P 500❹. Unfortunately, gold stocks quickly retreated back to their early May level. It was at the start of their seasonal period that they started to outperform the S&P 500. Even with the false start before the seasonal period, the trade was very profitable.

Exit Strategy–Sell Position on Exit Date–

XAU performed very well during its seasonal period and just started to flatten out at the end of the trade❺, when the FSO turned below 80❻ and the RSI turned below 70❼. At the same time, XAU started to underperform the S&P 500❽.

WEEK 29

Market Indices & Rates
Weekly Values**

Stock Markets	**2011**	**2012**
Dow	12,590	12,841
S&P500	1,329	1,366
Nasdaq	2,820	2,928
TSX	13,371	11,592
FTSE	5,846	5,669
DAX	7,228	6,643
Nikkei	10,010	8,737
Hang Seng	22,029	19,403
Commodities	**2011**	**2012**
Oil	98.02	90.32
Gold	1597.8	1582.1
Bond Yields	**2011**	**2012**
USA 5 Yr Treasury	1.50	0.61
USA 10 Yr T	2.97	1.52
USA 20 Yr T	3.93	2.20
Moody's Aaa	4.91	3.37
Moody's Baa	5.75	4.85
CAN 5 Yr T	2.21	1.17
CAN 10 Yr T	2.93	1.63
Money Market	**2011**	**2012**
USA Fed Funds	0.25	0.25
USA 3 Mo T-B	0.05	0.09
CAN tgt overnight rate	1.00	1.00
CAN 3 Mo T-B	0.92	0.91
Foreign Exchange	**2011**	**2012**
EUR/USD	1.43	1.23
GBP/USD	1.62	1.57
USD/CAD	0.95	1.01
USD/JPY	78.77	78.76

JULY

M	T	W	T	F	S	S
	1	2	3	4	5	6
7	8	9	10	11	12	13
14	15	16	17	18	19	20
21	22	23	24	25	26	27
28	29	30	31			

AUGUST

M	T	W	T	F	S	S
				1	2	3
4	5	6	7	8	9	10
11	12	13	14	15	16	17
18	19	20	21	22	23	24
25	26	27	27	29	30	31

SEPTEMBER

M	T	W	T	F	S	S
1	2	3	4	5	6	7
8	9	10	11	12	13	14
15	16	17	18	19	20	21
22	23	24	25	26	27	28
29	30					

OIL – SUMMER/AUTUMN STRATEGY

IInd of **II** Oil Stock Strategies for the Year
July 24th to October 3rd

Oil stocks tend to outperform the market from July 24th to October 3rd. Earlier in the year, there is a first wave of outperformance from late February to early May. Although the first wave has had an incredible record of outperformance, the second wave in July is still noteworthy.

While the first wave has more to do with inventories during the switch from producing heating oil to gasoline, the second wave is more related to the conversion of production from gasoline to heating oil and the effects of the hurricane season.

2.0% extra &
55% of the time better than S&P 500

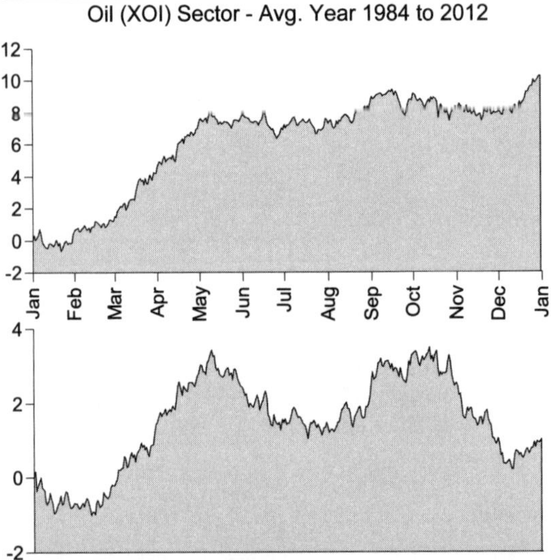

Oil (XOI) / S&P 500 Relative Strength - Avg Yr. 1984 - 2012

XOI vs. S&P 500
1984 to 2012

Positive (shaded)

Jul 24 to Oct 3	S&P 500	XOI	Diff
1984	9.1 %	9.0 %	-0.1 %
1985	-4.3	6.7	11.0
1986	-2.1	15.7	17.7
1987	6.6	-1.2	-7.8
1988	3.0	-3.6	-6.6
1989	5.6	5.7	0.1
1990	-12.4	-0.5	11.8
1991	1.3	0.7	-0.7
1992	-0.4	2.9	3.3
1993	3.2	7.8	4.6
1994	1.9	-3.6	-5.5
1995	5.2	-2.2	-7.4
1996	10.5	7.7	-2.8
1997	3.0	8.9	5.9
1998	-12.0	1.4	13.5
1999	-5.5	-2.1	3.3
2000	-3.6	12.2	15.8
2001	-10.0	-5.1	4.8
2002	2.7	7.3	4.6
2003	4.2	5.5	1.4
2004	4.2	10.9	6.7
2005	-0.6	14.3	14.9
2006	7.6	-8.5	-16.9
2007	-0.1	-4.2	-4.1
2008	-14.3	-18.1	-3.8
2009	5.0	3.0	-2.0
2010	4.0	8.5	4.5
2011	-18.3	-26.0	-7.7
2012	7.4	6.1	-1.3
Avg	0.0 %	2.0 %	2.0 %
Fq > 0	59 %	62 %	55 %

First, there is a large difference between how heating oil and gasoline are stored and consumed. For individuals and businesses, gasoline is consumed in an immediate fashion. It is stored by the local distributor and the supplies are drawn upon as needed. Heating oil, on the other hand, is largely inventoried by individuals, farms and business operations in rural areas.

The inventory process starts before the cold weather arrives. The production facilities have to start switching from gasoline to heating oil, dropping their inventory levels and boosting prices. Second, the hurricane season can play havoc with the production of oil and drive up prices substantially. The official duration of the hurricane season in the Gulf of Mexico is from June 1st to November 30th, but most major hurricanes occur in September and early October.

The threat of a strong hurricane can shut down the oil platforms temporarily, interrupting production. If a strong hurricane strikes the platforms, it can do significant damage and put the them out of commission for an extended period of time.

Amex Oil Index (XOI):
An index designed to represent a cross section of widely held oil corporations involved in various phases of the oil industry.

For more information on the XOI index, see www.cboe.com

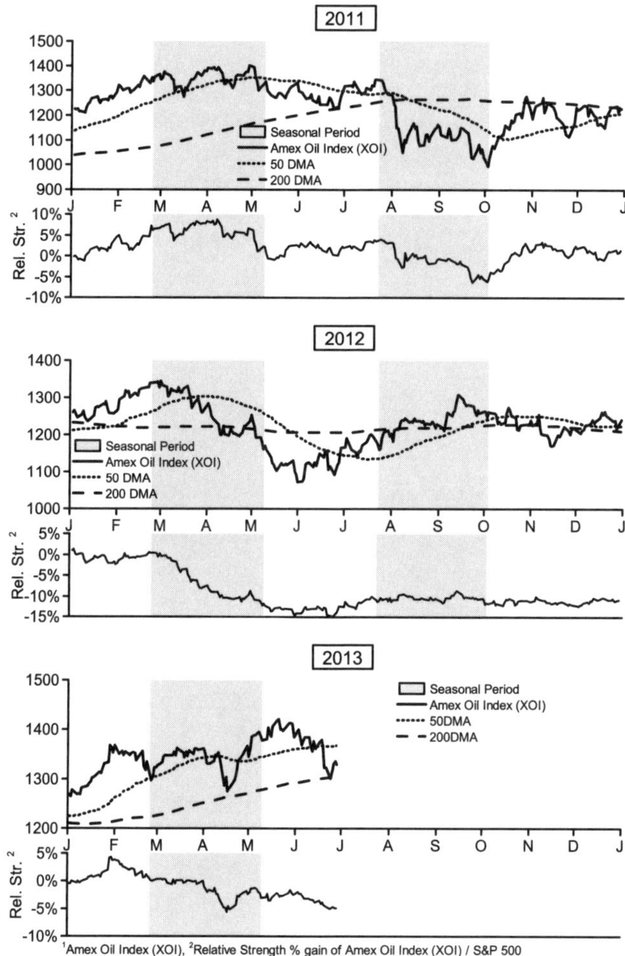

[1]Amex Oil Index (XOI), [2]Relative Strength % gain of Amex Oil Index (XOI) / S&P 500

WEEK 30

Market Indices & Rates
Weekly Values**

Stock Markets	2011	2012
Dow	12,356	12,796
S&P500	1,313	1,355
Nasdaq	2,794	2,892
TSX	13,153	11,582
FTSE	5,880	5,546
DAX	7,259	6,498
Nikkei	9,986	8,474
Hang Seng	22,484	19,000

Commodities	2011	2012
Oil	97.82	88.90
Gold	1618.7	1598.6

Bond Yields	2011	2012
USA 5 Yr Treasury	1.50	0.59
USA 10 Yr T	2.97	1.47
USA 20 Yr T	3.91	2.15
Moody's Aaa	4.84	3.26
Moody's Baa	5.72	4.77
CAN 5 Yr T	2.14	1.19
CAN 10 Yr T	2.87	1.63

Money Market	2011	2012
USA Fed Funds	0.25	0.25
USA 3 Mo T-B	0.10	0.11
CAN tgt overnight rate	1.00	1.00
CAN 3 Mo T-B	0.91	0.94

Foreign Exchange	2011	2012
EUR/USD	1.44	1.22
GBP/USD	1.64	1.56
USD/CAD	0.95	1.01
USD/JPY	77.72	78.28

JULY

M	T	W	T	F	S	S
	1	2	3	4	5	6
7	8	9	10	11	12	13
14	15	16	17	18	19	20
21	22	23	24	25	26	27
28	29	30	31			

AUGUST

M	T	W	T	F	S	S
				1	2	3
4	5	6	7	8	9	10
11	12	13	14	15	16	17
18	19	20	21	22	23	24
25	26	27	27	29	30	31

SEPTEMBER

M	T	W	T	F	S	S
1	2	3	4	5	6	7
8	9	10	11	12	13	14
15	16	17	18	19	20	21
22	23	24	25	26	27	28
29	30					

Amex Oil Index (XOI) Performance

In 2012, XOI started its seasonal period in July on a positive note, as it was rising and outperforming the S&P 500. In August, the performance of XOI started to flatten out, but managed to stay above its 200 day moving average and not break any key levels of support.

At the time, XOI was also performing at market. After a brief spike at the beginning of September, XOI started to retreat and underperform the S&P 500. In the end, the trade was successful on an absolute basis, but XOI underperformed the S&P 500 by 1%.

** Weekly avg closing values- except Fed Funds & CAN overnight tgt rate weekly closing values.

Seasonal Investment Timeline[1]

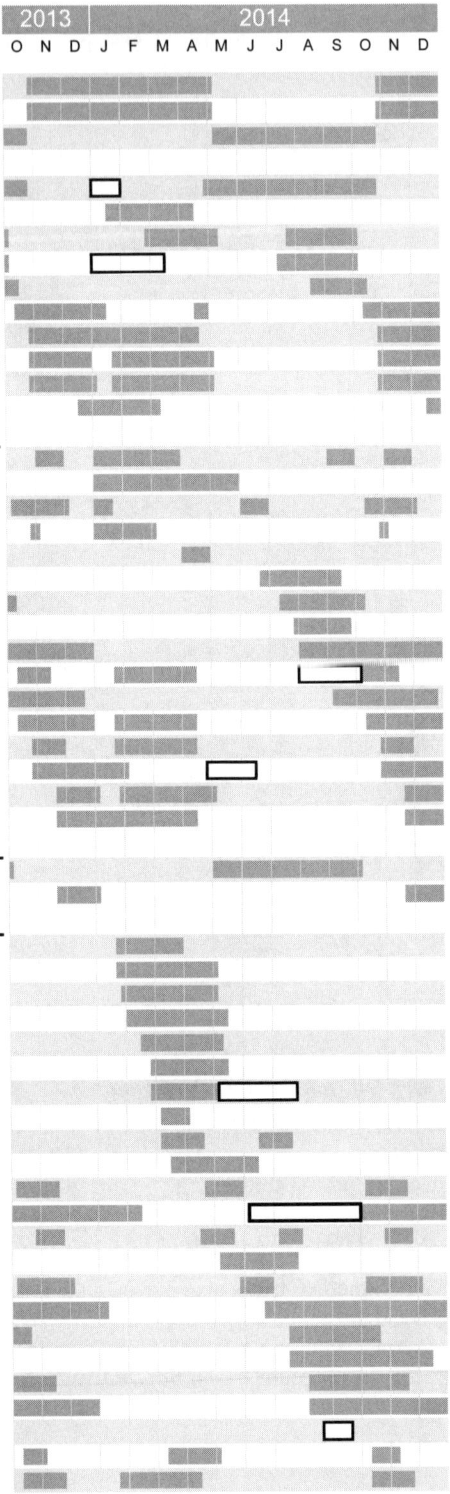

2013 | 2014

O N D J F M A M J J A S O N D

Investment	*Season*	
Core Positions		
S&P 500	Oct 28 - May 5	
TSX Composite	Oct 28 - May 5	
Cash	May 6 - Oct 27	
Primary Sectors		
Consumer Staples	Jan 1 - Jan 22 (S)	Apr 23 - Oct 27
Financials	Jan 19 - Apr 13	
Energy	Feb 25 - May 9	Jul 24 - Oct 3
[2]Utilities	Jul 17 - Oct 3	Jan 1 -Mar 13 (S)
Health Care	Aug 15 - Oct 18	
Information Tech	Oct 9 - Jan 17	Apr 16 - Apr 30
Consumer Disc.	Oct 28 - Apr 22	
Industrials	Oct 28 - Dec 31	Jan 23- May 5
Materials	Oct 28 - Jan 6	Jan 23 - May 5
Small Cap	Dec 19 - Mar 7	
Secondary Sectors		
Silver Bullion	Jan - Mar & Sep & Nov	
[2]Platinum	Jan 1 - May 31	
Software Jan1 - Jan19	Jun 1 - Jun 30	Oct 10 - Dec 5
Semiconductors	Jan 1 - Mar 7	Oct 28 - Nov 6
Canadian Dollar	Apr 1 - Apr 30	
Biotech	Jun 23 - Sep 13	
Gold Bullion	Jul 12 - Oct 9	
Gold Stocks (XAU)	Jul 27 - Sep 25	
Agriculture	Aug 1 - Dec 31	
Transportation Jan23-Apr16	Aug 1 - Oct 9 (S)	Oct 10 - Nov 13
Natural Gas	Sep 6 - Dec 21	
Canadian Banks	Oct 10 - Dec 31	Jan 23 - Apr 13
Retail	Oct 28 - Nov 29	Jan 21 - Apr 12
Homebuilders	Oct 28 - Feb 3	Apr 27- Jun 13
Metals & Mining	Nov 19 - Jan 5	Jan 23 - May 5
Emerging Markets	Nov 24 - April 18	
Fixed Income		
[3]U.S. Gov. Bonds	May 9 - Oct 3	
[3]U.S. High Yield	Nov 24 - Jan 8	
Stocks		
TJX Companies	Jan 22 - Mar 30	
Caterpillar	Jan 23 - May 5	
DuPont	Jan 28 - May 5	
[3]3M	Feb 3 - May 12	
[2]Suncor Energy	Feb 18 - May 9	
Waste Management	Feb 24 - May 14	
[3]AMD	Feb 24 - May 5	May 6 - Jul 29 (S)
[3]GE	Mar 5 - Apr 6	
Harley Davidson	Mar 9- Apr 18	Jun 22 - Jul 18
Boeing	Mar 13 - Jun 15	
Sysco	Apr 23 - May 30	Oct 11 - Nov 21
Disney	Jun 5 - Sep 30 (S)	Oct 1 - Feb 15
IBM Apr 14 - May 19	Jul 7 - Jul 30	Oct 28 - Nov 26
[3]Intel	May 6 - Jul 29	
Costco	May 26 - Jun 30	Oct 4 - Dec 1
[3]PotashCorp	Jun 23 - Jan 11	
[3]Johnson & Johnson	Jul 14 - Oct 21	
Altria	Jul 19 - Dec 19	
Procter and Gamble	Aug 7 - Nov 19	
Archer-Daniels Midland	Aug 7 - Dec 31	
[3]Alcoa	Aug 23 - Sep 26 (S)	
Union Pacific	Oct 10 - Nov 4	Mar 11 - May 5
Royal Bank	Oct 10 - Nov 28	Jan 23 - Apr 13

Long Investment ▬ Short Investment (S) ▭

[1] Holiday, End of Month, Witches' Hangover, - et al not included. [2]Thackray's 2012 Investor's Guide strategies. [3]Thackray's 2013 Investor's Guide strategies.

AUGUST

	MONDAY	TUESDAY	WEDNESDAY
WEEK 31	28	29	30
WEEK 32	4 27 CAN Market Closed- Civic Day	5 26	6 25
WEEK 33	11 20	12 19	13 18
WEEK 34	18 13	19 12	20 11
WEEK 35	25 6	26 5	27 4

THURSDAY		FRIDAY	
31		1	30
7	24	8	23
14	17	15	16
21	10	22	9
28	3	29	2

SEPTEMBER

M	T	W	T	F	S	S
1	2	3	4	5	6	7
8	9	10	11	12	13	14
15	16	17	18	19	20	21
22	23	24	25	26	27	28
29	30					

OCTOBER

M	T	W	T	F	S	S
		1	2	3	4	5
6	7	8	9	10	11	12
13	14	15	16	17	18	19
20	21	22	23	24	25	26
27	28	29	30	31		

NOVEMBER

M	T	W	T	F	S	S
					1	2
3	4	5	6	7	8	9
10	11	12	13	14	15	16
17	18	19	20	21	22	23
24	25	26	27	28	29	30

DECEMBER

M	T	W	T	F	S	S
1	2	3	4	5	6	7
8	9	10	11	12	13	14
15	16	17	18	19	20	21
22	23	24	25	26	27	28
29	30	31				

AUGUST
S U M M A R Y

	Dow Jones	S&P 500	Nasdaq	TSX Comp
Month Rank	4	6	11	10
# Up	39	34	21	15
# Down	24	29	20	13
% Pos	62	54	51	54
% Avg. Gain	1.2	1.0	0.1	-0.2

Dow & S&P 1950-2012, Nasdaq 1972-2012, TSX 1985-2012

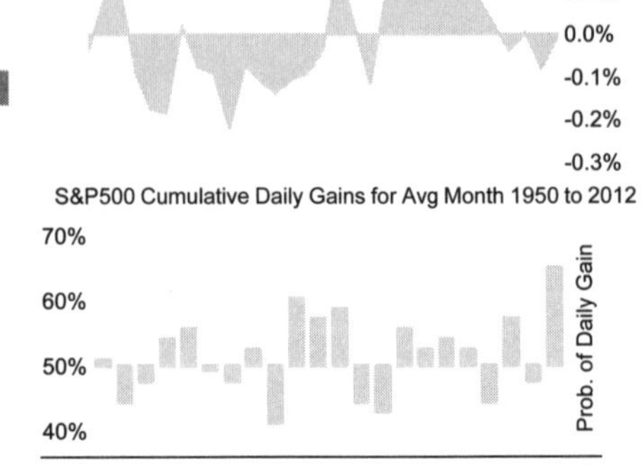

♦ August is typically a marginal month and has been the fourth worst month for the S&P 500 from 1950 to 2012, producing an average gain of 0%. ♦ If there is a summer rally in July, it is often in jeopardy in August. ♦ In 2012, July's rally carried over into August, with the S&P 500 producing a gain of 2.0%. Most of the gains were made at the beginning and the end of the month. ♦ During August, major seasonal trends start, such as: agriculture, health care and transportation sectors.

BEST / WORST AUGUST BROAD MKTS. 2003-2012

BEST AUGUST MARKETS

- Nikkei 225 (2003) 8.2%
- FTSE 100 (2009) 6.5%
- Russell 2000 (2003) 4.5%

WORST AUGUST MARKETS

- Nikkei 225 (2011) -8.9%
- Russell 2000 (2011) -8.8%
- Russell 2000 (2010) -7.5%

Index Values End of Month

	2003	2004	2005	2006	2007	2008	2009	2010	2011	2012
Dow	9,416	10,174	10,482	11,381	13,358	11,544	9,496	10,015	11,614	13,091
S&P 500	1,008	1,104	1,220	1,304	1,474	1,283	1,021	1,049	1,219	1,407
Nasdaq	1,810	1,838	2,152	2,184	2,596	2,368	2,009	2,114	2,579	3,067
TSX Comp.	7,510	8,377	10,669	12,074	13,660	13,771	10,868	11,914	12,769	11,949
Russell 1000	1,035	1,132	1,275	1,360	1,540	1,350	1,073	1,110	1,297	1,490
Russell 2000	1,236	1,362	1,656	1,791	1,970	1,838	1,422	1,496	1,806	2,018
FTSE 100	4,161	4,459	5,297	5,906	6,303	5,637	4,909	5,225	5,395	5,711
Nikkei 225	10,344	11,082	12,414	16,141	16,569	13,073	10,493	8,824	8,955	8,840

Percent Gain for August

	2003	2004	2005	2006	2007	2008	2009	2010	2011	2012
Dow	2.0	0.3	-1.5	1.7	1.1	1.5	3.5	-4.3	-4.4	0.6
S&P 500	1.8	0.2	-1.1	2.1	1.3	1.2	3.4	-4.7	-5.7	2.0
Nasdaq	4.3	-2.6	-1.5	4.4	2.0	1.8	1.5	-6.2	-6.4	4.3
TSX Comp.	3.5	-1.0	2.4	2.1	-1.5	1.3	0.8	1.7	-1.4	2.4
Russell 1000	1.9	0.3	-1.1	2.2	1.2	1.2	3.4	-4.7	-6.0	2.2
Russell 2000	4.5	-0.6	-1.9	2.9	2.2	3.5	2.8	-7.5	-8.8	3.2
FTSE 100	0.1	1.0	0.3	-0.4	-0.9	4.2	6.5	-0.6	-7.2	1.4
Nikkei 225	8.2	-2.2	4.3	4.4	-3.9	-2.3	1.3	-7.5	-8.9	1.7

August Market Avg. Performance 2003 to 2012(1)

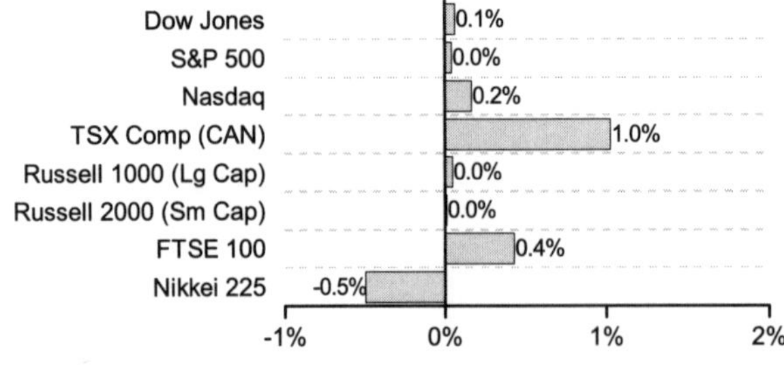

Interest Corner Aug(2)

	Fed Funds % (3)	3 Mo. T-Bill %(4)	10 Yr %(5)	20 Yr %(6)
2012	0.25	0.09	1.57	2.29
2011	0.25	0.02	2.23	3.19
2010	0.25	0.14	2.47	3.23
2009	0.25	0.15	3.40	4.14
2008	2.00	1.72	3.83	4.47

(1) Russell Data provided by Russell (2) Federal Reserve Bank of St. Louis- end of month values (3) Target rate set by FOMC (4)(5)(6) Constant yield maturities.

AUGUST SECTOR PERFORMANCE

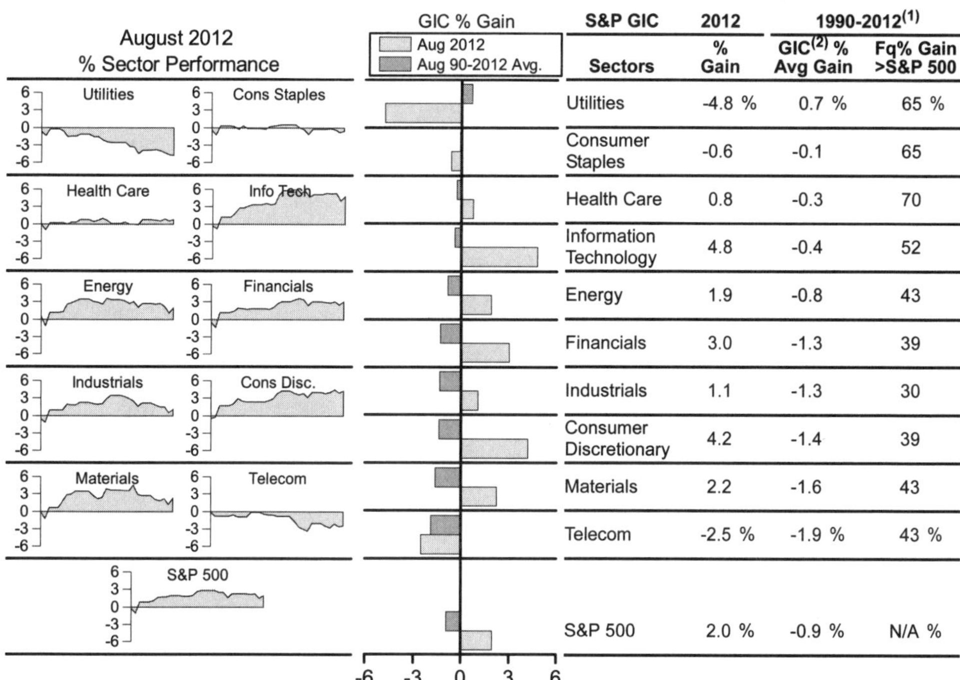

S&P GIC Sectors	2012 % Gain	1990-2012[1] GIC[2] % Avg Gain	1990-2012[1] Fq% Gain >S&P 500
Utilities	-4.8 %	0.7 %	65 %
Consumer Staples	-0.6	-0.1	65
Health Care	0.8	-0.3	70
Information Technology	4.8	-0.4	52
Energy	1.9	-0.8	43
Financials	3.0	-1.3	39
Industrials	1.1	-1.3	30
Consumer Discretionary	4.2	-1.4	39
Materials	2.2	-1.6	43
Telecom	-2.5 %	-1.9 %	43 %
S&P 500	2.0 %	-0.9 %	N/A %

Sector Commentary

♦ In August of 2012, the S&P 500 performed well, producing a gain of 2.0%.♦ Investors were becoming more positive about the future and shifted their focus from the previous month.♦ In July, investors were pushing up the defensive sectors. In August, they abandoned the defensive sectors and focused on the higher beta sectors. As a result, the technology and consumer discretionary sectors produced gains over 4%.

Sub-Sector Commentary

♦ As investors focused on the higher beta sectors, the winning sub-sector was the homebuilders, producing a gain of 12.6%. This was an out of season gain for the sector, which had been consolidating for a few months. When positive news was released on housing, the sub-sector responded very strongly.♦ Gold and silver produced gains strong gains. After a consolidation period in June and July, gold was starting to perform well in its seasonal period.♦ The sub-sectors that typically perform poorly in August lived up to their reputation: railroads, transportation and steel all produced losses.

SELECTED SUB-SECTORS[3]

Sub-Sector	2012 % Gain	GIC % Avg Gain	Fq% Gain >S&P 500
Biotech (1993-2012)	3.0 %	0.7 %	60 %
Agriculture (1994-2012)	2.5	0.4	53
Gold (London PM)	1.6	0.4	48
Home-builders	12.6	0.2	57
Pharma	-1.6	-0.3	65
SOX (1995-2012)	3.2	-0.4	50
Retail	4.8	-0.7	61
Software & Services	3.7	-0.7	57
Silver	8.2	-1.0	48
Banks	1.8	-1.2	39
Metals & Mining	4.6	-1.4	48
Chemicals	1.7	-1.7	39
Railroads	-1.5	-2.6	39
Transportation	-1.5	-3.0	26
Steel	-5.8	-4.0	43

(1) Sector data provided by Standard and Poors (2) GIC is short form for Global Industry Classification (3) Sub Sector data provided by Standard and Poors, except where marked by symbol.

ARCHER-DANIELS-MIDLAND PLANT YOUR SEEDS FOR GROWTH

August 7th to December 31st

The agriculture sector generally performs well in the last five months of the year and ADM is no exception. If you had to choose just one part of the year in which to invest in ADM, it would have to be the last five months. From August 7th to December 31st, for the years 1990 to 2012, ADM produced an average gain of 16.5% and was positive 91% of the time.

The business of "growing" really takes place in the last part of the year. This is the harvest season for the northern hemisphere and when the cash flows. It is the period when expenditures are made and investors are much more interested in committing money to the agriculture sector.

16.5% gain & positive 91% of the time positive

ADM vs. S&P 500
1990 to 2012

(Shaded = Positive)

Aug 7 to Dec 31	S&P 500	ADM	Diff
1990	-1.3%	0.1%	1.3%
1991	6.8	41.1	34.3
1992	3.6	3.1	-0.5
1993	4.0	1.7	-2.3
1994	0.5	31.9	31.4
1995	10.2	17.2	7.0
1996	11.8	27.5	15.6
1997	1.1	1.2	0.2
1998	12.8	9.4	-3.4
1999	13.0	-9.8	-22.8
2000	-9.8	58.5	68.2
2001	-4.4	14.6	19.0
2002	2.4	13.6	11.2
2003	15.0	16.7	1.7
2004	13.9	42.9	29.0
2005	1.8	18.7	16.9
2006	10.9	-21.9	-32.7
2007	0.1	34.5	34.5
2008	-29.9	5.4	35.3
2009	11.8	0.3	-2.6
2010	12.1	-0.3	-12.5
2011	4.9	-0.1	-5.0
2012	2.3	8.3	6.0
Avg	4.1%	16.5%	12.5%
Fq > 0	83%	91%	70%

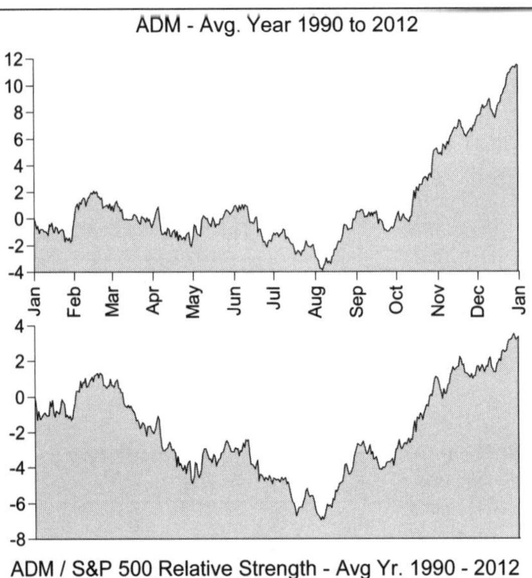

ADM / S&P 500 Relative Strength - Avg Yr. 1990 - 2012

Investing in ADM for the last five months of the year has produced very good results over the long-term. On the other hand, the first seven months leading up to the favorable season has produced an average loss of 3.9% and has only been positive 43% of the time.

Investors should avoid investing in ADM for the first seven months of the year. In fact, shorting ADM during the first seven months of the year and then switching to a long position for the last five months has proven to be a profitable strategy.

Seasonal investors can take advantage of the growing interest in the agriculture sector in the second half of the year by investing at the beginning of August. The idea is to get in before everyone else and get out when interest in the sector is at a maximum, towards the end of the year.

** ADM - stock symbol for Archer-Daniels-Midland which trades on the NYSE. Archer-Daniels-Midland Company engages in the manufacture and sale of protein meal, vegetable oil, corn sweeteners, flour, biodiesel, ethanol, and other value-added food and feed ingredients. Data adjusted for stock splits.*

2012-13 Strategy Performance

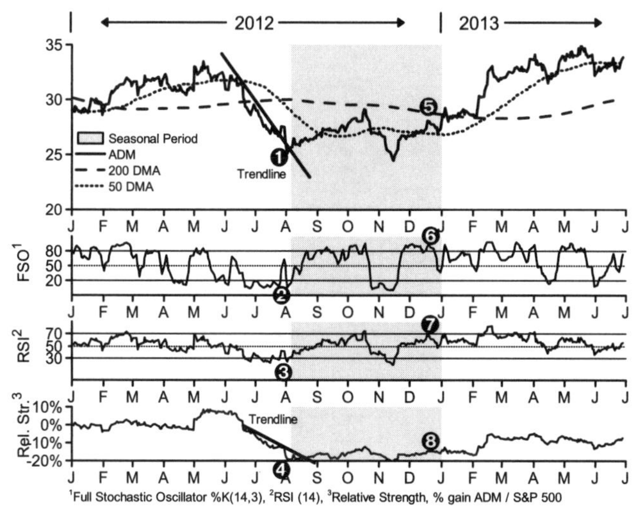

[1]Full Stochastic Oscillator %K(14,3), [2]RSI (14), [3]Relative Strength, % gain ADM / S&P 500

ADM Performance

In June 2012, ADM started to perform negatively and underperform the S&P 500. It continued its strong underperformance up until the end of July. Very often, a sharp correction before the beginning of a seasonally strong period can create a situation similar to a compressed spring, helping the investment to outperform at the beginning of its seasonal period. ADM was well setup for a bounce at the beginning of its seasonal period.

Technical Conditions August 7th to December 31st, 2012

Entry Strategy –Buy Position Early–

After a large correction that started in March of 2012, ADM's price bounced sharply upwards just before its seasonal period started❶. This caused the FSO to cross sharply above 20❷, triggering an early buy signal. At the same time, the RSI was above 30❸ and it appeared that ADM was about to start outperforming the S&P 500❹. On a poor earnings report, ADM retreated very quickly, below its previous July level. After a quick digestion of the news, ADM slowly started to outperform the S&P 500.

Exit Strategy–Sell Position Early–

Shortly after ADM moved above its 50 day moving average in December❺, the FSO turned below 80❻, triggering an early sell signal. In confirmation of the early sell signal, the RSI turned down from 70❼. At the same time, ADM was outperforming the S&P 500❽.

WEEK 31

Market Indices & Rates
Weekly Values**

Stock Markets	2011	2012
Dow	11,745	13,006
S&P500	1,240	1,379
Nasdaq	2,639	2,937
TSX	12,528	11,642
FTSE	5,543	5,698
DAX	6,608	6,755
Nikkei	9,681	8,636
Hang Seng	21,982	19,712

Commodities	2011	2012
Oil	90.82	89.06
Gold	1653.7	1607.6

Bond Yields	2011	2012
USA 5 Yr Treasury	1.23	0.62
USA 10 Yr T	2.62	1.54
USA 20 Yr T	3.54	2.24
Moody's Aaa	4.43	3.31
Moody's Baa	5.38	4.80
CAN 5 Yr T	1.85	1.29
CAN 10 Yr T	2.64	1.71

Money Market	2011	2012
USA Fed Funds	0.25	0.25
USA 3 Mo T-B	0.01	0.09
CAN tgt overnight rate	1.00	1.00
CAN 3 Mo T-B	0.87	0.98

Foreign Exchange	2011	2012
EUR/USD	1.42	1.23
GBP/USD	1.63	1.56
USD/CAD	0.97	1.00
USD/JPY	77.74	78.29

AUGUST

M	T	W	T	F	S	S
				1	2	3
4	5	6	7	8	9	10
11	12	13	14	15	16	17
18	19	20	21	22	23	24
25	26	27	27	29	30	31

SEPTEMBER

M	T	W	T	F	S	S
1	2	3	4	5	6	7
8	9	10	11	12	13	14
15	16	17	18	19	20	21
22	23	24	25	26	27	28
29	30					

OCTOBER

M	T	W	T	F	S	S
		1	2	3	4	5
6	7	8	9	10	11	12
13	14	15	16	17	18	19
20	21	22	23	24	25	26
27	28	29	30	31		

** Weekly avg closing values- except Fed Funds & CAN overnight tgt rate weekly closing values.

TRANSPORTATION— ON A ROLL

①LONG (Jan23-Apr16) ②SHORT (Aug1-Oct9) ③LONG (Oct10-Nov13)

The transportation sector can provide a "hilly" ride as the seasonal trends rise and fall throughout the year.

Activity in the transportation sub-sectors in rails, airlines and freight, tends to bottom in February.

17.2% gain & positive 91% of the time

Increased transportation activity in the spring, coupled with a typically positive economic outlook in the first part of the year, creates a positive seasonal trend, starting January 23rd and lasting until April 16th.

The next seasonal period is a weak period, giving investors an opportunity to sell short the sector and profit from its decline. This negative seasonal period lasts from August 1st to October 9th and is largely the result of investors questioning economic growth during at this time of the year.

The third seasonal period is positive and occurs from October 10th to November 13th. This trend is the result of a generally improved economic outlook at this time of the year and investors wanting to get into the sector ahead of earnings announcements.

Transportation Sector vs. S&P 500 1990 to 2012

Negative Short ☐ Positive Long ☐

	Jan 23 to Apr 16		Aug 1 to Oct 9		Oct 10 to Nov 13		Compound Growth	
Year	S&P 500	Transport	S&P 500	Transport	S&P 500	Transport	S&P 500	Transport
1990	4.4 %	4.1 %	-14.3 %	-19.2 %	4.1	3.3 %	-6.9 %	28.1 %
1991	18.1	11.4	-2.8	0.5	5.5	9.6	21.0	21.5
1992	-0.5	3.7	-5.1	-9.1	4.9	14.1	-0.9	29.1
1993	2.9	9.1	2.7	-0.3	1.1	6.4	6.9	16.5
1994	-6.0	-10.7	-0.7	-9.3	1.6	0.8	-5.2	-1.6
1995	9.6	10.5	2.9	-1.3	2.4	5.0	15.5	17.6
1996	5.2	9.4	8.9	4.9	4.9	6.1	20.1	10.4
1997	-2.9	-2.0	1.7	0.9	-5.6	-5.4	-6.7	-8.2
1998	15.1	12.2	-12.2	-16.5	14.4	12.5	15.6	47.0
1999	7.7	17.7	0.6	-11.0	4.5	4.0	13.1	35.8
2000	-5.9	-2.7	-2.0	-6.0	-3.6	13.0	-11.1	16.6
2001	12.2	0.1	-12.8	-20.0	7.8	14.1	-17.4	37.0
2002	0.8	6.9	-14.8	-11.2	13.6	8.2	-2.4	28.6
2003	0.2	0.6	4.9	4.9	1.9	8.0	7.1	3.3
2004	-0.8	-2.9	1.9	6.6	5.5	11.1	6.6	0.7
2005	-2.2	-5.1	-3.1	-0.5	3.3	9.0	-2.1	3.9
2006	2.2	13.2	5.8	6.4	2.5	3.8	10.8	9.9
2007	3.2	4.8	7.6	-0.2	-5.4	-2.9	5.0	1.9
2008	4.1	19.1	-28.2	-23.5	0.2	4.0	-25.1	52.9
2009	4.6	7.2	8.5	6.7	2.1	5.9	15.8	5.9
2010	9.2	17.4	5.8	7.9	2.9	2.5	18.9	10.9
2011	2.8	2.2	-10.6	-11.8	9.4	11.4	0.6	26.9
2012	4.1	-2.0	4.5	-3.5	-4.6	-1.1	3.8	0.3
Avg.	2.8 %	5.4 %	-2.2 %	-4.5 %	3.2 %	6.2 %	3.6 %	17.2 %
Fq>0	70 %	74 %	52	35 %	83 %	87 %	61 %	91 %

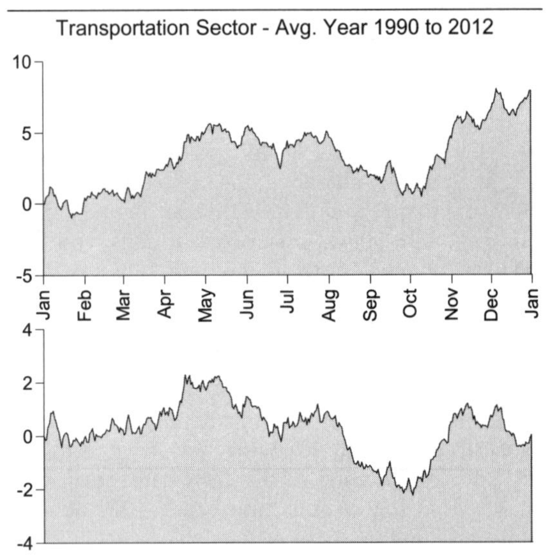

Transportation / S&P 500 Rel. Strength- Avg Yr. 1990-2012

> ℹ *The SP GICS Transportation Sector encompasses a wide range transportation based companies.*
> *For more information, see www.standardandpoors.com*

2012-13 Strategy Performance

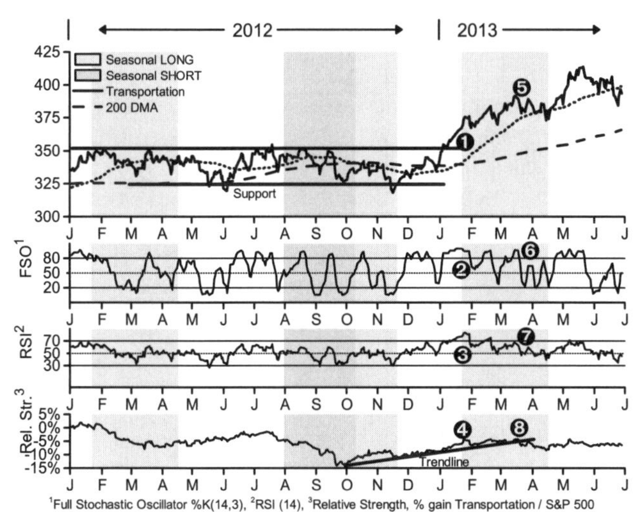

[1]Full Stochastic Oscillator %K(14,3), [2]RSI (14), [3]Relative Strength, % gain Transportation / S&P 500

Transportation Sector Performance

The transportation sector had been in a consolidation phase since the beginning of 2012. In October, the transportation sector started to outperform the S&P 500. The trend was sustained into the beginning of 2013.

Technical Conditions– January 23rd to April 16th, 2013

Entry Strategy –Buy Position on Entry Date–

The transportation sector started to increase its positive performance relative to the S&P 500 at the beginning of January 2013. After bouncing off its 50 day moving average, the transportation sector broke above its resistance line that had kept it in check for many months. Although there is a strong argument that this triggered a buy signal, the FSO had not dipped below 20 to trigger a buy signal. In addition, the first three weeks in January on average has a negative tendency. At the start of the seasonal period, the transportation sector was in an uptrend❶, with the FSO above 80❷ and the RSI above 70❸. In addition, the sector was outperforming the S&P 500❹. The sector was overbought, but performing well.

Exit Strategy–Sell Position Early–

The transportation sector slowed its ascent at the start of its seasonal period, but managed to outperform the S&P 500. In mid-March, the sector peaked❺ and the FSO dropped below 80❻, triggering an early sell signal. At the same time, the RSI bounced off 70❼ and was trending downwards. Shortly afterwards, the transportation sector started to underperform the S&P 500❽.

WEEK 32

Market Indices & Rates
Weekly Values**

Stock Markets	**2011**	**2012**
Dow	11,036	13,167
S&P500	1,153	1,401
Nasdaq	2,444	3,011
TSX	12,212	11,848
FTSE	5,145	5,839
DAX	5,850	6,952
Nikkei	9,005	8,856
Hang Seng	19,764	20,108
Commodities	**2011**	**2012**
Oil	82.92	93.09
Gold	1739.4	1613.6
Bond Yields	**2011**	**2012**
USA 5 Yr Treasury	0.99	0.71
USA 10 Yr T	2.27	1.65
USA 20 Yr T	3.23	2.36
Moody's Aaa	4.32	3.45
Moody's Baa	5.31	4.89
CAN 5 Yr T	1.49	1.38
CAN 10 Yr T	2.43	1.80
Money Market	**2011**	**2012**
USA Fed Funds	0.25	0.25
USA 3 Mo T-B	0.02	0.10
CAN tgt overnight rate	1.00	1.00
CAN 3 Mo T-B	0.81	0.97
Foreign Exchange	**2011**	**2012**
EUR/USD	1.42	1.24
GBP/USD	1.63	1.56
USD/CAD	0.99	0.99
USD/JPY	77.03	78.43

AUGUST

M	T	W	T	F	S	S
				1	2	3
4	5	6	7	8	9	10
11	12	13	14	15	16	17
18	19	20	21	22	23	24
25	26	27	27	29	30	31

SEPTEMBER

M	T	W	T	F	S	S
1	2	3	4	5	6	7
8	9	10	11	12	13	14
15	16	17	18	19	20	21
22	23	24	25	26	27	28
29	30					

OCTOBER

M	T	W	T	F	S	S
		1	2	3	4	5
6	7	8	9	10	11	12
13	14	15	16	17	18	19
20	21	22	23	24	25	26
27	28	29	30	31		

AGRICULTURE MOOOVES LAST 5 MONTHS OF THE YEAR – Aug to Dec

Agriculture, one of the hot sectors in recent years, has typically been hot during the last five months of the year (August to December).

This is the result of the major summer growing season in the northern hemisphere producing cash for the growers and subsequently increasing sales for the farming suppliers.

68% of the time better than the S&P 500

Although this sector can represent a good opportunity, investors should be wary of the wide performance swings. Out of the seventeen cycles from 1994 to 2012, during August to December, there have been six years with absolute returns greater than +25% or less than -25%, and nine years of returns greater than +10% or less than -10%. In other words, this sector is very volatile.

Agriculture vs. S&P 500 1994 to 2012

Aug 1 to Dec 31	S&P 500	Agri	Diff
		Positive	
1994	0.2 %	8.0 %	7.8 %
1995	9.6	31.7	22.1
1996	15.8	30.2	14.5
1997	1.7	14.7	13.0
1998	9.7	-3.4	-13.1
1999	10.6	-2.6	-13.2
2000	-7.7	68.0	75.7
2001	-5.2	12.5	17.7
2002	-3.5	6.0	9.5
2003	12.3	15.8	3.6
2004	10.0	44.6	34.6
2005	1.1	7.5	6.4
2006	11.1	-27.4	-38.5
2007	0.9	38.2	37.3
2008	-28.7	0.7	29.4
2009	12.9	4.0	-9.0
2010	14.2	9.9	-4.2
2011	-2.7	-5.9	-3.2
2012	3.4	5.0	1.6
Avg.	3.5 %	13.6 %	10.1 %
Fq > 0	74 %	79 %	68 %

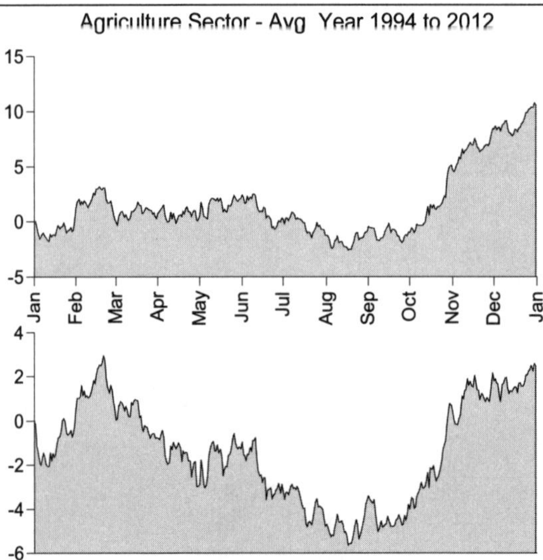

Agriculture / S&P 500 Relative Strength - Avg Yr. 1994-2012

On a year by year basis, the agriculture sector produced its biggest gain during its seasonally strong period in 2000, producing a gain of 68%. It is interesting to note that this is the same year that the technology sector's bubble burst. The agriculture sector benefited from the market correction because investors were looking for a safe haven to invest in – people need to eat, regardless of the performance of worldwide stock markets.

After realizing that technology stocks were not going to grow to the sky, investors started to have an epiphany– that the world might be running out of food and as a result, interest in the agriculture sector started to pick up.

In the second half of 2006, the agriculture sector corrected after a strong run in the first half of the year. In 2007 and the first half of 2008, the agriculture sector once again rocketed upwards due to the increase in prices of agricultural products.

Although food prices have had some reprieve with the global slowdown, the world population is still increasing and imbalances in food supply and demand will continue to exist in the future.

Investors should consider "mooov-ing" into the agriculture sector for the last five months of the year.

The SP GICS Agriculture Sector # 30202010

For more information on the agriculture sector, see www.standardandpoors.com

2012-13 Strategy Performance

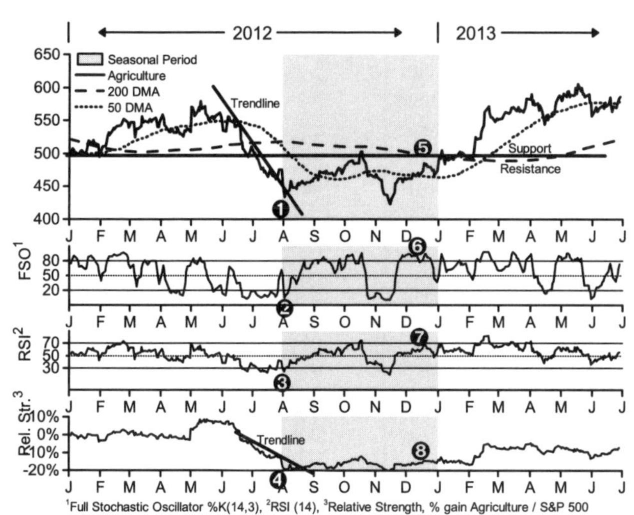

[1]Full Stochastic Oscillator %K(14,3), [2]RSI (14), [3]Relative Strength, % gain Agriculture / S&P 500

Agriculture Sector Performance

After performing at market for the beginning months of 2012, the agriculture sector had a spurt of outperformance in March and then subsequently turned down on an absolute basis and on a relative basis compared to the S&P 500. Coming into August, it dropped sharply, setting up for a bounce at the beginning of the seasonal period.

Technical Conditions August 1st to December 31st, 2012

Entry Strategy –Buy Position Early–

After a correction that started in March of 2012, the agriculture sector seemed to bottom just before its seasonal period was set to start❶. Towards the end of July, the FSO crossed above 20❷, triggering an early buy signal. The RSI crossed above 30❸ and the agriculture sector was poised to start outperforming the S&P 500❹. The early buy signal proved to be false, as the sector corrected for a few days sharply and then started to rally.

Exit Strategy– Sell Position Early–

In December, just prior to the exit date, the agriculture sector turned down❺ and the FSO crossed below 80❻ triggering an early sell signal, and the RSI turned down from 70❼. At the same time, the agriculture sector performing at market❽.

WEEK 33

Market Indices & Rates
Weekly Values**

Stock Markets	**2011**	**2012**
Dow	11,221	13,206
S&P500	1,171	1,409
Nasdaq	2,462	3,042
TSX	12,398	11,944
FTSE	5,235	5,843
DAX	5,810	6,974
Nikkei	8,983	8,999
Hang Seng	20,035	20,101

Commodities	**2011**	**2012**
Oil	85.35	94.42
Gold	1796.7	1608.3

Bond Yields	**2011**	**2012**
USA 5 Yr Treasury	0.93	0.78
USA 10 Yr T	2.17	1.76
USA 20 Yr T	3.13	2.49
Moody's Aaa	4.31	3.59
Moody's Baa	5.29	5.02
CAN 5 Yr T	1.51	1.47
CAN 10 Yr T	2.39	1.90

Money Market	**2011**	**2012**
USA Fed Funds	0.25	0.25
USA 3 Mo T-B	0.02	0.09
CAN tgt overnight rate	1.00	1.00
CAN 3 Mo T-B	0.87	1.00

Foreign Exchange	**2011**	**2012**
EUR/USD	1.44	1.23
GBP/USD	1.65	1.57
USD/CAD	0.98	0.99
USD/JPY	76.67	78.99

AUGUST

M	T	W	T	F	S	S
				1	2	3
4	5	6	7	8	9	10
11	12	13	14	15	16	17
18	19	20	21	22	23	24
25	26	27	27	29	30	31

SEPTEMBER

M	T	W	T	F	S	S
1	2	3	4	5	6	7
8	9	10	11	12	13	14
15	16	17	18	19	20	21
22	23	24	25	26	27	28
29	30					

OCTOBER

M	T	W	T	F	S	S
		1	2	3	4	5
6	7	8	9	10	11	12
13	14	15	16	17	18	19
20	21	22	23	24	25	26
27	28	29	30	31		

PG PROCTER AND GAMBLE
SOMETHING FOR EVERYONE – Aug 7 to Nov 19

In investors' eyes, Procter and Gamble is a relatively defensive investment, as the company is in the consumer packaged goods business and its revenues are generated in over 180 countries. Defensive stocks have a reputation of producing sub-par performance compared with the broad market. This is not the case with PG, as on average it has outperformed the S&P 500 over the last twenty-three years during its seasonally strong period.

10.4% gain & positive 87% of the time

Interestingly, on average, the gains have been produced largely in the second half of the year. In the first half of the year, PG has been relatively flat and has underperformed the S&P 500.

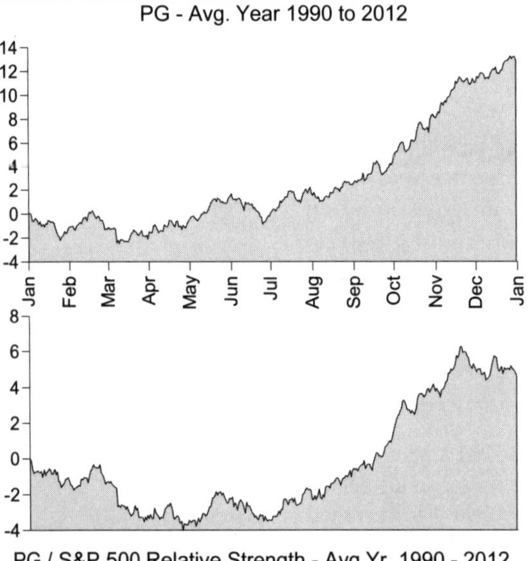

PG / S&P 500 Relative Strength - Avg Yr. 1990 - 2012

From a seasonal perspective, the best time to invest in PG has been from August 7th to November 19th. During this period, from 1990 to 2012, PG on average produced a gain of 10.4% and was positive 87% of the time. In addition, it substantially outperformed the S&P 500, generating an extra profit of 9.0% and beating its performance 83% of the time.

Investors will often seek sanctuary in defensive stocks in late summer and early autumn. Although August is not typically the worst month of the year, it does have a weak risk reward profile. With the dreaded month of September falling right after August, investors become "gun shy" and start to become more conservative in August.

PG vs. S&P 500 - 1990 to 2012

(Shaded = Positive)

Aug 7 to Nov 19	S&P 500	PG	Diff
1990	-4.5%	8.3%	12.8%
1991	-2.9	-2.2	0.7
1992	0.7	10.1	9.4
1993	3.1	17.7	14.6
1994	1.0	19.3	18.3
1995	7.4	27.8	20.4
1996	12.0	18.6	6.5
1997	-1.6	0.2	1.9
1998	5.8	14.0	8.2
1999	9.4	18.7	9.3
2000	-6.5	31.8	38.3
2001	-4.1	11.2	15.3
2002	4.3	-0.7	-5.0
2003	7.8	8.2	0.4
2004	10.0	2.5	-7.5
2005	1.8	6.2	4.4
2006	9.5	7.4	-2.1
2007	-2.3	12.0	14.4
2008	-37.4	-8.1	29.3
2009	9.8	20.8	11.0
2010	7.0	6.7	-0.3
2011	1.4	4.4	3.0
2012	-0.5	3.2	3.7
Avg	1.3%	10.4%	9.0%
Fq > 0	65%	87%	83%

This trend benefits PG as more investors switch over to defensive companies. PG's outperformance on average starts to occur just after it releases its fourth quarter earnings in the beginning of August.

PG continues to outperform the S&P 500 through September and October. For the S&P 500, September on average is the worst month of the year and October is the most volatile month. The outperformance of PG continues into mid-November.

It is interesting to note that PG's seasonally strong period extends past the seasonal period for the consumer staples sector. It is possible that investors wait until after PG's first quarter results are released in the beginning of November before adjusting their portfolios.

** The Procter and Gamble Company is a consumer packaged goods company. Its products are sold in more than 180 countries. Data adjusted for stock splits.*

2012-13 Strategy Performance

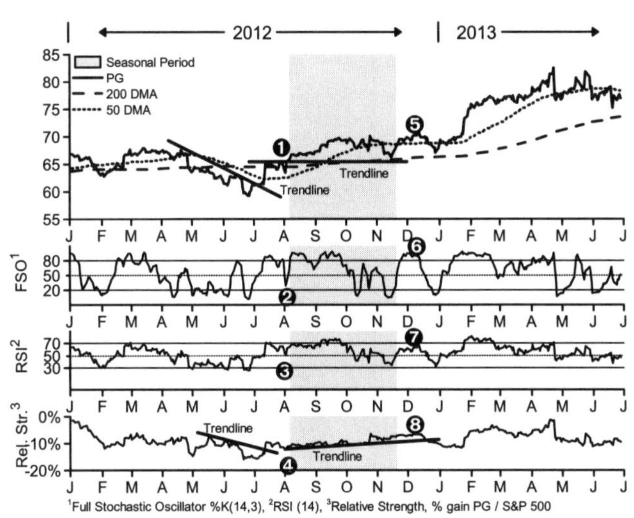

[1]Full Stochastic Oscillator %K(14,3), [2]RSI (14), [3]Relative Strength, % gain PG / S&P 500

Procter and Gamble (PG) Performance

In 2012, Procter and Gamble performed negatively and underperformed the S&P 500 for the first six months of the year. At the end of June, Procter and Gamble started to perform positively, boding well for its seasonal period which was due to start shortly afterwards.

Technical Conditions August 7th to November 19th, 2012
Entry Strategy –Buy Position on Entry Date–

In early July, Bill Ackman of Pershing Square Capital, an influential activist investor, was given permission from SEC to increase his purchases of Procter and Gamble shares. The price of Procter and Gamble shares rose as investors were excited with the possibility of Bill Ackman unlocking extra value in the company. On the seasonal entry date, Procter and Gamble broke above its 200 day moving average and started a new uptrend❶. Both the FSO and the RSI were already in their upper ranges❷❸ and PG was performing at market❹.

Exit Strategy – Sell Position after Exit Date–

After correcting in the weeks leading up to the seasonal period exit date, PG bounced off its 200 day moving average and then broke above its 50 day moving average. On the exit date, both the FSO and the RSI were rising. The technical picture was strong, justifying holding the position past the exit date. PG continued its positive performance for the next three weeks, but then turned down❺ and the FSO dropped below 80❻ and the RSI turned down from its upper range❼, triggering a full exit as PG started to underperform the S&P 500❽.

WEEK 34

Market Indices & Rates Weekly Values**

Stock Markets	**2011**	**2012**
Dow	11,157	13,173
S&P500	1,160	1,412
Nasdaq	2,432	3,068
TSX	12,272	12,091
FTSE	5,138	5,802
DAX	5,562	7,012
Nikkei	8,714	9,142
Hang Seng	19,633	20,021
Commodities	**2011**	**2012**
Oil	84.99	96.23
Gold	1808.1	1645.8
Bond Yields	**2011**	**2012**
USA 5 Yr Treasury	0.97	0.75
USA 10 Yr T	2.19	1.74
USA 20 Yr T	3.12	2.47
Moody's Aaa	4.37	3.54
Moody's Baa	5.40	4.96
CAN 5 Yr T	1.54	1.43
CAN 10 Yr T	2.39	1.87
Money Market	**2011**	**2012**
USA Fed Funds	0.25	0.25
USA 3 Mo T-B	0.01	0.10
CAN tgt overnight rate	1.00	1.00
CAN 3 Mo T-B	0.87	1.01
Foreign Exchange	**2011**	**2012**
EUR/USD	1.44	1.25
GBP/USD	1.64	1.58
USD/CAD	0.99	0.99
USD/JPY	76.91	78.89

AUGUST

M	T	W	T	F	S	S
				1	2	3
4	5	6	7	8	9	10
11	12	13	14	15	16	17
18	19	20	21	22	23	24
25	26	27	27	29	30	31

SEPTEMBER

M	T	W	T	F	S	S
1	2	3	4	5	6	7
8	9	10	11	12	13	14
15	16	17	18	19	20	21
22	23	24	25	26	27	28
29	30					

OCTOBER

M	T	W	T	F	S	S
		1	2	3	4	5
6	7	8	9	10	11	12
13	14	15	16	17	18	19
20	21	22	23	24	25	26
27	28	29	30	31		

** Weekly avg closing values- except Fed Funds & CAN overnight tgt rate weekly closing values.

HEALTH CARE
AUGUST PRESCRIPTION RENEWAL
August 15th to October 18th

Health care stocks have traditionally been classified as defensive stocks because of their stable earnings. Pharmaceutical and other health care companies typically still do well in an economic downturn.

Even in tough times, people still need to take their medication. As a result, investors have typically found comfort in this sector starting in the late summer doldrums and riding the momentum into early December.

2.7% extra & 15 out of 23 times better than the S&P 500

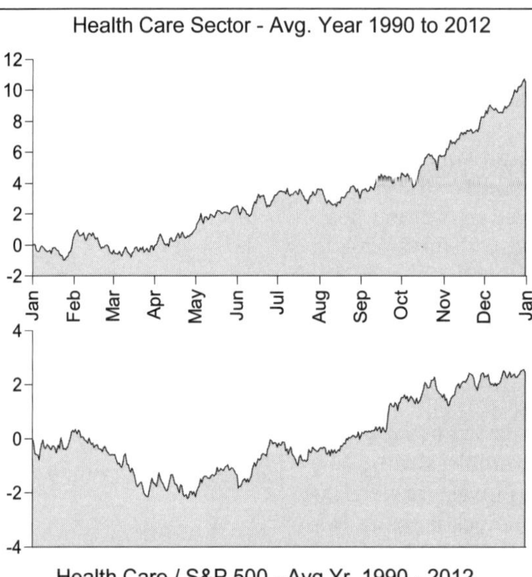

From August 15th to October 18th (1990 to 2012), health care stocks have had a tendency to outperform the S&P 500 on a yearly basis.

During this time period, the broad market (S&P 500) produced an average loss of 0.1%, compared with the health care stocks that produced a gain of 2.7%.

Despite competing with a runaway market in 2003 and legal problems which required drugs to be withdrawn from the market in 2004, the sector has beaten the S&P 500 fifteen out of twenty-three times from 1990 to 2012.

Health Care vs. S&P 500
Performance 1990 to 2012

Aug 15 to Oct 18	S&P 500	Positive Health Care	Diff
1990	-9.9 %	-1.3 %	8.6 %
1991	0.7	1.3	0.6
1992	-1.9	-9.0	-7.1
1993	4.1	13.5	9.5
1994	1.2	7.2	6.0
1995	4.9	11.7	6.7
1996	7.4	9.4	2.1
1997	2.1	5.8	3.7
1998	-0.6	3.0	3.6
1999	-5.5	-0.5	5.0
2000	-10.0	6.9	16.9
2001	-10.0	-0.4	9.6
2002	-3.8	2.4	6.2
2003	4.9	-0.5	-5.4
2004	4.6	-0.8	-5.4
2005	-4.2	-3.1	1.2
2006	7.7	6.4	-1.3
2007	8.0	6.0	-2.0
2008	-27.3	-20.4	6.8
2009	8.3	5.1	-3.3
2010	9.8	8.2	-1.6
2011	4.0	3.2	-0.8
2012	3.8	6.9	3.1
Avg	-0.1 %	2.7 %	2.7 %
Fq > 0	61 %	65 %	65 %

The real benefit of investing in the health care sector has been the positive returns that have been generated when the market has typically been negative.

Since 1950, August and September have been the worst two-month combination for gains in the broad stock market.

Having an alternative sector to invest in during the summer and early autumn is a valuable asset.

Alternate Strategy—As the health care sector has had a tendency to perform at par with the broad market from late October to early December, an alternative strategy is to continue holding the health care sector during this time period if the fundamentals or technicals are favorable.

Health Care SP GIC Sector# 35: An index designed to represent a cross section of health care companies. For more information on the health care sector, see www.standardandpoors.com.

2012-13 Strategy Performance

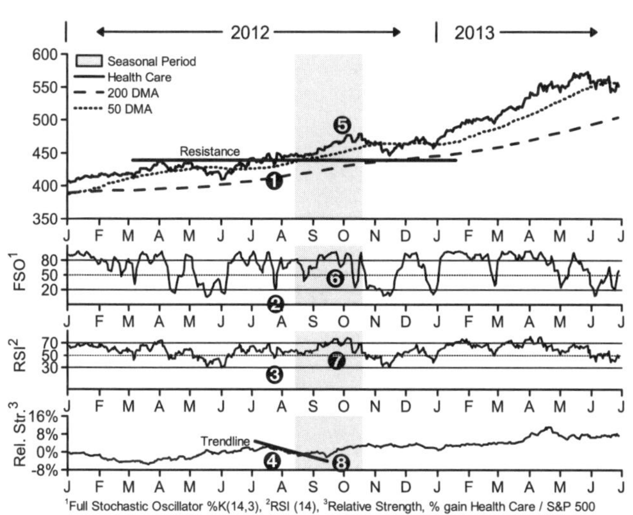

[1]Full Stochastic Oscillator %K(14,3), [2]RSI (14), [3]Relative Strength, % gain Health Care / S&P 500

Health Care Sector Performance

For the first seven months of 2012, the health care sector oscillated back and forth between outperforming and underperforming the S&P 500. Just prior to the start of its seasonal period, the health care sector managed to break above its resistance level, setting up well for a seasonal trade.

Technical Conditions August 15th to October 18th, 2012

Entry Strategy –Buy Position Early–

In late July 2012, after breaking above its resistance level, the health care sector retreated and then bounced upwards❶, causing the FSO to bounce off 20❷ and trigger an early buy signal. At the same time, the RSI also bounced off 50❸. The main concern was that the health care sector was still underperforming the S&P 500❹.

Exit Strategy– Sell Position Early–

In late September, the health care sector slowed is ascent❺ and the FSO crossed below 80❻, triggering an early sell signal. The RSI also crossed below 70❼ at the same time. Although an early sell signal was triggered, the health care sector was still outperforming the S&P 500❽, allowing for discretion to hold the trade longer.

WEEK 35

Market Indices & Rates Weekly Values**

Stock Markets	2011	2012
Dow	11,489	13,085
S&P500	1,204	1,407
Nasdaq	2,549	3,069
TSX	12,642	11,981
FTSE	5,343	5,738
DAX	5,674	6,985
Nikkei	8,954	9,002
Hang Seng	20,280	19,687
Commodities	**2011**	**2012**
Oil	88.07	95.68
Gold	1833.7	1659.3
Bond Yields	**2011**	**2012**
USA 5 Yr Treasury	0.93	0.67
USA 10 Yr T	2.17	1.63
USA 20 Yr T	3.11	2.35
Moody's Aaa	4.34	3.41
Moody's Baa	5.40	4.83
CAN 5 Yr T	1.60	1.37
CAN 10 Yr T	2.41	1.79
Money Market	**2011**	**2012**
USA Fed Funds	0.25	0.25
USA 3 Mo T-B	0.02	0.09
CAN tgt overnight rate	1.00	1.00
CAN 3 Mo T-B	0.94	1.03
Foreign Exchange	**2011**	**2012**
EUR/USD	1.44	1.25
GBP/USD	1.63	1.58
USD/CAD	0.98	0.99
USD/JPY	76.79	78.60

AUGUST

M	T	W	T	F	S	S
				1	2	3
4	5	6	7	8	9	10
11	12	13	14	15	16	17
18	19	20	21	22	23	24
25	26	27	27	29	30	31

SEPTEMBER

M	T	W	T	F	S	S
1	2	3	4	5	6	7
8	9	10	11	12	13	14
15	16	17	18	19	20	21
22	23	24	25	26	27	28
29	30					

OCTOBER

M	T	W	T	F	S	S
		1	2	3	4	5
6	7	8	9	10	11	12
13	14	15	16	17	18	19
20	21	22	23	24	25	26
27	28	29	30	31		

** Weekly avg closing values- except Fed Funds & CAN overnight tgt rate weekly closing values.

SEPTEMBER

	MONDAY	TUESDAY	WEDNESDAY
WEEK 36	1 29 USA Market Closed- Labour Day CAN Market Closed- Labour Day	2 28	3 27
WEEK 37	8 22	9 21	10 20
WEEK 38	15 15	16 14	17 13
WEEK 39	22 8	23 7	24 6
WEEK 40	29 1	30	1

THURSDAY		FRIDAY	
4	26	5	25
11	19	12	18
18	12	19	11
25	5	26	4
2		3	

OCTOBER

M	T	W	T	F	S	S
		1	2	3	4	5
6	7	8	9	10	11	12
13	14	15	16	17	18	19
20	21	22	23	24	25	26
27	28	29	30	31		

NOVEMBER

M	T	W	T	F	S	S
					1	2
3	4	5	6	7	8	9
10	11	12	13	14	15	16
17	18	19	20	21	22	23
24	25	26	27	28	29	30

DECEMBER

M	T	W	T	F	S	S
1	2	3	4	5	6	7
8	9	10	11	12	13	14
15	16	17	18	19	20	21
22	23	24	25	26	27	28
29	30	31				

JANUARY

M	T	W	T	F	S	S
			1	2	3	4
5	6	7	8	9	10	11
12	13	14	15	16	17	18
19	20	21	22	23	24	25
26	27	28	29	30	31	

SEPTEMBER
S U M M A R Y

	Dow Jones	S&P 500	Nasdaq	TSX Comp
Month Rank	12	12	12	12
# Up	25	28	22	11
# Down	38	35	19	17
% Pos	40	44	54	39
% Avg. Gain	-0.8	-0.5	-0.6	-1.6

Dow & S&P 1950-2012, Nasdaq 1972-2012, TSX 1985-2012

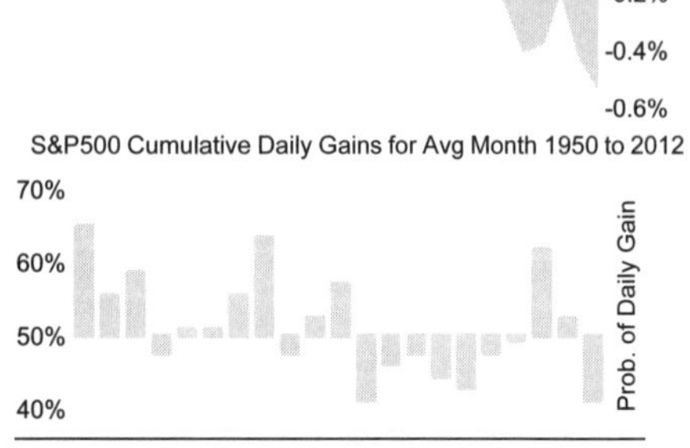

♦ September has the reputation of being the worst month of the year. From 1950 to 2012, September produced an average loss of 0.5% and has only been positive 44% of the time. ♦ When rallies occur in September it is usually the result of a large external event, such as an increase in monetary stimulus. ♦ The last part of September tends to be negative. ♦ Gold is typically one of the stronger sectors in September.

BEST / WORST SEPTEMBER BROAD MKTS. 2003-2012

BEST SEPTEMBER MARKETS

- Russell 2000 (2010) 12.3%
- Nasdaq (2010) 12.0%
- Nikkei 225 (2005) 9.4%

WORST SEPTEMBER MARKETS

- TSX Comp. (2008) -14.7%
- Nikkei 225 (2008) -13.9%
- FTSE 100 (2008) -13.0%

Index Values End of Month

	2003	2004	2005	2006	2007	2008	2009	2010	2011	2012
Dow	9,275	10,080	10,569	11,679	13,896	10,851	9,712	10,788	10,913	13,437
S&P 500	996	1,115	1,229	1,336	1,527	1,166	1,057	1,141	1,131	1,441
Nasdaq	1,787	1,897	2,152	2,258	2,702	2,092	2,122	2,369	2,415	3,116
TSX Comp.	7,421	8,668	11,012	11,761	14,099	11,753	11,395	12,369	11,624	12,317
Russell 1000	1,023	1,145	1,285	1,391	1,597	1,219	1,115	1,211	1,198	1,526
Russell 2000	1,212	1,424	1,660	1,803	2,002	1,689	1,502	1,680	1,601	2,081
FTSE 100	4,091	4,571	5,478	5,961	6,467	4,902	5,134	5,549	5,128	5,742
Nikkei 225	10,219	10,824	13,574	16,128	16,786	11,260	10,133	9,369	8,700	8,870

Percent Gain for September

	2003	2004	2005	2006	2007	2008	2009	2010	2011	2012
Dow	-1.5	-0.9	0.8	2.6	4.0	-6.0	2.3	7.7	-6.0	2.6
S&P 500	-1.2	0.9	0.7	2.5	3.6	-9.1	3.6	8.8	-7.2	2.4
Nasdaq	-1.3	3.2	0.0	3.4	4.0	-11.6	5.6	12.0	-6.4	1.6
TSX Comp.	-1.2	3.5	3.2	-2.6	3.2	-14.7	4.8	3.8	-9.0	3.1
Russell 1000	-1.2	1.1	0.8	2.3	3.7	-9.8	3.9	9.0	-7.6	2.4
Russell 2000	-2.0	4.6	0.2	0.7	1.6	-8.1	5.6	12.3	-11.4	3.1
FTSE 100	-1.7	2.5	3.4	0.9	2.6	-13.0	4.6	6.2	-4.9	0.5
Nikkei 225	-1.2	-2.3	9.4	-0.1	1.3	-13.9	-3.4	6.2	-2.8	0.3

September Market Avg. Performance 2003 to 2012(1)

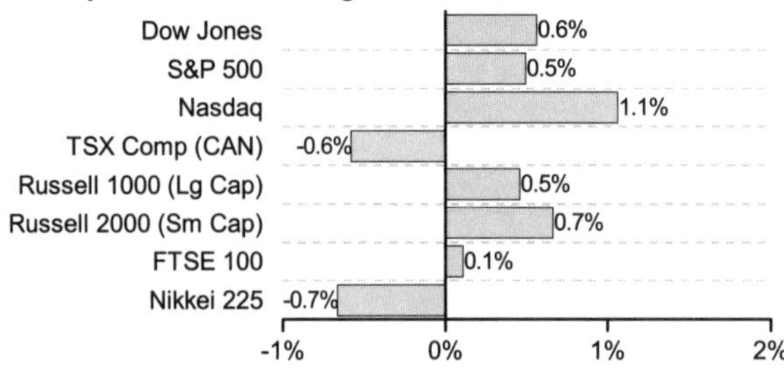

Interest Corner Sep(2)

	Fed Funds % (3)	3 Mo. T-Bill % (4)	10 Yr % (5)	20 Yr % (6)
2012	0.25	0.10	1.65	2.42
2011	0.25	0.02	1.92	2.66
2010	0.25	0.16	2.53	3.38
2009	0.25	0.14	3.31	4.02
2008	2.00	0.92	3.85	4.43

(1) Russell Data provided by Russell (2) Federal Reserve Bank of St. Louis- end of month values (3) Target rate set by FOMC (4)(5)(6) Constant yield maturities.

SEPTEMBER SECTOR PERFORMANCE

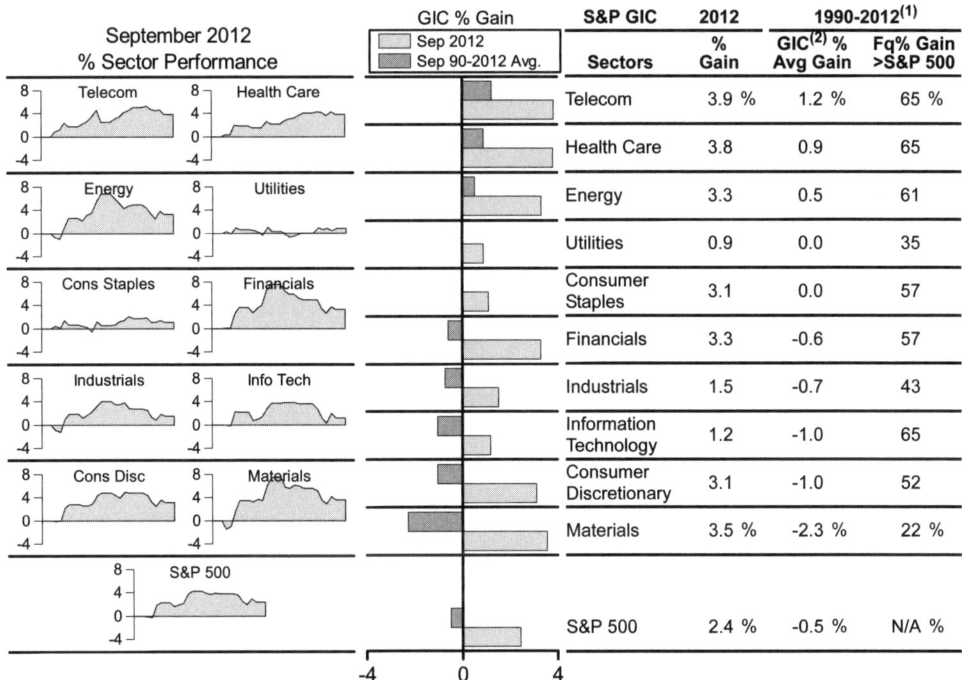

S&P GIC Sectors	2012 % Gain	1990-2012[1] GIC[2] % Avg Gain	1990-2012[1] Fq% Gain >S&P 500
Telecom	3.9 %	1.2 %	65 %
Health Care	3.8	0.9	65
Energy	3.3	0.5	61
Utilities	0.9	0.0	35
Consumer Staples	3.1	0.0	57
Financials	3.3	-0.6	57
Industrials	1.5	-0.7	43
Information Technology	1.2	-1.0	65
Consumer Discretionary	3.1	-1.0	52
Materials	3.5 %	-2.3 %	22 %
S&P 500	2.4 %	-0.5 %	N/A %

Sector Commentary

♦ September, on average is the worst month of the year, but in 2012 it was a strongly positive month.♦ There was a mixture of sectors that performed well, including the sectors that typically perform well in September: telecom, health care and energy.♦ The two sectors that are typically the worst performing sectors, consumer discretionary and materials, outperformed the S&P 500 with returns of 3.1% and 3.5% respectively.

Sub-Sector Commentary

♦ Gold and silver typically perform well in September and 2012 was no exception.♦ The biotech sub-sector was still performing well in its seasonal period.♦ Generally speaking, the top performing sub-sectors in September 2012 were the ones that typically perform well at this time of the year. ♦The notable exceptions were the metals and mining, and steel, which produced gains of 7.7% and 3.7% respectively. Both of these sub-sectors performed very poorly the month before, and as a result a bounce was not totally unexpected.

SELECTED SUB-SECTORS[3]

Sub-Sector	2012 % Gain	GIC % Avg Gain	Fq% Gain >S&P 500
Gold (London PM)	7.7 %	3.3 %	70 %
Silver	13.5	2.7	74
Biotech (1993-2012)	5.5	1.8	65
Pharma	3.8	1.0	65
Software & Services	3.5	0.7	70
Agriculture (1994-2012)	1.6	-0.3	53
Retail	1.1	-0.7	43
Home-builders	9.6	-0.9	61
Banks	2.9	-0.9	57
Transporta-tion	-3.9	-1.1	48
Railroads	-5.7	-1.2	30
Metals & Mining	7.7	-1.9	43
Chemicals	1.9	-2.1	26
SOX (1995-2012)	-3.5	-3.7	33
Steel	3.7	-4.0	43

(1) Sector data provided by Standard and Poors (2) GIC is short form for Global Industry Classification (3) Sub Sector data provided by Standard and Poors, except where marked by symbol.

GAS FIRES UP IN SEPTEMBER

Natural Gas (Commodity) – Outperforms
Cash price increases from Sep 5th to Dec 21st

A lot of investors are still "gun-shy" from investing in natural gas a few years ago when it was in a multi-year decline. The decline was caused by the increased supply of natural gas from "fracking." This procedure involves creating fractures in rock formations by injecting liquids into them, in order to let oil and natural gas flow more freely and has greatly increased the amount of natural gas available to be tapped.

After a multi-year collapse in price, natural gas put in a strong performance in 2012. Although prices will fluctuate in the future, the effects of the large supply shock have largely played out and natural gas is likely to be more influenced by its seasonal trends.

If there is one time of the year that investors should consider investing in natural gas, it is from September 5th to December 21st.

47.2% gain & positive 83% of the time

We may not use natural gas ourselves, but most of us depend on it in one way or another. It is used for furnaces and hot water tanks and is usually responsible for producing some portion of the electrical power that we consume.

Natural Gas (Henry Hub Spot)- Avg. Year 1995 to 2012

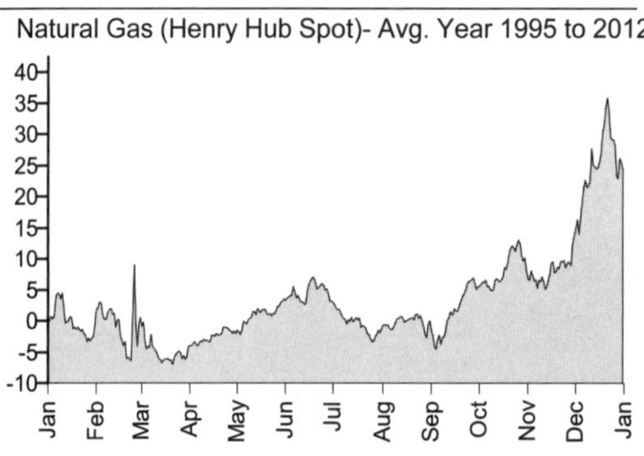

As a result, there are two high consumption times for natural gas: winter and summer. The colder it gets in winter, the more natural gas is consumed to keep the furnaces going. The warmer it gets in the summer, the more natural gas is used to produce power for air conditioners. On the supply side, weather also plays a large factor in determining

Natural Gas (Cash) Henry Hub LA
Seasonal Gains 1995 to 2012

	Negative	Positive	Negative
	Jan 1 to Sep 4	Sep 5 to Dec 21	Dec 22 to Dec 31
1995	-2.9 %	103.0 %	1.2 %
1996	-50.2	170.4	-46.2
1997	11.4	-13.1	-6.3
1998	-22.9	20.9	-6.7
1999	26.8	5.3	-11.2
2000	104.4	121.9	0.7
2001	-79.1	21.5	1.5
2002	15.9	61.3	-9.1
2003	2.6	47.1	-16.3
2004	-24.1	54.6	-11.6
2005	96.5	14.5	-29.6
2006	-45.6	17.4	-9.5
2007	-3.8	32.7	2.0
2008	1.0	-21.4	-0.9
2009	-66.6	208.0	0.7
2010	-35.9	10.4	2.4
2011	-3.1	-26.1	-1.7
2012	-5.7	21.7	0.6
Avg.	-4.5 %	47.2 %	-7.8 %

price. During the hurricane season in the Gulf of Mexico, the price of natural gas is affected by the forecast of the number, severity and impact of hurricanes.

The tail end of the hurricane season occurs in late autumn and early winter, at the same time distributors are accumulating natural gas inventories for the winter heating season. As a result, the price of natural gas tends to rise from the beginning of September. As the price is very dependent on the weather, it is also extremely volatile. Large percentage moves are not uncommon.

As a result of the hurricane season ending and the slowdown in accumulating natural gas inventories for winter heating, the price of natural gas frequently decreases during the last part of December.

Caution:
The cash price for natural gas is extremely volatile and extreme caution should be used. Care must be taken to ensure that investments are within risk tolerances.

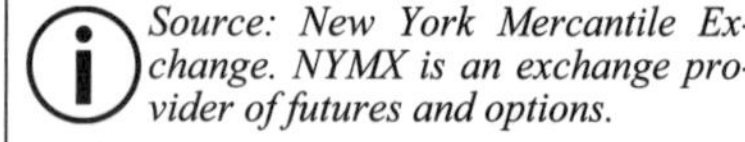

Source: New York Mercantile Exchange. NYMX is an exchange provider of futures and options.

2012-13 Strategy Performance

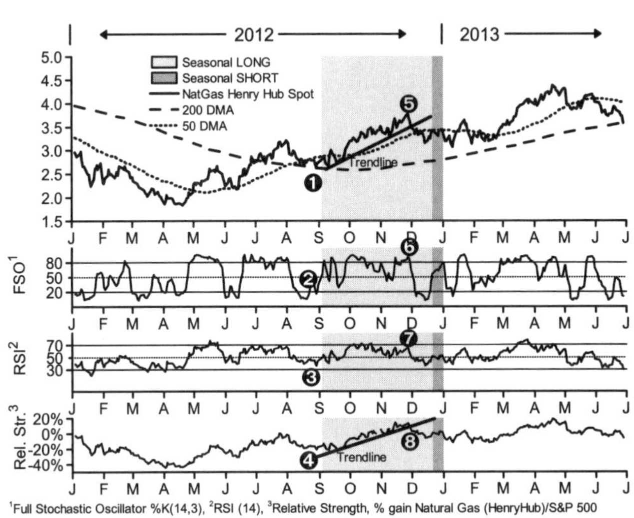

¹Full Stochastic Oscillator %K(14,3), ²RSI (14), ³Relative Strength, % gain Natural Gas (HenryHub)/S&P 500

Natural Gas Performance

For the first part of 2012, up until mid-April, natural gas prices fell sharply. After a rally into August, natural gas corrected briefly before consolidating before the start of its seasonal period.

Technical Conditions September 5th to December 21st, 2012

Entry Strategy –Buy Position Early–

As natural gas was consolidating just before the start of its seasonal trade, a price spike❶ caused the FSO to cross above 20❷, generating an early buy signal. At the same time, the RSI was neutral in its lower range❸ and natural gas was just starting to show signs of starting to outperform the S&P 500❹.

Exit Strategy– Sell Position Early–

After performing strongly for the first two and a half months of its seasonal trade, natural gas started to correct and break its upward trend❺. At the same time, the FSO crossed below 80❻ and shortly afterwards the RSI turned down from its upper range❼. Natural gas started to underperform the S&P 500, as it broke its upward relative trendline❽. As a result, an early exit from the position was justified.

WEEK 36

Market Indices & Rates
Weekly Values**

Stock Markets	**2011**	**2012**
Dow	11,211	13,171
S&P500	1,176	1,420
Nasdaq	2,505	3,104
TSX	12,578	12,085
FTSE	5,227	5,732
DAX	5,289	7,059
Nikkei	8,734	8,758
Hang Seng	19,831	19,429
Commodities	**2011**	**2012**
Oil	87.91	95.65
Gold	1861.2	1701.5
Bond Yields	**2011**	**2012**
USA 5 Yr Treasury	0.87	0.64
USA 10 Yr T	1.99	1.64
USA 20 Yr T	2.90	2.36
Moody's Aaa	4.11	3.43
Moody's Baa	5.24	4.82
CAN 5 Yr T	1.40	1.37
CAN 10 Yr T	2.23	1.79
Money Market	**2011**	**2012**
USA Fed Funds	0.25	0.25
USA 3 Mo T-B	0.01	0.11
CAN tgt overnight rate	1.00	1.00
CAN 3 Mo T-B	0.88	1.00
Foreign Exchange	**2011**	**2012**
EUR/USD	1.39	1.26
GBP/USD	1.60	1.59
USD/CAD	0.99	0.98
USD/JPY	77.39	78.44

SEPTEMBER

M	T	W	T	F	S	S
1	2	3	4	5	6	7
8	9	10	11	12	13	14
15	16	17	18	19	20	21
22	23	24	25	26	27	28
29	30					

OCTOBER

M	T	W	T	F	S	S
		1	2	3	4	5
6	7	8	9	10	11	12
13	14	15	16	17	18	19
20	21	22	23	24	25	26
27	28	29	30	31		

NOVEMBER

M	T	W	T	F	S	S
					1	2
3	4	5	6	7	8	9
10	11	12	13	14	15	16
17	18	19	20	21	22	23
24	25	26	27	28	29	30

SOFTWARE POSITIVE ACTION TRIPLE PLAY

①Jan1-Jan19 ②Jun1-Jun30 ③Oct10-Dec5

The software sector starts off the year on a strong seasonal note as it echoes the outperformance of the technology sector in the first part of January.

15.8% gain & positive 83% of time

The software sector's next period of seasonal strength occurs from June 1st to June 30th. This mid-summer period of outperformance is largely the result of one company: Oracle, which is considered a bellwether for the sector.

Oracle, a software solutions based company realizes a disproportionate amount of sales just before their year-end on May 31st. They announce their year-end earnings approximately in the third week of June. At this time of the year, the market has not started its "official" earnings season and investors gravitate to Oracle before it announces earnings in June, anticipating positive announcements.

The software sector has its biggest seasonal run starting in October as investors enter the sector to take advantage of the corporate purchases before year-end, and the positive impact on earnings as a result.

Software SP GIC Sector: An index designed to represent a cross section of software companies.

For more information, see www.standardandpoors.com.

Software vs. S&P 500 1990 to 2012 Positive

	Jan 1 to Jan 19		Jun 1 to Jun 30		Oct 10 to Dec 5		Compound Growth	
Year	S&P 500	Software	S&P 500	Software	S&P 500	Software	S&P 500	Software
1990	-4.0 %	-4.0 %	-0.9 %	1.8 %	8.1	22.7 %	2.9 %	19.8 %
1991	0.6	-0.4	-4.8	-4.2	0.2	3.0	-4.1	-1.7
1992	0.4	6.1	-1.7	-6.8	7.3	14.5	5.9	13.2
1993	-0.1	1.6	0.1	2.6	1.0	17.0	0.9	22.0
1994	1.7	6.1	-2.7	-2.8	-0.4	9.5	-1.4	12.9
1995	1.7	3.7	2.1	7.6	6.8	15.3	10.9	28.6
1996	-0.7	4.4	0.2	2.5	6.8	8.9	6.4	16.5
1997	4.8	2.0	4.4	2.0	1.4	0.9	10.8	5.0
1998	-0.9	1.4	3.9	21.4	19.5	30.3	23.1	60.4
1999	1.9	8.8	5.4	9.4	7.3	14.3	15.2	35.9
2000	-0.9	-8.8	2.4	12.5	-1.8	-4.3	-0.4	-1.8
2001	1.7	29.3	-2.5	9.2	10.8	25.8	9.8	77.5
2002	-1.8	2.6	-7.3	2.5	16.7	29.2	6.3	35.9
2003	2.5	1.3	1.1	1.4	2.2	-5.3	5.9	-2.7
2004	2.5	2.9	1.8	6.0	6.2	9.6	10.8	19.6
2005	-2.3	-4.0	0.0	-2.3	5.5	9.7	3.1	3.0
2006	2.9	1.9	0.0	2.4	4.8	6.6	7.8	11.2
2007	0.9	2.3	-1.8	-1.5	-5.1	2.9	-6.0	3.7
2008	-9.8	-10.3	-8.6	-7.5	-3.7	-9.7	-20.6	-25.1
2009	-5.9	-1.6	0.0	4.6	3.2	9.6	-2.8	12.8
2010	3.2	0.6	-5.4	-6.2	5.1	8.1	2.6	2.0
2011	1.9	3.7	-1.8	-0.7	8.8	7.0	8.9	10.2
2012	4.5	3.6	4.0	4.5	-2.2	-3.1	6.2	4.8
Avg.	0.2 %	2.3 %	-0.5 %	2.5 %	4.7 %	9.7 %	4.4 %	15.8 %
Fq>0	61 %	74 %	52	65 %	78 %	83 %	74 %	83 %

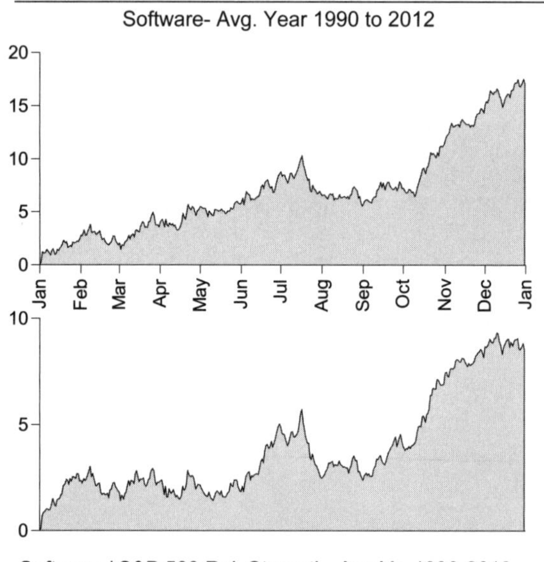

Software / S&P 500 Rel. Strength- Avg Yr. 1990-2012

2012-13 Strategy Performance

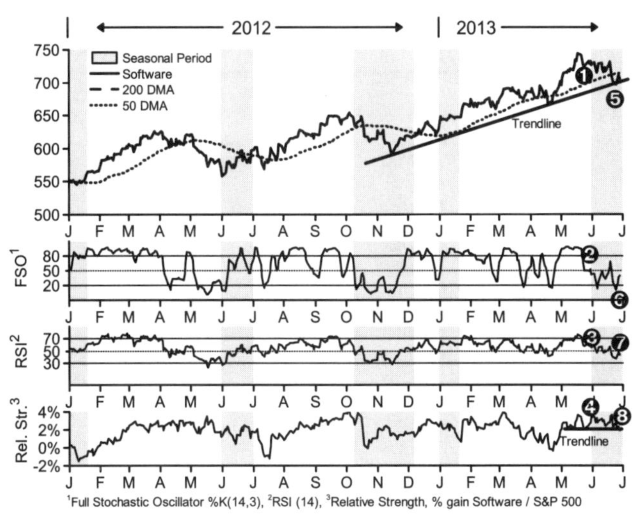

¹Full Stochastic Oscillator %K(14,3), ²RSI (14), ³Relative Strength, % gain Software / S&P 500

Software Performance

After a strong run at the end of April 2012, the software and services sector consolidated in mid-May and turned down before the start its seasonal trade.

Technical Conditions June 1st to June 30th, 2013

Entry Strategy –Buy Position on Entry Date–

At the start of the June 2013 seasonal time period, the software sector was performing negatively, after peaking a week earlier❶. On the entry date, the FSO was at 50❷ and the RSI was turning down in its upper range❸. On a relative basis to the S&P 500, the sector was performing at market❹.

Exit Strategy – Sell Position on Exit Date–

During its seasonal time period, the software sector corrected to its upward sloping trendline and then had a slight bounce to finish the trade❺. Both the FSO and the RSI ended below 50❻❼ and the sector ended on its market performance line❽. In the end, this leg of the software trade was unsuccessful. With a short term trade, very often the sector does not have time to overcome the negative start.

WEEK 37

Market Indices & Rates
Weekly Values**

Stock Markets	**2011**	**2012**
Dow	11,271	13,409
S&P500	1,190	1,445
Nasdaq	2,566	3,133
TSX	12,267	12,306
FTSE	5,247	5,821
DAX	5,332	7,318
Nikkei	8,641	8,958
Hang Seng	19,178	20,088

Commodities	**2011**	**2012**
Oil	88.93	97.61
Gold	1809.7	1742.9

Bond Yields	**2011**	**2012**
USA 5 Yr Treasury	0.91	0.68
USA 10 Yr T	2.03	1.76
USA 20 Yr T	2.92	2.52
Moody's Aaa	4.14	3.55
Moody's Baa	5.33	4.94
CAN 5 Yr T	1.47	1.43
CAN 10 Yr T	2.23	1.89

Money Market	**2011**	**2012**
USA Fed Funds	0.25	0.25
USA 3 Mo T-B	0.01	0.11
CAN tgt overnight rate	1.00	1.00
CAN 3 Mo T-B	0.87	1.00

Foreign Exchange	**2011**	**2012**
EUR/USD	1.38	1.29
GBP/USD	1.58	1.61
USD/CAD	0.99	0.97
USD/JPY	76.86	77.96

SEPTEMBER

M	T	W	T	F	S	S
1	2	3	4	5	6	7
8	9	10	11	12	13	14
15	16	17	18	19	20	21
22	23	24	25	26	27	28
29	30					

OCTOBER

M	T	W	T	F	S	S
		1	2	3	4	5
6	7	8	9	10	11	12
13	14	15	16	17	18	19
20	21	22	23	24	25	26
27	28	29	30	31		

NOVEMBER

M	T	W	T	F	S	S
					1	2
3	4	5	6	7	8	9
10	11	12	13	14	15	16
17	18	19	20	21	22	23
24	25	26	27	28	29	30

INFORMATION TECHNOLOGY USE IT OR LOSE IT

October 9th to January 17th

Information technology– the sector that investors love to love and love to hate. In recent years, most investors have made and lost money in this sector. When the sector is performing well, it can perform really well. When it is performing poorly, it can perform really poorly.

4.8% extra compared with the S&P 500

Technology stocks get bid up at the end of the year for three reasons.

First, a lot of companies operate with year end budgets and if they do not spend the money in their budget, they lose it.

In the last few months of the year, whatever money they have, they spend. Hence, the saying "use it or lose it."

The number one purchase item for this budget flush is technology equipment. An upgrade in technology equipment is something which a large number of employees in the company can benefit from and is easy to justify.

Second, consumers indirectly help push up technology stocks by purchasing electronic items during the holiday season.

Retail sales ramp up significantly on Black Friday, the Friday after Thanksgiving. Investors anticipate the upswing in sales and buy technology stocks.

Third, the "Conference Effect" helps maintain the momentum in January. This phenomenon is the result of investors increasing positions ahead of major conferences in order to benefit from positive announcements.

In the case of Information Technology, investors increase their holdings ahead of the Las Vegas Consumer Electronics Conference that typically occurs in the second week of January.

Info Tech & Nasdaq vs S&P 500
Oct 9 to Jan 17, 1989/90-2012/13

Positive [shaded]

	S&P 500	Info Tech	Nas daq	Diff IT- S&P500	Diff Nas- S&P500
1989/90	-6.0 %	-6.9 %	-9.3 %	-1.0 %	-3.3 %
1990/91	4.6	13.4	8.0	8.8	3.3
1991/92	10.0	16.4	21.2	6.4	11.2
1992/93	7.2	11.2	21.5	4.0	14.3
1993/94	2.8	12.5	3.7	9.7	0.8
1994/95	3.3	16.0	3.0	12.7	-0.3
1995/96	4.1	-8.9	-1.4	-13.0	-5.5
1996/97	10.8	21.2	8.8	10.4	-2.0
1997/98	-1.3	-14.2	-10.3	-12.9	-9.0
1998/99	29.6	71.8	65.5	42.2	35.9
1999/00	9.7	29.2	40.8	19.5	31.1
2001/01	-5.6	-21.7	-20.2	-16.1	-14.5
2001/02	7.2	26.8	23.7	19.6	16.5
2002/03	12.9	30.0	21.9	17.0	8.9
2003/04	10.3	14.2	13.0	4.0	2.8
2004/05	5.6	6.8	8.7	1.2	3.2
2005/06	7.3	9.7	10.2	2.4	2.9
2006/07	6.0	7.1	7.8	1.1	1.8
2007/08	-14.1	-14.9	-15.8	-0.7	-1.7
2008/09	-13.7	-12.0	-12.1	1.6	1.6
2009/10	6.6	9.9	7.7	3.3	1.1
2010/11	11.0	13.6	14.7	2.6	3.7
2011/12	12.0	8.4	10.0	-3.6	-1.9
2012/13	1.7	-2.9	0.8	-4.8	-1.0
Avg	5.1 %	9.9 %	9.2 %	4.8 %	4.2 %
Fq > 0	79 %	71 %	75 %	71 %	63 %

InfoTech Sector % Gain Avg. Year 1990 to 2012

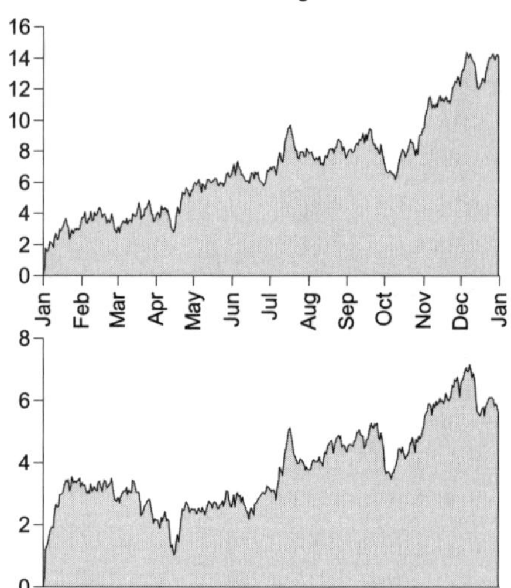

Info Tech / S&P 500 - Avg Yr. 1990 - 2012

Information Technology SP GIC Sector 45: An index designed to represent a cross section of information technology companies.

For more information on the information technology sector, see www.standardandpoors.com.

2012-13 Strategy Performance

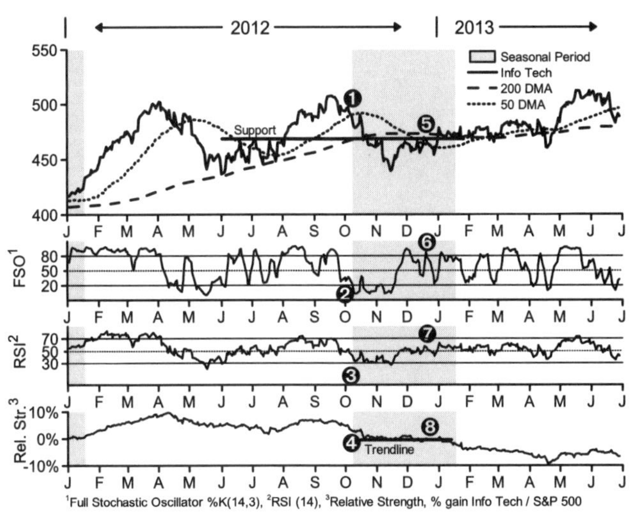

[1]Full Stochastic Oscillator %K(14,3), [2]RSI (14), [3]Relative Strength, % gain Info Tech / S&P 500

Information Technology Sector Performance

In 2012, the technology sector strongly outperformed the S&P 500 for the first four months and then underperformed for the next four months. Coming into the seasonal trade, the technology sector was pulling back and underperforming the S&P 500.

Technical Conditions October 9th to January 17th, 2013

Entry Strategy –Buy Position on Entry Date–

At the beginning of the seasonal trade in October 2012, the technology sector had just broken through its 50 day moving average and was falling❶. The FSO had just broken below 20❷ and the RSI was dropping to 30❸. Although these were negative signs, they did not preclude the trade from starting. The one concerning aspect was technology's negative relative performance compared to the S&P 500❹.

Exit Strategy – Sell Position Early–

Starting in mid-November, the technology sector started to increase, but only performed at market. Two-thirds the way through December and within the four week sell window before the seasonal end date, the FSO turned below 80❻, triggering an early sell signal. At the same time, the technology sector was pushing up against resistance❺, unsuccessfully for the third time in a month and the RSI responded by crossing below 50❼. It was not until the end of the month that the technology sector started to underperform the market, confirming the sell signal by the FSO. At the end of the trade, the technology sector was underperforming❽ and it continued this trend for the next four months.

WEEK 38

Market Indices & Rates
Weekly Values**

Stock Markets	2011	2012
Dow	11,088	13,574
S&P500	1,168	1,460
Nasdaq	2,536	3,179
TSX	11,872	12,420
FTSE	5,204	5,871
DAX	5,356	7,397
Nikkei	8,674	9,138
Hang Seng	18,468	20,686

Commodities	2011	2012
Oil	83.64	93.67
Gold	1759.4	1769.9

Bond Yields	2011	2012
USA 5 Yr Treasury	0.85	0.70
USA 10 Yr T	1.87	1.81
USA 20 Yr T	2.68	2.60
Moody's Aaa	3.98	3.55
Moody's Baa	5.18	4.88
CAN 5 Yr T	1.38	1.42
CAN 10 Yr T	2.12	1.89

Money Market	2011	2012
USA Fed Funds	0.25	0.25
USA 3 Mo T-B	0.01	0.11
CAN tgt overnight rate	1.00	1.00
CAN 3 Mo T-B	0.83	1.00

Foreign Exchange	2011	2012
EUR/USD	1.36	1.30
GBP/USD	1.55	1.62
USD/CAD	1.01	0.97
USD/JPY	76.47	78.46

SEPTEMBER

M	T	W	T	F	S	S
1	2	3	4	5	6	7
8	9	10	11	12	13	14
15	16	17	18	19	20	21
22	23	24	25	26	27	28
29	30					

OCTOBER

M	T	W	T	F	S	S
		1	2	3	4	5
6	7	8	9	10	11	12
13	14	15	16	17	18	19
20	21	22	23	24	25	26
27	28	29	30	31		

NOVEMBER

M	T	W	T	F	S	S
					1	2
3	4	5	6	7	8	9
10	11	12	13	14	15	16
17	18	19	20	21	22	23
24	25	26	27	28	29	30

CANADIAN BANKS — IN-OUT-IN AGAIN

①Oct 10-Dec 31 ②Jan 23-Apr 13

During the financial crisis of 2007/08, the Canadian banks were touted as being the best in the world. Canadians love to invest in their banks because the banks operate in a regulated environment and for long periods of time have grown their earnings and dividends. Although a lot of sectors in the Canadian market have very similar seasonally strong periods compared with the US, the seasonality for Canadian banks starts earlier than the US banks.

The difference in seasonally strong periods is driven by the difference in fiscal year-ends. The US banks have their year-end on December 31st and the Canadian banks on October 31st. Why does this make a difference? Typically, banks clean up their "books" at their year-end, by announcing any bad news. In addition, this is often the time period when the banks announce their positive news, including increases in dividends.

11.6% gain & and positive 79% of the time

The Canadian bank sector, from October 10th to December 31st for the years 1989 to 2012, has been positive 83% of the time and has produced an average gain of 5.5%. From January 23rd to April 13th, the sector has been positive 71% of the time and has produced an average gain of 5.8%. On a compounded basis, the strategy has been positive 79% of the time and produced an average gain of 11.6%.

Investors have a choice to either invest in each seasonal strategy separately and avoid the short time period between the strategies, or to hold the Canadian banking sector from October 10th to April 13th. Investors should consider that from January 1st to the 22nd, from 1990 to 2013, the sector has produced an average loss of 1.7% and has only been positive 46% of the time.

CDN Banks* vs. S&P/TSX Comp 1989/90 to 2012/13 Positive

Year	Oct 10 to Dec 31 TSX Comp	Oct 10 to Dec 31 CDN Banks	Jan 23 to Apr 13 TSX Comp	Jan 23 to Apr 13 CDN Banks	Compound Growth TSX Comp	Compound Growth CDN Banks
1989/90	-1.7 %	-1.8 %	-6.3 %	-9.1 %	-7.9 %	-10.8 %
1990/91	3.7	8.9	9.8	14.6	13.9	24.8
1991/92	5.2	10.2	-6.8	-11.6	-2.0	-2.6
1992/93	4.1	2.5	10.7	14.4	15.2	17.3
1993/94	6.3	6.8	-5.6	-13.3	0.3	-7.4
1994/95	-1.8	3.4	5.0	10.0	3.1	13.8
1995/96	4.9	3.5	3.6	-3.2	8.6	0.1
1996/97	9.0	15.1	-6.2	0.7	2.3	15.9
1997/98	-6.1	7.6	19.9	38.8	12.6	49.4
1998/99	18.3	28.0	4.8	13.0	24.0	44.6
1999/00	18.2	5.1	3.8	22.1	22.8	28.3
2000/01	-14.4	1.7	-14.1	-6.7	-26.4	-5.1
2001/02	11.9	6.5	2.3	8.2	14.5	15.1
2002/03	16.1	21.3	-4.3	2.6	11.1	24.4
2003/04	8.1	5.1	2.0	2.1	10.3	7.4
2004/05	4.9	6.2	4.5	6.9	9.6	13.5
2005/06	6.2	8.4	5.5	2.7	12.1	11.3
2006/07	10.4	8.4	6.9	3.2	18.0	11.8
2007/08	-3.0	-10.4	8.2	-3.5	5.0	-13.5
2008/09	-6.4	-14.8	9.4	24.4	2.4	6.1
2009/10	2.7	2.4	6.7	15.2	9.6	18.0
2010/11	7.2	-0.2	4.3	9.1	11.9	8.9
2011/12	3.2	3.1	-2.9	1.1	0.2	4.2
2012/13	1.3	4.4	-3.8	-2.0	-2.5	2.0
Avg.	4.5 %	5.5 %	2.4 %	5.8 %	7.0 %	11.6 %
Fq > 0	75 %	83 %	69 %	71 %	83 %	79 %

CDN Bank Sector* S&P GIC- Avg. Year 1990 to 2012

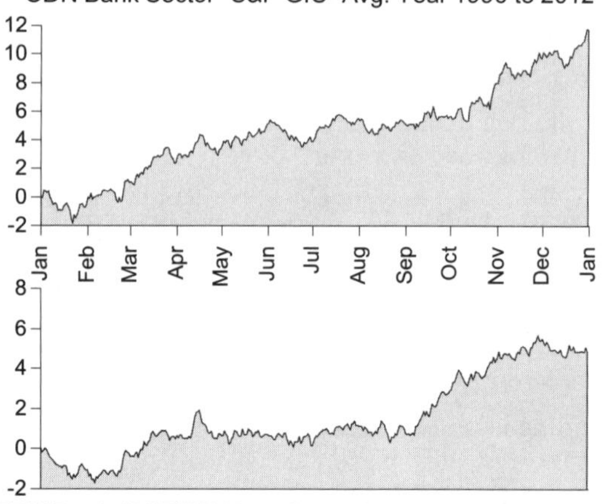

CDN Banks/S&P/TSX Rel. Strength - Avg Yr. 1990 - 2012

Alternate Strategy—
Investors can bridge the gap between the two positive seasonal trends for the bank sector by holding from October 10th to April 13th. Longer term investors may prefer this strategy, shorter term investors can use technical tools to determine the appropriate strategy.

** Banks SP GIC Canadian Sector Level 2*
An index designed to represent a cross section of Canadian banking companies. For more information on the bank sector, see www.standardandpoors.com.

2012-13 Strategy Performance

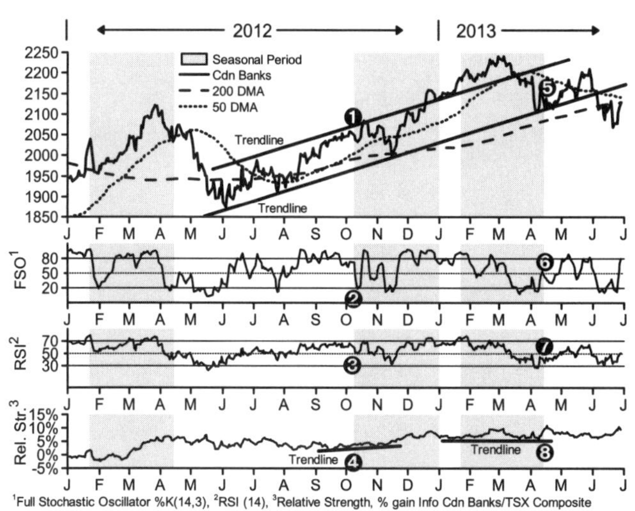

[1]Full Stochastic Oscillator %K(14,3), [2]RSI (14), [3]Relative Strength, % gain Info Cdn Banks/TSX Composite

Canadian Bank Sector Performance

The Canadian bank sector was on an uptrend since the beginning of June 2012 and was performing flat compared to the TSX Composite, setting up well for the October entry date into the trade.

Technical Conditions– October 10th to April 13th, 2013

Entry Strategy –Buy Position on Entry Date–

At the beginning of the trade in October 2012, the Canadian bank sector was at the upper boundary level of its trading range❶. Both the FSO and the RSI were in their upper bands❷❸. Most importantly, the sector was starting to show signs of outperforming the TSX Composite❹.

Exit Strategy – Sell Position on Exit Date–

The Canadian bank sector corrected sharply at the beginning of April 2013, just two weeks before the end of the seasonal period for the sector. It bounced off the upward trendline and settled back on the trendline at the end of the trade❺. The FSO and the RSI were in their neutral ranges❻❼. Large gains were made relative to the TSX Composite in the last few days of the trade as the sector strongly outperformed❽.

WEEK 39

Market Indices & Rates
Weekly Values**

Stock Markets	**2011**	**2012**
Dow	11,063	13,471
S&P500	1,156	1,444
Nasdaq	2,490	3,125
TSX	11,685	12,292
FTSE	5,185	5,798
DAX	5,539	7,324
Nikkei	8,600	8,978
Hang Seng	17,785	20,705

Commodities	**2011**	**2012**
Oil	81.45	91.33
Gold	1626.6	1763.6

Bond Yields	**2011**	**2012**
USA 5 Yr Treasury	0.96	0.65
USA 10 Yr T	1.97	1.68
USA 20 Yr T	2.74	2.45
Moody's Aaa	4.06	3.40
Moody's Baa	5.31	4.72
CAN 5 Yr T	1.44	1.33
CAN 10 Yr T	2.18	1.77

Money Market	**2011**	**2012**
USA Fed Funds	0.25	0.25
USA 3 Mo T-B	0.02	0.10
CAN tgt overnight rate	1.00	1.00
CAN 3 Mo T-B	0.80	0.97

Foreign Exchange	**2011**	**2012**
EUR/USD	1.35	1.29
GBP/USD	1.56	1.62
USD/CAD	1.03	0.98
USD/JPY	76.73	77.79

SEPTEMBER

M	T	W	T	F	S	S
1	2	3	4	5	6	7
8	9	10	11	12	13	14
15	16	17	18	19	20	21
22	23	24	25	26	27	28
29	30					

OCTOBER

M	T	W	T	F	S	S
		1	2	3	4	5
6	7	8	9	10	11	12
13	14	15	16	17	18	19
20	21	22	23	24	25	26
27	28	29	30	31		

NOVEMBER

M	T	W	T	F	S	S
					1	2
3	4	5	6	7	8	9
10	11	12	13	14	15	16
17	18	19	20	21	22	23
24	25	26	27	28	29	30

** Weekly avg closing values- except Fed Funds & CAN overnight tgt rate weekly closing values.

OCTOBER

	MONDAY	TUESDAY	WEDNESDAY
WEEK 40	29	30	1 30
WEEK 41	6 25	7 24	8 23
WEEK 42	13 18 USA Bond Market Closed-Columbus Day CAN Market Closed-Thanksgiving Day	14 17	15 16
WEEK 43	20 11	21 10	22 9
WEEK 44	27 4	28 3	29 2

OCTOBER

THURSDAY		FRIDAY	
2	29	**3**	28
9	22	**10**	21
16	15	**17**	14
23	8	**24**	7
30	1	**31**	

NOVEMBER

M	T	W	T	F	S	S
					1	2
3	4	5	6	7	8	9
10	11	12	13	14	15	16
17	18	19	20	21	22	23
24	25	26	27	28	29	30

DECEMBER

M	T	W	T	F	S	S
1	2	3	4	5	6	7
8	9	10	11	12	13	14
15	16	17	18	19	20	21
22	23	24	25	26	27	28
29	30	31				

JANUARY

M	T	W	T	F	S	S
			1	2	3	4
5	6	7	8	9	10	11
12	13	14	15	16	17	18
19	20	21	22	23	24	25
26	27	28	29	30	31	

FEBRUARY

M	T	W	T	F	S	S
						1
2	3	4	5	6	7	8
9	10	11	12	13	14	15
16	17	18	19	20	21	22
23	24	25	26	27	28	

OCTOBER
SUMMARY

	Dow Jones	S&P 500	Nasdaq	TSX Comp
Month Rank	7	7	8	9
# Up	37	37	22	18
# Down	26	26	19	20
% Pos	59	59	54	64
% Avg. Gain	0.5	0.7	0.6	0.0

Dow & S&P 1950-2012, Nasdaq 1972-2012, TSX 1985-2012

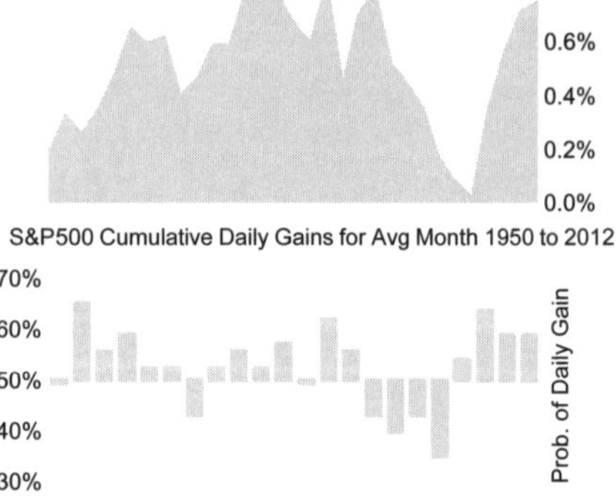

♦ October, on average is the most volatile month of the year and often provides opportunities for short-term traders. The first half of October tends to be positive. ♦ The second half of the month, leading up to the last four days, tends to be negative, and prone to large drops. ♦ Seasonal opportunities in mid-October include Canadian banks, technology and transportation. ♦ In late October, a lot of sectors start their seasonal period, including the materials, industrials, consumer discretionary and retail sectors.

BEST / WORST OCTOBER BROAD MKTS. 2003-2012

BEST OCTOBER MARKETS

- Russell 2000 (2011) 15.0%
- Nasdaq (2011) 11.1%
- Russell 1000 (2011) 11.1%

WORST OCTOBER MARKETS

- Nikkei 225 (2008) -23.8%
- Russell 2000 (2008) -20.9%
- Nasdaq (2008) -17.7%

Index Values End of Month

	2003	2004	2005	2006	2007	2008	2009	2010	2011	2012
Dow	9,801	10,027	10,440	12,081	13,930	9,325	9,713	11,118	11,955	13,096
S&P 500	1,051	1,130	1,207	1,378	1,549	969	1,036	1,183	1,253	1,412
Nasdaq	1,932	1,975	2,120	2,367	2,859	1,721	2,045	2,507	2,684	2,977
TSX Comp.	7,773	8,871	10,383	12,345	14,625	9,763	10,911	12,676	12,252	12,423
Russell 1000	1,081	1,162	1,261	1,437	1,623	1,004	1,089	1,256	1,331	1,498
Russell 2000	1,313	1,451	1,607	1,906	2,058	1,336	1,399	1,748	1,842	2,035
FTSE 100	4,288	4,624	5,317	6,129	6,722	4,377	5,045	5,675	5,544	5,783
Nikkei 225	10,560	10,771	13,607	16,399	16,738	8,577	10,035	9,202	8,988	8,928

Percent Gain for October

	2003	2004	2005	2006	2007	2008	2009	2010	2011	2012
Dow	5.7	-0.5	-1.2	3.4	0.2	-14.1	0.0	3.1	9.5	-2.5
S&P 500	5.5	1.4	-1.8	3.2	1.5	-16.9	-2.0	3.7	10.8	-2.0
Nasdaq	8.1	4.1	-1.5	4.8	5.8	-17.7	-3.6	5.9	11.1	-4.5
TSX Comp.	4.7	2.3	-5.7	5.0	3.7	-16.9	-4.2	2.5	5.4	0.9
Russell 1000	5.7	1.5	-1.9	3.3	1.6	-17.5	-2.3	3.8	11.1	-1.8
Russell 2000	8.3	1.9	-3.2	5.7	2.8	-20.9	-6.9	4.0	15.0	-2.2
FTSE 100	4.8	1.2	-2.9	2.8	3.9	-10.7	-1.7	2.3	8.1	0.7
Nikkei 225	3.3	-0.5	0.2	1.7	-0.3	-23.8	-1.0	-1.8	3.3	0.7

October Market Avg. Performance 2003 to 2012(1)

Dow Jones	0.4%
S&P 500	0.3%
Nasdaq	1.3%
TSX Comp (CAN)	-0.2%
Russell 1000 (Lg Cap)	0.3%
Russell 2000 (Sm Cap)	0.5%
FTSE 100	0.8%
Nikkei 225	-1.8%

-3% -2% -1% 0% 1% 2%

Interest Corner Oct(2)

	Fed Funds % (3)	3 Mo. T-Bill %(4)	10 Yr %(5)	20 Yr %(6)
2012	0.25	0.11	1.72	2.46
2011	0.25	0.01	2.17	2.89
2010	0.25	0.12	2.63	3.64
2009	0.25	0.05	3.41	4.19
2008	1.00	0.46	4.01	4.74

(1) Russell Data provided by Russell (2) Federal Reserve Bank of St. Louis- end of month values (3) Target rate set by FOMC (4)(5)(6) Constant yield maturities.

OCTOBER SECTOR PERFORMANCE

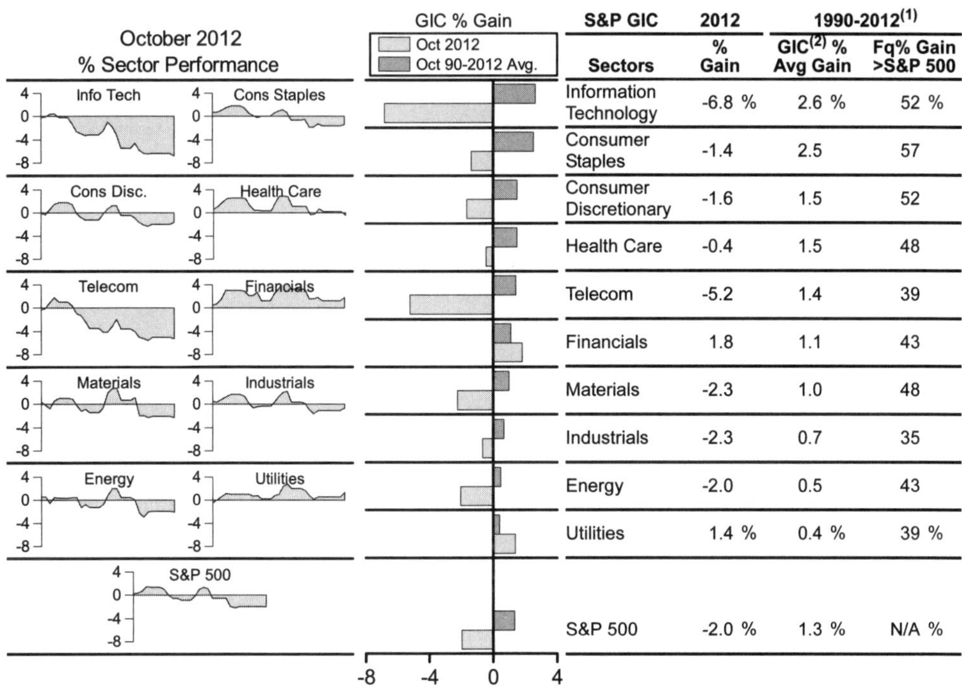

S&P GIC Sectors	2012 % Gain	1990-2012[1] GIC[2] % Avg Gain	1990-2012[1] Fq% Gain >S&P 500
Information Technology	-6.8 %	2.6 %	52 %
Consumer Staples	-1.4	2.5	57
Consumer Discretionary	-1.6	1.5	52
Health Care	-0.4	1.5	48
Telecom	-5.2	1.4	39
Financials	1.8	1.1	43
Materials	-2.3	1.0	48
Industrials	-2.3	0.7	35
Energy	-2.0	0.5	43
Utilities	1.4 %	0.4 %	39 %
S&P 500	-2.0 %	1.3 %	N/A %

Sector Commentary

♦ After a positive September 2012, the S&P 500 had a lackluster performance for most of October. Towards the end of October, the market started to correct. In the end, it produced a loss of 2% for the month.♦ After a strong August and a positive September, the technology sector faded quickly in October and ended up producing a loss of 6.8%.♦ After a strong month in September, the telecom sector produced a large loss of 5.2%.♦ On a positive note, the financial sector produced a strong gain of 1.8%, outperforming its average performance since 1990. The outperformance of this sector was indicating positive times ahead.

Sub-Sector Commentary

♦ The top performing sub-sector was the homebuilders sector, producing a strong gain of 6.9%. ♦ The bottom performing sub-sectors in 2012 were the ones that typically underperform. The metals and mining sub-sector produced a loss of 2.0%, gold produced a loss of 3.2% and silver, a loss of 6.8%.♦ Gold typically finishes its seasonal run towards the beginning of October and then performs poorly for the rest of the month.

SELECTED SUB-SECTORS[3]

Sub-Sector	2012 % Gain	GIC % Avg Gain	Fq% Gain >S&P 500
Agriculture (1994-2012)	-1.3 %	6.4 %	79 %
Railroads	1.1	4.4	74
Software & Services	-4.5	4.3	65
Transportation	2.5	3.9	74
Pharma	0.2	2.1	57
Steel	-0.9	2.0	39
Chemicals	-2.6	1.9	57
SOX (1995-2012)	-4.0	1.8	44
Retail	-1.8	1.6	52
Biotech (1993-2012)	-3.0	1.3	45
Homebuilders	6.9	0.7	39
Banks	-3.7	0.7	39
Metals & Mining	-2.0	-0.1	35
Gold (London PM)	-3.2	-1.0	26
Silver	-6.8	-1.5	35

UNION PACIFIC – JUMP ON BOARD
①Oct10-Nov4 ②Mar11-May5

Union Pacific follows the general seasonal pattern of the transportation sector: a strong spring, weak summer and a strong autumn.

The success of this trade can be seen in the frequency of how often the compound gains of Union Pacific, across both of its seasonal periods, outperforms the S&P 500. The seasonal period from October 10th to November 4th, for the years 1989 to 2012, has a positive success rate of 79%, and it has produced more than double the average gain (6.4% vs. 2.7%) of the S&P 500. The period from March 11th to May 5th, for the years 1990 to 2013, has a positive success rate of 75%, and almost triple the average gain (9.1% vs. 3.4%) compared with the S&P 500.

Union Pacific vs. S&P 500 1989/90 to 2012/13 Positive

	Oct10 to Nov4		Mar11 to May5		Compound Growth	
Year	S&P 500	UNP	S&P 500	UNP	S&P 500	UNP
1989/90	-6.2	-7.0 %	0.1	-5.1 %	-6.0	-11.8 %
1990/91	2.2	-3.4	1.6	9.3	3.8	5.6
1991/92	3.6	7.9	2.5	14.0	6.1	23.1
1992/93	3.6	9.6	-2.6	6.3	0.9	16.5
1993/94	-0.6	2.1	-2.7	-0.4	-3.3	1.6
1994/95	1.6	0.5	6.2	7.6	7.9	8.1
1995/96	2.1	4.0	1.3	1.1	3.4	5.1
1996/97	1.4	13.3	2.1	5.9	3.5	19.9
1997/98	-3.1	-3.8	4.8	9.1	1.6	4.9
1998/99	13.6	10.8	4.7	26.6	19.0	40.3
1999/00	2.0	6.8	2.7	20.7	4.7	28.9
2000/01	1.8	19.7	2.7	-1.6	4.5	17.8
2001/02	2.9	16.5	-7.8	-4.4	-5.2	11.3
2002/03	16.9	9.9	14.8	13.9	34.2	25.2
2003/04	1.4	8.6	-0.2	-4.5	1.2	3.7
2004/05	3.5	5.8	-3.0	-2.5	0.4	3.2
2005/06	2.0	-0.9	3.5	8.7	5.6	7.7
2006/07	1.0	1.0	7.3	18.1	8.4	19.3
2007/08	-3.6	6.7	10.5	23.6	6.6	31.9
2008/09	10.5	22.1	25.6	45.5	38.8	77.6
2009/10	-2.3	-1.1	1.8	3.8	-0.6	2.6
2010/11	4.8	8.1	3.1	8.1	8.0	16.9
2011/12	8.5	14.0	-0.1	5.5	8.3	20.3
2012/13	-1.9	2.3	4.1	7.7	2.1	10.2
Avg.	2.7 %	6.4 %	3.4 %	9.1 %	6.4 %	16.4 %
Fq>0	75 %	79 %	75 %	75 %	83 %	96 %

16.4% gain

Both of these seasonal trades are strong trades by themselves, as the average gain for the Union Pacific trade is more than double the S&P 500 for each trade.

In addition, Union Pacific's frequency of positive performance over both seasonal periods is a very strong 96%, which is better than the S&P 500's success rate of 83%. It should also be noted that the only losing compound trade took place twenty-three years ago. Not only has this trade produced large returns, with a high frequency, but the drawdowns have also been small.

Investors should note that Union Pacific typically has a weak summer period, and if it is held past the end of its seasonal period in May, a sell criteria should be established for when the stock starts to weaken.

UNP - stock symbol for Union Pacific which trades on the NYSE exchange. Data adjusted for stock splits.

Union Pacific- Avg. Year 1990 to 2012

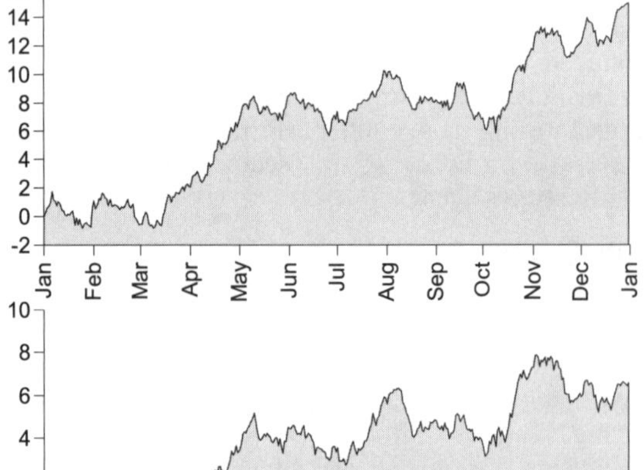

Union Pacific / S&P 500 Rel. Strength- Avg Yr. 1990-2012

2012-13 Strategy Performance

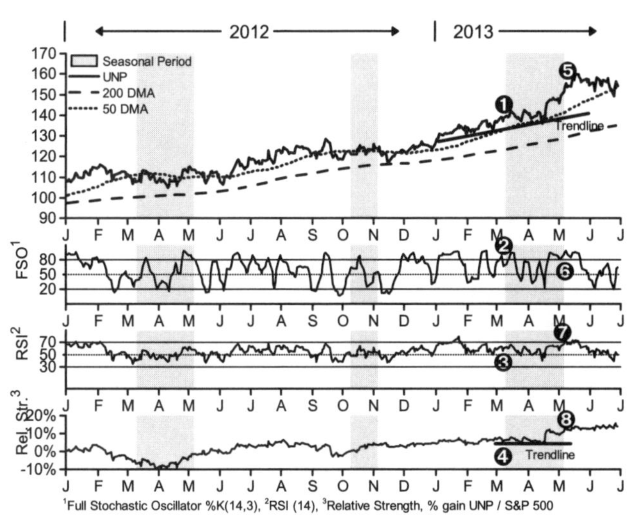

¹Full Stochastic Oscillator %K(14,3), ²RSI (14), ³Relative Strength, % gain UNP / S&P 500

Union Pacific Performance

After consolidating in price from August to November 2012, UNP bounced off its 200 day moving average and started to increase into its seasonal period which starts in March.

Technical Conditions– March 11th to May 5th, 2013

Entry Strategy –Buy Position on Entry Date–

At the beginning of the seasonal trade in March 2013, UNP was in a steady uptrend❶, but performing at market❹. The FSO was just below 80❷ and the RSI was just below 70❸. In other words, there was nothing remarkable about the entry into the seasonal trade.

Exit Strategy– Sell Position Late–

On April 18th, 2013, UNP released earnings that beat estimates. As a result, the stock jumped in price. After the initial reaction, the stock settled down and performed at market. On the seasonal exit date, the stock was rising rapidly in price❺, slightly outperforming the S&P 500❽, the FSO was above 80❻ and had not turned down and the RSI was just below 70❼. As a result, there was technical justification to maintain the trade until the FSO crossed below 80 later in May. Although holding the trade provided extra value, the seasonal trade without adjustment was a success both on an absolute basis and relative to the S&P 500.

WEEK 40

Market Indices & Rates
Weekly Values**

Stock Markets	**2011**	**2012**
Dow	10,926	13,536
S&P500	1,138	1,453
Nasdaq	2,437	3,131
TSX	11,451	12,398
FTSE	5,143	5,831
DAX	5,477	7,332
Nikkei	8,502	8,803
Hang Seng	16,988	20,936
Commodities	**2011**	**2012**
Oil	79.71	90.82
Gold	1639.5	1782.7
Bond Yields	**2011**	**2012**
USA 5 Yr Treasury	0.96	0.63
USA 10 Yr T	1.93	1.67
USA 20 Yr T	2.63	2.45
Moody's Aaa	3.91	3.44
Moody's Baa	5.26	4.69
CAN 5 Yr T	1.40	1.31
CAN 10 Yr T	2.15	1.75
Money Market	**2011**	**2012**
USA Fed Funds	0.25	0.25
USA 3 Mo T-B	0.01	0.11
CAN tgt overnight rate	1.00	1.00
CAN 3 Mo T-B	0.85	0.96
Foreign Exchange	**2011**	**2012**
EUR/USD	1.33	1.30
GBP/USD	1.55	1.61
USD/CAD	1.05	0.98
USD/JPY	76.74	78.36

OCTOBER

M	T	W	T	F	S	S
		1	2	3	4	5
6	7	8	9	10	11	12
13	14	15	16	17	18	19
20	21	22	23	24	25	26
27	28	29	30	31		

NOVEMBER

M	T	W	T	F	S	S
					1	2
3	4	5	6	7	8	9
10	11	12	13	14	15	16
17	18	19	20	21	22	23
24	25	26	27	28	29	30

DECEMBER

M	T	W	T	F	S	S
1	2	3	4	5	6	7
8	9	10	11	12	13	14
15	16	17	18	19	20	21
22	23	24	25	26	27	28
29	30	31				

HOMEBUILDERS— TIME TO BREAK & TIME TO BUILD

①SELL SHORT (Apr27-Jun13) & ②LONG (Oct28-Feb3)

The homebuilders sector has been in the spotlight for the last few years: first when the mortgage meltdown occurred in 2007 and 2008, and more recently as the housing market has bounced back giving the homebuilders sector a boost.

18.6% extra & positive 18 times out of 23

Historically, the best time to be in the homebuilders sector has been from October 28th to February 3rd. In this time period, during the years 1990/91 to 2012/13, the homebuilders sector has produced an average gain of 18.8% and have been positive 91% of the time.

In the three years where losses occurred, the drawdowns were relatively small, at least compared to the large gains that the homebuilders sector has produced during its strong seasonal time period.

Generally the rest of the year, other than the strong seasonal period, is a time that seasonal investors should avoid, as not only has the average performance relative to the S&P 500 been negative, but the homebuilders sector has produced both large gains and losses. In other words, the risk is substantially higher that a large drawdown will occur.

This is particularly true for the time period from April 27th to June 13th. In this time period from 1990 to 2012, the homebuilders sector produced an average loss of 3.8% and was only positive 30% of the time.

Homebuilders: SP GIC Sector: An index designed to represent a cross section of homebuilding companies. For more information, see www.standardandpoors.com.

Homebuilders (HB) vs. S&P 500 1990 to 2012

Negative Short ☐ Positive Long ▒

	SHORT Apr 27 to Jun 13		LONG Oct 28 to Feb 3		Compound Growth	
Year	S&P 500	HB	S&P 500	HB	S&P 500	HB
1990	9.6 %	7.9 %	12.6 %	58.0 %	1.8 %	45.5 %
1991	-0.4	-4.8	6.6	41.2	7.0	48.0
1992	0.2	-11.5	6.9	26.7	6.7	41.2
1993	3.2	12.6	3.5	8.6	0.2	-5.1
1994	1.6	-4.0	2.8	-4.0	1.1	-0.2
1995	4.6	11.1	9.7	16.7	4.7	3.7
1996	2.2	10.6	12.2	6.3	9.8	-4.9
1997	16.7	22.6	14.7	24.8	-4.5	-3.4
1998	-0.8	-10.6	19.4	12.4	20.4	24.2
1999	-4.9	-7.1	9.9	-3.9	15.3	2.9
2000	0.6	-3.8	-2.2	18.6	-2.7	23.1
2001	0.6	-17.5	1.6	43.1	1.0	68.1
2002	-6.2	-5.3	-4.2	6.7	1.8	12.3
2003	10.0	31.5	10.2	7.6	-0.8	-26.3
2004	0.1	-2.6	5.7	23.7	5.6	26.9
2005	4.3	11.9	7.2	14.8	2.7	1.1
2006	-6.3	-27.1	5.2	16.8	11.7	48.4
2007	1.4	-7.9	-9.1	8.8	-10.4	17.4
2008	-2.7	-25.3	-1.2	27.7	1.4	60.0
2009	9.2	-25.1	3.2	15.5	-6.3	44.4
2010	-9.9	-22.9	10.5	12.9	21.5	38.7
2011	-5.6	-11.2	4.7	35.0	10.6	50.1
2012	-6.1	-9.3	7.2	13.7	13.7	24.3
Avg.	0.9 %	-3.8 %	6.0 %	18.8 %	4.9 %	23.5 %
Fq>0	61	30	83	91	78	78

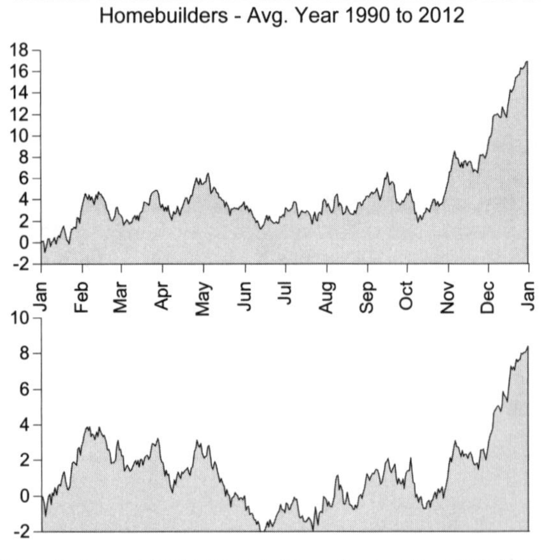

Homebuilders / S&P 500 Rel. Strength- Avg Yr. 1990-2012

2012-13 Strategy Performance

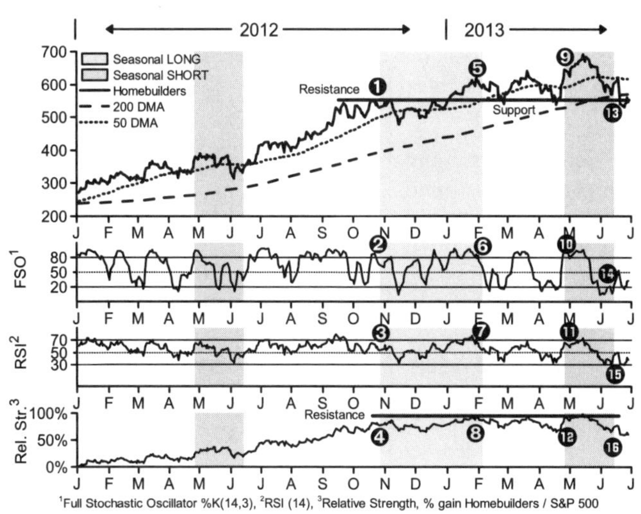

[1]Full Stochastic Oscillator %K(14,3), [2]RSI (14), [3]Relative Strength, % gain Homebuilders / S&P 500

Homebuilders Sector Performance

The homebuilders sector performed very well in 2012, doubling in price as the housing market was on the mend from the 2008 crash. Coming into the long trade in October, the sector paused and consolidated starting in mid-September.

Technical Conditions– October 28 to February 3 (LONG)

Entry Strategy –Buy Position on Entry Date–

Despite the strong performance of the homebuilders sector earlier in 2012, it was still set up for a buy at the beginning of its seasonal period, pushing up against its resistance level❶. At the same time, both the FSO and RSI were in their upper bands❷❸ and the sector was outperforming the S&P 500❹.

Exit Strategy –Exit Position Early–

Just before the seasonal trade ended, the homebuilders sector started to turn down❺, and the FSO dropped below 80❻, and the RSI dropped below 70❼. The sector outperformed the S&P 500 in its seasonal trade, but was starting to turn down❽.

Technical Conditions– April 27 to June 13 (SHORT)

Entry Strategy –Buy Position on Entry Date–

The trade was well setup after the homebuilders sector spiked just before the start date❾. The FSO was above 80❿ and the RSI was close to 70⓫. Relative performance to the S&P 500 was just starting to roll over⓬.

Exit Strategy –Sell Position on Exit Date–

After falling starting in mid-May, the homebuilders sector reached its support level in June⓭, close to the exit date. The FSO was below 30⓮ and the RSI touching 20⓯ and the sector finished successfully by underperforming the S&P 500⓰.

WEEK 41

Market Indices & Rates Weekly Values**

Stock Markets	**2011**	**2012**
Dow	11,498	13,411
S&P500	1,205	1,438
Nasdaq	2,608	3,065
TSX	11,975	12,230
FTSE	5,421	5,810
DAX	5,918	7,249
Nikkei	8,771	8,612
Hang Seng	18,288	20,963

Commodities	**2011**	**2012**
Oil	85.56	91.38
Gold	1668.0	1768.9

Bond Yields	**2011**	**2012**
USA 5 Yr Treasury	1.14	0.67
USA 10 Yr T	2.22	1.71
USA 20 Yr T	2.92	2.47
Moody's Aaa	4.10	3.44
Moody's Baa	5.52	4.60
CAN 5 Yr T	1.55	1.37
CAN 10 Yr T	2.32	1.80

Money Market	**2011**	**2012**
USA Fed Funds	0.25	0.25
USA 3 Mo T-B	0.02	0.11
CAN tgt overnight rate	1.00	1.00
CAN 3 Mo T-B	0.87	0.98

Foreign Exchange	**2011**	**2012**
EUR/USD	1.37	1.29
GBP/USD	1.57	1.60
USD/CAD	1.02	0.98
USD/JPY	76.94	78.31

OCTOBER

M	T	W	T	F	S	S
		1	2	3	4	5
6	7	8	9	10	11	12
13	14	15	16	17	18	19
20	21	22	23	24	25	26
27	28	29	30	31		

NOVEMBER

M	T	W	T	F	S	S
					1	2
3	4	5	6	7	8	9
10	11	12	13	14	15	16
17	18	19	20	21	22	23
24	25	26	27	28	29	30

DECEMBER

M	T	W	T	F	S	S
1	2	3	4	5	6	7
8	9	10	11	12	13	14
15	16	17	18	19	20	21
22	23	24	25	26	27	28
29	30	31				

CONSUMER DISCRETIONARY TIME TO SHOP
October 28th to April 12th

Consumers keep holding up the economy by spending money. In recent years, they have been assisted by the Fed's easy money policy keeping interest rates low.

Consumers tend to increase their spending starting in October as the holiday season approaches. This trend peaks later in the beginning of December and there is a brief pullback in spending with a low being formed in December. Spending quickly starts to ramp up again in March.

5.5% gain & positive 79% of the time positive

Investors take advantage of this trend by investing in consumer discretionary companies that benefit from a corresponding increase in earnings.

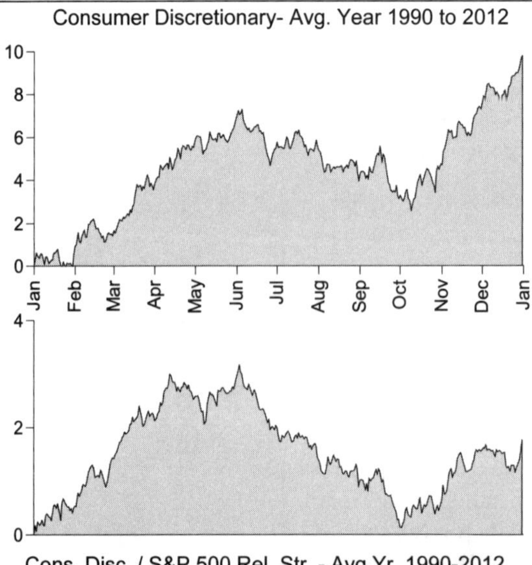

Consumer Discretionary vs. S&P 500
1989 to 2013

Positive (shaded)

Oct 28 to Apr 12	S&P 500	Cons. Disc.	Diff
1989-90	-2.6%	-0.4%	2.2%
1990-91	15.2	25.0	9.8
1991-92	-3.1	4.4	7.4
1992-93	2.9	3.9	1.0
1993-94	-4.1	-3.3	0.7
1994-95	10.4	6.9	-3.5
1995-96	3.4	6.9	3.5
1996-97	-0.4	0.9	1.4
1997-98	14.5	19.8	5.3
1998-99	10.5	19.4	8.9
1999-00	-0.1	-1.0	-0.9
2000-01	-10.4	0.4	10.7
2001-02	-3.2	2.0	5.2
2002-03	-1.3	3.1	4.4
2003-04	3.0	2.3	-0.7
2004-05	-2.0	-6.4	-4.4
2005-06	3.2	2.4	-0.8
2006-07	2.1	1.3	-0.8
2007-08	-9.2	-6.3	3.0
2008-09	-5.2	2.3	7.4
2009-10	7.3	13.9	6.6
2010-11	4.5	4.3	-0.3
2011-12	10.3	14.5	4.2
2012-13	11.4	14.6	3.2
Avg	2.4%	5.5%	3.1%
Fq > 0	54%	79%	71%

On an absolute basis, the consumer discretionary sector tends to weaken in June, providing average negative returns until October. Relative to the S&P 500, the sector peaks in mid-April.

From 1989/90 to 2012/13, during the time period from October 28th to April 12th, the consumer discretionary sector produced an average rate of return of 5.5% and was positive 79% of the time. In this time period, there were two periods of negative performance, with losses of 6% that took place in 2004/05 and 2007/08. Underperformance relative to the S&P 500 were relatively small, with the worst loss being 4.4% (2004/05).

The worst string of underperformance relative to the S&P 500 occurred from 2003/04 to 2006/07. In this time period, the U.S. GDP was declining at a steady rate.

In the other underperformance years, the GDP was also heading lower (1994/95, 1999/00, 2012/11). Although the consumer discretionary sector has performed very well during its seasonal period, investors should be cautious during time periods of economic contraction.

** Consumer Discretionary- SP GIC Sector: An index designed to represent a cross section of consumer discretionary companies.*

For more information, see www.standardandpoors.com.

2012-13 Strategy Performance

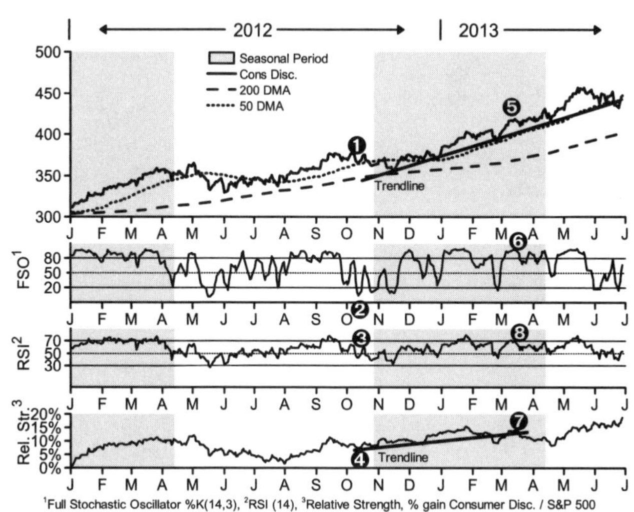

¹Full Stochastic Oscillator %K(14,3), ²RSI (14), ³Relative Strength, % gain Consumer Disc. / S&P 500

Consumer Discretionary Performance

The consumer discretionary sector was positive during the unfavourable period in the summer of 2012, but it underperformed the S&P 500. It corrected one month before the start of its seasonally strong period, setting up well for the start of its seasonal period.

Technical Conditions– October 28th to April 12th, 2013

Entry Strategy –Buy Position Early–

Just before the start of its seasonal period in October 2012, the consumer discretionary sector corrected❶ bringing the FSO below 20. It then rose above 20❷, triggering an early buy signal. The RSI crossed above 50❸ and the sector started to show outperformance relative to the S&P 500❹. In the end, it would have been better to wait for the "official" start date as the sector corrected once again, before starting to perform well.

Exit Strategy– Exit Position Early–

After performing strongly for the first three months of the trade, the consumer discretionary sector started to underperform the S&P 500. At the same time, the sector was still in an uptrend and above its 50 day moving average❺. Within the four week sell window, the FSO turned below 80❻, triggering an early sell signal. The RSI had previously turned down from 70❼. At the same time, the sector was performing at market❽. The trade ended up being positive and outperforming the S&P 500.

WEEK 42

Market Indices & Rates
Weekly Values**

Stock Markets	**2011**	**2012**
Dow	11,566	13,485
S&P500	1,218	1,449
Nasdaq	2,622	3,070
TSX	11,921	12,396
FTSE	5,434	5,880
DAX	5,878	7,370
Nikkei	8,751	8,814
Hang Seng	18,254	21,368
Commodities	**2011**	**2012**
Oil	86.67	91.64
Gold	1645.6	1742.3
Bond Yields	**2011**	**2012**
USA 5 Yr Treasury	1.07	0.74
USA 10 Yr T	2.20	1.79
USA 20 Yr T	2.92	2.55
Moody's Aaa	3.98	3.50
Moody's Baa	5.41	4.55
CAN 5 Yr T	1.56	1.38
CAN 10 Yr T	2.32	1.86
Money Market	**2011**	**2012**
USA Fed Funds	0.25	0.25
USA 3 Mo T-B	0.02	0.10
CAN tgt overnight rate	1.00	1.00
CAN 3 Mo T-B	0.88	0.96
Foreign Exchange	**2011**	**2012**
EUR/USD	1.38	1.30
GBP/USD	1.58	1.61
USD/CAD	1.02	0.98
USD/JPY	76.71	79.01

OCTOBER

M	T	W	T	F	S	S
		1	2	3	4	5
6	7	8	9	10	11	12
13	14	15	16	17	18	19
20	21	22	23	24	25	26
27	28	29	30	31		

NOVEMBER

M	T	W	T	F	S	S
					1	2
3	4	5	6	7	8	9
10	11	12	13	14	15	16
17	18	19	20	21	22	23
24	25	26	27	28	29	30

DECEMBER

M	T	W	T	F	S	S
1	2	3	4	5	6	7
8	9	10	11	12	13	14
15	16	17	18	19	20	21
22	23	24	25	26	27	28
29	30	31				

** Weekly avg closing values- except Fed Funds & CAN overnight tgt rate weekly closing values.

RETAIL - SHOP EARLY

IInd of **II** Retail Strategies for the Year
October 28th to November 29th

The *Retail – Shop Early* strategy is the second retail sector strategy of the year and it occurs before the biggest shopping season of the year – the Christmas holiday season.

3.0% extra & 78% of the time better than S&P 500

The time to go shopping for retail stocks is at the end of October, which is about one month before Thanksgiving. It is the time when two favorable influences happen at the same time.

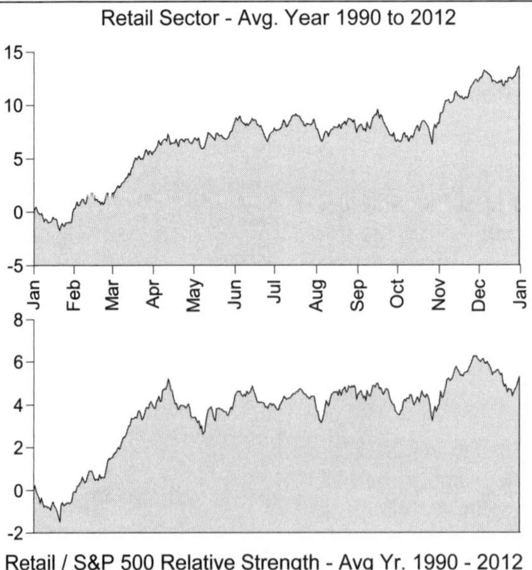

Retail / S&P 500 Relative Strength - Avg Yr. 1990 - 2012

First, historically the three best months in a row for the stock market have been November, December and January. The end of October usually represents an excellent buying opportunity, not only for the next three months, but the next six months.

Second, investors tend to buy retail stocks in anticipation of a strong holiday sales season. At the same time that the market tends to increase, investors are attracted back into the retail sector.

Retail sales tend to be lower in the summer and a lot of investors view investing in retail stocks at this time as dead money. During the summertime, investors prefer not to invest in this sector until it comes back into favor towards the end of October.

The trick to investing is not to be too early, but early. If an investor gets into a sector too early, they can suffer from the frustration of having dead money– having an investment that goes nowhere, while the rest of the market increases.

If an investor moves into a sector too late, there is very little upside potential. In fact, this can be a dangerous strategy because if the sales or earnings numbers disappoint the analysts, the sector can severely correct.

For the *Retail – Shop Early* strategy the time to enter is approximately one month before Black Friday.

Coincidentally, the end of October is also typically a good time to enter the broad market.

Retail Sector vs. S&P 500 1990 to 2012

Oct 28 to Nov 29	S&P 500	Retail	Diff
1990	3.8 %	9.9 %	6.0 %
1991	-2.3	2.7	5.0
1992	2.8	5.5	2.8
1993	-0.6	6.3	6.9
1994	-2.3	0.4	2.7
1995	4.8	9.5	4.7
1996	8.0	0.4	-7.6
1997	8.9	16.9	7.9
1998	11.9	20.4	8.4
1999	8.6	14.1	5.5
2000	-2.7	9.9	12.6
2001	3.2	7.9	4.7
2002	4.3	-1.7	-6.0
2003	2.6	2.5	-0.1
2004	4.7	7.0	2.3
2005	6.7	9.9	3.2
2006	1.6	0.2	-1.4
2007	-4.3	-7.5	-3.2
2008	5.6	7.5	1.9
2009	2.6	3.6	1.0
2010	0.5	5.2	4.7
2011	-7.0	-4.5	2.5
2012	0.3	5.1	4.8
Avg.	2.7 %	5.7 %	3.0 %
Fq > 0	74 %	87 %	78 %

(Shaded: Positive)

2011-12-13 Strategy Performance

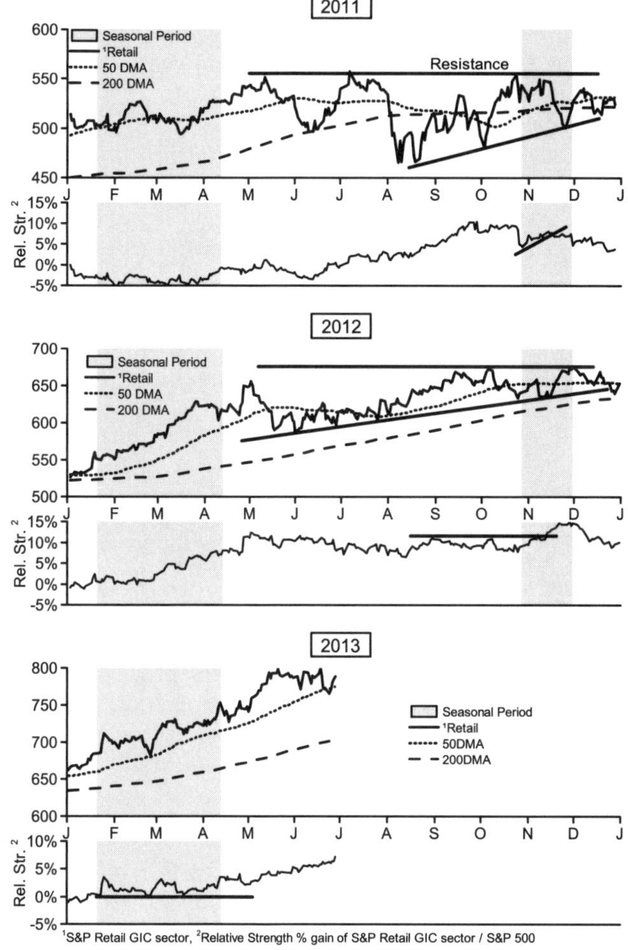

¹S&P Retail GIC sector, ²Relative Strength % gain of S&P Retail GIC sector / S&P 500

Retail Sector Performance– October to November 2012

The retail sector in the autumn leg of its seasonal performance in 2012 had been correcting as the seasonal entry date approached and dropped below its 50 day moving average one week before the start date. It corrected at its trendline as the seasonal period started. At the same time, it started to strongly outperform the S&P 500.

At the end of the trade, the sector reached its peak at its resistance level and started to underperform the S&P 500. Overall, it was a very successful trade, producing a 5.1% gain and outperforming the S&P 500.

WEEK 43

Market Indices & Rates
Weekly Values**

Stock Markets	**2011**	**2012**
Dow	11,986	13,147
S&P500	1,259	1,416
Nasdaq	2,693	2,993
TSX	12,289	12,285
FTSE	5,609	5,819
DAX	6,160	7,225
Nikkei	8,866	8,994
Hang Seng	19,303	21,704
Commodities	**2011**	**2012**
Oil	92.33	86.47
Gold	1696.4	1715.2
Bond Yields	**2011**	**2012**
USA 5 Yr Treasury	1.11	0.78
USA 10 Yr T	2.28	1.81
USA 20 Yr T	3.02	2.56
Moody's Aaa	3.97	3.50
Moody's Baa	5.36	4.54
CAN 5 Yr T	1.62	1.40
CAN 10 Yr T	2.38	1.86
Money Market	**2011**	**2012**
USA Fed Funds	0.25	0.25
USA 3 Mo T-B	0.01	0.12
CAN tgt overnight rate	1.00	1.00
CAN 3 Mo T-B	0.91	1.00
Foreign Exchange	**2011**	**2012**
EUR/USD	1.40	1.30
GBP/USD	1.60	1.60
USD/CAD	1.00	0.99
USD/JPY	76.03	79.91

OCTOBER

M	T	W	T	F	S	S
		1	2	3	4	5
6	7	8	9	10	11	12
13	14	15	16	17	18	19
20	21	22	23	24	25	26
27	28	29	30	31		

NOVEMBER

M	T	W	T	F	S	S
					1	2
3	4	5	6	7	8	9
10	11	12	13	14	15	16
17	18	19	20	21	22	23
24	25	26	27	28	29	30

DECEMBER

M	T	W	T	F	S	S
1	2	3	4	5	6	7
8	9	10	11	12	13	14
15	16	17	18	19	20	21
22	23	24	25	26	27	28
29	30	31				

** Weekly avg closing values- except Fed Funds & CAN overnight tgt rate weekly closing values.

INDUSTRIAL STRENGTH
①Oct 28-Dec 31 ②Jan 23-May 5

The industrial sector's seasonal trends are largely the same as the broad market, such as the S&P 500. Although the trends are similar, there still exists an opportunity to take advantage of the time period when the industrials tend to outperform.

12.4% gain & positive 92% of the time

Industrials tend to outperform in the favorable six months, but there is an opportunity to temporarily get out of the sector to avoid a time period when the sector has, on average, decreased before turning positive again.

The overall strategy is to be invested in the industrial sector from October 28th to December 31st, sell at the end of the day on the 31st and re-enter the sector to be invested from January 23rd to May 5th.

Using the complete *Industrial Strength* strategy; from 1989/90 to 2012/13 the industrial sector has produced a total compounded average annual gain of 12.4%.

In addition, it has been positive 92% of the time and has outperformed the S&P 500, 75% of the time.

During the time period from January 1st to January 22nd, the industrial sector has on average lost 0.7% and has only been positive 54% of the time.

It should be noted that longer term investors may decide to be invested during the whole time period from October 28th to May 5th.

Shorter term investors may decide to use technical analysis to determine if and when they should temporarily sell the industrials sector during its weak period from January 1st to January 22nd.

Industrials vs. S&P 500 1989/90 to 2012/123 Positive

Year	Oct 28 to Dec 31 S&P 500	Oct 28 to Dec 31 Ind.	Jan 23 to May 5 S&P 500	Jan 23 to May 5 Ind.	Compound Growth S&P 500	Compound Growth Ind.
1989/90	5.5 %	6.9 %	2.4 %	5.5 %	8.0 %	12.7 %
1990/91	8.4	10.7	16.0	15.2	25.7	27.5
1991/92	8.6	7.2	-0.3	-1.0	8.2	6.1
1992/93	4.1	6.3	1.9	5.4	6.1	12.0
1993/94	0.4	5.1	-4.9	-6.7	-4.5	-2.0
1994/95	-1.4	-0.5	11.9	12.4	10.3	11.8
1995/96	6.3	10.7	4.6	7.6	11.1	19.1
1996/97	5.7	4.5	5.6	5.2	11.6	9.9
1997/98	10.7	10.5	15.8	11.5	28.2	23.2
1998/99	15.4	10.5	10.0	19.5	26.9	32.1
1999/00	13.3	10.8	-0.6	4.5	12.6	15.8
2000/01	-4.3	1.8	-5.7	4.7	-9.7	6.6
2001/02	3.9	8.1	-4.1	-5.3	-0.3	2.4
2002/03	-2.0	-1.3	5.5	8.6	3.4	7.1
2003/04	7.8	11.6	-2.0	-3.3	5.7	7.9
2004/05	7.7	8.7	0.4	0.2	8.1	8.9
2005/06	5.9	7.6	5.1	14.3	11.3	23.0
2006/07	3.0	3.1	5.8	6.8	9.0	10.1
2007/08	-4.4	-3.4	7.4	9.7	2.7	6.0
2008/09	6.4	7.1	9.2	6.1	16.2	13.7
2009/10	4.9	6.4	6.8	13.4	12.0	20.6
2010/11	6.4	8.1	4.0	4.9	10.6	13.5
2011/12	-2.1	-1.0	4.1	0.3	1.9	-0.7
2012/13	1.0	4.1	8.2	4.9	9.3	9.2
Avg.	4.6 %	6.0 %	4.5 %	6.0 %	9.3 %	12.4 %
Fq > 0	79 %	83 %	75 %	83 %	88 %	92 %

Industrial Sector - Avg. Year 1990 to 2012

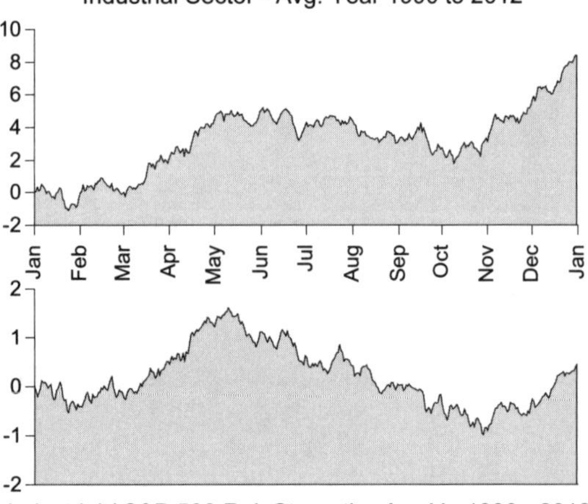

Industrial / S&P 500 Rel. Strength - Avg Yr. 1990 - 2012

Alternate Strategy—
Investors can bridge the gap between the two positive seasonal trends for the industrials sector by holding from October 28th to May 5th. Longer term investors may prefer this strategy, shorter term investors can use technical tools to determine the appropriate strategy.

The SP GICS Industrial Sector encompasses a wide range industrial based companies.
For more information on the information technology sector, see www.standardandpoors.com

2012-13 Strategy Performance

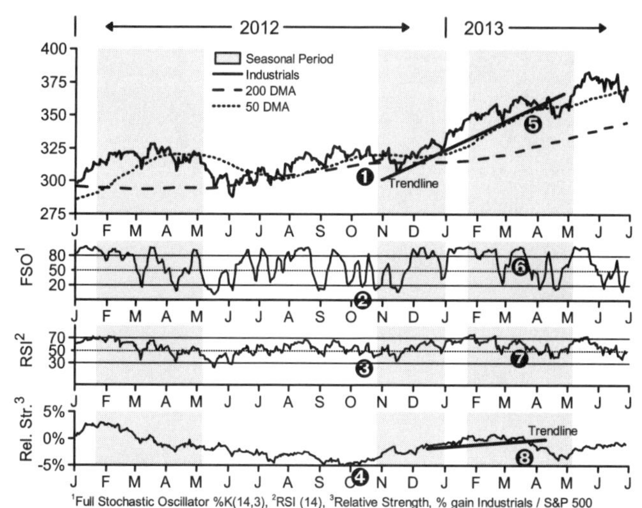

¹Full Stochastic Oscillator %K(14,3), ²RSI (14), ³Relative Strength, % gain Industrials / S&P 500

Industrials Sector Performance

Coming into the seasonal trade in October 2012, the industrial sector was slowly rolling over, but performing at market.

Technical Conditions– October 28th to May 5th, 2013

Entry Strategy –Buy Position Early–

In the beginning part of October 2012, the industrial sector was bouncing off its 50 day moving average❶ and the FSO crossed above 20❷, triggering an early buy signal. At the same time, the RSI crossed above 50❸ and the industrial sector was starting to show signs of outperforming the S&P 500❹.

Entry Strategy –Exit Position Early–

After performing well and outperforming the S&P 500 for five months, the industrial sector's performance started to wane❺. The FSO turned down below 80❻, but it was outside the four week sell window and as a result, could not trigger an early sell signal. The RSI was also bouncing off 70❼, supporting the weakening FSO. Most importantly, the industrial sector broke a key trendline of performance relative to the S&P 500❽. Given that the industrial sector had broken down on a absolute basis and relative basis, an early sell signal was triggered in March.

WEEK 44

Market Indices & Rates Weekly Values**

Stock Markets	2011	2012
Dow	11,895	13,141
S&P500	1,245	1,418
Nasdaq	2,663	2,993
TSX	12,297	12,399
FTSE	5,505	5,832
DAX	6,008	7,290
Nikkei	8,816	8,940
Hang Seng	19,611	21,703

Commodities	2011	2012
Oil	93.24	85.86
Gold	1734.2	1707.5

Bond Yields	2011	2012
USA 5 Yr Treasury	0.91	0.73
USA 10 Yr T	2.07	1.74
USA 20 Yr T	2.80	2.49
Moody's Aaa	3.84	3.44
Moody's Baa	5.11	4.49
CAN 5 Yr T	1.45	1.35
CAN 10 Yr T	2.20	1.79

Money Market	2011	2012
USA Fed Funds	0.25	0.25
USA 3 Mo T-B	0.01	0.09
CAN tgt overnight rate	1.00	1.00
CAN 3 Mo T-B	0.89	0.99

Foreign Exchange	2011	2012
EUR/USD	1.38	1.29
GBP/USD	1.60	1.61
USD/CAD	1.01	1.00
USD/JPY	78.18	79.95

OCTOBER

M	T	W	T	F	S	S
		1	2	3	4	5
6	7	8	9	10	11	12
13	14	15	16	17	18	19
20	21	22	23	24	25	26
27	28	29	30	31		

NOVEMBER

M	T	W	T	F	S	S
					1	2
3	4	5	6	7	8	9
10	11	12	13	14	15	16
17	18	19	20	21	22	23
24	25	26	27	28	29	30

DECEMBER

M	T	W	T	F	S	S
1	2	3	4	5	6	7
8	9	10	11	12	13	14
15	16	17	18	19	20	21
22	23	24	25	26	27	28
29	30	31				

** Weekly avg closing values- except Fed Funds & CAN overnight tgt rate weekly closing values.

NOVEMBER

	MONDAY	TUESDAY	WEDNESDAY
WEEK 45	3 27	4 26	5 25
WEEK 46	10 20	11 19	12 18
WEEK 47	17 13	18 12	19 11
WEEK 48	24 6	25 5	26 4
WEEK 49	1	2	3

THURSDAY		FRIDAY	
6	24	**7**	23
13	17	**14**	16
20	10	**21**	9
27	3	**28**	2
USA Market Closed-Thanksgiving Day		USA Early Market Close Thanksgiving	
4		**5**	

DECEMBER

M	T	W	T	F	S	S
1	2	3	4	5	6	7
8	9	10	11	12	13	14
15	16	17	18	19	20	21
22	23	24	25	26	27	28
29	30	31				

JANUARY

M	T	W	T	F	S	S
			1	2	3	4
5	6	7	8	9	10	11
12	13	14	15	16	17	18
19	20	21	22	23	24	25
26	27	28	29	30	31	

FEBRUARY

M	T	W	T	F	S	S
						1
2	3	4	5	6	7	8
9	10	11	12	13	14	15
16	17	18	19	20	21	22
23	24	25	26	27	28	

MARCH

M	T	W	T	F	S	S
						1
2	3	4	5	6	7	8
9	10	11	12	13	14	15
16	17	18	19	20	21	22
23	24	25	26	27	28	29
30	31					

NOVEMBER
S U M M A R Y

	Dow Jones	S&P 500	Nasdaq	TSX Comp
Month Rank	3	3	3	8
# Up	41	41	27	16
# Down	22	22	14	12
% Pos	65	65	66	57
% Avg. Gain	1.5	1.5	1.6	2.3

Dow & S&P 1950-2012, Nasdaq 1972-2012, TSX 1985-2012

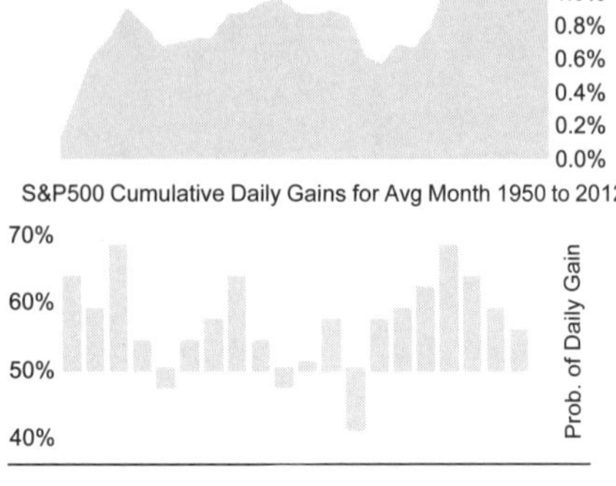

♦ November on average, is one of the better months of the year. From 1950 to 2012, the S&P 500 produced an average gain of 1.5% and has been positive 65% of the time. ♦ In November, the cyclical sectors start to increase their relative performance to the S&P 500, with the metals and mining sector starting its period of seasonal strength on November 16. ♦ For investors looking for a short-term investment, the day before and the day after Thanksgiving, are on average the two strongest days of the years.

BEST / WORST NOVEMBER BROAD MKTS. 2003-2012

BEST NOVEMBER MARKETS

- Nikkei 225 (2005) 9.3%
- Russell 2000 (2004) 8.6%
- Nikkei 225 (2010) 8.0%

WORST NOVEMBER MARKETS

- Russell 2000 (2008) -12.0%
- Nasdaq (2008) -10.8%
- Russell 1000 (2008) -7.9%

Index Values End of Month

	2003	2004	2005	2006	2007	2008	2009	2010	2011	2012
Dow	9,782	10,428	10,806	12,222	13,372	8,829	10,345	11,006	12,046	13,026
S&P 500	1,058	1,174	1,249	1,401	1,481	896	1,096	1,181	1,247	1,416
Nasdaq	1,960	2,097	2,233	2,432	2,661	1,536	2,145	2,498	2,620	3,010
TSX Comp.	7,859	9,030	10,824	12,752	13,689	9,271	11,447	12,953	12,204	12,239
Russell 1000	1,093	1,210	1,306	1,464	1,550	925	1,150	1,258	1,324	1,506
Russell 2000	1,358	1,575	1,683	1,954	1,908	1,176	1,441	1,807	1,833	2,043
FTSE 100	4,343	4,703	5,423	6,049	6,433	4,288	5,191	5,528	5,505	5,867
Nikkei 225	10,101	10,899	14,872	16,274	15,681	8,512	9,346	9,937	8,435	9,446

Percent Gain for November

	2003	2004	2005	2006	2007	2008	2009	2010	2011	2012
Dow	-0.2	4.0	3.5	1.2	-4.0	-5.3	6.5	-1.0	0.8	-0.5
S&P 500	0.7	3.9	3.5	1.6	-4.4	-7.5	5.7	-0.2	-0.5	0.3
Nasdaq	1.5	6.2	5.3	2.7	-6.9	-10.8	4.9	-0.4	-2.4	1.1
TSX Comp.	1.1	1.8	4.2	3.3	-6.4	-5.0	4.9	2.2	-0.4	-1.5
Russell 1000	1.0	4.1	3.5	1.9	-4.5	-7.9	5.6	0.1	-0.5	0.5
Russell 2000	3.5	8.6	4.7	2.5	-7.3	-12.0	3.0	3.4	-0.5	0.4
FTSE 100	1.3	1.7	2.0	-1.3	-4.3	-2.0	2.9	-2.6	-0.7	1.5
Nikkei 225	-4.3	1.2	9.3	-0.8	-6.3	-0.8	-6.9	8.0	-6.2	5.8

November Market Avg. Performance 2003 to 2012(1)

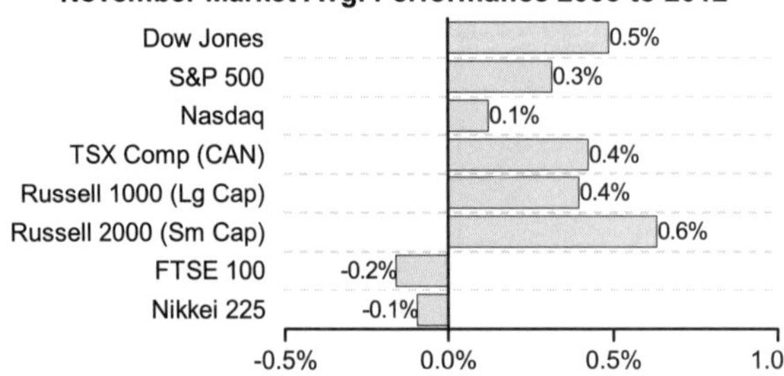

Interest Corner Nov(2)

	Fed Funds % (3)	3 Mo. T-Bill %(4)	10 Yr %(5)	20 Yr %(6)
2012	0.25	0.08	1.62	2.37
2011	0.25	0.01	2.08	2.77
2010	0.25	0.17	2.81	3.80
2009	0.25	0.06	3.21	4.07
2008	1.00	0.01	2.93	3.71

(1) Russell Data provided by Russell (2) Federal Reserve Bank of St. Louis- end of month values (3) Target rate set by FOMC (4)(5)(6) Constant yield maturities.

NOVEMBER SECTOR PERFORMANCE

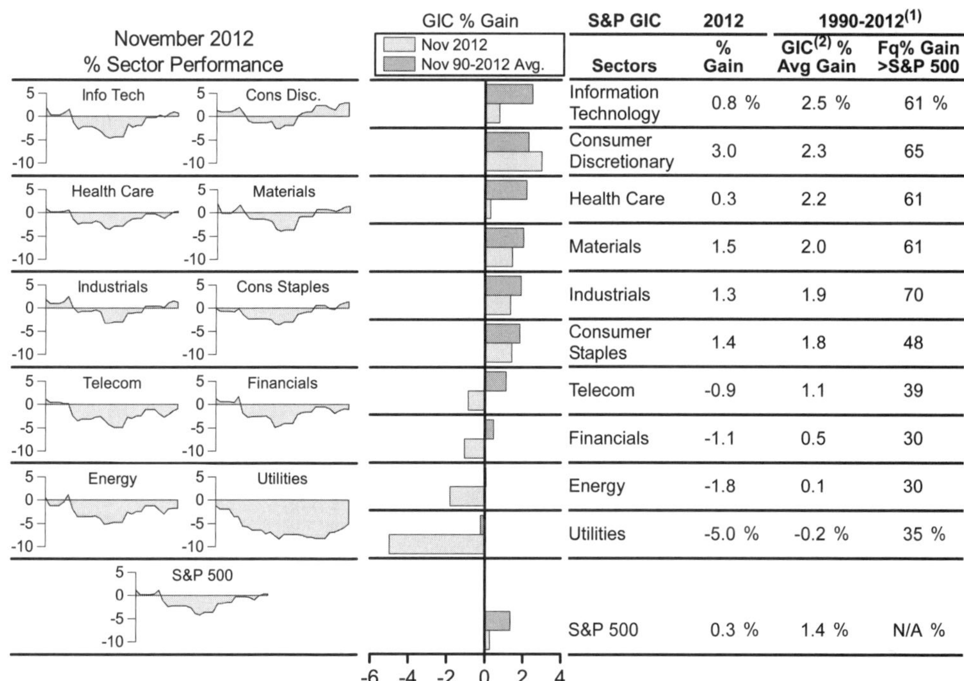

S&P GIC Sectors	2012 % Gain	1990-2012[1] GIC[2] % Avg Gain	1990-2012[1] Fq% Gain >S&P 500
Information Technology	0.8 %	2.5 %	61 %
Consumer Discretionary	3.0	2.3	65
Health Care	0.3	2.2	61
Materials	1.5	2.0	61
Industrials	1.3	1.9	70
Consumer Staples	1.4	1.8	48
Telecom	-0.9	1.1	39
Financials	-1.1	0.5	30
Energy	-1.8	0.1	30
Utilities	-5.0 %	-0.2 %	35 %
S&P 500	0.3 %	1.4 %	N/A %

Sector Commentary

♦ In November 2012, the S&P 500 dipped in the middle of the month, but ended up producing a 0.3% gain. ♦ November proved to be a very well behaved seasonal month, with the sectors that typically outperform, performing well and the sectors that tend to be weaker, underperforming the S&P 500. ♦ The largest sector gain in the month was produced by the consumer discretionary sector, which gained 3.0%. The consumer discretionary sector typically performs well in November, as it starts its seasonal run towards the end of October.

Sub-Sector Commentary

♦ The best performing sub-sector was biotech, which can sometimes produce a strong run into the end of the year, starting in mid-December. Biotech appeared to be starting its seasonal run early. ♦ The worst performing sub-sector was metals and mining, which typically starts its seasonal run in late November. ♦ The homebuilders sub-sector performed poorly, producing a loss of 2.8%. This sector was having trouble gaining traction during the start of its seasonal period.

SELECTED SUB-SECTORS[3]

Sub-Sector	2012 % Gain	GIC % Avg Gain	Fq% Gain >S&P 500
Agriculture (1994-2012)	-0.5 %	4.2 %	47 %
Retail	5.0	3.3	65
SOX (1995-2012)	2.0	3.3	56
Steel	-2.5	3.2	57
Home-builders	-2.8	2.3	48
Software & Services	0.8	2.3	65
Pharma	-0.8	2.0	57
Gold (London PM)	0.4	2.0	61
Silver	6.2	2.0	57
Metals & Mining	-4.1	1.9	57
Transporta-tion	-0.5	1.9	43
Biotech (1993-2012)	6.8	1.8	45
Chemicals	2.7	1.8	52
Railroads	-1.2	0.8	52
Banks	-2.3	0.5	43

(1) Sector data provided by Standard and Poors (2) GIC is short form for Global Industry Classification (3) Sub Sector data provided by Standard and Poors, except where marked by symbol.

MATERIAL STOCKS — MATERIAL GAINS

①Oct 28-Jan 6 ②Jan 23-May 5

> *Materials Composition – CAUTION*
>
> The U.S. materials sector is substantially different from the Canadian materials sector. The U.S. sector has over a 60% weight in chemical companies, versus the Canadian sector which has over a 60% weight in gold companies.

The materials sector (U.S.) generally does well during the favorable six months of the year, from the end of October to the beginning of May. The sector is economically sensitive and is leveraged to the economic forecasts. Generally, if the economy is expected to slow, the materials sector tends to decline and vice versa.

Positive 96% of the time

The materials sector has two seasonal periods. The first is from October 28th to January 6th and second period is from January 23rd to May 5th.

In the first seasonal period, the materials sector has produced an average gain of 7.5% in the years from 1990 to 2012 and has been positive 88% of the time.

The second seasonal period from January 23rd to May 5th has produced an average gain of 7.6% (almost double the S&P 500) and has been positive 75% of the time.

The time period in between the two seasonal periods, from January 7th to January 22nd, has had an average loss of 3.2% and only been positive 30% of the time (1989/90 to 2012/13). Investors may decide to bridge the gap between the two seasonal periods if the materials sector has strong momentum at the beginning of January.

The complete materials strategy is to be invested from October 28th to January 6th, out from January 7th to the 22nd, and back in from January 23rd to May 5th. This strategy has produced an average gain of 15.6% and has been positive 96% of the time.

Materials vs. S&P 500 1989/90 to 2012/13 Positive (shaded)

	Oct 28 to Jan6		Jan 23 to May 5		Compound Growth	
Year	S&P 500	Mat.	S&P 500	Mat.	S&P 500	Mat.
1989/90	5.1 %	9.1 %	2.4 %	-3.1 %	7.7 %	5.7 %
1990/91	5.4	9.2	16.0	15.3	22.2	26.0
1991/92	8.8	1.5	-0.3	5.5	8.5	7.1
1992/93	3.8	5.6	1.9	4.3	5.8	10.2
1993/94	0.5	9.4	-4.9	-5.3	-4.4	3.6
1994/95	-1.1	-3.5	11.9	6.1	10.7	2.4
1995/96	6.4	7.6	4.6	11.1	11.3	19.5
1996/97	6.7	2.3	5.6	2.3	12.6	4.6
1997/98	10.2	1.4	15.8	20.9	27.7	22.6
1998/99	19.4	6.1	10.0	31.5	31.3	39.6
1999/00	8.2	15.7	-0.6	-7.1	7.6	7.5
2000/01	-5.9	19.2	-5.7	15.1	-11.2	37.2
2001/02	6.2	8.5	-4.1	14.9	1.8	24.7
2002/03	3.5	9.2	5.5	2.7	9.2	12.1
2003/04	9.0	16.6	-2.0	-3.0	6.8	13.1
2004/05	5.6	5.4	0.4	0.3	6.0	5.8
2005/06	9.0	16.3	5.1	14.7	14.6	33.5
2006/07	2.4	3.2	5.8	10.7	8.3	14.2
2007/08	-8.1	-5.1	7.4	16.7	-1.2	10.8
2008/09	10.1	12.0	9.2	23.3	20.3	38.1
2009/10	6.9	13.8	6.8	3.0	14.2	17.2
2010/11	7.7	11.7	4.0	4.2	12.1	16.4
2011/12	-0.5	-2.3	4.1	-2.7	3.5	-4.9
2012/13	3.9	7.2	8.2	0.0	12.3	7.2
Avg.	5.1 %	7.5 %	4.5 %	7.6 %	9.9 %	15.6 %
Fq > 0	83 %	88 %	75 %	75 %	88 %	96 %

Materials Sector - Avg. Year 1990 to 2012

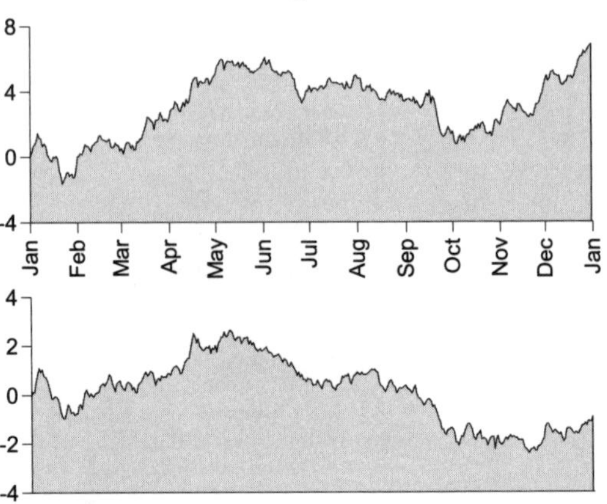

Materials / S&P 500 Rel. Strength - Avg Yr. 1990 - 2012

> *Alternate Strategy—*
> *Investors can bridge the gap between the two positive seasonal trends for the materials sector by holding from October 28th to May 5th. Longer term investors may prefer this strategy. Shorter term investors can use technical tools to determine the appropriate strategy.*

> *The SP GICS Materials Sector encompasses a wide range of materials based companies.*
> *For more information on the materials sector, see www.standardandpoors.com*

2012-13 Strategy Performance

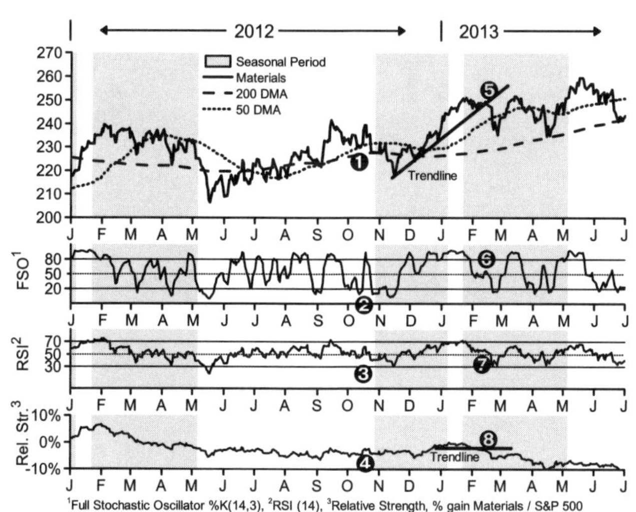

¹Full Stochastic Oscillator %K(14,3), ²RSI (14), ³Relative Strength, % gain Materials / S&P 500

Materials Sector Performance

The materials sector started its rise mid-May 2012 and continued to increase with higher highs and higher lows for the next four months. At the same time, the sector was underperforming the S&P 500. The sector peaked in September and corrected down to its 50 day moving average in the first part of October.

Technical Conditions– October 28th to May 5th, 2013

Entry Strategy –Buy Position Early–

Two weeks into October 2012, after a small correction, the materials sector started to turn up❶ and the FSO crossed above 20❷, triggering an early buy signal. In support, the RSI crossed above 50❸. The sector was still performing at market❹. After a brief increase, the sector corrected once again and it was not until three weeks into November before it bottomed.

Exit Strategy –Sell Position Early–

The materials sector continued to perform well until the start of its second seasonal leg in late January. At the time, the sector started to fade while the market was increasing. At the end of January, the sector broke its upward trendline❺. Previously the FSO had crossed below 80❻ and the RSI crossed below 70❼. The most important indicator to back up the fading absolute price was the break down of the sector relative to the S&P 500 that took place in mid-February❽. This underperformance justified an early exit from the trade.

WEEK 45

Market Indices & Rates Weekly Values**

Stock Markets	2011	2012
Dow	12,013	12,984
S&P500	1,254	1,400
Nasdaq	2,670	2,950
TSX	12,299	12,266
FTSE	5,506	5,812
DAX	5,929	7,261
Nikkei	8,639	8,910
Hang Seng	19,494	21,800

Commodities	2011	2012
Oil	96.97	85.99
Gold	1778.0	1709.0

Bond Yields	2011	2012
USA 5 Yr Treasury	0.90	0.68
USA 10 Yr T	2.05	1.68
USA 20 Yr T	2.79	2.42
Moody's Aaa	3.88	3.42
Moody's Baa	5.12	4.46
CAN 5 Yr T	1.39	1.32
CAN 10 Yr T	2.14	1.75

Money Market	2011	2012
USA Fed Funds	0.25	0.25
USA 3 Mo T-B	0.01	0.09
CAN tgt overnight rate	1.00	1.00
CAN 3 Mo T-B	0.89	0.98

Foreign Exchange	2011	2012
EUR/USD	1.37	1.28
GBP/USD	1.60	1.60
USD/CAD	1.02	1.00
USD/JPY	77.69	79.92

NOVEMBER

M	T	W	T	F	S	S
					1	2
3	4	5	6	7	8	9
10	11	12	13	14	15	16
17	18	19	20	21	22	23
24	25	26	27	28	29	30

DECEMBER

M	T	W	T	F	S	S
1	2	3	4	5	6	7
8	9	10	11	12	13	14
15	16	17	18	19	20	21
22	23	24	25	26	27	28
29	30	31				

JANUARY

M	T	W	T	F	S	S
			1	2	3	4
5	6	7	8	9	10	11
12	13	14	15	16	17	18
19	20	21	22	23	24	25
26	27	28	29	30	31	

SOX (SEMICONDUCTOR) TIME TO PUT ON YOUR SOX TRADE

①Oct 28- Nov 6 ②Jan 1- Feb 15

Many investors think of the semiconductor sector as the technology sector on steroids, but there are some differences.

The seasonal trends in the semiconductor sector are largely driven by the ordering cycle of semiconductors and economic expectations.

15.5% gain & positive 84% of the time

SOX Semiconductor vs. S&P 500 Positive
1994/95 to 2012/13

Year	Oct 28 to Nov 6 S&P 500	Oct 28 to Nov 6 SOX	Jan 1 to Feb 15 S&P 500	Jan 1 to Feb 15 SOX	Compound Growth S&P 500	Compound Growth SOX
1994/95	-0.8 %	1.4 %	5.5 %	13.9 %	4.7 %	15.5 %
1995/96	1.5	1.5	5.8	-4.5	7.3	-3.1
1996/97	3.4	7.6	9.1	19.5	12.8	28.6
1997/98	7.0	9.9	5.1	16.4	12.4	27.9
1998/99	7.1	11.1	0.1	11.8	7.2	24.2
1999/00	5.7	25.9	-4.6	35.4	0.8	70.5
2000/01	3.8	8.8	0.5	23.4	4.3	34.2
2001/02	1.3	8.2	-3.8	6.2	-2.6	14.9
2002/03	2.9	12.8	-5.1	-3.1	-2.3	9.2
2003/04	2.6	13.8	3.1	0.5	5.7	14.3
2004/05	3.6	1.7	-0.2	1.4	3.5	3.1
2005/06	3.5	5.7	2.5	12.3	6.1	18.6
2006/07	0.2	1.1	2.7	1.3	2.9	2.4
2007/08	-1.0	0.8	-8.1	-14.8	-9.0	-14.2
2008/09	6.6	3.2	-8.5	4.0	-2.4	7.3
2009/10	0.6	-2.5	-3.6	-7.5	-3.0	-9.8
2010/11	3.7	5.8	5.6	12.0	9.5	18.6
2011/12	-2.4	-1.1	6.8	16.8	4.2	15.5
2012/13	1.2	4.5	6.6	11.6	7.8	16.5
Avg.	2.6 %	6.3 %	1.0 %	8.2 %	3.7 %	15.5 %
Fq > 0	84 %	89 %	63 %	79 %	74 %	84 %

Demand for semiconductors tends to reach a low in the second quarter and the beginning of the third quarter. It tends to reach a peak towards the end of the third quarter and into the forth quarter. Most of the major semiconductor companies report their third quarter earnings in mid-October. Although this quarter realizes some of the seasonal earnings peak, the market tends to be volatile in this month and investors defer their entry into the sector until the market shows consistent strength, typically towards the end of October.

The first quarter tends to be positive for semiconductor companies and as a result, this sector in the stock market tends to perform well into mid-February.

As a result of the cyclical demand for semiconductors, the semiconductor sector has two periods of seasonal strength, with a short period of market performance in between.

The first period of seasonal strength is very short, starting on October 28th and finishing on November 6th and has produced an average gain of 6.3% and has been positive 89% of the time, from 1994 to 2012. Although the remainder of the year, from November 7th to December 31st, can be positive, previous returns in this time period have been very volatile and on average the sector has underperformed the S&P 500.

SOX PHLX Semiconductor - Avg. Year 1995 to 2012

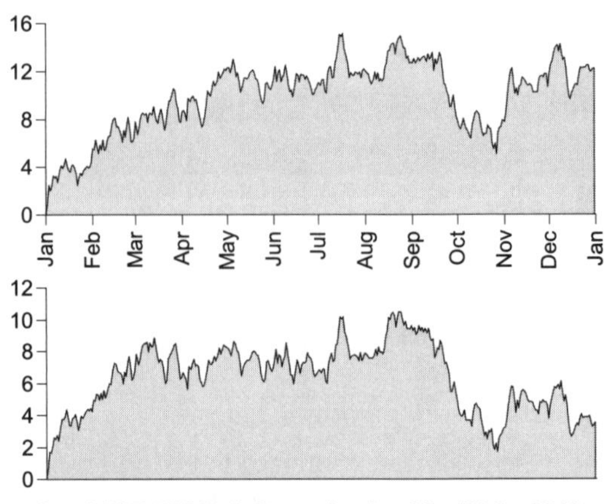

Sox / S&P 500 Rel. Strength - Avg Yr. 1990 - 2012

Alternate Strategy—
Investors can bridge the gap between the two positive seasonal trends for the semiconductor sector by holding from October 28th to March 1st. Longer term investors may prefer this strategy, shorter term investors can use technical tools to determine the appropriate strategy.

PHLX Semiconductor Index (SOX):
For more information on the PHLX Semiconductor Index (SOX), see www.nasdaq.com.

2012-13 Strategy Performance

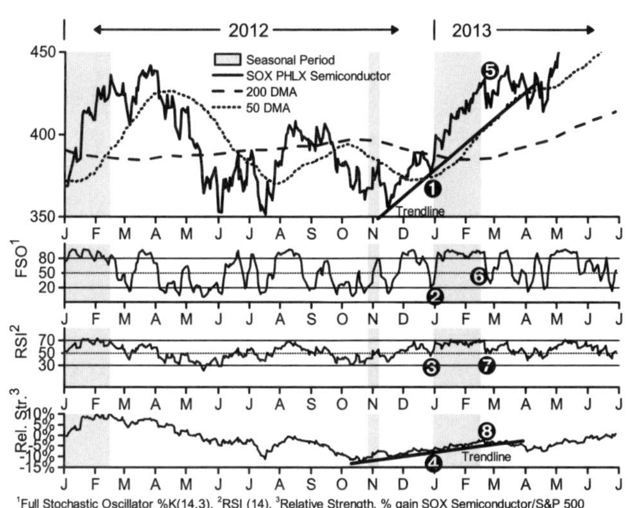

[1]Full Stochastic Oscillator %K(14,3), [2]RSI (14), [3]Relative Strength, % gain SOX Semiconductor/S&P 500

SOX (PHLX Semiconductor) Performance

The semiconductor sector performed well in its first seasonal period from October 28th to November 6th, 2012. At the end of this seasonal period, the sector started to correct and reached a low in mid-November. It then started to outperform the S&P 500, setting up for the second seasonal period beginning January 1st.

Technical Conditions– January 1st to February 15th, 2013

Entry Strategy –Buy Position on Entry Date–

At the start of this seasonal period, the semiconductor sector bounced off its 50 day moving average❶. At the same time, the FSO bounced higher off 20❷ and the RSI crossed above 50❸. The semiconductor sector continued to outperform the S&P 500❹.

Exit Strategy– Exit Position Late–

The sector strongly outperformed the S&P 500 from the start of its seasonal period and continued to outperform at the end of its seasonal period. At this time, the FSO was above 80, the RSI was at 70 and was continuing to outperform the S&P 500, justifying holding the position past the exit date. A few days after the end of the seasonal period, the semiconductor sector corrected sharply❺, and as a result the FSO crossed below 80❻, triggering a sell signal. At the same time, the RSI turned lower from 70❼ and the sector started to underperform the S&P 500❽.

WEEK 46

Market Indices & Rates
Weekly Values**

Stock Markets	2011	2012
Dow	11,930	12,655
S&P500	1,236	1,365
Nasdaq	2,629	2,865
TSX	12,087	11,989
FTSE	5,466	5,712
DAX	5,896	7,087
Nikkei	8,493	8,771
Hang Seng	19,025	21,266
Commodities	**2011**	**2012**
Oil	99.27	85.88
Gold	1755.7	1722.2
Bond Yields	**2011**	**2012**
USA 5 Yr Treasury	0.91	0.63
USA 10 Yr T	2.02	1.59
USA 20 Yr T	2.73	2.31
Moody's Aaa	3.89	3.46
Moody's Baa	5.16	4.47
CAN 5 Yr T	1.37	1.30
CAN 10 Yr T	2.11	1.71
Money Market	**2011**	**2012**
USA Fed Funds	0.25	0.25
USA 3 Mo T-B	0.01	0.06
CAN tgt overnight rate	1.00	1.00
CAN 3 Mo T-B	0.89	0.97
Foreign Exchange	**2011**	**2012**
EUR/USD	1.35	1.27
GBP/USD	1.58	1.59
USD/CAD	1.02	1.00
USD/JPY	77.01	80.32

NOVEMBER

M	T	W	T	F	S	S
					1	2
3	4	5	6	7	8	9
10	11	12	13	14	15	16
17	18	19	20	21	22	23
24	25	26	27	28	29	30

DECEMBER

M	T	W	T	F	S	S
1	2	3	4	5	6	7
8	9	10	11	12	13	14
15	16	17	18	19	20	21
22	23	24	25	26	27	28
29	30	31				

JANUARY

M	T	W	T	F	S	S
			1	2	3	4
5	6	7	8	9	10	11
12	13	14	15	16	17	18
19	20	21	22	23	24	25
26	27	28	29	30	31	

** Weekly avg closing values- except Fed Funds & CAN overnight tgt rate weekly closing values.

METALS AND MINING — STRONG TWO TIMES

①Nov 19-Jan 5 ②Jan 23-May 5

At the macro level, the metals and mining (M&M) sector is driven by future economic growth expectations. When worldwide growth expectations are increasing, there is a greater need for raw materials– when growth expectations are decreasing, the need is less.

Within the macro trend, the M&M sector has traditionally followed the overall market cycle of performing well from autumn until spring. This is the time of year that investors have a positive outlook on the economy and as a result, the cyclical sectors tend to outperform, including the metals and mining sector.

13.5% gain and positive 71% of the time

The metals and mining sector has two seasonal "sweet spots" – the first from November 19th to January 5th and the second from January 23rd to May 5th.

Investors have the option to hold and "bridge the gap" across the two sweet spots, but over the long-term, nimble traders have been able to capture extra value by being out of the sector from January 6th to the 22nd. During this period, the metals and mining sector produced an average loss of 2.7% and has only been positive 50% of the time.

From a portfolio perspective, it is important to consider reducing exposure at the beginning of May. The danger of holding on too long is that the sector tends not to do well in the late summer, particularly in September.

For more information on the metals and mining sector, see www.standardandpoors.com

Metals & Mining Sector vs. S&P 500 1989/90 to 2012/13

Positive (shaded)

	Nov 19 to Jan 5		Jan 23 to May 5		Compound Growth	
Year	S&P 500	M&M	S&P 500	M&M	S&P 500	M&M
1989/90	3.1 %	6.3 %	2.4 %	-4.6 %	5.6 %	1.4 %
1990/91	1.2	6.4	16.0	7.1	17.4	13.9
1991/92	8.9	1.0	-0.3	-1.7	8.5	-0.7
1992/93	2.7	12.5	1.9	3.2	4.7	16.1
1993/94	0.9	9.0	-4.9	-11.1	-4.1	-3.1
1994/95	-0.2	-1.2	11.9	-3.0	11.6	-4.1
1995/96	2.8	8.3	4.6	5.8	7.5	14.6
1996/97	1.5	-1.9	5.6	-1.2	7.2	-3.0
1997/98	4.1	-4.5	15.8	19.3	20.6	13.9
1998/99	8.8	-7.9	10.0	31.0	19.6	20.6
1999/00	-1.6	21.7	-0.6	-10.4	-2.2	9.1
2000/01	-5.1	17.0	-5.7	19.6	-10.5	40.0
2001/02	3.0	5.5	-4.1	12.8	-1.3	19.0
2002/03	0.9	9.3	5.5	3.2	6.4	12.8
2003/04	8.5	18.2	-2.0	-12.1	6.4	3.9
2004/05	0.0	-8.4	0.4	-4.0	0.4	-12.0
2005/06	2.0	17.3	5.1	27.3	7.2	49.4
2006/07	0.6	3.0	5.8	17.2	6.5	20.8
2007/08	-3.2	0.9	7.4	27.4	3.0	20.5
2008/09	8.0	43.8	9.2	30.6	17.9	87.8
2009/10	2.4	6.3	6.8	4.8	9.4	11.3
2010/11	6.7	15.0	4.0	-1.6	11.0	13.1
2011/12	5.4	1.2	4.1	-16.0	9.7	-15.0
2012/13	7.8	3.9	8.2	-16.8	16.6	-13.6
Avg.	2.9 %	7.6 %	4.5 %	5.3 %	7.5 %	13.5 %
Fq > 0	83 %	79 %	75 %	54 %	83 %	71 %

Metals & Mining Sector - Avg. Year 1990 to 2012

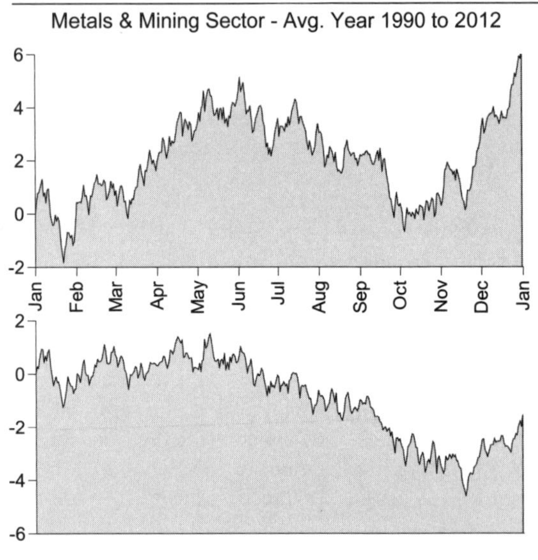

Metals & Mining / S&P 500 Rel. Strength- Avg Yr. 1990-2012

2012-13 Strategy Performance

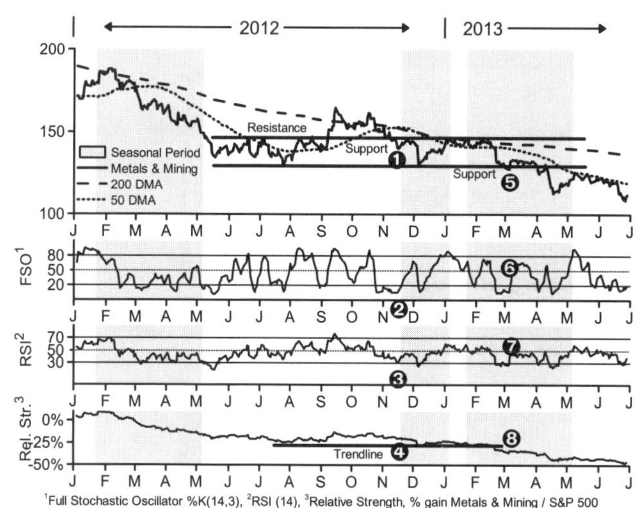

¹Full Stochastic Oscillator %K(14,3), ²RSI (14), ³Relative Strength, % gain Metals & Mining / S&P 500

Metals and Mining Sector Performance

After falling for the first four months of 2012, the metals and mining sub-sector consolidated for the next six months up until the start of the seasonal period in November. The last part of the consolidation was a downtrend that started in September.

Technical Conditions– November 19th to May 5th, 2013

Entry Strategy –Buy Position on Entry Date–

On the seasonal entry date, the metals and mining sub-sector had corrected to the top of its consolidation band❶. The FSO crossed above 20❷, reaffirming a buy signal and the RSI bounced off 30❸. The sector was still in a downtrend relative to the S&P 500❹. The technical picture was not strong, but still supportive of establishing a position.

Exit Strategy –Sell Position Early–

After an initial correction in late November and December, the metals and mining sector started to perform at market. In the beginning of February, the sector was not able to break above its resistance level and promptly turned down❺. The FSO and the RSI both turned down❻❼, but the real damage was done by the underperformance relative to the S&P 500❽, which became evident in mid-February, triggering an early sell signal.

WEEK 47

Market Indices & Rates Weekly Values**

Stock Markets	2011	2012
Dow	11,383	12,858
S&P500	1,175	1,394
Nasdaq	2,487	2,932
TSX	11,620	12,111
FTSE	5,172	5,770
DAX	5,504	7,207
Nikkei	8,247	9,221
Hang Seng	17,993	21,534

Commodities	2011	2012
Oil	96.76	87.64
Gold	1692.6	1730.5

Bond Yields	2011	2012
USA 5 Yr Treasury	0.91	0.68
USA 10 Yr T	1.94	1.67
USA 20 Yr T	2.60	2.40
Moody's Aaa	3.81	3.58
Moody's Baa	5.11	4.56
CAN 5 Yr T	1.36	1.35
CAN 10 Yr T	2.07	1.76

Money Market	2011	2012
USA Fed Funds	0.25	0.25
USA 3 Mo T-B	0.02	0.10
CAN tgt overnight rate	1.00	1.00
CAN 3 Mo T-B	0.85	0.96

Foreign Exchange	2011	2012
EUR/USD	1.34	1.29
GBP/USD	1.55	1.60
USD/CAD	1.04	1.00
USD/JPY	77.20	82.10

NOVEMBER

M	T	W	T	F	S	S
					1	2
3	4	5	6	7	8	9
10	11	12	13	14	15	16
17	18	19	20	21	22	23
24	25	26	27	28	29	30

DECEMBER

M	T	W	T	F	S	S
1	2	3	4	5	6	7
8	9	10	11	12	13	14
15	16	17	18	19	20	21
22	23	24	25	26	27	28
29	30	31				

JANUARY

M	T	W	T	F	S	S
			1	2	3	4
5	6	7	8	9	10	11
12	13	14	15	16	17	18
19	20	21	22	23	24	25
26	27	28	29	30	31	

THANKSGIVING
GIVE THANKS & TAKE RETURNS
Day Before and After – Two of the Best Days

We have a lot to be thankful for on Thanksgiving Day. As a bonus, the market day before and the market day after Thanksgiving have been two of the best days of the year in the stock market.

Each day by itself has produced spectacular results. From 1950 to 2012, the S&P 500 has had an average gain of 0.4% on the days before and after Thanksgiving.

The day before Thanksgiving and the day after have had an average cumulative return of 0.7% and together have been positive 84% of the time

To put the performance of these two days in perspective, the average daily return of the market over the same time period is 0.03%.

The gains the day before Thanksgiving and the day after are almost ten times better than the average market and have a much greater frequency of being positive.

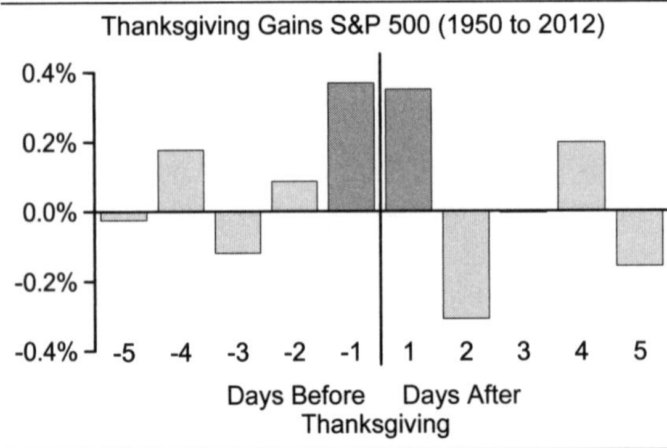

Alternate Strategy — Although the focus has been on the performance of two specific days, the day before and the day after Thanksgiving, the holiday occurs at the end of November which tends to be a strong month. December, the next month is also strong. Investors have a good option of expanding their trade is to include the "Santa Arrives Early & Stays Late" Strategy.

History of Thanksgiving:
It was originally a "thanksgiving feast" by the pilgrims for surviving their first winter. Initially it was celebrated sporadically and the holiday, when it was granted, had its date changed several times. It was not until 1941 that it was proclaimed to be the 4th Thursday in November.

(Shaded = Positive)

THANKSGIVING DAY

S&P500	Day Before	Day After
1950	1.4	0.8
1951	-0.2	-1.1
1952	0.6	0.5
1953	0.1	0.6
1954	0.6	1.0
1955	0.1	-0.1
1956	-0.5	1.1
1957	2.9	1.1
1958	1.7	1.1
1959	0.2	0.5
1960	0.1	0.6
1961	-0.1	0.2
1962	0.6	1.2
1963	-0.2	1.4
1964	-0.3	-0.3
1965	0.2	0.1
1966	0.7	0.8
1967	0.6	0.3
1968	0.5	0.6
1969	0.4	0.6
1970	0.4	1.0
1971	0.2	1.8
1972	0.6	0.3
1073	1.1	0.3
1974	0.7	0.0
1975	0.3	0.3
1976	0.4	0.7
1977	0.4	0.2
1978	0.5	0.3
1979	0.2	0.8
1980	0.6	0.2
1981	0.4	0.8
1982	0.7	0.7
1983	0.1	0.1
1984	0.2	1.5
1985	0.9	-0.2
1986	0.2	0.2
1987	-0.9	-1.5
1988	0.7	-0.7
1989	0.7	0.6
1990	0.2	-0.3
1991	-0.4	-0.4
1992	0.4	0.2
1993	0.3	0.2
1994	0.0	0.5
1995	-0.3	0.3
1996	-0.1	0.3
1997	0.1	0.4
1998	0.3	0.5
1999	0.9	0.0
2000	-1.9	1.5
2001	-0.5	1.2
2002	2.8	-0.3
2003	0.4	0.0
2004	0.4	0.1
2005	0.3	0.2
2006	0.2	-0.4
2007	-1.6	1.7
2008	3.5	1.0
2009	0.5	-1.7
2010	1.5	-0.7
2011	-2.2	-0.3
2012	0.2	1.3
Total Avg %	0.4%	0.4%
Fq > 0	78 %	75 %

2010-12 Strategy Performance

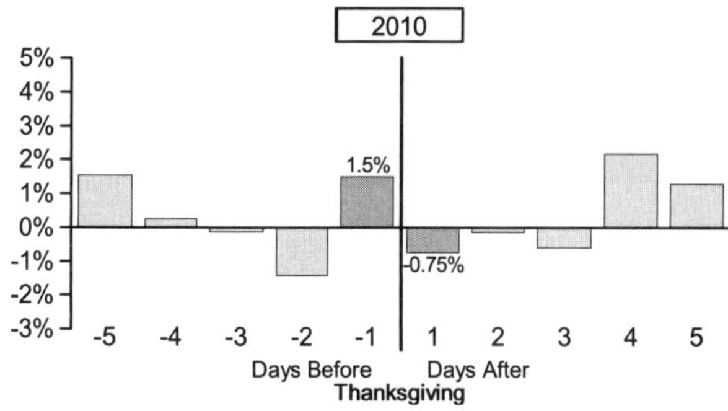

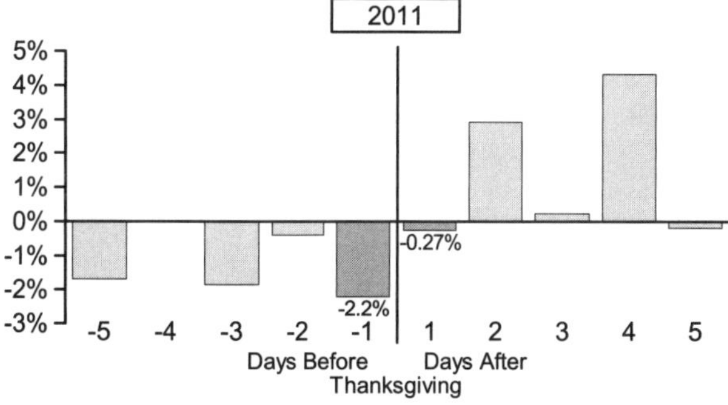

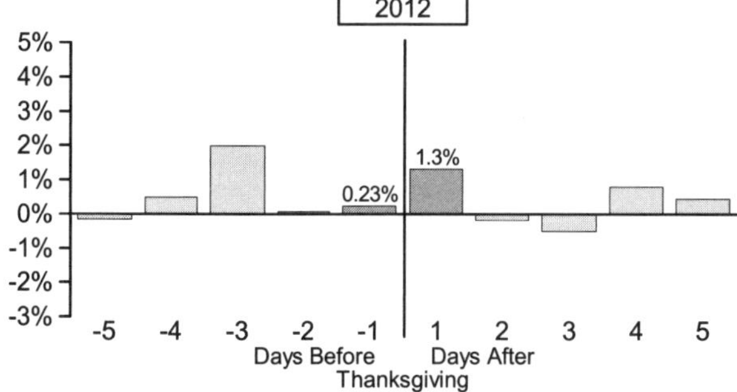

Thanksgiving Strategy Performance 2012

After a sharp correction in the first half of November 2012, the S&P 500 bounced sharply, providing a good base for the Thanksgiving trade. The day before Thanksgiving produced a respectable 0.2% and the day after Thanksgiving produced an exceptionally strong gain of 1.3%.

WEEK 48

Market Indices & Rates
Weekly Values**

Stock Markets	**2011**	**2012**
Dow	11,833	12,976
S&P500	1,225	1,409
Nasdaq	2,583	2,992
TSX	11,953	12,176
FTSE	5,439	5,825
DAX	5,950	7,355
Nikkei	8,488	9,393
Hang Seng	18,465	21,874
Commodities	**2011**	**2012**
Oil	99.90	87.68
Gold	1735.2	1731.2
Bond Yields	**2011**	**2012**
USA 5 Yr Treasury	0.94	0.64
USA 10 Yr T	2.04	1.63
USA 20 Yr T	2.72	2.37
Moody's Aaa	4.00	3.56
Moody's Baa	5.28	4.56
CAN 5 Yr T	1.42	1.31
CAN 10 Yr T	2.13	1.72
Money Market	**2011**	**2012**
USA Fed Funds	0.25	0.25
USA 3 Mo T-B	0.02	0.08
CAN tgt overnight rate	1.00	1.00
CAN 3 Mo T-B	0.84	0.96
Foreign Exchange	**2011**	**2012**
EUR/USD	1.34	1.30
GBP/USD	1.56	1.60
USD/CAD	1.02	0.99
USD/JPY	77.84	82.18

NOVEMBER

M	T	W	T	F	S	S
					1	2
3	4	5	6	7	8	9
10	11	12	13	14	15	16
17	18	19	20	21	22	23
24	25	26	27	28	29	30

DECEMBER

M	T	W	T	F	S	S
1	2	3	4	5	6	7
8	9	10	11	12	13	14
15	16	17	18	19	20	21
22	23	24	25	26	27	28
29	30	31				

JANUARY

M	T	W	T	F	S	S
			1	2	3	4
5	6	7	8	9	10	11
12	13	14	15	16	17	18
19	20	21	22	23	24	25
26	27	28	29	30	31	

** Weekly avg closing values- except Fed Funds & CAN overnight tgt rate weekly closing values.

DECEMBER

	MONDAY	TUESDAY	WEDNESDAY
WEEK 49	1 30	2 29	3 28
WEEK 50	8 23	9 22	10 21
WEEK 51	15 16	16 15	17 14
WEEK 52	22 9	23 8	24 7 USA Early Market Close
WEEK 01	29 2	30 1	31

THURSDAY		FRIDAY	
4	27	**5**	26
11	20	**12**	19
18	13	**19**	12
25	6	**26**	5
CAN Market Closed-Christmas Day USA Market Closed-Christmas Day		CAN Market Closed-Boxing Day	
1		**2**	

JANUARY

M	T	W	T	F	S	S
			1	2	3	4
5	6	7	8	9	10	11
12	13	14	15	16	17	18
19	20	21	22	23	24	25
26	27	28	29	30	31	

FEBRUARY

M	T	W	T	F	S	S
						1
2	3	4	5	6	7	8
9	10	11	12	13	14	15
16	17	18	19	20	21	22
23	24	25	26	27	28	

MARCH

M	T	W	T	F	S	S
						1
2	3	4	5	6	7	8
9	10	11	12	13	14	15
16	17	18	19	20	21	22
23	24	25	26	27	28	29
30	31					

APRIL

M	T	W	T	F	S	S
		1	2	3	4	5
6	7	8	9	10	11	12
13	14	15	16	17	18	19
20	21	22	23	24	25	26
27	28	29	30			

DECEMBER
SUMMARY

	Dow Jones	S&P 500	Nasdaq	TSX Comp
Month Rank	2	1	2	1
# Up	45	49	24	25
# Down	18	14	17	3
% Pos	71	78	59	89
% Avg. Gain	1.7	1.7	1.8	2.3

Dow & S&P 1950-2012, Nasdaq 1972-2012, TSX 1985-2012

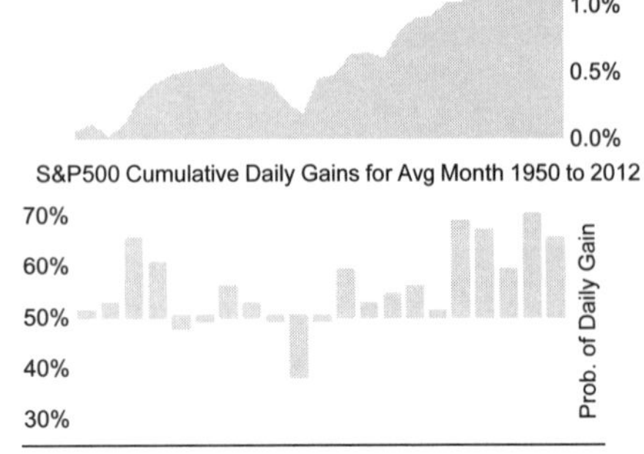

♦ December is typically one of the strongest months of the year for the S&P 500. From 1950 to 2012, the S&P 500 produced an average gain of 1.7% and was positive 78% of the time. In the last five years in a row, the S&P 500 has been positive in December. ♦ Most of the gains for the S&P 500 are in the second half of the month.♦ The Nasdaq tends to outperform the S&P 500 starting mid-December.♦ The small cap sector also starts to outperform mid-month.

BEST / WORST DECEMBER BROAD MKTS. 2003-2012

BEST DECEMBER MARKETS

- Nikkei 225 (2009) 12.8%
- Nikkei 225 (2012) 10.0%
- Nikkei 225 (2005) 8.3%

WORST DECEMBER MARKETS

- TSX Comp. (2008) -3.1%
- Nikkei 225 (2007) -2.4%
- TSX Comp. (2011) -2.0%

Index Values End of Month

	2003	2004	2005	2006	2007	2008	2009	2010	2011	2012
Dow	10,454	10,783	10,718	12,463	13,265	8,776	10,428	11,578	12,218	13,104
S&P 500	1,112	1,212	1,248	1,418	1,468	903	1,115	1,258	1,258	1,426
Nasdaq	2,003	2,175	2,205	2,415	2,652	1,577	2,269	2,653	2,605	3,020
TSX Comp.	8,221	9,247	11,272	12,908	13,833	8,988	11,746	13,443	11,955	12,434
Russell 1000	1,143	1,251	1,306	1,480	1,538	938	1,176	1,340	1,333	1,518
Russell 2000	1,384	1,619	1,673	1,958	1,904	1,241	1,554	1,948	1,841	2,111
FTSE 100	4,477	4,814	5,619	6,221	6,457	4,434	5,413	5,900	5,572	5,898
Nikkei 225	10,677	11,489	16,111	17,226	15,308	8,860	10,546	10,229	8,455	10,395

Percent Gain for December

	2003	2004	2005	2006	2007	2008	2009	2010	2011	2012
Dow	6.9	3.4	-0.8	2.0	-0.8	-0.6	0.8	5.2	1.4	0.6
S&P 500	5.1	3.2	-0.1	1.3	-0.9	0.8	1.8	6.5	0.9	0.7
Nasdaq	2.2	3.7	-1.2	-0.7	-0.3	2.7	5.8	6.2	-0.6	0.3
TSX Comp.	4.6	2.4	4.1	1.2	1.1	-3.1	2.6	3.8	-2.0	1.6
Russell 1000	4.6	3.5	0.0	1.1	-0.8	1.3	2.3	6.5	0.7	0.8
Russell 2000	1.9	2.8	-0.6	0.2	-0.2	5.6	7.9	7.8	0.5	3.3
FTSE 100	3.1	2.4	3.6	2.8	0.4	3.4	4.3	6.7	1.2	0.5
Nikkei 225	5.7	5.4	8.3	5.8	-2.4	4.1	12.8	2.9	0.2	10.0

December Market Avg. Performance 2003 to 2012[1]

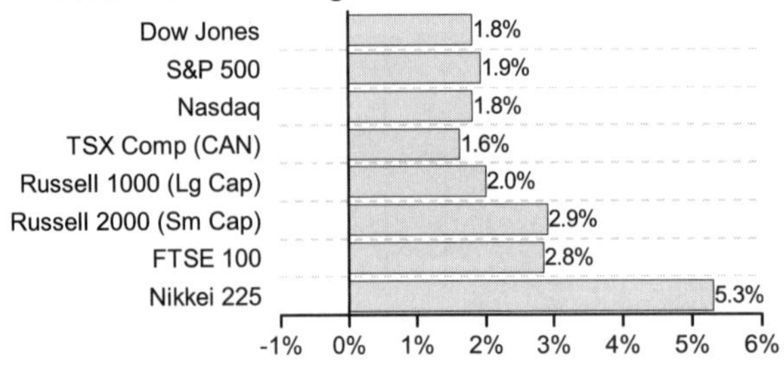

Interest Corner Dec[2]

	Fed Funds % [3]	3 Mo. T-Bill %[4]	10 Yr %[5]	20 Yr %[6]
2012	0.25	0.05	1.78	2.54
2011	0.25	0.02	1.89	2.57
2010	0.25	0.12	3.30	4.13
2009	0.25	0.06	3.85	4.58
2008	0.25	0.11	2.25	3.05

(1) Russell Data provided by Russell (2) Federal Reserve Bank of St. Louis- end of month values (3) Target rate set by FOMC (4)(5)(6) Constant yield maturities.

DECEMBER SECTOR PERFORMANCE

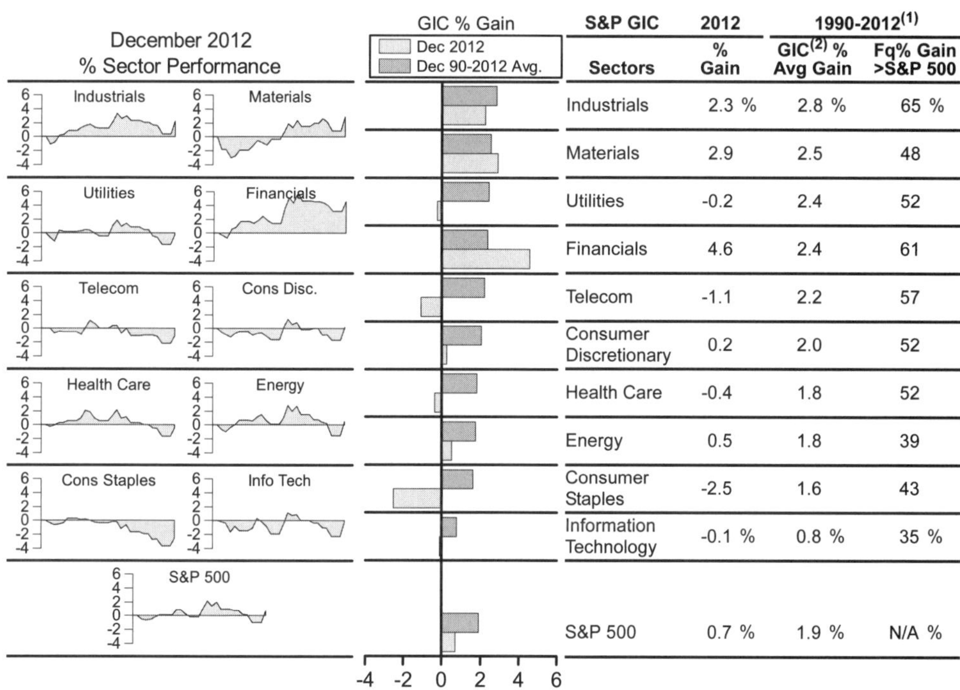

S&P GIC Sectors	2012 % Gain	1990-2012[1] GIC[2] % Avg Gain	1990-2012[1] Fq% Gain >S&P 500
Industrials	2.3 %	2.8 %	65 %
Materials	2.9	2.5	48
Utilities	-0.2	2.4	52
Financials	4.6	2.4	61
Telecom	-1.1	2.2	57
Consumer Discretionary	0.2	2.0	52
Health Care	-0.4	1.8	52
Energy	0.5	1.8	39
Consumer Staples	-2.5	1.6	43
Information Technology	-0.1 %	0.8 %	35 %
S&P 500	0.7 %	1.9 %	N/A %

Sector Commentary

♦ In December, the S&P 500 produced a gain of 0.7%. Although this was positive, it was less than the average gain of 1.9% since 1990. ♦The sectors that on average outperform, lived up to their trends by performing well. ♦The top performing sector was the financials sector with a gain of 4.6%. Very often this sector will start its seasonal run in mid-December. ♦The next best performing sector was the materials sector, producing a gain of 2.9%.

Sub-Sector Commentary

♦ The top performing sub-sector was steel, producing a gain of 12.2%. As the market shifted back to a risk on mode, the cyclicals became the favoured sectors. ♦The chemicals sub-sector produced a strong gain of 4.3%.♦ Homebuilders also produced a very strong performance with a gain of 3.7%. Nevertheless, it still underperformed its average gain of 8.3% since 1990. ♦ Silver produced a big loss of 12.6% and gold lost 4.0%. December tends not to be a strong month for gold and silver, and 2012 was not an exception.♦ The retail sector was a weak performer which mirrors its long-term trend in December. Despite its December loss, the retail sector has a very strong seasonal trend starting in January that investors should consider.

SELECTED SUB-SECTORS[3]

Sub-Sector	2012 % Gain	Avg Gain	Fq% Gain >S&P 500
Home-builders	3.7 %	8.3 %	91 %
Steel	12.2	5.6	70
Biotech (1993-2012)	-1.9	4.8	55
Metals & Mining	-1.9	3.4	57
Chemicals	4.3	2.1	57
Agriculture (1994-2012)	2.6	2.1	53
Banks	2.8	2.1	57
Railroads	1.9	1.8	48
Software & Services	1.5	1.7	43
Silver	-12.6	1.4	48
Pharma	-1.0	1.4	43
Transporta-tion	2.1	1.2	35
SOX (1995-2012)	2.6	1.0	39
Retail	-3.4	1.0	30
Gold (London PM)	-4.0	0.0	30

EMERGING MARKETS(USD)– TRUNCATED SIX MONTH SEASONAL

November 24th to April 18th

Emerging markets become popular periodically, mainly after they have had a strong run, or if they have suffered a major correction and investors perceive them to have a lot of value.

Markets around the world tend to have the same broad seasonal trends, including the emerging markets. Typically, emerging markets will outperform when the U.S. market is increasing and underperform when it is decreasing.

The exceptions to this usually occurs if there is a global economic contraction underway, or economic growth is in question, and investors seek the "safety" of the U.S. market. In this case the emerging markets can underperform the U.S. market.

11.5% gain & positive 83% of the time positive

Seasonal investors have benefited from concentrating their emerging market exposure in a truncated, or shorter version of the favorable six month seasonal period.

Emerging Markets (USD) vs. S&P 500
1990/91 to 2012/13

Positive (shaded)

Nov 24 to Apr 18	S&P 500	Em. Mkts.	Diff
1990/91	23.8%	33.8%	10.5%
1991/92	10.6	37.5	26.8
1992/93	5.6	11.8	6.2
1993/94	-4.0	3.7	7.8
1994/95	12.3	-16.4	-28.7
1995/96	7.6	14.7	7.1
1996/97	2.4	7.1	4.7
1997/98	16.6	6.7	-9.9
1998/99	11.0	18.1	7.1
1999/00	2.6	3.5	0.8
2000/01	-6.4	-4.6	1.8
2001/02	-2.3	22.3	24.5
2002/03	-4.0	0.0	4.0
2003/04	9.6	19.5	9.9
2004/05	-2.6	4.3	7.0
2005/06	3.3	24.7	21.4
2006/07	4.7	13.2	8.5
2007/08	-3.5	-0.9	2.6
2008/09	8.7	37.6	28.9
2009/10	7.8	5.6	-2.2
2010/11	10.5	6.6	-3.9
2011/12	19.2	15.6	-3.6
2012/13	9.4	0.1	-9.3
Avg	6.2%	11.5%	5.3%
Fq > 0	74%	83%	74%

Emerging Mkts. (USD)- Avg. Year 1990 to 2012

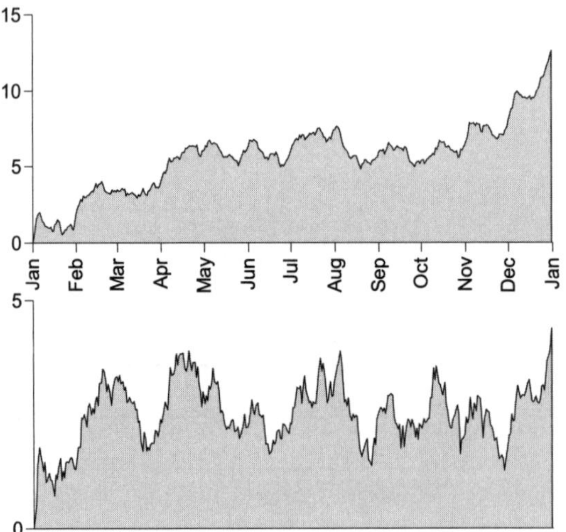

Emerg. Mkts. (USD)/S&P 500 Rel. Str. - Avg Yr. 1990-2012

The seasonally strong period for the emerging markets sector is from November 24th to April 18th. In this time period, from 1990/91 to 2012/13 the emerging markets sector (USD) produced an average rate of return of 11.5% and has been positive 83% of the time.

As the world has grappled with the sub-prime crisis and then the EU crisis in the last few years, investors have sought the safety of the U.S. markets and as a result emerging markets have underperformed.

As worldwide economic growth gains traction in the future, seasonal investors should consider adding emerging markets to their portfolio from November 24th to April 18th.

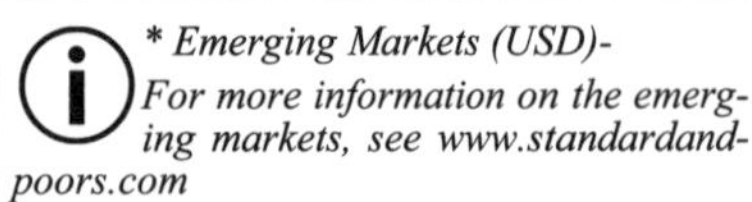

** Emerging Markets (USD)- For more information on the emerging markets, see www.standardandpoors.com*

2011-12 Strategy Performance

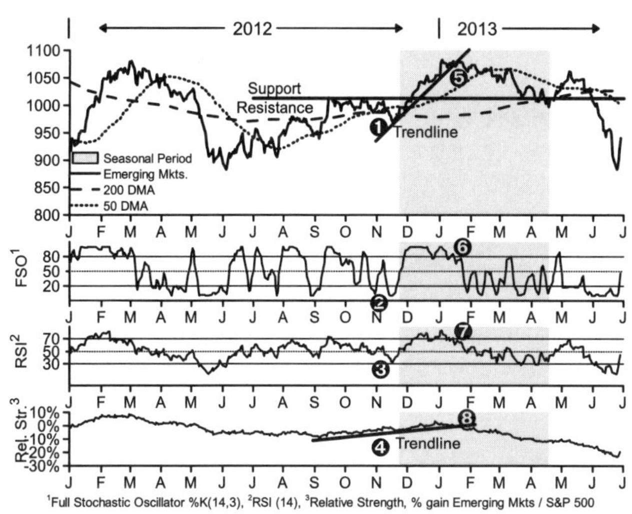

[1]Full Stochastic Oscillator %K(14,3), [2]RSI (14), [3]Relative Strength, % gain Emerging Mkts / S&P 500

Emerging Markets Performance

After underperforming in the spring and summer of 2012, emerging markets started to outperform the S&P 500 in September, setting up for a positive seasonal trade starting in November.

Technical Conditions– November 24th to April 18th, 2013

Entry Strategy –Buy Position Early–

Starting at the beginning of September, emerging markets tried to push through its resistance level❶, and as a result, an early buy signal was generated when the FSO crossed above 20❷. At the same time, the RSI crossed above 50❸ and emerging markets was outperforming the S&P 500❹.

Exit Strategy –Exit Position Early–

After a correction preceding the seasonal start date, emerging markets broke through its 200 and 50 day moving averages and broke through its resistance level. In January, the emerging markets' performance started to wane and it broke its uptrend line❺. At the same time, the FSO broke below 80❻ and the RSI broke below 70❼. The trade broke down at the end of January when emerging markets started to underperform the S&P 500❽, justifying an early exit from the trade.

WEEK 49

Market Indices & Rates Weekly Values**

Stock Markets	**2011**	**2012**
Dow	12,125	13,036
S&P500	1,253	1,412
Nasdaq	2,640	2,988
TSX	12,067	12,155
FTSE	5,539	5,890
DAX	5,998	7,475
Nikkei	8,639	9,486
Hang Seng	19,011	22,056
Commodities	**2011**	**2012**
Oil	100.10	87.53
Gold	1722.3	1701.5
Bond Yields	**2011**	**2012**
USA 5 Yr Treasury	0.90	0.62
USA 10 Yr T	2.04	1.62
USA 20 Yr T	2.74	2.36
Moody's Aaa	4.02	3.57
Moody's Baa	5.30	4.57
CAN 5 Yr T	1.33	1.27
CAN 10 Yr T	2.07	1.70
Money Market	**2011**	**2012**
USA Fed Funds	0.25	0.25
USA 3 Mo T-B	0.01	0.09
CAN tgt overnight rate	1.00	1.00
CAN 3 Mo T-B	0.83	0.96
Foreign Exchange	**2011**	**2012**
EUR/USD	1.34	1.30
GBP/USD	1.57	1.61
USD/CAD	1.02	0.99
USD/JPY	77.70	82.30

DECEMBER

M	T	W	T	F	S	S
1	2	3	4	5	6	7
8	9	10	11	12	13	14
15	16	17	18	19	20	21
22	23	24	25	26	27	28
29	30	31				

JANUARY

M	T	W	T	F	S	S
			1	2	3	4
5	6	7	8	9	10	11
12	13	14	15	16	17	18
19	20	21	22	23	24	25
26	27	28	29	30	31	

FEBRUARY

M	T	W	T	F	S	S
						1
2	3	4	5	6	7	8
9	10	11	12	13	14	15
16	17	18	19	20	21	22
23	24	25	26	27	28	

** Weekly avg closing values- except Fed Funds & CAN overnight tgt rate weekly closing values.

SMALL CAP (SMALL COMPANY) EFFECT

Small Companies Outperform - Dec 19th to Mar 7th

At different stages of the business cycle, small capitalization companies (small caps represented by Russell 2000), perform better than large capitalization companies (large caps represented by Russell 1000).

Evidence shows that the small caps relative outperformance also has a seasonal component as they typically outperform large caps from December 19th to March 7th.

24 times out of 34 better than the Russell 1000

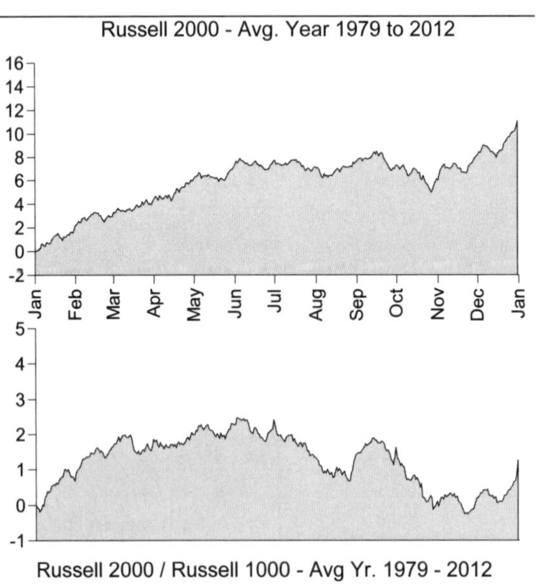

Russell 2000 / Russell 1000 - Avg Yr. 1979 - 2012

Russell 2000 vs. Russell 1000 Gains 19th Dec to Mar 7th 1979 to 2013

Positive [shaded]

Dec 19 - Mar7	Russell 1000	Russell 2000	Diff
79 / 80	-1.3 %	-0.4 %	0.9 %
80 / 81	-2.8	4.0	6.8
81 / 82	-12.4	-12.1	0.3
82 / 83	11.8	19.8	8.0
83 / 84	-6.4	-7.5	-1.1
84 / 85	7.7	17.1	9.4
85 / 86	8.2	11.7	3.5
86 / 87	17.2	21.3	4.1
87 / 88	8.3	16.4	8.0
88 / 89	6.9	9.1	2.5
89 / 90	-2.0	-1.9	0.2
90 / 91	14.6	29.0	14.4
91 / 92	6.0	16.8	10.8
92 / 93	1.4	5.0	3.5
93 / 94	0.5	5.7	5.3
94 / 95	5.3	5.5	0.2
95 / 96	8.3	7.8	-0.5
96 / 97	9.5	3.5	-6.0
97 / 98	10.2	10.3	0.1
98 / 99	7.3	0.2	-7.2
99 / 00	-1.7	27.7	20.4
00 / 01	-5.2	4.7	9.8
01 / 02	1.6	1.9	0.4
02 / 03	-6.7	-7.8	-1.0
03 / 04	6.4	9.6	3.3
04 / 05	2.8	0.3	-2.5
05 / 06	0.8	5.6	4.7
06 / 07	-1.6	-0.8	0.9
07 / 08	-10.9	-12.5	-1.5
08 / 09	-22.2	-26.7	-4.5
09 / 10	3.6	9.1	5.5
10 / 11	5.5	4.2	-1.3
11 / 12	11.3	10.2	-1.1
12 / 13	7.1	10.3	3.1
Avg.	2.6 %	5.8 %	3.2 %
Fq > 0	68 %	76 %	68 %

The core part of the small cap seasonal strategy occurs in January and includes what has been described as the January Effect (Wachtel 1942, 184).

This well documented anomaly of superior performance of stocks in the month of January is based upon the tenet that investors sell stocks in December for tax loss reasons, artificially driving down prices, and creating a great opportunity for astute investors.

In recent times, the January Effect start date has shifter to mid-December and is more pronounced for small caps as their prices are more volatile than large caps. At the beginning of the year, small cap stocks benefit from a phenomenon that I have coined, "beta out of the gate, and coast." If small cap stocks are outperforming at the beginning of the year, money managers will gravitate to the sector in order to produce returns that are above their index benchmark. Once above average returns have been "locked in," the managers then rotate from their small cap overweight positions back to index large cap positions and coast for the rest of the year with above average returns. The overall process boosts small cap stocks at the beginning of the year.

Russell 2000 (small cap index): The 2000 smallest companies in the Russell 3000 stock index (a broad market index). Russell 1000 (large cap index): The 1000 largest companies in the Russell 3000 stock index

For more information on the Russell indexes, see www.Russell.com

Wachtel, S.B. 1942. Certain observations on seasonal movements in stock prices. The Journal of Business and Economics (Winter): 184.

2012-13 Strategy Performance

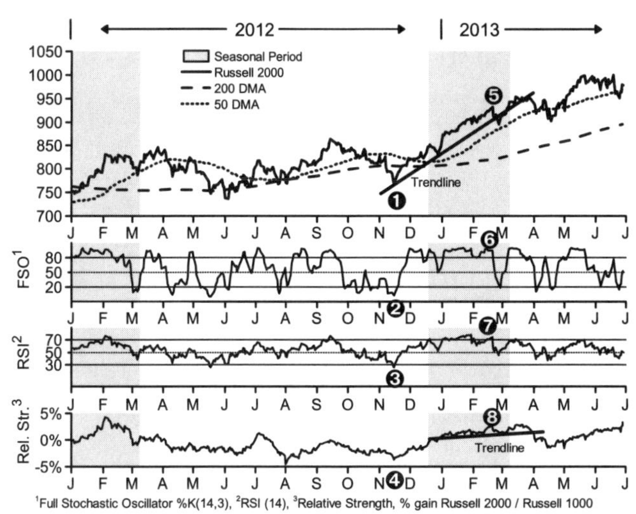

[1]Full Stochastic Oscillator %K(14,3), [2]RSI (14), [3]Relative Strength, % gain Russell 2000 / Russell 1000

Small Cap Sector Russell 2000 Performance

After performing at market for most of 2012, the Russell 2000 (small cap sector) hit a low in mid-November, setting up well for a positive seasonal trade.

Technical Conditions– December 19th to March 7th, 2013

Entry Strategy –Buy Position Early–

When the Russell 2000 bottomed out in mid-November 2012 and bounced back above its 200 and 50 day moving averages❶, it caused the FSO to rise above 20❷, triggering an early buy signal. The RSI action was supportive as it rose above 30❸. At the same time, the Russell 2000 started to outperform the Russell 1000 (large cap sector)❹.

Exit Strategy –Sell Position Early–

After bottoming in November, the Russell 2000 performed strongly and produced a strong uptrend❺. In mid-February, the FSO turned down below 80❻, triggering an early sell signal. The RSI was supportive as it corrected below 70❼. The Russell 2000 briefly retreated from its strong performance relative to the Russell 1000❽.

WEEK 50

Market Indices & Rates
Weekly Values**

Stock Markets	2011	2012
Dow	11,907	13,194
S&P500	1,222	1,422
Nasdaq	2,565	2,997
TSX	11,670	12,290
FTSE	5,415	5,929
DAX	5,733	7,583
Nikkei	8,501	9,624
Hang Seng	18,338	22,431
Commodities	**2011**	**2012**
Oil	96.05	86.15
Gold	1620.6	1705.6
Bond Yields	**2011**	**2012**
USA 5 Yr Treasury	0.85	0.66
USA 10 Yr T	1.94	1.69
USA 20 Yr T	2.63	2.44
Moody's Aaa	3.92	3.65
Moody's Baa	5.20	4.63
CAN 5 Yr T	1.24	1.33
CAN 10 Yr T	1.95	1.76
Money Market	**2011**	**2012**
USA Fed Funds	0.25	0.25
USA 3 Mo T-B	0.00	0.04
CAN tgt overnight rate	1.00	1.00
CAN 3 Mo T-B	0.81	0.96
Foreign Exchange	**2011**	**2012**
EUR/USD	1.31	1.31
GBP/USD	1.55	1.61
USD/CAD	1.03	0.99
USD/JPY	77.93	83.06

DECEMBER

M	T	W	T	F	S	S
1	2	3	4	5	6	7
8	9	10	11	12	13	14
15	16	17	18	19	20	21
22	23	24	25	26	27	28
29	30	31				

JANUARY

M	T	W	T	F	S	S
			1	2	3	4
5	6	7	8	9	10	11
12	13	14	15	16	17	18
19	20	21	22	23	24	25
26	27	28	29	30	31	

FEBRUARY

M	T	W	T	F	S	S
						1
2	3	4	5	6	7	8
9	10	11	12	13	14	15
16	17	18	19	20	21	22
23	24	25	26	27	28	

** Weekly avg closing values- except Fed Funds & CAN overnight tgt rate weekly closing values.

DO THE "NAZ" WITH SANTA

Nasdaq Gives More at Christmas – Dec 15th to Jan 23rd

One of the best times to invest in the major markets is Christmas time. What few investors know is that this seasonally strong time favors the Nasdaq market.

From December 15th to January 23rd, starting in 1972 and ending in 2013, the Nasdaq has outperformed the S&P 500 by an average 2.2% per year.

This rate of return is considered to be very high given that the length of the favorable period is just over one month.

2.2% extra & 83% of time better than S&P 500

Looking for reasons that the Nasdaq outperforms? Interestingly, the Nasdaq starts to outperform at the same time as small companies in December (see *Small Company Effect* strategy).

As investors move into the market to scoop up bargains that have been sold for tax losses, smaller companies and stocks with greater volatility tend to outperform.

Compared with the S&P 500 and Dow Jones, the Nasdaq market tends to be a much greater recipient of the upward move created by investors picking up cheap stocks at this time of the year.

Nasdaq vs. S&P 500 Dec 15th to Jan 23rd 1971/72 To 2012/13

Positive (shaded)

Dec 15 to Jan 23	S&P 500	Nasdaq	Diff
1971/72	6.1 %	7.5 %	1.3 %
1972/73	0.0	-0.7	-0.7
1973/74	4.1	6.8	2.8
1974/75	7.5	8.9	1.4
1975/76	13.0	13.8	0.9
1976/77	-1.7	2.8	4.5
1977/78	-5.1	-3.5	1.6
1978/79	4.7	6.2	1.4
1979/80	4.1	5.6	1.5
1980/81	0.8	3.3	2.5
1981/82	-6.0	-5.0	1.0
1982/83	4.7	5.5	0.8
1983/84	0.9	1.4	0.4
1984/85	9.0	13.3	4.3
1985/86	-2.7	0.8	3.5
1986/87	9.2	10.2	1.0
1987/88	1.8	9.1	7.3
1988/89	3.3	4.6	1.3
1989/90	-5.5	-3.8	1.7
1990/91	1.0	4.1	3.1
1991/92	7.9	15.2	7.2
1992/93	0.8	7.2	6.4
1993/94	2.5	5.7	3.2
1994/95	2.4	4.7	2.3
1995/96	-0.7	-1.0	-0.3
1996/97	6.7	7.3	0.6
1997/98	0.4	2.6	2.1
1998/99	7.4	18.9	11.6
1999/00	2.7	18.6	15.9
2000/01	1.5	4.1	2.6
2001/02	0.5	-1.6	-2.0
2002/03	-0.2	1.9	2.1
2003/04	6.3	9.0	2.7
2004/05	-3.0	-5.8	-2.9
2005/06	-0.7	-0.6	0.1
2006/07	0.2	-0.9	-1.1
2007/08	-8.8	-12.1	-3.3
2008/09	-5.4	-4.1	1.3
2009/10	-2.0	-0.3	1.7
2010/11	3.4	2.4	-1.0
2011/12	8.6	9.6	1.1
2012/13	5.8	6.1	0.4
Avg	2.0 %	4.2 %	2.2 %
Fq > 0	69 %	71 %	83 %

Nasdaq - Avg. Year 1972 to 2012

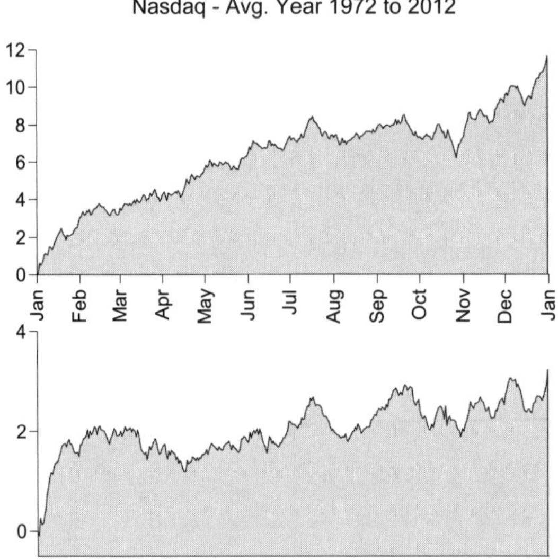

Nasdaq / SP 500 Relative Strength - Avg Yr. 1972 - 2012

Alternate Strategy — For those investors who favor the Nasdaq, an alternative strategy is to invest in the Nasdaq at an earlier date: October 28th. Historically, on average the Nasdaq has started its outperformance at this time. The "Do the Naz with Santa" strategy focuses on the sweet spot of the Nasdaq's outperformance.

Nasdaq is a market with a number of sectors. It is more focused on technology and is typically more volatile than the S&P 500.

2012-13 Strategy Performance

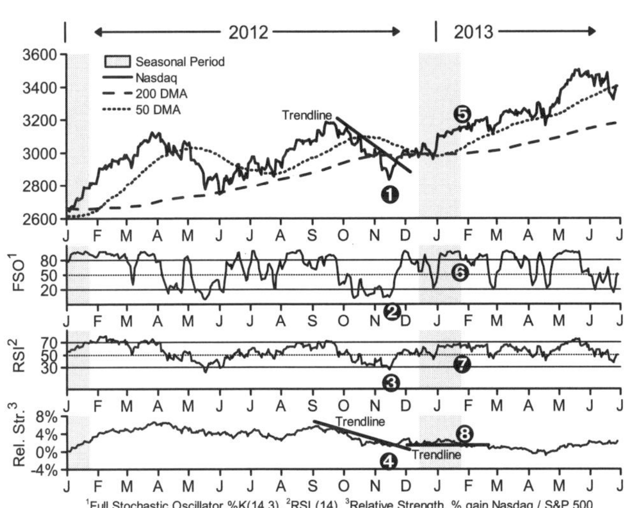

¹Full Stochastic Oscillator %K(14,3), ²RSI (14), ³Relative Strength, % gain Nasdaq / S&P 500

Nasdaq Performance

The Nasdaq started to correct in September 2012 and at the same time, started to underperform the S&P 500. It crossed below the 50 and 200 day moving averages and then bottomed in mid-November, along with the rest of the market.

Technical Conditions– December 15 to January 23, 2013

Entry Strategy –Buy Position Early–

When the Nasdaq bounced in mid-November 2012❶ the FSO crossed above 20❷, triggering an early buy signal. At the same time, the RSI crossed above 30❸ and shortly after in late November the Nasdaq started to outperform the S&P 500❹. Entering the trade early provided a large net benefit to the seasonally successful trade.

Exit Strategy –Sell Position on Exit Date–

In late December, the Nasdaq bounced up sharply off its 50 and 200 moving averages and then continued with a strong performance right to the end of its seasonal period❺. At the end of its seasonal trade, the FSO crossed below 80❻, confirming a sell on the seasonal exit date. The RSI also turned down from 70❼. The exit date proved to be apropos, as the Nasdaq started to underperform the S&P 500❽.

WEEK 51

Market Indices & Rates
Weekly Values**

Stock Markets	2011	2012
Dow	12,088	13,268
S&P500	1,242	1,437
Nasdaq	2,585	3,036
TSX	11,763	12,359
FTSE	5,429	5,942
DAX	5,808	7,647
Nikkei	8,372	9,978
Hang Seng	18,315	22,560
Commodities	**2011**	**2012**
Oil	97.75	88.53
Gold	1606.5	1671.4
Bond Yields	**2011**	**2012**
USA 5 Yr Treasury	0.90	0.76
USA 10 Yr T	1.95	1.80
USA 20 Yr T	2.63	2.56
Moody's Aaa	3.88	3.73
Moody's Baa	5.24	4.70
CAN 5 Yr T	1.25	1.39
CAN 10 Yr T	1.94	1.83
Money Market	**2011**	**2012**
USA Fed Funds	0.25	0.25
USA 3 Mo T-B	0.01	0.06
CAN tgt overnight rate	1.00	1.00
CAN 3 Mo T-B	0.82	0.92
Foreign Exchange	**2011**	**2012**
EUR/USD	1.30	1.32
GBP/USD	1.56	1.62
USD/CAD	1.03	0.99
USD/JPY	78.05	84.23

DECEMBER

M	T	W	T	F	S	S
1	2	3	4	5	6	7
8	9	10	11	12	13	14
15	16	17	18	19	20	21
22	23	24	25	26	27	28
29	30	31				

JANUARY

M	T	W	T	F	S	S
			1	2	3	4
5	6	7	8	9	10	11
12	13	14	15	16	17	18
19	20	21	22	23	24	25
26	27	28	29	30	31	

FEBRUARY

M	T	W	T	F	S	S
						1
2	3	4	5	6	7	8
9	10	11	12	13	14	15
16	17	18	19	20	21	22
23	24	25	26	27	28	

** Weekly avg closing values- except Fed Funds & CAN overnight tgt rate weekly closing values.

CONSUMER STAPLES — NOT NEEDED

SHORT SELL – January 1st to January 22nd

January has the reputation of being a strong month. Since 1950, the S&P 500 has produced an average gain of 1.2% and been positive 63% of the time. One of the weaker sectors in the market in the month of January has been consumer staples. From 1990 to 2012, the sector has produced an average monthly loss of 1.6%.

1.5% gain & successful 67% of the time

The worst performance for the sector is focused on the time period from January 1st to January 22nd. In this time period, the consumer staples sector has produced an average loss of 1.5% (gain for short position) and has been negative 67% (rate of success for short position) of the time.

Con. Staples vs. S&P 500 1990 to 2013

Jan 1 to Jan 22	S&P 500	Negative Staples	Diff
1990	-6.5 %	-8.3 %	-1.8 %
1991	-0.6	-1.1	-0.5
1992	0.3	-3.2	-3.4
1993	0.1	-3.5	-3.6
1994	1.8	-0.6	-2.4
1995	1.2	-1.1	-2.3
1996	-0.4	1.4	1.8
1997	6.1	6.2	0.0
1998	-0.8	-0.9	-0.1
1999	-0.3	-6.8	-6.4
2000	-1.9	-2.0	-0.1
2001	1.7	-8.4	-10.1
2002	-2.5	0.5	3.0
2003	-0.2	1.0	1.1
2004	2.9	-1.0	-3.9
2005	-3.6	0.4	4.1
2006	1.1	-0.8	-1.8
2007	0.3	1.7	1.4
2008	-10.8	-6.7	4.1
2009	-8.4	-4.9	3.5
2010	-2.1	-1.1	1.0
2011	2.0	0.2	-1.9
2012	4.6	-0.4	-5.0
2013	4.7	4.5	-0.2
Avg.	-0.5 %	-1.5 %	-1.0 %
Fq >0	50 %	33 %	38 %

Staples / S&P 500 Relative Strength - Avg Yr. 1990 - 2012

The Consumer Staples vs. S&P 500 table illustrates the relationship between the consumer staples sector and the S&P 500. In general, when the S&P 500 is positive or slightly negative, the consumer staples sector tends to underperform. On the other hand, when the S&P 500 suffers large losses the consumer staples sector tends to outperform the S&P 500.

The direction of the US dollar has an impact on the performance of the consumer staples sector. When the US dollar is rising, the sector tends to fall and when the dollar is falling, the sector tends to increase.

The reason that this relationship exists is that consumer staples companies receive a higher percentage of their revenues from offshore compared with the S&P 500.

This means that if the US dollar is falling, consumer staples companies will benefit from increased revenues because of the lower exchange rate and vice versa. This relationship is important because the US dollar tends to rise in January and therefore put downward pressure on the consumer staples sector.

The SP GICS Consumer Staples Sector encompasses a wide range of consumer staples based companies. For more information on the consumer staples sector, see www.standardandpoors.com

2011-12-13 Strategy Performance

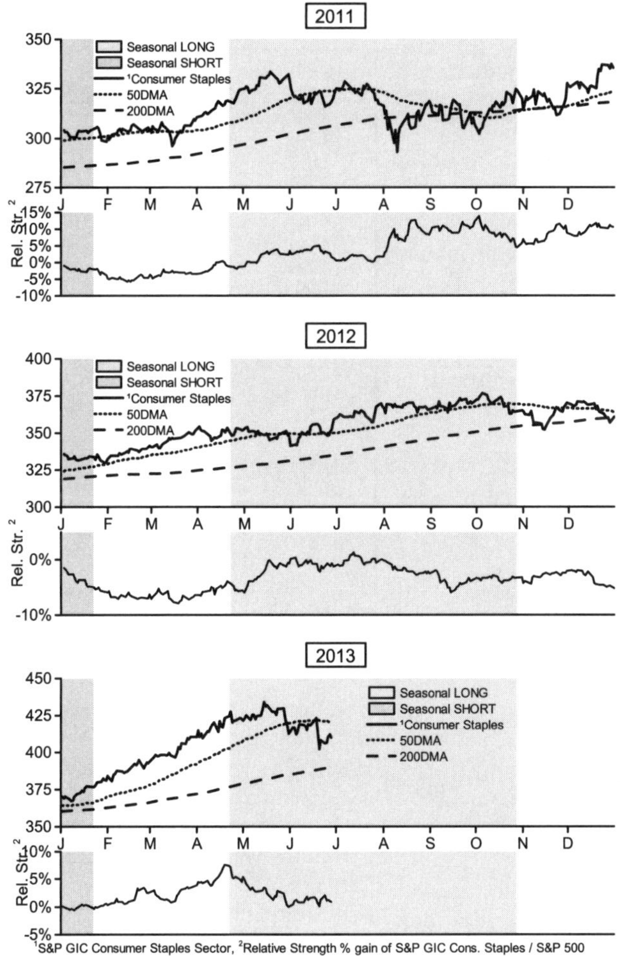

[1]S&P GIC Consumer Staples Sector, [2]Relative Strength % gain of S&P GIC Cons. Staples / S&P 500

Consumer Staples SHORT Performance– 2012-2013

In 2012, the consumer staples sector produced a slightly negative performance in its seasonally weak period from January 1st to January 22nd. The big benefit was not in its absolute performance, but rather its underperformance relative to the S&P 500. It underperformed by 5%.

In 2013, the consumer staples sector performed positively from January 1st to January 22nd as the overall market was strong and all of the major sectors of the market were positive. Nevertheless, the consumer staples sector still managed to slightly underperform the S&P 500 for a successful pair trade against the market.

WEEK 52

Market Indices & Rates
Weekly Values**

Stock Markets	2011	2012
Dow	12,237	13,072
S&P500	1,259	1,417
Nasdaq	2,609	2,987
TSX	11,842	12,354
FTSE	5,549	5,945
DAX	5,852	7,634
Nikkei	8,440	10,257
Hang Seng	18,450	22,609
Commodities	**2011**	**2012**
Oil	99.80	90.23
Gold	1551.0	1656.5
Bond Yields	**2011**	**2012**
USA 5 Yr Treasury	0.90	0.74
USA 10 Yr T	1.94	1.76
USA 20 Yr T	2.62	2.50
Moody's Aaa	3.83	3.65
Moody's Baa	5.21	4.61
CAN 5 Yr T	1.29	1.37
CAN 10 Yr T	1.97	1.80
Money Market	**2011**	**2012**
USA Fed Funds	0.25	0.25
USA 3 Mo T-B	0.02	0.01
CAN tgt overnight rate	1.00	1.00
CAN 3 Mo T-B	0.82	0.92
Foreign Exchange	**2011**	**2012**
EUR/USD	1.30	1.32
GBP/USD	1.55	1.61
USD/CAD	1.02	0.99
USD/JPY	77.67	85.48

DECEMBER

M	T	W	T	F	S	S
1	2	3	4	5	6	7
8	9	10	11	12	13	14
15	16	17	18	19	20	21
22	23	24	25	26	27	28
29	30	31				

JANUARY

M	T	W	T	F	S	S
			1	2	3	4
5	6	7	8	9	10	11
12	13	14	15	16	17	18
19	20	21	22	23	24	25
26	27	28	29	30	31	

FEBRUARY

M	T	W	T	F	S	S
						1
2	3	4	5	6	7	8
9	10	11	12	13	14	15
16	17	18	19	20	21	22
23	24	25	26	27	28	

** Weekly avg closing values- except Fed Funds & CAN overnight tgt rate weekly closing values.

FINANCIALS (U.S.) YEAR END CLEAN UP

Outperform January 19th to April 13th

The U.S. financial sector often starts its strong performance in October and then steps up its performance in mid-December and then strongly outperforms the S&P 500 starting in mid-January.

Extra 2.6% &
18 out of 24 times better than the S&P 500

If fundamental and technical indicators are favorable, then a justification to enter the market early can exist, otherwise a mid-January date represents the start of the seasonal sweet spot.

Financials Sector - Avg. Year 1990 to 2012

Financials / S&P 500 Relative Strength - Avg Yr. 1990-2012

Financials Sector vs. S&P 500
1990 to 2013

Jan 19 to Apr 13	S&P 500	Positive Financials	Diff
1990	1.8 %	-4.3 %	-6.1 %
1991	14.5	27.7	13.2
1992	-3.1	-2.8	0.2
1993	2.8	11.3	8.5
1994	-5.9	-2.7	3.2
1995	8.4	10.4	1.9
1996	4.7	5.6	1.0
1997	-5.0	-2.6	2.4
1998	15.4	22.3	6.9
1999	8.6	13.2	4.6
1900	-1.0	5.9	6.9
2001	-12.2	-6.3	5.9
2002	-1.5	2.6	4.1
2003	-3.7	-5.2	-1.5
2004	-0.9	0.6	1.5
2005	-1.9	-6.2	-4.4
2006	0.9	1.1	0.2
2007	1.9	-3.1	-5.0
2008	0.6	-1.4	-2.0
2009	1.0	15.4	14.4
2010	5.4	11.2	5.8
2011	1.5	-2.1	-3.6
2012	4.8	8.3	3.6
2013	6.9	7.7	0.7
Avg.	1.8 %	4.4 %	2.6 %
Fq > 0	63 %	58 %	75 %

In the 1990s and early 2000s, financial stocks benefited from the tailwind of falling interest rates. During this period, with a few exceptions, this sector has participated in both the rallies and the declines.

The real sweet spot on average each year, from 1989/90 to 2012/13, has been from mid-January to mid-April.

The main driver for the strong seasonal performance of the financial sector has been the year-end earnings of the banks that start to report in mid-January. A strong performance from mid-January has been the result of investors getting into the market early to take advantage of positive year-end earnings.

Interest rates are at historic lows and although they may move lower over the next few years, it is not possible for them to have the same decline that they have had since the 1980s. The Federal Reserve, through its quantitative easing policies, is pushing down the rates on the long part of the yield curve and as a result, flattening the curve and making it difficult for banks to increase profits.

Given this situation, investors should concentrate their financial investments during the strong seasonal period.

It should be noted that Canadian banks have their year-ends at the end of October (reporting in November) and as such, their seasonally strong period starts in October.

Financial SP GIC Sector # 40:
An index that contains companies involved in activities such as banking, mortgage finance, consumer finance, specialized finance, investment banking and brokerage, asset management and custody, corporate lending, insurance, financial investment, and real estate, including REITs.

2012-13 Strategy Performance

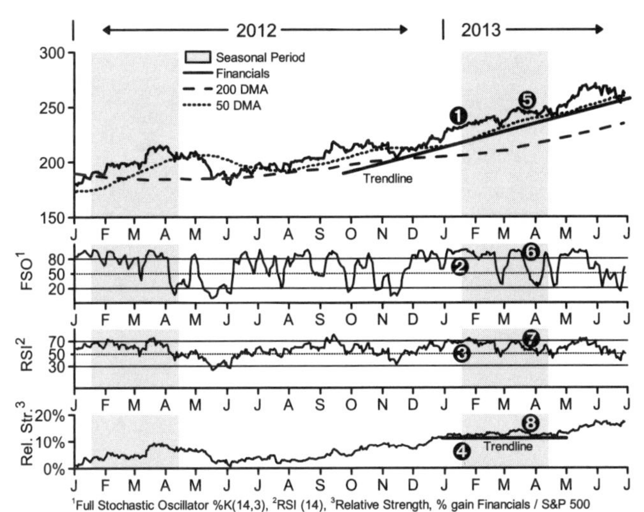

¹Full Stochastic Oscillator %K(14,3), ²RSI (14), ³Relative Strength, % gain Financials / S&P 500

Financial Sector Performance

The financial sector started to perform positively and outperform the S&P 500 in August of 2012. After a brief correction in November, the sector bounced off its 200 day moving average and once again resumed its positive performance, setting up well for its seasonal trade.

Technical Conditions– January 19th to April 13th, 2013

Entry Strategy –Buy Position on Entry Date–

After putting in a positive performance from mid-December 2012, the financial sector rose steadily into the start date of its seasonal period❶. At the same time, the FSO was above 80❷ and the RSI touching 70❸, but the trend was still positive for the sector, even though it was performing at market❹.

Exit Strategy– Sell Position Early–

After a bounce off its 50 day moving average in mid-February, the financial sector rose into mid-March and then started to roll over❺. As the sector performance weakened, the FSO crossed below 80❻, triggering an early sell signal and the RSI bounced off 70❼. Shortly afterwards, the sector's relative performance to the S&P 500 started to weaken❽. Although exiting the trade early produced extra value, the full seasonal trade was successful.

JANUARY

M	T	W	T	F	S	S
			1	2	3	4
5	6	7	8	9	10	11
12	13	14	15	16	17	18
19	20	21	22	23	24	25
26	27	28	29	30	31	

FEBRUARY

M	T	W	T	F	S	S
						1
2	3	4	5	6	7	8
9	10	11	12	13	14	15
16	17	18	19	20	21	22
23	24	25	26	27	28	

MARCH

M	T	W	T	F	S	S
						1
2	3	4	5	6	7	8
9	10	11	12	13	14	15
16	17	18	19	20	21	22
23	24	25	26	27	28	29
30	31					

APRIL

M	T	W	T	F	S	S
		1	2	3	4	5
6	7	8	9	10	11	12
13	14	15	16	17	18	19
20	21	22	23	24	25	26
27	28	29	30			

MAY

M	T	W	T	F	S	S
				1	2	3
4	5	6	7	8	9	10
11	12	13	14	15	16	17
18	19	20	21	22	23	24
25	26	27	28	29	30	31

JUNE

M	T	W	T	F	S	S
1	2	3	4	5	6	7
8	9	10	11	12	13	14
15	16	17	18	19	20	21
22	23	24	25	26	27	28
29	30					

** Weekly avg closing values- except Fed Funds & CAN overnight tgt rate weekly closing values.

APPENDIX

STOCK MARKET RETURNS

S&P 500 PERCENT CHANGES

	JAN	FEB	MAR	APR	MAY	JUN
1950	1.7 %	1.0 %	0.4 %	4.5 %	3.9 %	— 5.8 %
1951	6.1	0.6	— 1.8	4.8	— 4.1	— 2.6
1952	1.6	— 3.6	4.8	— 4.3	2.3	4.6
1953	— 0.7	— 1.8	— 2.4	— 2.6	— 0.3	— 1.6
1954	5.1	0.3	3.0	4.9	3.3	0.1
1955	1.8	0.4	— 0.5	3.8	— 0.1	8.2
1956	— 3.6	3.5	6.9	— 0.2	— 6.6	3.9
1957	— 4.2	— 3.3	2.0	3.7	3.7	— 0.1
1958	4.3	2.1	3.1	3.2	1.5	2.6
1959	0.4	— 0.1	0.1	3.9	1.9	— 0.4
1960	— 7.1	0.9	— 1.4	— 1.8	2.7	2.0
1961	6.3	2.7	2.6	0.4	1.9	— 2.9
1962	— 3.8	1.6	— 0.6	— 6.2	— 8.6	— 8.2
1963	4.9	— 2.9	3.5	4.9	1.4	— 2.0
1964	2.7	1.0	1.5	0.6	1.1	1.6
1965	3.3	— 0.1	— 1.5	3.4	— 0.8	— 4.9
1966	0.5	— 1.8	— 2.2	2.1	— 5.4	— 1.6
1967	7.8	0.2	3.9	4.2	— 5.2	1.8
1968	— 4.4	— 3.1	0.9	8.0	1.3	0.9
1969	— 0.8	— 4.7	3.4	2.1	— 0.2	— 5.6
1970	— 7.6	5.3	0.1	— 9.0	— 6.1	— 5.0
1971	4.0	0.9	3.7	3.6	— 4.2	— 0.9
1972	1.8	2.5	0.6	0.4	1.7	— 2.2
1973	— 1.7	— 3.7	— 0.1	— 4.1	— 1.9	— 0.7
1974	— 1.0	— 0.4	— 2.3	— 3.9	— 3.4	— 1.5
1975	12.3	6.0	2.2	4.7	4.4	4.4
1976	11.8	— 1.1	3.1	— 1.1	— 1.4	4.1
1977	— 5.1	— 2.2	— 1.4	0.0	— 2.4	4.5
1978	— 6.2	— 2.5	2.5	8.5	0.4	— 1.8
1979	4.0	— 3.7	5.5	0.2	— 2.6	3.9
1980	5.8	— 0.4	— 10.2	4.1	4.7	2.7
1981	— 4.6	1.3	3.6	— 2.3	— 0.2	— 1.0
1982	— 1.8	— 6.1	— 1.0	4.0	— 3.9	— 2.0
1983	3.3	1.9	3.3	7.5	— 1.2	3.2
1984	— 0.9	— 3.9	1.3	0.5	— 5.9	1.7
1985	7.4	0.9	— 0.3	— 0.5	5.4	1.2
1986	0.2	7.1	5.3	— 1.4	5.0	1.4
1987	13.2	3.7	2.6	— 1.1	0.6	4.8
1988	4.0	4.2	— 3.3	0.9	0.3	4.3
1989	7.1	— 2.9	2.1	5.0	3.5	— 0.8
1990	— 6.9	0.9	2.4	— 2.7	9.2	— 0.9
1991	4.2	6.7	2.2	0.0	3.9	— 4.8
1992	— 2.0	1.0	— 2.2	2.8	0.1	— 1.7
1993	0.7	1.0	1.9	— 2.5	2.3	0.1
1994	3.3	— 3.0	— 4.6	1.2	1.2	— 2.7
1995	2.4	3.6	2.7	2.8	3.6	2.1
1996	3.3	0.7	0.8	1.3	2.3	0.2
1997	6.1	0.6	— 4.3	5.8	5.9	4.3
1998	1.0	7.0	5.0	0.9	— 1.9	3.9
1999	4.1	— 3.2	3.9	3.8	— 2.5	5.4
2000	— 5.1	— 2.0	9.7	— 3.1	— 2.2	2.4
2001	3.5	— 9.2	— 6.4	7.7	0.5	— 2.5
2002	— 1.6	— 2.1	3.7	— 6.1	— 0.9	— 7.2
2003	— 2.7	— 1.7	0.8	8.1	5.1	1.1
2004	1.7	1.2	— 1.6	— 1.7	1.2	1.8
2005	— 2.5	1.9	— 1.9	— 2.0	3.0	0.0
2006	2.5	0.0	1.1	1.2	— 3.1	0.0
2007	1.4	— 2.2	1.0	4.3	3.3	— 1.8
2008	— 6.1	— 3.5	— 0.6	4.8	1.1	— 8.6
2009	— 8.6	— 11.0	8.5	9.4	5.3	0.0
2010	— 3.7	2.9	5.9	1.5	— 8.2	— 5.4
2011	2.3	3.2	— 0.1	2.8	— 1.4	— 1.8
2012	4.4	4.1	3.1	— 0.7	— 6.3	4.0
FQ POS*	39 / 63	34 / 63	41 / 63	43 / 63	35 / 63	32 / 63
% FQ POS*	61 %	54 %	65 %	68 %	56 %	51 %
AVG GAIN*	1.1 %	-0.1 %	1.2 %	1.5 %	0.1 %	0.0 %
RANK GAIN*	5	11	4	2	8	10

S&P 500 PERCENT CHANGES

JUL	AUG	SEP	OCT	NOV	DEC		YEAR
0.8 %	3.3 %	5.6 %	0.4 %	— 0.1 %	4.6 %	**1950**	21.8 %
6.9	3.9	— 0.1	— 1.4	— 0.3	3.9	**1951**	16.5
1.8	— 1.5	— 2.0	— 0.1	4.6	3.5	**1952**	11.8
2.5	— 5.8	0.1	5.1	0.9	0.2	**1953**	— 6.6
5.7	— 3.4	8.3	— 1.9	8.1	5.1	**1954**	45.0
6.1	— 0.8	1.1	— 3.0	7.5	— 0.1	**1955**	26.4
5.2	— 3.8	— 4.5	0.5	— 1.1	3.5	**1956**	2.6
1.1	— 5.6	— 6.2	— 3.2	1.6	— 4.1	**1957**	— 14.3
4.3	1.2	4.8	2.5	2.2	5.2	**1958**	38.1
3.5	— 1.5	— 4.6	1.1	1.3	2.8	**1959**	8.5
— 2.5	2.6	— 6.0	— 0.2	4.0	4.6	**1960**	— 3.0
3.3	2.0	— 2.0	2.8	3.9	0.3	**1961**	23.1
6.4	1.5	— 4.8	0.4	10.2	1.3	**1962**	— 11.8
— 0.3	4.9	— 1.1	3.2	— 1.1	2.4	**1963**	18.9
1.8	— 1.6	2.9	0.8	— 0.5	0.4	**1964**	13.0
1.3	2.3	3.2	2.7	— 0.9	0.9	**1965**	9.1
— 1.3	— 7.8	— 0.7	4.8	0.3	— 0.1	**1966**	— 13.1
4.5	— 1.2	3.3	— 3.5	0.8	2.6	**1967**	20.1
— 1.8	1.1	3.9	0.7	4.8	— 4.2	**1968**	7.7
— 6.0	4.0	— 2.5	4.3	— 3.4	— 1.9	**1969**	— 11.4
7.3	4.4	3.4	— 1.2	4.7	5.7	**1970**	0.1
— 3.2	3.6	— 0.7	— 4.2	— 0.3	8.6	**1971**	10.8
0.2	3.4	— 0.5	0.9	4.6	1.2	**1972**	15.6
3.8	— 3.7	4.0	— 0.1	— 11.4	1.7	**1973**	— 17.4
— 7.8	— 9.0	— 11.9	16.3	— 5.3	— 2.0	**1974**	— 29.7
— 6.8	— 2.1	— 3.5	6.2	2.5	— 1.2	**1975**	31.5
— 0.8	— 0.5	2.3	— 2.2	— 0.8	5.2	**1976**	19.1
— 1.6	— 2.1	— 0.2	— 4.3	2.7	0.3	**1977**	— 11.5
5.4	2.6	— 0.7	— 9.2	1.7	1.5	**1978**	1.1
0.9	5.3	0.0	— 6.9	4.3	1.7	**1979**	12.3
6.5	0.6	2.5	1.6	10.2	— 3.4	**1980**	25.8
— 0.2	— 6.2	— 5.4	4.9	3.7	— 3.0	**1981**	— 9.7
— 2.3	11.6	0.8	11.0	3.6	1.5	**1982**	14.8
— 3.0	1.1	1.0	— 1.5	1.7	— 0.9	**1983**	17.3
— 1.6	10.6	— 0.3	0.0	— 1.5	2.2	**1984**	1.4
— 0.5	— 1.2	— 3.5	4.3	6.5	4.5	**1985**	26.3
— 5.9	7.1	— 8.5	5.5	2.1	— 2.8	**1986**	14.6
4.8	3.5	— 2.4	— 21.8	— 8.5	7.3	**1987**	2.0
— 0.5	— 3.9	4.0	2.6	— 1.9	1.5	**1988**	12.4
8.8	1.6	— 0.7	— 2.5	1.7	2.1	**1989**	27.3
— 0.5	— 9.4	— 5.1	— 0.7	6.0	2.5	**1990**	— 6.6
4.5	2.0	— 1.9	1.2	— 4.4	11.2	**1991**	26.3
3.9	— 2.4	0.9	0.2	3.0	1.0	**1992**	4.5
— 0.5	3.4	— 1.0	1.9	— 1.3	1.0	**1993**	7.1
3.1	3.8	— 2.7	2.1	— 4.0	1.2	**1994**	— 1.5
3.2	0.0	4.0	— 0.5	4.1	1.7	**1995**	34.1
— 4.6	1.9	5.4	2.6	7.3	— 2.2	**1996**	20.3
7.8	— 5.7	5.3	— 3.4	4.5	1.6	**1997**	31.0
— 1.2	— 14.6	6.2	8.0	5.9	5.6	**1998**	26.7
— 3.2	— 0.6	— 2.9	6.3	1.9	5.8	**1999**	19.5
— 1.6	6.1	— 5.3	— 0.5	— 8.0	0.4	**2000**	— 10.1
— 1.1	— 6.4	— 8.2	1.8	7.5	0.8	**2001**	— 13.0
— 7.9	0.5	— 11.0	8.6	5.7	— 6.0	**2002**	— 23.4
1.6	1.8	— 1.2	5.5	0.7	5.1	**2003**	26.4
-3.4	0.2	0.9	1.4	3.9	3.2	**2004**	9.0
3.6	— 1.1	0.7	— 1.8	3.5	— 0.1	**2005**	3.0
0.5	2.1	2.5	3.2	1.6	1.3	**2006**	13.6
— 3.2	1.3	3.6	1.5	— 4.4	— 0.9	**2007**	3.5
— 1.0	1.2	— 9.2	— 16.8	— 7.5	0.8	**2008**	-38.5
7.4	3.4	3.6	— 2.0	5.7	1.8	**2009**	23.5
6.9	— 4.7	8.8	3.7	— 0.2	6.5	**2010**	12.8
— 2.1	— 5.7	— 7.2	10.8	— 0.5	0.9	**2011**	0.0
1.3	2.0	2.4	— 2.0	0.3	0.7	**2012**	13.4
34 / 63	35 / 63	28 / 63	37 / 63	41/ 63	49 / 63		46 / 63
54 %	56 %	44 %	59 %	65 %	78 %		73 %
1.0 %	0.0 %	— 0.5 %	0.7 %	1.5 %	1.7 %		8.7 %
6	9	12	7	3	1		

STOCK MKT

S&P 500 MONTH CLOSING VALUES

	JAN	FEB	MAR	APR	MAY	JUN
1950	17	17	17	18	19	18
1951	22	22	21	22	22	21
1952	24	23	24	23	24	25
1953	26	26	25	25	25	24
1954	26	26	27	28	29	29
1955	37	37	37	38	38	41
1956	44	45	48	48	45	47
1957	45	43	44	46	47	47
1958	42	41	42	43	44	45
1959	55	55	55	58	59	58
1960	56	56	55	54	56	57
1961	62	63	65	65	67	65
1962	69	70	70	65	60	55
1963	66	64	67	70	71	69
1964	77	78	79	79	80	82
1965	88	87	86	89	88	84
1966	93	91	89	91	86	85
1967	87	87	90	94	89	91
1968	92	89	90	97	99	100
1969	103	98	102	104	103	98
1970	85	90	90	82	77	73
1971	96	97	100	104	100	99
1972	104	107	107	108	110	107
1973	116	112	112	107	105	104
1974	97	96	94	90	87	86
1975	77	82	83	87	91	95
1976	101	100	103	102	100	104
1977	102	100	98	98	96	100
1978	89	87	89	97	97	96
1979	100	96	102	102	99	103
1980	114	114	102	106	111	114
1981	130	131	136	133	133	131
1982	120	113	112	116	112	110
1983	145	148	153	164	162	168
1984	163	157	159	160	151	153
1985	180	181	181	180	190	192
1986	212	227	239	236	247	251
1987	274	284	292	288	290	304
1988	257	268	259	261	262	274
1989	297	289	295	310	321	318
1990	329	332	340	331	361	358
1991	344	367	375	375	390	371
1992	409	413	404	415	415	408
1993	439	443	452	440	450	451
1994	482	467	446	451	457	444
1995	470	487	501	515	533	545
1996	636	640	646	654	669	671
1997	786	791	757	801	848	885
1998	980	1049	1102	1112	1091	1134
1999	1280	1238	1286	1335	1302	1373
2000	1394	1366	1499	1452	1421	1455
2001	1366	1240	1160	1249	1256	1224
2002	1130	1107	1147	1077	1067	990
2003	856	841	848	917	964	975
2004	1131	1145	1126	1107	1121	1141
2005	1181	1204	1181	1157	1192	1191
2006	1280	1281	1295	1311	1270	1270
2007	1438	1407	1421	1482	1531	1503
2008	1379	1331	1323	1386	1400	1280
2009	826	735	798	873	919	919
2010	1074	1104	1169	1187	1089	1031
2011	1286	1327	1326	1364	1345	1321
2012	1312	1366	1408	1398	1310	1362

S&P 500 MONTH CLOSING VALUES

JUL	AUG	SEP	OCT	NOV	DEC	
18	18	19	20	20	20	**1950**
22	23	23	23	23	24	**1951**
25	25	25	25	26	27	**1952**
25	23	23	25	25	25	**1953**
31	30	32	32	34	36	**1954**
44	43	44	42	46	45	**1955**
49	48	45	46	45	47	**1956**
48	45	42	41	42	40	**1957**
47	48	50	51	52	55	**1958**
61	60	57	58	58	60	**1959**
56	57	54	53	56	58	**1960**
67	68	67	69	71	72	**1961**
58	59	56	57	62	63	**1962**
69	73	72	74	73	75	**1963**
83	82	84	85	84	85	**1964**
85	87	90	92	92	92	**1965**
84	77	77	80	80	80	**1966**
95	94	97	93	94	96	**1967**
98	99	103	103	108	104	**1968**
92	96	93	97	94	92	**1969**
78	82	84	83	87	92	**1970**
96	99	98	94	94	102	**1971**
107	111	111	112	117	118	**1972**
108	104	108	108	96	98	**1973**
79	72	64	74	70	69	**1974**
89	87	84	89	91	90	**1975**
103	103	105	103	102	107	**1976**
99	97	97	92	95	95	**1977**
101	103	103	93	95	96	**1978**
104	109	109	102	106	108	**1979**
122	122	125	127	141	136	**1980**
131	123	116	122	126	123	**1981**
107	120	120	134	139	141	**1982**
163	164	166	164	166	165	**1983**
151	167	166	166	164	167	**1984**
191	189	182	190	202	211	**1985**
236	253	231	244	249	242	**1986**
319	330	322	252	230	247	**1987**
272	262	272	279	274	278	**1988**
346	351	349	340	346	353	**1989**
356	323	306	304	322	330	**1990**
388	395	388	392	375	417	**1991**
424	414	418	419	431	436	**1992**
448	464	459	468	462	466	**1993**
458	475	463	472	454	459	**1994**
562	562	584	582	605	616	**1995**
640	652	687	705	757	741	**1996**
954	899	947	915	955	970	**1997**
1121	957	1017	1099	1164	1229	**1998**
1329	1320	1283	1363	1389	1469	**1999**
1431	1518	1437	1429	1315	1320	**2000**
1211	1134	1041	1060	1139	1148	**2001**
912	916	815	886	936	880	**2002**
990	1008	996	1051	1058	1112	**2003**
1102	1104	1115	1130	1174	1212	**2004**
1234	1220	1229	1207	1249	1248	**2005**
1277	1304	1336	1378	1401	1418	**2006**
1455	1474	1527	1549	1481	1468	**2007**
1267	1283	1165	969	896	903	**2008**
987	1021	1057	1036	1096	1115	**2009**
1102	1049	1141	1183	1181	1258	**2010**
1292	1219	1131	1253	1247	1258	**2011**
1379	1407	1441	1412	1416	1426	**2012**

STOCK MKT

DOW JONES PERCENT MONTH CHANGES

	JAN	FEB	MAR	APR	MAY	JUN
1950	0.8 %	0.8 %	1.3 %	4.0 %	4.2 %	— 6.4 %
1951	5.7	1.3	— 1.7	4.5	— 3.6	— 2.8
1952	0.6	— 3.9	3.6	— 4.4	2.1	4.3
1953	— 0.7	— 2.0	— 1.5	— 1.8	— 0.9	— 1.5
1954	4.1	0.7	3.1	5.2	2.6	1.8
1955	1.1	0.8	— 0.5	3.9	— 0.2	6.2
1956	— 3.6	2.8	5.8	0.8	— 7.4	3.1
1957	— 4.1	— 3.0	2.2	4.1	2.1	— 0.3
1958	3.3	— 2.2	1.6	2.0	1.5	3.3
1959	1.8	1.6	— 0.3	3.7	3.2	0.0
1960	— 8.4	1.2	— 2.1	— 2.4	4.0	2.4
1961	5.2	2.1	2.2	0.3	2.7	— 1.8
1962	— 4.3	1.2	— 0.2	— 5.9	— 7.8	— 8.5
1963	4.7	— 2.9	3.0	5.2	1.3	— 2.8
1964	2.9	1.9	1.6	— 0.3	1.2	1.3
1965	3.3	0.1	— 1.6	3.7	— 0.5	— 5.4
1966	1.5	— 3.2	— 2.8	1.0	— 5.3	— 1.6
1967	8.2	— 1.2	3.2	3.6	— 5.0	0.9
1968	— 5.5	— 1.8	0.0	8.5	— 1.4	— 0.1
1969	0.2	— 4.3	3.3	1.6	— 1.3	— 6.9
1970	— 7.0	4.5	1.0	— 6.3	— 4.8	— 2.4
1971	3.5	1.2	2.9	4.1	— 3.6	— 1.8
1972	1.3	2.9	1.4	1.4	0.7	— 3.3
1973	— 2.1	— 4.4	— 0.4	— 3.1	— 2.2	— 1.1
1974	0.6	0.6	— 1.6	— 1.2	— 4.1	0.0
1975	14.2	5.0	3.9	6.9	1.3	5.6
1976	14.4	— 0.3	2.8	— 0.3	— 2.2	2.8
1977	— 5.0	— 1.9	— 1.8	0.8	— 3.0	2.0
1978	— 7.4	— 3.6	2.1	10.5	0.4	— 2.6
1979	4.2	— 3.6	6.6	— 0.8	— 3.8	2.4
1980	4.4	— 1.5	— 9.0	4.0	4.1	2.0
1981	— 1.7	2.9	3.0	— 0.6	— 0.6	— 1.5
1982	— 0.4	— 5.4	— 0.2	3.1	— 3.4	— 0.9
1983	2.8	3.4	1.6	8.5	— 2.1	1.8
1984	— 3.0	— 5.4	0.9	0.5	— 5.6	2.5
1985	6.2	— 0.2	— 1.3	— 0.7	4.6	1.5
1986	1.6	8.8	6.4	— 1.9	5.2	0.9
1987	13.8	3.1	3.6	— 0.8	0.2	5.5
1988	1.0	5.8	— 4.0	2.2	— 0.1	5.4
1989	8.0	— 3.6	1.6	5.5	2.5	— 1.6
1990	— 5.9	1.4	3.0	— 1.9	8.3	0.1
1991	3.9	5.3	1.1	— 0.9	4.8	— 4.0
1992	1.7	1.4	— 1.0	3.8	1.1	— 2.3
1993	0.3	1.8	1.9	— 0.2	2.9	— 0.3
1994	6.0	— 3.7	— 5.1	1.3	2.1	— 3.5
1995	0.2	4.3	3.7	3.9	3.3	2.0
1996	5.4	1.7	1.9	— 0.3	1.3	0.2
1997	5.7	0.9	— 4.3	6.5	4.6	4.7
1998	0.0	8.1	3.0	3.0	— 1.8	0.6
1999	1.9	— 0.6	5.2	10.2	— 2.1	3.9
2000	— 4.5	— 7.4	7.8	— 1.7	— 2.0	— 0.7
2001	0.9	— 3.6	— 5.9	8.7	1.6	— 3.8
2002	— 1.0	1.9	2.9	— 4.4	— 0.2	— 6.9
2003	— 3.5	— 2.0	1.3	6.1	4.4	1.5
2004	0.3	0.9	— 2.1	— 1.3	— 0.4	2.4
2005	— 2.7	2.6	— 2.4	— 3.0	2.7	— 1.8
2006	1.4	1.2	1.1	2.3	— 1.7	— 0.2
2007	1.3	— 2.8	0.7	5.7	4.3	— 1.6
2008	— 4.6	— 3.0	0.0	4.5	— 1.4	— 10.2
2009	— 8.8	— 11.7	7.7	7.3	4.1	— 0.6
2010	— 3.5	2.6	5.1	1.4	— 7.9	— 3.6
2011	2.7	2.8	0.8	4.0	— 1.9	— 1.2
2012	3.4	3.8	2.0	0.0	— 6.2	3.9
FQ POS	41 / 63	36 / 63	41 / 63	41 / 63	31 / 63	29 / 63
% FQ POS	65 %	57 %	65 %	65 %	49 %	46 %
AVG GAIN	1.1 %	0.1 %	1.1 %	2.0 %	— 0.1 %	— 0.3 %
RANK GAIN	6	8	5	1	8	11

DOW JONES PERCENT MONTH CHANGES

STOCK MKT

JUL	AUG	SEP	OCT	NOV	DEC		YEAR
0.1 %	3.6 %	4.4 %	— 0.6 %	1.2 %	3.4 %	**1950**	17.6 %
6.3	4.8	0.3	— 3.2	— 0.4	3.0	**1951**	14.4
1.9	— 1.6	— 1.6	— 0.5	5.4	2.9	**1952**	8.4
2.6	— 5.2	1.1	4.5	2.0	— 0.2	**1953**	— 3.8
4.3	— 3.5	7.4	— 2.3	9.9	4.6	**1954**	44.0
3.2	0.5	— 0.3	— 2.5	6.2	1.1	**1955**	20.8
5.1	— 3.1	— 5.3	1.0	— 1.5	5.6	**1956**	2.3
1.0	— 4.7	— 5.8	— 3.4	2.0	— 3.2	**1957**	— 12.8
5.2	1.1	4.6	2.1	2.6	4.7	**1958**	34.0
4.9	— 1.6	— 4.9	2.4	1.9	3.1	**1959**	16.4
— 3.7	1.5	— 7.3	0.1	2.9	3.1	**1960**	— 9.3
3.1	2.1	— 2.6	0.4	2.5	1.3	**1961**	18.7
6.5	1.9	— 5.0	1.9	10.1	0.4	**1962**	— 10.8
— 1.6	4.9	0.5	3.1	— 0.6	1.7	**1963**	17.0
1.2	— 0.3	4.4	— 0.3	0.3	— 0.1	**1964**	14.6
1.6	1.3	4.2	3.2	— 1.5	2.4	**1965**	10.9
— 2.6	— 7.0	— 1.8	4.2	— 1.9	— 0.7	**1966**	— 18.9
5.1	— 0.3	2.8	— 5.1	— 0.4	3.3	**1967**	15.2
— 1.6	1.5	4.4	1.8	3.4	— 4.2	**1968**	4.3
— 6.6	2.6	— 2.8	5.3	— 5.1	— 1.5	**1969**	— 15.2
7.4	4.2	— 0.5	— 0.7	5.1	5.6	**1970**	4.8
— 3.7	4.6	— 1.2	— 5.4	— 0.9	7.1	**1971**	6.1
— 0.5	4.2	— 1.1	0.2	6.6	0.2	**1972**	14.6
3.9	— 4.2	6.7	1.0	— 14.0	3.5	**1973**	— 16.6
— 5.6	— 10.4	— 10.4	9.5	— 7.0	— 0.4	**1974**	— 27.6
— 5.4	0.5	— 5.0	5.3	3.0	— 1.0	**1975**	38.3
— 1.8	— 1.1	1.7	— 2.6	— 1.8	6.1	**1976**	17.9
— 2.9	— 3.2	— 1.7	— 3.4	1.4	0.2	**1977**	— 17.3
5.3	1.7	— 1.3	— 8.5	0.8	0.8	**1978**	— 3.2
0.5	4.9	— 1.0	— 7.2	0.8	2.0	**1979**	4.2
7.8	— 0.3	0.0	— 0.8	7.4	— 2.9	**1980**	14.9
— 2.5	— 7.4	— 3.6	0.3	4.3	— 1.6	**1981**	— 9.2
— 0.4	11.5	— 0.6	10.6	4.8	0.7	**1982**	19.6
— 1.9	1.4	1.4	— 0.6	4.1	— 1.4	**1983**	20.3
— 1.5	9.8	— 1.4	0.1	— 1.5	1.9	**1984**	— 3.7
0.9	— 1.0	— 0.4	3.4	7.1	5.1	**1985**	27.7
— 6.2	6.9	— 6.9	6.2	1.9	— 1.0	**1986**	22.6
6.4	3.5	— 2.5	— 23.2	— 8.0	5.7	**1987**	2.3
— 0.6	— 4.6	4.0	1.7	— 1.6	2.6	**1988**	11.9
9.0	2.9	— 1.6	— 1.8	2.3	1.7	**1989**	27.0
0.9	— 10.0	— 6.2	— 0.4	4.8	2.9	**1990**	— 4.3
4.1	0.6	— 0.9	1.7	— 5.7	9.5	**1991**	20.3
2.3	— 4.0	0.4	— 1.4	2.4	— 0.1	**1992**	4.2
0.7	3.2	— 2.6	3.5	0.1	1.9	**1993**	13.7
3.8	4.0	— 1.8	1.7	— 4.3	2.5	**1994**	2.1
3.3	— 2.1	3.9	— 0.7	6.7	0.8	**1995**	33.5
— 2.2	1.6	4.7	2.5	8.2	— 1.1	**1996**	26.0
7.2	— 7.3	4.2	— 6.3	5.1	1.1	**1997**	22.6
— 0.8	— 15.1	4.0	9.6	6.1	0.7	**1998**	16.1
— 2.9	1.6	— 4.5	3.8	1.4	5.3	**1999**	24.7
0.7	6.6	— 5.0	3.0	— 5.1	3.6	**2000**	— 5.8
0.2	— 5.4	— 11.1	2.6	8.6	1.7	**2001**	— 7.1
— 5.5	— 0.8	— 12.4	10.6	5.9	— 6.2	**2002**	— 16.8
2.8	2.0	— 1.5	5.7	— 0.2	6.9	**2003**	25.3
— 2.8	0.3	— 0.9	— 0.5	4.0	3.4	**2004**	3.1
3.6	— 1.5	0.8	— 1.2	3.5	— 0.8	**2005**	— 0.6
0.3	1.7	2.6	3.4	1.2	2.0	**2006**	16.3
— 1.5	1.1	4.0	0.2	— 4.0	— 0.8	**2007**	6.4
0.2	1.5	— 6.0	— 14.1	— 5.3	— 0.6	**2008**	— 33.8
8.6	3.5	2.3	0.0	6.5	0.8	**2009**	18.8
7.1	— 4.3	7.7	3.1	— 1.0	5.2	**2010**	11.0
— 2.2	— 4.4	— 6.0	9.5	0.8	1.4	**2011**	5.5
1.0	0.6	2.6	— 2.5	— 0.5	0.6	**2012**	7.3
39 / 63	36 / 63	25 / 63	37 / 63	41 / 63	45 / 63		45 / 63
62 %	57 %	40 %	59 %	65 %	71 %		71 %
1.2 %	— 0.1 %	— 0.8 %	0.5 %	1.5 %	1.7 %		8.1 %
4	9	12	7	3	2		

DOW JONES MONTH CLOSING VALUES

	JAN	FEB	MAR	APR	MAY	JUN
1950	202	203	206	214	223	209
1951	249	252	248	259	250	243
1952	271	260	270	258	263	274
1953	290	284	280	275	272	268
1954	292	295	304	319	328	334
1955	409	412	410	426	425	451
1956	471	484	512	516	478	493
1957	479	465	475	494	505	503
1958	450	440	447	456	463	478
1959	594	604	602	624	644	644
1960	623	630	617	602	626	641
1961	648	662	677	679	697	684
1962	700	708	707	665	613	561
1963	683	663	683	718	727	707
1964	785	800	813	811	821	832
1965	903	904	889	922	918	868
1966	984	952	925	934	884	870
1967	850	839	866	897	853	860
1968	856	841	841	912	899	898
1969	946	905	936	950	938	873
1970	744	778	786	736	700	684
1971	869	879	904	942	908	891
1972	902	928	941	954	961	929
1973	999	955	951	921	901	892
1974	856	861	847	837	802	802
1975	704	739	768	821	832	879
1976	975	973	1000	997	975	1003
1977	954	936	919	927	899	916
1978	770	742	757	837	841	819
1979	839	809	862	855	822	842
1980	876	863	786	817	851	868
1981	947	975	1004	998	992	977
1982	871	824	823	848	820	812
1983	1076	1113	1130	1226	1200	1222
1984	1221	1155	1165	1171	1105	1132
1985	1287	1284	1267	1258	1315	1336
1986	1571	1709	1819	1784	1877	1893
1987	2158	2224	2305	2286	2292	2419
1988	1958	2072	1988	2032	2031	2142
1989	2342	2258	2294	2419	2480	2440
1990	2591	2627	2707	2657	2877	2881
1991	2736	2882	2914	2888	3028	2907
1992	3223	3268	3236	3359	3397	3319
1993	3310	3371	3435	3428	3527	3516
1994	3978	3832	3636	3682	3758	3625
1995	3844	4011	4158	4321	4465	4556
1996	5395	5486	5587	5569	5643	5655
1997	6813	6878	6584	7009	7331	7673
1998	7907	8546	8800	9063	8900	8952
1999	9359	9307	9786	10789	10560	10971
2000	10941	10128	10922	10734	10522	10448
2001	10887	10495	9879	10735	10912	10502
2002	9920	10106	10404	9946	9925	9243
2003	8054	7891	7992	8480	8850	8985
2004	10488	10584	10358	10226	10188	10435
2005	10490	10766	10504	10193	10467	10275
2006	10865	10993	11109	11367	11168	11150
2007	12622	12269	12354	13063	13628	13409
2008	12650	12266	12263	12820	12638	11350
2009	8001	7063	7609	8168	8500	8447
2010	10067	10325	10857	11009	10137	9774
2011	11892	12226	12320	12811	12570	12414
2012	12633	12952	13212	13214	12393	12880

DOW JONES MONTH CLOSING VALUES

JUL	AUG	SEP	OCT	NOV	DEC	
209	217	226	225	228	235	**1950**
258	270	271	262	261	269	**1951**
280	275	271	269	284	292	**1952**
275	261	264	276	281	281	**1953**
348	336	361	352	387	404	**1954**
466	468	467	455	483	488	**1955**
518	502	475	480	473	500	**1956**
509	484	456	441	450	436	**1957**
503	509	532	543	558	584	**1958**
675	664	632	647	659	679	**1959**
617	626	580	580	597	616	**1960**
705	720	701	704	722	731	**1961**
598	609	579	590	649	652	**1962**
695	729	733	755	751	763	**1963**
841	839	875	873	875	874	**1964**
882	893	931	961	947	969	**1965**
847	788	774	807	792	786	**1966**
904	901	927	880	876	905	**1967**
883	896	936	952	985	944	**1968**
816	837	813	856	812	800	**1969**
734	765	761	756	794	839	**1970**
858	898	887	839	831	890	**1971**
925	964	953	956	1018	1020	**1972**
926	888	947	957	822	851	**1973**
757	679	608	666	619	616	**1974**
832	835	794	836	861	852	**1975**
985	974	990	965	947	1005	**1976**
890	862	847	818	830	831	**1977**
862	877	866	793	799	805	**1978**
846	888	879	816	822	839	**1979**
935	933	932	925	993	964	**1980**
952	882	850	853	889	875	**1981**
809	901	896	992	1039	1047	**1982**
1199	1216	1233	1225	1276	1259	**1983**
1115	1224	1207	1207	1189	1212	**1984**
1348	1334	1329	1374	1472	1547	**1985**
1775	1898	1768	1878	1914	1896	**1986**
2572	2663	2596	1994	1834	1939	**1987**
2129	2032	2113	2149	2115	2169	**1988**
2661	2737	2693	2645	2706	2753	**1989**
2905	2614	2453	2442	2560	2634	**1990**
3025	3044	3017	3069	2895	3169	**1991**
3394	3257	3272	3226	3305	3301	**1992**
3540	3651	3555	3681	3684	3754	**1993**
3765	3913	3843	3908	3739	3834	**1994**
4709	4611	4789	4756	5075	5117	**1995**
5529	5616	5882	6029	6522	6448	**1996**
8223	7622	7945	7442	7823	7908	**1997**
8883	7539	7843	8592	9117	9181	**1998**
10655	10829	10337	10730	10878	11453	**1999**
10522	11215	10651	10971	10415	10788	**2000**
10523	9950	8848	9075	9852	10022	**2001**
8737	8664	7592	8397	8896	8342	**2002**
9234	9416	9275	9801	9782	10454	**2003**
10140	10174	10080	10027	10428	10783	**2004**
10641	10482	10569	10440	10806	10718	**2005**
11186	11381	11679	12801	12222	12463	**2006**
13212	13358	13896	13930	13372	13265	**2007**
11378	11544	10851	9325	8829	8776	**2008**
9172	9496	9712	9713	10345	10428	**2009**
10466	10015	10788	11118	11006	11578	**2010**
12143	11614	10913	11955	12046	12218	**2011**
13009	13091	13437	13096	13026	13104	**2012**

STOCK MKT

NASDAQ PERCENT MONTH CHANGES

	JAN	FEB	MAR	APR	MAY	JUN
1972	4.2	5.5	2.2	2.5	0.9	— 1.8
1973	— 4.0	— 6.2	— 2.4	— 8.2	— 4.8	— 1.6
1974	3.0	— 0.6	— 2.2	— 5.9	— 7.7	— 5.3
1975	16.6	4.6	3.6	3.8	5.8	4.7
1976	12.1	3.7	0.4	— 0.6	— 2.3	2.6
1977	— 2.4	— 1.0	— 0.5	1.4	0.1	4.3
1978	— 4.0	0.6	4.7	8.5	4.4	0.0
1979	6.6	— 2.6	7.5	1.6	— 1.8	5.1
1980	7.0	— 2.3	— 17.1	6.9	7.5	4.9
1981	— 2.2	0.1	6.1	3.1	3.1	— 3.5
1982	— 3.8	— 4.8	— 2.1	5.2	— 3.3	— 4.1
1983	6.9	5.0	3.9	8.2	5.3	3.2
1984	— 3.7	— 5.9	— 0.7	— 1.3	— 5.9	2.9
1985	12.8	2.0	— 1.8	0.5	3.6	1.9
1986	3.4	7.1	4.2	2.3	4.4	1.3
1987	12.4	8.4	1.2	— 2.9	— 0.3	2.0
1988	4.3	6.5	2.1	1.2	— 2.3	6.6
1989	5.2	— 0.4	1.8	5.1	4.3	— 2.4
1990	— 8.6	2.4	2.3	— 3.5	9.3	0.7
1991	10.8	9.4	6.4	0.5	4.4	— 6.0
1992	5.8	2.1	— 4.7	— 4.2	1.1	— 3.7
1993	2.9	— 3.7	2.9	— 4.2	5.9	0.5
1994	3.0	— 1.0	— 6.2	— 1.3	0.2	— 4.0
1995	0.4	5.1	3.0	3.3	2.4	8.0
1996	0.7	3.8	0.1	8.1	4.4	— 4.7
1997	6.9	— 5.1	— 6.7	3.2	11.1	3.0
1998	3.1	9.3	3.7	1.8	— 4.8	6.5
1999	14.3	— 8.7	7.6	3.3	— 2.8	8.7
2000	— 3.2	19.2	— 2.6	— 15.6	— 11.9	16.6
2001	12.2	— 22.4	— 14.5	15.0	— 0.3	2.4
2002	— 0.8	— 10.5	6.6	— 8.5	— 4.3	— 9.4
2003	— 1.1	1.3	0.3	9.2	9.0	1.7
2004	3.1	— 1.8	— 1.8	— 3.7	3.5	3.1
2005	— 5.2	— 0.5	— 2.6	— 3.9	7.6	— 0.5
2006	4.6	— 1.1	2.6	— 0.7	— 6.2	— 0.3
2007	2.0	— 1.9	0.2	4.3	3.1	0.0
2008	— 9.9	— 5.0	0.3	5.9	4.6	— 9.1
2009	— 6.4	— 6.7	10.9	12.3	3.3	3.4
2010	— 5.4	4.2	7.1	2.6	— 8.3	— 6.5
2011	1.8	3.0	0.0	3.3	— 1.3	— 2.2
2012	8.0	5.4	4.2	— 1.5	— 7.2	3.8
FQ POS	27/41	21/41	26/41	26/41	24/41	24/41
% FQ POS	66 %	51 %	63 %	63 %	59 %	59 %
AVG GAIN	2.8 %	0.4 %	0.7 %	1.4 %	0.8 %	0.8 %
RANK GAIN	1	9	7	4	5	6

NASDAQ PERCENT MONTH CHANGES

STOCK MKT

JUL	AUG	SEP	OCT	NOV	DEC		YEAR
— 1.8	1.7	— 0.3	0.5	2.1	0.6	**1972**	17.2
7.6	— 3.5	6.0	— 0.9	— 15.1	— 1.4	**1973**	— 31.1
— 7.9	— 10.9	— 10.7	17.2	— 3.5	— 5.0	**1974**	— 35.1
— 4.4	— 5.0	— 5.9	3.6	2.4	— 1.5	**1975**	29.8
1.1	— 1.7	1.7	— 1.0	0.9	7.4	**1976**	26.1
0.9	— 0.5	0.7	— 3.3	5.8	1.8	**1977**	7.3
5.0	6.9	— 1.6	— 16.4	3.2	2.9	**1978**	12.3
2.3	6.4	— 0.3	— 9.6	6.4	4.8	**1979**	28.1
8.9	5.7	3.4	2.7	8.0	— 2.8	**1980**	33.9
— 1.9	— 7.5	— 8.0	8.4	3.1	— 2.7	**1981**	— 3.2
— 2.3	6.2	5.6	13.3	9.3	0.0	**1982**	18.7
— 4.6	— 3.8	1.4	— 7.4	4.1	— 2.5	**1983**	19.9
— 4.2	10.9	— 1.8	— 1.2	— 1.9	1.9	**1984**	— 11.3
1.7	— 1.2	— 5.8	4.4	7.4	3.5	**1985**	31.5
— 8.4	3.1	— 8.4	2.9	— 0.3	— 3.0	**1986**	7.4
2.4	4.6	— 2.4	— 27.2	— 5.6	8.3	**1987**	— 5.2
— 1.9	— 2.8	2.9	— 1.3	— 2.9	2.7	**1988**	15.4
4.2	3.4	0.8	— 3.7	0.1	— 0.3	**1989**	19.2
— 5.2	— 13.0	— 9.6	— 4.3	8.9	4.1	**1990**	— 17.8
5.5	4.7	0.2	3.1	— 3.5	11.9	**1991**	56.9
3.1	— 3.0	3.6	3.8	7.9	3.7	**1992**	15.5
0.1	5.4	2.7	2.2	— 3.2	3.0	**1993**	14.7
2.3	6.0	— 0.2	1.7	— 3.5	0.2	**1994**	— 3.2
7.3	1.9	2.3	— 0.7	2.2	— 0.7	**1995**	39.9
— 8.8	5.6	7.5	— 0.4	5.8	— 0.1	**1996**	22.7
10.5	— 0.4	6.2	— -5.5	0.4	— 1.9	**1997**	21.6
— 1.2	— 19.9	13.0	4.6	10.1	12.5	**1998**	39.6
— 1.8	3.8	0.2	8.0	12.5	22.0	**1999**	85.6
— 5.0	11.7	— 12.7	— 8.3	— 22.9	— 4.9	**2000**	— 39.3
— 6.2	— 10.9	— 17.0	12.8	14.2	1.0	**2001**	— 21.1
— 9.2	— 1.0	— 10.9	13.5	11.2	— 9.7	**2002**	— 31.5
6.9	4.3	— 1.3	8.1	1.5	2.2	**2003**	50.0
— 7.8	— 2.6	3.2	4.1	6.2	3.7	**2004**	8.6
6.2	— 1.5	0.0	— 1.5	5.3	— 1.2	**2005**	1.4
— 3.7	4.4	3.4	4.8	2.7	— 0.7	**2006**	9.5
— 2.2	2.0	4.0	5.8	— 6.9	— 0.3	**2007**	9.8
1.4	1.8	— 11.6	— 17.7	— 10.8	2.7	**2008**	— 40.5
7.8	1.5	5.6	— 3.6	4.9	5.8	**2009**	43.9
6.9	— 6.2	12.0	5.9	— 0.4	6.2	**2010**	16.9
— 0.6	— 6.4	— 6.4	11.1	— 2.4	— 0.6	**2011**	— 1.8
0.2	4.3	1.6	— 4.5	1.1	0.3	**2012**	15.9
21/41	22/41	22/41	22/41	27/41	24/41		29/41
51 %	54 %	54 %	54 %	66 %	59 %		71 %
0.1 %	0.1 %	— 0.6 %	0.6 %	1.6 %	1.8 %		11.7 %
11	10	12	8	3	2		

STOCK MKT

NASDAQ MONTH CLOSING VALUES

	JAN	FEB	MAR	APR	MAY	JUN
1972	119	125	128	131	133	130
1973	128	120	117	108	103	101
1974	95	94	92	87	80	76
1975	70	73	76	79	83	87
1976	87	90	91	90	88	90
1977	96	95	94	95	96	100
1978	101	101	106	115	120	120
1979	126	123	132	134	131	138
1980	162	158	131	140	150	158
1981	198	198	210	217	223	216
1982	188	179	176	185	179	171
1983	248	261	271	293	309	319
1984	268	253	251	247	233	240
1985	279	284	279	281	291	296
1986	336	360	375	383	400	406
1987	392	425	430	418	417	425
1988	345	367	375	379	370	395
1989	401	400	407	428	446	435
1990	416	426	436	420	459	462
1991	414	453	482	485	506	476
1992	620	633	604	579	585	564
1993	696	671	690	661	701	704
1994	800	793	743	734	735	706
1995	755	794	817	844	865	933
1996	1060	1100	1101	1191	1243	1185
1997	1380	1309	1222	1261	1400	1442
1998	1619	1771	1836	1868	1779	1895
1999	2506	2288	2461	2543	2471	2686
2000	3940	4697	4573	3861	3401	3966
2001	2773	2152	1840	2116	2110	2161
2002	1934	1731	1845	1688	1616	1463
2003	1321	1338	1341	1464	1596	1623
2004	2066	2030	1994	1920	1987	2048
2005	2062	2052	1999	1922	2068	2057
2006	2306	2281	2340	2323	2179	2172
2007	2464	2416	2422	2525	2605	2603
2008	2390	2271	2279	2413	2523	2293
2009	1476	1378	1529	1717	1774	1835
2010	2147	2238	2398	2461	2257	2109
2011	2700	2782	2781	2874	2835	2774
2012	2814	2967	3092	3046	2827	2935

NASDAQ MONTH CLOSING VALUES

JUL	AUG	SEP	OCT	NOV	DEC	
128	130	130	130	133	134	**1972**
109	105	111	110	94	92	**1973**
70	62	56	65	63	60	**1974**
83	79	74	77	79	78	**1975**
91	90	91	90	91	98	**1976**
101	100	101	98	103	105	**1977**
126	135	133	111	115	118	**1978**
141	150	150	136	144	151	**1979**
172	182	188	193	208	202	**1980**
212	196	180	195	201	196	**1981**
167	178	188	213	232	232	**1982**
304	292	297	275	286	279	**1983**
230	255	250	247	242	247	**1984**
301	298	280	293	314	325	**1985**
371	383	351	361	360	349	**1986**
435	455	444	323	305	331	**1987**
387	377	388	383	372	381	**1988**
454	469	473	456	456	455	**1989**
438	381	345	330	359	374	**1990**
502	526	527	543	524	586	**1991**
581	563	583	605	653	677	**1992**
705	743	763	779	754	777	**1993**
722	766	764	777	750	752	**1994**
1001	1020	1044	1036	1059	1052	**1995**
1081	1142	1227	1222	1293	1291	**1996**
1594	1587	1686	1594	1601	1570	**1997**
1872	1499	1694	1771	1950	2193	**1998**
2638	2739	2746	2966	3336	4069	**1999**
3767	4206	3673	3370	2598	2471	**2000**
2027	1805	1499	1690	1931	1950	**2001**
1328	1315	1172	1330	1479	1336	**2002**
1735	1810	1787	1932	1960	2003	**2003**
1887	1838	1897	1975	2097	2175	**2004**
2185	2152	2152	2120	2233	2205	**2005**
2091	2184	2258	2367	2432	2415	**2006**
2546	2596	2702	2859	2661	2652	**2007**
2326	2368	2092	1721	1536	1577	**2008**
1979	2009	2122	2045	2145	2269	**2009**
2255	2114	2369	2507	2498	2653	**2010**
2756	2579	2415	2684	2620	2605	**2011**
2940	3067	3116	2977	3010	3020	**2012**

STOCK MKT

S&P/TSX MONTH PERCENT CHANGES

	JAN	FEB	MAR	APR	MAY	JUN
1985	8.1	0.0	0.7	0.8	3.8	— 0.8
1986	— 1.7	0.5	6.7	1.1	1.4	— 1.2
1987	9.2	4.5	6.9	— 0.6	— 0.9	1.5
1988	— 3.3	4.8	3.4	0.8	— 2.7	5.9
1989	6.7	— 1.2	0.2	1.4	2.2	1.5
1990	— 6.7	— 0.5	— 1.3	— 8.2	6.7	— 0.6
1991	0.5	5.8	1.0	-0.8	2.2	— 2.3
1992	2.4	— 0.4	— 4.7	— 1.7	1.0	0.0
1993	— 1.3	4.4	4.4	5.2	2.5	2.2
1994	5.4	— 2.9	— 2.1	— 1.4	1.4	— 7.0
1995	— 4.7	2.7	4.6	— -0.8	4.0	1.8
1996	5.4	— 0.7	0.8	3.5	1.9	— 3.9
1997	3.1	0.8	— 5.0	2.2	6.8	0.9
1998	0.0	5.9	6.6	1.4	— 1.0	— 2.9
1999	3.8	— 6.2	4.5	6.3	— 2.5	2.5
2000	0.8	7.6	3.7	— 1.2	— 1.0	10.2
2001	4.3	— 13.3	— 5.8	4.5	2.7	— 5.2
2002	— 0.5	— 0.1	2.8	— 2.4	— 0.1	— 6.7
2003	— 0.7	— 0.2	— 3.2	3.8	4.2	1.8
2004	3.7	3.1	— 2.3	— 4.0	2.1	1.5
2005	— 0.5	5.0	— 0.6	— 3.5	3.6	3.1
2006	6.0	— 2.2	3.6	0.8	— 3.8	— 1.1
2007	1.0	0.1	0.9	1.9	4.8	— 1.1
2008	— 4.9	3.3	— 1.7	4.4	5.6	— 1.7
2009	— 3.3	— 6.6	7.4	6.9	11.2	0.0
2010	— 5.5	4.8	3.5	1.4	— 3.7	— 4.0
2011	0.8	4.3	— 0.1	— 1.2	— 1.0	— 3.6
2012	4.2	1.5	— 2.0	— 0.8	— 6.3	0.7
FQ POS	17/28	16/28	17/28	16/28	18/28	13/28
% FQ POS	61 %	57 %	61 %	57 %	64 %	46 %
AVG GAIN	1.2 %	0.9 %	1.2 %	0.7 %	1.6 %	-0.3 %
RANK GAIN	4	5	3	7	2	11

S&P/TSX MONTH PERCENT CHANGES

STOCK MKT

JUL	AUG	SEP	OCT	NOV	DEC		YEAR
2.4	1.5	— 6.7	1.6	6.8	1.3	**1985**	20.5
— 4.9	3.2	— 1.6	1.6	0.7	0.6	**1986**	6.0
7.8	— 0.9	— 2.3	— 22.6	— 1.4	6.1	**1987**	3.1
— 1.9	— 2.7	— 0.1	3.4	— 3.0	2.9	**1988**	7.3
5.6	1.0	— 1.7	— 0.6	0.6	0.7	**1989**	17.1
0.5	— 6.0	— 5.6	— 2.5	2.3	3.4	**1990**	— 18.0
2.1	— 0.6	— 3.7	3.8	— 1.9	1.9	**1991**	7.8
1.6	— 1.2	— 3.1	1.2	— 1.6	2.1	**1992**	— 4.6
0.0	4.3	— 3.6	6.6	— 1.8	3.4	**1993**	29.0
3.8	4.1	0.1	— 1.4	— 4.6	2.9	**1994**	— 2.5
1.9	— 2.1	0.3	— 1.6	4.5	1.1	**1995**	11.9
— 2.3	4.3	2.9	5.8	7.5	— 1.5	**1996**	25.7
6.8	— 3.9	6.5	— 2.8	— 4.8	2.9	**1997**	13.0
— 5.9	— 20.2	1.5	10.6	2.2	2.2	**1998**	— 3.2
1.0	— 1.6	— 0.2	4.3	3.6	11.9	**1999**	29.7
2.1	8.1	— 7.7	— 7.1	— 8.5	1.3	**2000**	6.2
— 0.6	— 3.8	— 7.6	0.7	7.8	3.5	**2001**	— 13.9
— 7.6	0.1	— 6.5	1.1	5.1	0.7	**2002**	— 14.0
3.9	3.6	— 1.3	4.7	1.1	4.6	**2003**	24.3
— 1.0	— 1.0	3.5	2.3	1.8	2.4	**2004**	12.5
5.3	2.4	3.2	— 5.7	4.2	4.1	**2005**	21.9
1.9	2.1	— 2.6	5.0	3.3	1.2	**2006**	14.5
— 0.3	— 1.5	3.2	3.7	— 6.4	1.1	**2007**	7.2
— 6.0	1.3	— 14.7	— 16.9	— 5.0	— 3.1	**2008**	— 35.0
4.0	0.8	4.8	— 4.2	4.9	2.6	**2009**	30.7
3.7	1.7	3.8	2.5	2.2	3.8	**2010**	14.4
— 2.7	— 1.4	— 9.0	5.4	— 0.4	— 2.0	**2011**	— 11.1
0.6	2.4	3.1	0.9	— 1.5	1.6	**2012**	4.0
18/28	15/28	11/28	18/28	16/28	25/28		20/28
64 %	54 %	39 %	64 %	57 %	89 %		71 %
0.8 %	— 0.2 %	— 1.6 %	0.0 %	0.6 %	2.3 %		7.3 %
6	10	12	9	8	1		

S&P/TSX MONTH CLOSING VALUES

	JAN	FEB	MAR	APR	MAY	JUN
1985	2595	2595	2613	2635	2736	2713
1986	2843	2856	3047	3079	3122	3086
1987	3349	3499	3739	3717	3685	3740
1988	3057	3205	3314	3340	3249	3441
1989	3617	3572	3578	3628	3707	3761
1990	3704	3687	3640	3341	3565	3544
1991	3273	3462	3496	3469	3546	3466
1992	3596	3582	3412	3356	3388	3388
1993	3305	3452	3602	3789	3883	3966
1994	4555	4424	4330	4267	4327	4025
1995	4018	4125	4314	4280	4449	4527
1996	4968	4934	4971	5147	5246	5044
1997	6110	6158	5850	5977	6382	6438
1998	6700	7093	7559	7665	7590	7367
1999	6730	6313	6598	7015	6842	7010
2000	8481	9129	9462	9348	9252	10196
2001	9322	8079	7608	7947	8162	7736
2002	7649	7638	7852	7663	7656	7146
2003	6570	6555	6343	6586	6860	6983
2004	8521	8789	8586	8244	8417	8546
2005	9204	9668	9612	9275	9607	9903
2006	11946	11688	12111	12204	11745	11613
2007	13034	13045	13166	13417	14057	13907
2008	13155	13583	13350	13937	14715	14467
2009	8695	8123	8720	9325	10370	10375
2010	11094	11630	12038	12211	11763	11294
2011	13552	14137	14116	13945	13803	13301
2012	12452	12644	12392	12293	11513	11597

S&P/TSX PERCENT CLOSING VALUES

JUL	AUG	SEP	OCT	NOV	DEC	
2779	2820	2632	2675	2857	2893	**1985**
2935	3028	2979	3027	3047	3066	**1986**
4030	3994	3902	3019	2978	3160	**1987**
3377	3286	3284	3396	3295	3390	**1988**
3971	4010	3943	3919	3943	3970	**1989**
3561	3346	3159	3081	3151	3257	**1990**
3540	3518	3388	3516	3449	3512	**1991**
3443	3403	3298	3336	3283	3350	**1992**
3967	4138	3991	4256	4180	4321	**1993**
4179	4350	4354	4292	4093	4214	**1994**
4615	4517	4530	4459	4661	4714	**1995**
4929	5143	5291	5599	6017	5927	**1996**
6878	6612	7040	6842	6513	6699	**1997**
6931	5531	5614	6208	6344	6486	**1998**
7081	6971	6958	7256	7520	8414	**1999**
10406	11248	10378	9640	8820	8934	**2000**
7690	7399	6839	6886	7426	7688	**2001**
6605	6612	6180	6249	6570	6615	**2002**
7258	7517	7421	7773	7859	8221	**2003**
8458	8377	8668	8871	9030	9247	**2004**
10423	10669	11012	10383	10824	11272	**2005**
11831	12074	11761	12345	12752	12908	**2006**
13869	13660	14099	14625	13689	13833	**2007**
13593	13771	11753	9763	9271	8988	**2008**
10787	10868	11935	10911	11447	11746	**2009**
11713	11914	12369	12676	12953	13443	**2010**
12946	12769	11624	12252	12204	11955	**2011**
11665	11949	12317	12423	12239	12434	**2012**

S&P 500 1950 - 2012 BEST - WORST

10 BEST

YEARS

	Close	Change	Change
1954	36	11 pt	45.0 %
1958	55	15	38.1
1995	616	157	34.1
1975	90	22	31.5
1997	970	230	31.0
1989	353	76	27.3
1998	1229	259	26.7
1955	45	10	26.4
2003	1112	232	26.4
1985	211	44	26.3

MONTHS

	Close	Change	Change
Oct 1974	74	10 pt	16.3 %
Aug 1982	120	12	11.6
Dec 1991	417	42	11.2
Oct 1982	134	13	11.0
Oct 2011	1253	122	10.8
Aug 1984	167	16	10.6
Nov 1980	141	13	10.2
Nov 1962	62	6	10.2
Mar 2000	1499	132	9.7
Apr 2009	798	75	9.4

DAYS

		Close	Change	Change
Mon	2008 Oct 13	1003	104 pt	11.6 %
Tue	2008 Oct 28	941	92	10.8
Wed	1987 Oct 21	258	22	9.1
Mon	2009 Mar 23	883	54	7.1
Thu	2008 Nov 13	911	59	6.9
Mon	2008 Nov 24	852	52	6.5
Tues	2009 Mar 10	720	43	6.4
Fri	2008 Nov 21	800	48	6.3
Wed	2002 Jul 24	843	46	5.7
Tue	2008 Sep 30	1166	60	5.4

10 WORST

YEARS

	Close	Change	Change
2008	903	– 566 pt	– 38.5 %
1974	69	– 29	– 29.7
2002	880	– 268	– 23.4
1973	98	– 21	– 17.4
1957	40	– 7	– 14.3
1966	80	– 12	– 13.1
2001	1148	– 172	– 13.0
1962	63	– 8	– 11.8
1977	95	– 12	– 11.5
1969	92	– 12	– 11.4

MONTHS

	Close	Change	Change
Oct 1987	252	– 70 pt	– 21.8 %
Oct 2008	969	– 196	– 16.8
Aug 1998	957	– 163	– 14.6
Sep 1974	64	– 9	– 11.9
Nov 1973	96	– 12	– 11.4
Sep 2002	815	– 101	– 11.0
Feb 2009	735	– 91	– 11.0
Mar 1980	102	– 12	– 10.2
Aug 1990	323	– 34	– 9.4
Feb 2001	1240	– 126	– 9.2

DAYS

		Close	Change	Change
Mon	1987 Oct 19	225	– 58 pt	– 20.5 %
Wed	2008 Oct 15	908	– 90	– 9.0
Mon	2008 Dec 01	816	– 80	– 8.9
Mon	2008 Sep 29	1106	– 107	– 8.8
Mon	1987 Oct 26	228	– 21	– 8.3
Thu	2008 Oct 09	910	– 75	– 7.6
Mon	1997 Oct 27	877	– 65	– 6.9
Mon	1998 Aug 31	957	– 70	– 6.8
Fri	1988 Jan 8	243	– 18	– 6.8
Thu	2008 Nov 20	752	– 54	– 6.7

DOW JONES 1950 - 2012 BEST - WORST

STOCK MKT

10 BEST

YEARS

	Close	Change	Change
1954	404	124 pt	44.0 %
1975	852	236	38.3
1958	584	148	34.0
1995	5117	1283	33.5
1985	1547	335	27.7
1989	2753	585	27.0
1996	6448	1331	26.0
2003	10454	2112	25.3
1999	11453	2272	25.2
1997	7908	1460	22.6

MONTHS

	Close	Change	Change
Aug 1982	901	93 pt	11.5 %
Oct 1982	992	95	10.6
Oct 2002	8397	805	10.6
Apr 1978	837	80	10.5
Apr 1999	10789	1003	10.2
Nov 1962	649	60	10.1
Nov 1954	387	35	9.9
Aug 1984	1224	109	9.8
Oct 1998	8592	750	9.6
Oct 2011	11955	1042	9.5

DAYS

		Close	Change	Change
Mon	2008 Oct 13	9388	936 pt	11.1 %
Tue	2008 Oct 28	9065	889	10.9
Wed	1987 Oct 21	2028	187	10.2
Mon	2009 Mar 23	7776	497	6.8
Thu	2008 Nov 13	8835	553	6.7
Fri	2008 Nov 21	8046	494	6.5
Wed	2002 Jul 24	8191	489	6.3
Tue	1987 Oct 20	1841	102	5.9
Tue	2009 Mar 10	6926	379	5.8
Mon	2002 Jul 29	8712	448	5.4

10 WORST

YEARS

	Close	Change	Change
2008	8776	– 4488 pt	– 33.8 %
1974	616	– 235	– 27.6
1966	786	– 184	– 18.9
1977	831	– 174	– 17.3
2002	8342	– 1680	– 16.8
1973	851	– 169	– 16.6
1969	800	– 143	– 15.2
1957	436	– 64	– 12.8
1962	652	– 79	– 10.8
1960	616	– 64	– 9.3

MONTHS

	Close	Change	Change
Oct 1987	1994	– 603 pt	– 23.2 %
Aug 1998	7539	– 1344	– 15.1
Oct 2008	9325	– 1526	– 14.1
Nov 1973	822	– 134	– 14.0
Sep 2002	7592	– 1072	– 12.4
Feb 2009	7063	– 938	– 11.7
Sep 2001	8848	– 1102	– 11.1
Sep 1974	608	– 71	– 10.4
Aug 1974	679	– 79	– 10.4
Jun 2008	11350	– 1288	– 10.2

DAYS

		Close	Change	Change
Mon	1987 Oct 19	1739	– 508 pt	– 22.6 %
Mon	1987 Oct 26	1794	– 157	– 8.0
Wed	2008 Oct 15	8578	– 733	– 7.9
Mon	2008 Dec 01	8149	– 680	– 7.7
Thu	2008 Oct 09	8579	– 679	– 7.3
Mon	1997 Oct 27	8366	– 554	– 7.2
Mon	2001 Sep 17	8921	– 685	– 7.1
Mon	2008 Sep 29	10365	– 778	– 7.0
Fri	1989 Oct 13	2569	– 191	– 6.9
Fri	1988 Jan 8	1911	– 141	– 6.9

STOCK MKT

NASDAQ 1972- 2012 BEST - WORST

10 BEST

YEARS

	Close	Change	Change
1999	4069	1877 pt	85.6 %
1991	586	213	56.9
2003	2003	668	50.0
2009	2269	692	43.9
1995	1052	300	39.9
1998	2193	622	39.6
1980	202	51	33.9
1985	325	78	31.5
1975	78	18	29.8
1979	151	33	28.1

MONTHS

	Close	Change	Change
Dec 1999	4069	733 pt	22.0 %
Feb 2000	4697	756	19.2
Oct 1974	65	10	17.2
Jun 2000	3966	565	16.6
Apr 2001	2116	276	15.0
Nov 2001	1931	240	14.2
Oct 2002	1330	158	13.5
Oct 1982	1771	25	13.3
Sep 1998	1694	195	13.0
Oct 2001	1690	191	12.8

DAYS

		Close	Change	Change
Wed	2001 Jan 3	2617	325 pt	14.2 %
Mon	2008 Oct 13	1844	195	11.8
Tue	2000 Dec 5	2890	274	10.5
Tue	2008 Oct 28	1649	144	9.5
Thu	2001 Apr 5	1785	146	8.9
Wed	2001 Apr 18	2079	156	8.1
Tue	2000 May 30	3459	254	7.9
Fri	2000 Oct 13	3317	242	7.9
Thu	2000 Oct 19	3419	247	7.8
Wed	2002 May 8	1696	122	7.8

10 WORST

YEARS

	Close	Change	Change
2008	1577	– 1075 pt	– 40.5 %
2000	2471	– 1599	– 39.3
1974	60	– 32	– 35.1
2002	1336	– 615	– 31.5
1973	92	– 42	– 31.1
2001	1950	– 520	– 21.1
1990	374	– 81	– 17.8
1984	247	– 32	– 11.3
1987	331	– 18	– 5.2
1981	196	– 7	– 3.2

MONTHS

	Close	Change	Change
Oct 1987	323	– 121 pt	– 27.2 %
Nov 2000	2598	– 772	– 22.9
Feb 2001	2152	– 621	– 22.4
Aug 1998	1499	– 373	– 19.9
Oct 2008	1721	– 371	– 17.7
Mar 1980	131	– 27	– 17.1
Sep 2001	1499	– 307	– 17.0
Oct 1978	111	– 22	– 16.4
Apr 2000	3861	– 712	– 15.6
Nov 1973	94	– 17	– 15.1

DAYS

		Close	Change	Change
Mon	1987 Oct 19	360	– 46 pt	– 11.3 %
Fri	2000 Apr 14	3321	– 355	– 9.7
Mon	2008 Sep 29	1984	– 200	– 9.1
Mon	1987 Oct 26	299	– 30	– 9.0
Tue	1987 Oct 20	328	– 32	– 9.0
Mon	2008 Dec 01	1398	– 138	– 9.0
Mon	1998 Aug 31	1499	– 140	– 8.6
Wed	2008 Oct 15	1628	– 151	– 8.5
Mon	2000 Apr 03	4224	– 349	– 7.6
Tue	2001 Jan 02	2292	– 179	– 7.2

S&P /TSX (CANADA) 1985 - 2012 BEST - WORST

STOCK MKT

10 BEST

YEARS

	Close	Change	Change
2009	8414	2758 pt	30.7 %
1999	4321	1928	29.7
1993	5927	971	29.0
1996	8221	1213	25.7
2003	11272	1606	24.3
2005	2893	2026	21.9
1985	3970	500	20.8
1989	12908	580	17.1
2006	6699	1636	14.5
2010	13433	1697	14.4

MONTHS

	Close	Change	Change
Dec 1999	8414	891 pt	11.8 %
May 2009	8500	1045	11.2
Oct 1998	6208	594	10.6
Jun 2000	10196	943	10.2
Jan 1985	2595	195	8.1
Aug 2000	11248	842	8.1
Nov 2001	7426	540	7.8
Jul 1987	4030	290	7.8
Feb 2000	9129	648	7.6
Nov 1996	6017	418	7.5

DAYS

		Close	Change	Change
Tue	2008 Oct 14	9956	891 pt	9.8 %
Wed	1987 Oct 21	3246	269	9.0
Mon	2008 Oct 20	10251	689	7.2
Tue	2008 Oct 28	9152	614	7.2
Fri	2008 Sep 19	12913	848	7.0
Fri	2008 Nov 28	9271	517	5.9
Fri	2008 Nov 21	8155	431	5.6
Mon	2008 Dec 08	8567	450	5.5
Mon	2009 Mar 23	8959	452	5.3
Fri	1987 Oct 30	3019	147	5.1

10 WORST

YEARS

	Close	Change	Change
2008	8988	– 4845 pt	– 35.0 %
1990	3257	– 713	– 18.0
2002	6615	– 1074	– 14.0
2001	7688	– 1245	– 13.9
2011	11955	– 1488	– 11.1
1992	3350	– 162	– 4.6
1998	6486	– 214	– 3.2
1994	4214	– 108	– 2.5
1987	3160	94	3.1
2012	12434	479	4.0

MONTHS

	Close	Change	Change
Oct 1987	3019	– 883 pt	– 22.6 %
Aug 1998	5531	– 1401	– 20.2
Oct 2008	9763	– 1990	– 16.9
Sep 2008	11753	– 2018	– 14.7
Feb 2001	8079	– 1243	– 13.3
Nov 2000	8820	– 820	– 8.5
Apr 1990	3341	– 299	– 8.2
Sep 2000	10378	– 870	– 7.7
Sep 2001	6839	– 561	– 7.6
Jul 2002	6605	– 540	– 7.6

DAYS

		Close	Change	Change
Mon	1987 Oct 19	3192	– 407 pt	– 11.3 %
Mon	2008 Dec 01	8406	– 864	– 9.3
Thu	2008 Nov 20	7725	– 766	– 9.0
Mon	2008 Oct 27	8537	– 757	– 8.1
Wed	2000 Oct 25	9512	– 840	– 8.1
Mon	1987 Oct 26	2846	– 233	– 7.6
Thu	2008 Oct 02	10901	– 814	– 6.9
Mon	2008 Sep 29	11285	– 841	– 6.9
Tue	1987 Oct 20	2977	– 215	– 6.7
Fri	2001 Feb 16	8393	– 574	– 6.4

BOND YIELDS

BOND YIELDS 10 YEAR TREASURY*

	JAN	FEB	MAR	APR	MAY	JUN
1954	2.48	2.47	2.37	2.29	2.37	2.38
1955	2.61	2.65	2.68	2.75	2.76	2.78
1956	2.9	2.84	2.96	3.18	3.07	3
1957	3.46	3.34	3.41	3.48	3.6	3.8
1958	3.09	3.05	2.98	2.88	2.92	2.97
1959	4.02	3.96	3.99	4.12	4.31	4.34
1960	4.72	4.49	4.25	4.28	4.35	4.15
1961	3.84	3.78	3.74	3.78	3.71	3.88
1962	4.08	4.04	3.93	3.84	3.87	3.91
1963	3.83	3.92	3.93	3.97	3.93	3.99
1964	4.17	4.15	4.22	4.23	4.2	4.17
1965	4.19	4.21	4.21	4.2	4.21	4.21
1966	4.61	4.83	4.87	4.75	4.78	4.81
1967	4.58	4.63	4.54	4.59	4.85	5.02
1968	5.53	5.56	5.74	5.64	5.87	5.72
1969	6.04	6.19	6.3	6.17	6.32	6.57
1970	7.79	7.24	7.07	7.39	7.91	7.84
1971	6.24	6.11	5.7	5.83	6.39	6.52
1972	5.95	6.08	6.07	6.19	6.13	6.11
1973	6.46	6.64	6.71	6.67	6.85	6.9
1974	6.99	6.96	7.21	7.51	7.58	7.54
1975	7.5	7.39	7.73	8.23	8.06	7.86
1976	7.74	7.79	7.73	7.56	7.9	7.86
1977	7.21	7.39	7.46	7.37	7.46	7.28
1978	7.96	8.03	8.04	8.15	8.35	8.46
1979	9.1	9.1	9.12	9.18	9.25	8.91
1980	10.8	12.41	12.75	11.47	10.18	9.78
1981	12.57	13.19	13.12	13.68	14.1	13.47
1982	14.59	14.43	13.86	13.87	13.62	14.3
1983	10.46	10.72	10.51	10.4	10.38	10.85
1984	11.67	11.84	12.32	12.63	13.41	13.56
1985	11.38	11.51	11.86	11.43	10.85	10.16
1986	9.19	8.7	7.78	7.3	7.71	7.8
1987	7.08	7.25	7.25	8.02	8.61	8.4
1988	8.67	8.21	8.37	8.72	9.09	8.92
1989	9.09	9.17	9.36	9.18	8.86	8.28
1990	8.21	8.47	8.59	8.79	8.76	8.48
1991	8.09	7.85	8.11	8.04	8.07	8.28
1992	7.03	7.34	7.54	7.48	7.39	7.26
1993	6.6	6.26	5.98	5.97	6.04	5.96
1994	5.75	5.97	6.48	6.97	7.18	7.1
1995	7.78	7.47	7.2	7.06	6.63	6.17
1996	5.65	5.81	6.27	6.51	6.74	6.91
1997	6.58	6.42	6.69	6.89	6.71	6.49
1998	5.54	5.57	5.65	5.64	5.65	5.5
1999	4.72	5	5.23	5.18	5.54	5.9
2000	6.66	6.52	6.26	5.99	6.44	6.1
2001	5.16	5.1	4.89	5.14	5.39	5.28
2002	5.04	4.91	5.28	5.21	5.16	4.93
2003	4.05	3.9	3.81	3.96	3.57	3.33
2004	4.15	4.08	3.83	4.35	4.72	4.73
2005	4.22	4.17	4.5	4.34	4.14	4.00
2006	4.42	4.57	4.72	4.99	5.11	5.11
2007	4.76	4.72	4.56	4.69	4.75	5.10
2008	3.74	3.74	3.51	3.68	3.88	4.10
2009	2.52	2.87	2.82	2.93	3.29	3.72
2010	3.73	3.69	3.73	3.85	3.42	3.20
2011	3.39	3.58	3.41	3.46	3.17	3.00
2012	1.97	1.97	2.17	2.05	1.80	1.62

* Source: Federal Reserve Bank of St. Louis, monthly data calculated as average of business days

JUL	AUG	SEP	OCT	NOV	DEC	
2.3	2.36	2.38	2.43	2.48	2.51	**1954**
2.9	2.97	2.97	2.88	2.89	2.96	**1955**
3.11	3.33	3.38	3.34	3.49	3.59	**1956**
3.93	3.93	3.92	3.97	3.72	3.21	**1957**
3.2	3.54	3.76	3.8	3.74	3.86	**1958**
4.4	4.43	4.68	4.53	4.53	4.69	**1959**
3.9	3.8	3.8	3.89	3.93	3.84	**1960**
3.92	4.04	3.98	3.92	3.94	4.06	**1961**
4.01	3.98	3.98	3.93	3.92	3.86	**1962**
4.02	4	4.08	4.11	4.12	4.13	**1963**
4.19	4.19	4.2	4.19	4.15	4.18	**1964**
4.2	4.25	4.29	4.35	4.45	4.62	**1965**
5.02	5.22	5.18	5.01	5.16	4.84	**1966**
5.16	5.28	5.3	5.48	5.75	5.7	**1967**
5.5	5.42	5.46	5.58	5.7	6.03	**1968**
6.72	6.69	7.16	7.1	7.14	7.65	**1969**
7.46	7.53	7.39	7.33	6.84	6.39	**1970**
6.73	6.58	6.14	5.93	5.81	5.93	**1971**
6.11	6.21	6.55	6.48	6.28	6.36	**1972**
7.13	7.4	7.09	6.79	6.73	6.74	**1973**
7.81	8.04	8.04	7.9	7.68	7.43	**1974**
8.06	8.4	8.43	8.14	8.05	8	**1975**
7.83	7.77	7.59	7.41	7.29	6.87	**1976**
7.33	7.4	7.34	7.52	7.58	7.69	**1977**
8.64	8.41	8.42	8.64	8.81	9.01	**1978**
8.95	9.03	9.33	10.3	10.65	10.39	**1979**
10.25	11.1	11.51	11.75	12.68	12.84	**1980**
14.28	14.94	15.32	15.15	13.39	13.72	**1981**
13.95	13.06	12.34	10.91	10.55	10.54	**1982**
11.38	11.85	11.65	11.54	11.69	11.83	**1983**
13.36	12.72	12.52	12.16	11.57	11.5	**1984**
10.31	10.33	10.37	10.24	9.78	9.26	**1985**
7.3	7.17	7.45	7.43	7.25	7.11	**1986**
8.45	8.76	9.42	9.52	8.86	8.99	**1987**
9.06	9.26	8.98	8.8	8.96	9.11	**1988**
8.02	8.11	8.19	8.01	7.87	7.84	**1989**
8.47	8.75	8.89	8.72	8.39	8.08	**1990**
8.27	7.9	7.65	7.53	7.42	7.09	**1991**
6.84	6.59	6.42	6.59	6.87	6.77	**1992**
5.81	5.68	5.36	5.33	5.72	5.77	**1993**
7.3	7.24	7.46	7.74	7.96	7.81	**1994**
6.28	6.49	6.2	6.04	5.93	5.71	**1995**
6.87	6.64	6.83	6.53	6.2	6.3	**1996**
6.22	6.3	6.21	6.03	5.88	5.81	**1997**
5.46	5.34	4.81	4.53	4.83	4.65	**1998**
5.79	5.94	5.92	6.11	6.03	6.28	**1999**
6.05	5.83	5.8	5.74	5.72	5.24	**2000**
5.24	4.97	4.73	4.57	4.65	5.09	**2001**
4.65	4.26	3.87	3.94	4.05	4.03	**2002**
3.98	4.45	4.27	4.29	4.3	4.27	**2003**
4.5	4.28	4.13	4.1	4.19	4.23	**2004**
4.18	4.26	4.20	4.46	4.54	4.47	**2005**
5.09	4.88	4.72	4.73	4.60	4.56	**2006**
5.00	4.67	4.52	4.53	4.15	4.10	**2007**
4.01	3.89	3.69	3.81	3.53	2.42	**2008**
3.56	3.59	3.40	3.39	3.40	3.59	**2009**
3.01	2.70	2.65	2.54	2.76	3.29	**2010**
3.00	2.30	1.98	2.15	2.01	1.98	**2011**
1.53	1.68	1.72	1.75	1.65	1.72	**2012**

BOND YIELDS 5 YEAR TREASURY*

	JAN	FEB	MAR	APR	MAY	JUN
1954	2.17	2.04	1.93	1.87	1.92	1.92
1955	2.32	2.38	2.48	2.55	2.56	2.59
1956	2.84	2.74	2.93	3.20	3.08	2.97
1957	3.47	3.39	3.46	3.53	3.64	3.83
1958	2.88	2.78	2.64	2.46	2.41	2.46
1959	4.01	3.96	3.99	4.12	4.35	4.50
1960	4.92	4.69	4.31	4.29	4.49	4.12
1961	3.67	3.66	3.60	3.57	3.47	3.81
1962	3.94	3.89	3.68	3.60	3.66	3.64
1963	3.58	3.66	3.68	3.74	3.72	3.81
1964	4.07	4.03	4.14	4.15	4.05	4.02
1965	4.10	4.15	4.15	4.15	4.15	4.15
1966	4.86	4.98	4.92	4.83	4.89	4.97
1967	4.70	4.74	4.54	4.51	4.75	5.01
1968	5.54	5.59	5.76	5.69	6.04	5.85
1969	6.25	6.34	6.41	6.30	6.54	6.75
1970	8.17	7.82	7.21	7.50	7.97	7.85
1971	5.89	5.56	5.00	5.65	6.28	6.53
1972	5.59	5.69	5.87	6.17	5.85	5.91
1973	6.34	6.60	6.80	6.67	6.80	6.69
1974	6.95	6.82	7.31	7.92	8.18	8.10
1975	7.41	7.11	7.30	7.99	7.72	7.51
1976	7.46	7.45	7.49	7.25	7.59	7.61
1977	6.58	6.83	6.93	6.79	6.94	6.76
1978	7.77	7.83	7.86	7.98	8.18	8.36
1979	9.20	9.13	9.20	9.25	9.24	8.85
1980	10.74	12.60	13.47	11.84	9.95	9.21
1981	12.77	13.41	13.41	13.99	14.63	13.95
1982	14.65	14.54	13.98	14.00	13.75	14.43
1983	10.03	10.26	10.08	10.02	10.03	10.63
1984	11.37	11.54	12.02	12.37	13.17	13.48
1985	10.93	11.13	11.52	11.01	10.34	9.60
1986	8.68	8.34	7.46	7.05	7.52	7.64
1987	6.64	6.79	6.79	7.57	8.26	8.02
1988	8.18	7.71	7.83	8.19	8.58	8.49
1989	9.15	9.27	9.51	9.30	8.91	8.29
1990	8.12	8.42	8.60	8.77	8.74	8.43
1991	7.70	7.47	7.77	7.70	7.70	7.94
1992	6.24	6.58	6.95	6.78	6.69	6.48
1993	5.83	5.43	5.19	5.13	5.20	5.22
1994	5.09	5.40	5.94	6.52	6.78	6.70
1995	7.76	7.37	7.05	6.86	6.41	5.93
1996	5.36	5.38	5.97	6.30	6.48	6.69
1997	6.33	6.20	6.54	6.76	6.57	6.38
1998	5.42	5.49	5.61	5.61	5.63	5.52
1999	4.60	4.91	5.14	5.08	5.44	5.81
2000	6.58	6.68	6.50	6.26	6.69	6.30
2001	4.86	4.89	4.64	4.76	4.93	4.81
2002	4.34	4.30	4.74	4.65	4.49	4.19
2003	3.05	2.90	2.78	2.93	2.52	2.27
2004	3.12	3.07	2.79	3.39	3.85	3.93
2005	3.71	3.77	4.17	4.00	3.85	3.77
2006	4.35	4.57	4.72	4.90	5.00	5.07
2007	4.75	4.71	4.48	4.59	4.67	5.03
2008	2.98	2.78	2.48	2.84	3.15	3.49
2009	1.60	1.87	1.82	1.86	2.13	2.71
2010	2.48	2.36	2.43	2.58	2.18	2.00
2011	1.99	2.26	2.11	2.17	1.84	1.58
2012	0.84	0.83	1.02	0.89	0.76	0.71

* Source: Federal Reserve Bank of St. Louis, monthly data calculated as average of business days

5 YEAR TREASURY BOND YIELDS

JUL	AUG	SEP	OCT	NOV	DEC	
1.85	1.90	1.96	2.02	2.09	2.16	**1954**
2.72	2.86	2.85	2.76	2.81	2.93	**1955**
3.12	3.41	3.47	3.40	3.56	3.70	**1956**
4.00	4.00	4.03	4.08	3.72	3.08	**1957**
2.77	3.29	3.69	3.78	3.70	3.82	**1958**
4.58	4.57	4.90	4.72	4.75	5.01	**1959**
3.79	3.62	3.61	3.76	3.81	3.67	**1960**
3.84	3.96	3.90	3.80	3.82	3.91	**1961**
3.80	3.71	3.70	3.64	3.60	3.56	**1962**
3.89	3.89	3.96	3.97	4.01	4.04	**1963**
4.03	4.05	4.08	4.07	4.04	4.09	**1964**
4.15	4.20	4.25	4.34	4.46	4.72	**1965**
5.17	5.50	5.50	5.27	5.36	5.00	**1966**
5.23	5.31	5.40	5.57	5.78	5.75	**1967**
5.60	5.50	5.48	5.55	5.66	6.12	**1968**
7.01	7.03	7.57	7.51	7.53	7.96	**1969**
7.59	7.57	7.29	7.12	6.47	5.95	**1970**
6.85	6.55	6.14	5.93	5.78	5.69	**1971**
5.97	6.02	6.25	6.18	6.12	6.16	**1972**
7.33	7.63	7.05	6.77	6.92	6.80	**1973**
8.38	8.63	8.37	7.97	7.68	7.31	**1974**
7.92	8.33	8.37	7.97	7.80	7.76	**1975**
7.49	7.31	7.13	6.75	6.52	6.10	**1976**
6.84	7.03	7.04	7.32	7.34	7.48	**1977**
8.54	8.33	8.43	8.61	8.84	9.08	**1978**
8.90	9.06	9.41	10.63	10.93	10.42	**1979**
9.53	10.84	11.62	11.86	12.83	13.25	**1980**
14.79	15.56	15.93	15.41	13.38	13.60	**1981**
14.07	13.00	12.25	10.80	10.38	10.22	**1982**
11.21	11.63	11.43	11.28	11.41	11.54	**1983**
13.27	12.68	12.53	12.06	11.33	11.07	**1984**
9.70	9.81	9.81	9.69	9.28	8.73	**1985**
7.06	6.80	6.92	6.83	6.76	6.67	**1986**
8.01	8.32	8.94	9.08	8.35	8.45	**1987**
8.66	8.94	8.69	8.51	8.79	9.09	**1988**
7.83	8.09	8.17	7.97	7.81	7.75	**1989**
8.33	8.44	8.51	8.33	8.02	7.73	**1990**
7.91	7.43	7.14	6.87	6.62	6.19	**1991**
5.84	5.60	5.38	5.60	6.04	6.08	**1992**
5.09	5.03	4.73	4.71	5.06	5.15	**1993**
6.91	6.88	7.08	7.40	7.72	7.78	**1994**
6.01	6.24	6.00	5.86	5.69	5.51	**1995**
6.64	6.39	6.60	6.27	5.97	6.07	**1996**
6.12	6.16	6.11	5.93	5.80	5.77	**1997**
5.46	5.27	4.62	4.18	4.54	4.45	**1998**
5.68	5.84	5.80	6.03	5.97	6.19	**1999**
6.18	6.06	5.93	5.78	5.70	5.17	**2000**
4.76	4.57	4.12	3.91	3.97	4.39	**2001**
3.81	3.29	2.94	2.95	3.05	3.03	**2002**
2.87	3.37	3.18	3.19	3.29	3.27	**2003**
3.69	3.47	3.36	3.35	3.53	3.60	**2004**
3.98	4.12	4.01	4.33	4.45	4.39	**2005**
5.04	4.82	4.67	4.69	4.58	4.53	**2006**
4.88	4.43	4.20	4.20	3.67	3.49	**2007**
3.30	3.14	2.88	2.73	2.29	1.52	**2008**
2.46	2.57	2.37	2.33	2.23	2.34	**2009**
1.76	1.47	1.41	1.18	1.35	1.93	**2010**
1.54	1.02	0.90	1.06	0.91	0.89	**2011**
0.62	0.71	0.67	0.71	0.67	0.70	**2012**

BOND YIELDS 3 MONTH TREASURY

	JAN	FEB	MAR	APR	MAY	JUN
1982	12.92	14.28	13.31	13.34	12.71	13.08
1983	8.12	8.39	8.66	8.51	8.50	9.14
1984	9.26	9.46	9.89	10.07	10.22	10.26
1985	8.02	8.56	8.83	8.22	7.73	7.18
1986	7.30	7.29	6.76	6.24	6.33	6.40
1987	5.58	5.75	5.77	5.82	5.85	5.85
1988	6.00	5.84	5.87	6.08	6.45	6.66
1999	8.56	8.84	9.14	8.96	8.74	8.43
1990	7.90	8.00	8.17	8.04	8.01	7.99
1991	6.41	6.12	6.09	5.83	5.63	5.75
1992	3.91	3.95	4.14	3.84	3.72	3.75
1993	3.07	2.99	3.01	2.93	3.03	3.14
1994	3.04	3.33	3.59	3.78	4.27	4.25
1995	5.90	5.94	5.91	5.84	5.85	5.64
1996	5.15	4.96	5.10	5.09	5.15	5.23
1997	5.17	5.14	5.28	5.30	5.20	5.07
1998	5.18	5.23	5.16	5.08	5.14	5.12
1999	4.45	4.56	4.57	4.41	4.63	4.72
2000	5.50	5.73	5.86	5.82	5.99	5.86
2001	5.29	5.01	4.54	3.97	3.70	3.57
2002	1.68	1.76	1.83	1.75	1.76	1.73
2003	1.19	1.19	1.15	1.15	1.09	0.94
2004	0.90	0.94	0.95	0.96	1.04	1.29
2005	2.37	2.58	2.80	2.84	2.90	3.04
2006	4.34	4.54	4.63	4.72	4.84	4.92
2007	5.11	5.16	5.08	5.01	4.87	4.74
2008	2.82	2.17	1.28	1.31	1.76	1.89
2009	0.13	0.30	0.22	0.16	0.18	0.18
2010	0.06	0.11	0.15	0.16	0.16	0.12
2011	0.15	0.13	0.10	0.06	0.04	0.04
2012	0.03	0.09	0.08	0.08	0.09	0.09

* Source: Federal Reserve Bank of St. Louis, monthly data calculated as average of business days

3 MONTH TREASURY 

JUL	AUG	SEP	OCT	NOV	DEC	
11.86	9.00	8.19	7.97	8.35	8.20	**1982**
9.45	9.74	9.36	8.99	9.11	9.36	**1983**
10.53	10.90	10.80	10.12	8.92	8.34	**1984**
7.32	7.37	7.33	7.40	7.48	7.33	**1985**
6.00	5.69	5.35	5.32	5.50	5.68	**1986**
5.88	6.23	6.62	6.35	5.89	5.96	**1987**
6.95	7.30	7.48	7.60	8.03	8.35	**1988**
8.15	8.17	8.01	7.90	7.94	7.88	**1999**
7.87	7.69	7.60	7.40	7.29	6.95	**1990**
5.75	5.50	5.37	5.14	4.69	4.18	**1991**
3.28	3.20	2.97	2.93	3.21	3.29	**1992**
3.11	3.09	3.01	3.09	3.18	3.13	**1993**
4.46	4.61	4.75	5.10	5.45	5.76	**1994**
5.59	5.57	5.43	5.44	5.52	5.29	**1995**
5.30	5.19	5.24	5.12	5.17	5.04	**1996**
5.19	5.28	5.08	5.11	5.28	5.30	**1997**
5.09	5.04	4.74	4.07	4.53	4.50	**1998**
4.69	4.87	4.82	5.02	5.23	5.36	**1999**
6.14	6.28	6.18	6.29	6.36	5.94	**2000**
3.59	3.44	2.69	2.20	1.91	1.72	**2001**
1.71	1.65	1.66	1.61	1.25	1.21	**2002**
0.92	0.97	0.96	0.94	0.95	0.91	**2003**
1.36	1.50	1.68	1.79	2.11	2.22	**2004**
3.29	3.52	3.49	3.79	3.97	3.97	**2005**
5.08	5.09	4.93	5.05	5.07	4.97	**2006**
4.96	4.32	3.99	4.00	3.35	3.07	**2007**
1.66	1.75	1.15	0.69	0.19	0.03	**2008**
0.18	0.17	0.12	0.07	0.05	0.05	**2009**
0.16	0.16	0.15	0.13	0.14	0.14	**2010**
0.04	0.02	0.01	0.02	0.01	0.01	**2011**
0.10	0.10	0.11	0.10	0.09	0.07	**2012**

BOND YIELDS

MOODY'S SEASONED CORPORATE Aaa*

	JAN	FEB	MAR	APR	MAY	JUN
1950	2.57	2.58	2.58	2.60	2.61	2.62
1951	2.66	2.66	2.78	2.87	2.89	2.94
1952	2.98	2.93	2.96	2.93	2.93	2.94
1953	3.02	3.07	3.12	3.23	3.34	3.40
1954	3.06	2.95	2.86	2.85	2.88	2.90
1955	2.93	2.93	3.02	3.01	3.04	3.05
1956	3.11	3.08	3.10	3.24	3.28	3.26
1957	3.77	3.67	3.66	3.67	3.74	3.91
1958	3.60	3.59	3.63	3.60	3.57	3.57
1959	4.12	4.14	4.13	4.23	4.37	4.46
1960	4.61	4.56	4.49	4.45	4.46	4.45
1961	4.32	4.27	4.22	4.25	4.27	4.33
1962	4.42	4.42	4.39	4.33	4.28	4.28
1963	4.21	4.19	4.19	4.21	4.22	4.23
1964	4.39	4.36	4.38	4.40	4.41	4.41
1965	4.43	4.41	4.42	4.43	4.44	4.46
1966	4.74	4.78	4.92	4.96	4.98	5.07
1967	5.20	5.03	5.13	5.11	5.24	5.44
1968	6.17	6.10	6.11	6.21	6.27	6.28
1969	6.59	6.66	6.85	6.89	6.79	6.98
1970	7.91	7.93	7.84	7.83	8.11	8.48
1971	7.36	7.08	7.21	7.25	7.53	7.64
1972	7.19	7.27	7.24	7.30	7.30	7.23
1973	7.15	7.22	7.29	7.26	7.29	7.37
1974	7.83	7.85	8.01	8.25	8.37	8.47
1975	8.83	8.62	8.67	8.95	8.90	8.77
1976	8.60	8.55	8.52	8.40	8.58	8.62
1977	7.96	8.04	8.10	8.04	8.05	7.95
1978	8.41	8.47	8.47	8.56	8.69	8.76
1979	9.25	9.26	9.37	9.38	9.50	9.29
1980	11.09	12.38	12.96	12.04	10.99	10.58
1981	12.81	13.35	13.33	13.88	14.32	13.75
1982	15.18	15.27	14.58	14.46	14.26	14.81
1983	11.79	12.01	11.73	11.51	11.46	11.74
1984	12.20	12.08	12.57	12.81	13.28	13.55
1985	12.08	12.13	12.56	12.23	11.72	10.94
1986	10.05	9.67	9.00	8.79	9.09	9.13
1987	8.36	8.38	8.36	8.85	9.33	9.32
1988	9.88	9.40	9.39	9.67	9.90	9.86
1989	9.62	9.64	9.80	9.79	9.57	9.10
1990	8.99	9.22	9.37	9.46	9.47	9.26
1991	9.04	8.83	8.93	8.86	8.86	9.01
1992	8.20	8.29	8.35	8.33	8.28	8.22
1993	7.91	7.71	7.58	7.46	7.43	7.33
1994	6.92	7.08	7.48	7.88	7.99	7.97
1995	8.46	8.26	8.12	8.03	7.65	7.30
1996	6.81	6.99	7.35	7.50	7.62	7.71
1997	7.42	7.31	7.55	7.73	7.58	7.41
1998	6.61	6.67	6.72	6.69	6.69	6.53
1999	6.24	6.40	6.62	6.64	6.93	7.23
2000	7.78	7.68	7.68	7.64	7.99	7.67
2001	7.15	7.10	6.98	7.20	7.29	7.18
2002	6.55	6.51	6.81	6.76	6.75	6.63
2003	6.17	5.95	5.89	5.74	5.22	4.97
2004	5.54	5.50	5.33	5.73	6.04	6.01
2005	5.36	5.20	5.40	5.33	5.15	4.96
2006	5.29	5.35	5.53	5.84	5.95	5.89
2007	5.40	5.39	5.30	5.47	5.47	5.79
2008	5.33	5.53	5.51	5.55	5.57	5.68
2009	5.05	5.27	5.50	5.39	5.54	5.61
2010	5.26	5.35	5.27	5.29	4.96	4.88
2011	5.04	5.22	5.13	5.16	4.96	4.99
2012	3.85	3.85	3.99	3.96	3.80	3.64

* Source: Federal Reserve Bank of St. Louis, monthly data calculated as average of business days

MOODY'S SEASONED CORPORATE Aaa BOND YIELDS

JUL	AUG	SEP	OCT	NOV	DEC	
2.65	2.61	2.64	2.67	2.67	2.67	**1950**
2.94	2.88	2.84	2.89	2.96	3.01	**1951**
2.95	2.94	2.95	3.01	2.98	2.97	**1952**
3.28	3.24	3.29	3.16	3.11	3.13	**1953**
2.89	2.87	2.89	2.87	2.89	2.90	**1954**
3.06	3.11	3.13	3.10	3.10	3.15	**1955**
3.28	3.43	3.56	3.59	3.69	3.75	**1956**
3.99	4.10	4.12	4.10	4.08	3.81	**1957**
3.67	3.85	4.09	4.11	4.09	4.08	**1958**
4.47	4.43	4.52	4.57	4.56	4.58	**1959**
4.41	4.28	4.25	4.30	4.31	4.35	**1960**
4.41	4.45	4.45	4.42	4.39	4.42	**1961**
4.34	4.35	4.32	4.28	4.25	4.24	**1962**
4.26	4.29	4.31	4.32	4.33	4.35	**1963**
4.40	4.41	4.42	4.42	4.43	4.44	**1964**
4.48	4.49	4.52	4.56	4.60	4.68	**1965**
5.16	5.31	5.49	5.41	5.35	5.39	**1966**
5.58	5.62	5.65	5.82	6.07	6.19	**1967**
6.24	6.02	5.97	6.09	6.19	6.45	**1968**
7.08	6.97	7.14	7.33	7.35	7.72	**1969**
8.44	8.13	8.09	8.03	8.05	7.64	**1970**
7.64	7.59	7.44	7.39	7.26	7.25	**1971**
7.21	7.19	7.22	7.21	7.12	7.08	**1972**
7.45	7.68	7.63	7.60	7.67	7.68	**1973**
8.72	9.00	9.24	9.27	8.89	8.89	**1974**
8.84	8.95	8.95	8.86	8.78	8.79	**1975**
8.56	8.45	8.38	8.32	8.25	7.98	**1976**
7.94	7.98	7.92	8.04	8.08	8.19	**1977**
8.88	8.69	8.69	8.89	9.03	9.16	**1978**
9.20	9.23	9.44	10.13	10.76	10.74	**1979**
11.07	11.64	12.02	12.31	12.97	13.21	**1980**
14.38	14.89	15.49	15.40	14.22	14.23	**1981**
14.61	13.71	12.94	12.12	11.68	11.83	**1982**
12.15	12.51	12.37	12.25	12.41	12.57	**1983**
13.44	12.87	12.66	12.63	12.29	12.13	**1984**
10.97	11.05	11.07	11.02	10.55	10.16	**1985**
8.88	8.72	8.89	8.86	8.68	8.49	**1986**
9.42	9.67	10.18	10.52	10.01	10.11	**1987**
9.96	10.11	9.82	9.51	9.45	9.57	**1988**
8.93	8.96	9.01	8.92	8.89	8.86	**1989**
9.24	9.41	9.56	9.53	9.30	9.05	**1990**
9.00	8.75	8.61	8.55	8.48	8.31	**1991**
8.07	7.95	7.92	7.99	8.10	7.98	**1992**
7.17	6.85	6.66	6.67	6.93	6.93	**1993**
8.11	8.07	8.34	8.57	8.68	8.46	**1994**
7.41	7.57	7.32	7.12	7.02	6.82	**1995**
7.65	7.46	7.66	7.39	7.10	7.20	**1996**
7.14	7.22	7.15	7.00	6.87	6.76	**1997**
6.55	6.52	6.40	6.37	6.41	6.22	**1998**
7.19	7.40	7.39	7.55	7.36	7.55	**1999**
7.65	7.55	7.62	7.55	7.45	7.21	**2000**
7.13	7.02	7.17	7.03	6.97	6.77	**2001**
6.53	6.37	6.15	6.32	6.31	6.21	**2002**
5.49	5.88	5.72	5.70	5.65	5.62	**2003**
5.82	5.65	5.46	5.47	5.52	5.47	**2004**
5.06	5.09	5.13	5.35	5.42	5.37	**2005**
5.85	5.68	5.51	5.51	5.33	5.32	**2006**
5.73	5.79	5.74	5.66	5.44	5.49	**2007**
5.67	5.64	5.65	6.28	6.12	5.05	**2008**
5.41	5.26	5.13	5.15	5.19	5.26	**2009**
4.72	4.49	4.53	4.68	4.87	5.02	**2010**
4.93	4.37	4.09	3.98	3.87	3.93	**2011**
3.40	3.48	3.49	3.47	3.50	3.65	**2012**

BOND YIELDS

MOODY'S SEASONED CORPORATE Baa*

	JAN	FEB	MAR	APR	MAY	JUN
1950	3.24	3.24	3.24	3.23	3.25	3.28
1951	3.17	3.16	3.23	3.35	3.40	3.49
1952	3.59	3.53	3.51	3.50	3.49	3.50
1953	3.51	3.53	3.57	3.65	3.78	3.86
1954	3.71	3.61	3.51	3.47	3.47	3.49
1955	3.45	3.47	3.48	3.49	3.50	3.51
1956	3.60	3.58	3.60	3.68	3.73	3.76
1957	4.49	4.47	4.43	4.44	4.52	4.63
1958	4.83	4.66	4.68	4.67	4.62	4.55
1959	4.87	4.89	4.85	4.86	4.96	5.04
1960	5.34	5.34	5.25	5.20	5.28	5.26
1961	5.10	5.07	5.02	5.01	5.01	5.03
1962	5.08	5.07	5.04	5.02	5.00	5.02
1963	4.91	4.89	4.88	4.87	4.85	4.84
1964	4.83	4.83	4.83	4.85	4.85	4.85
1965	4.80	4.78	4.78	4.80	4.81	4.85
1966	5.06	5.12	5.32	5.41	5.48	5.58
1967	5.97	5.82	5.85	5.83	5.96	6.15
1968	6.84	6.80	6.85	6.97	7.03	7.07
1969	7.32	7.30	7.51	7.54	7.52	7.70
1970	8.86	8.78	8.63	8.70	8.98	9.25
1971	8.74	8.39	8.46	8.45	8.62	8.75
1972	8.23	8.23	8.24	8.24	8.23	8.20
1973	7.90	7.97	8.03	8.09	8.06	8.13
1974	8.48	8.53	8.62	8.87	9.05	9.27
1975	10.81	10.65	10.48	10.58	10.69	10.62
1976	10.41	10.24	10.12	9.94	9.86	9.89
1977	9.08	9.12	9.12	9.07	9.01	8.91
1978	9.17	9.20	9.22	9.32	9.49	9.60
1979	10.13	10.08	10.26	10.33	10.47	10.38
1980	12.42	13.57	14.45	14.19	13.17	12.71
1981	15.03	15.37	15.34	15.56	15.95	15.80
1982	17.10	17.18	16.82	16.78	16.64	16.92
1983	13.94	13.95	13.61	13.29	13.09	13.37
1984	13.65	13.59	13.99	14.31	14.74	15.05
1985	13.26	13.23	13.69	13.51	13.15	12.40
1986	11.44	11.11	10.50	10.19	10.29	10.34
1987	9.72	9.65	9.61	10.04	10.51	10.52
1988	11.07	10.62	10.57	10.90	11.04	11.00
1989	10.65	10.61	10.67	10.61	10.46	10.03
1990	9.94	10.14	10.21	10.30	10.41	10.22
1991	10.45	10.07	10.09	9.94	9.86	9.96
1992	9.13	9.23	9.25	9.21	9.13	9.05
1993	8.67	8.39	8.15	8.14	8.21	8.07
1994	7.65	7.76	8.13	8.52	8.62	8.65
1995	9.08	8.85	8.70	8.60	8.20	7.90
1996	7.47	7.63	8.03	8.19	8.30	8.40
1997	8.09	7.94	8.18	8.34	8.20	8.02
1998	7.19	7.25	7.32	7.33	7.30	7.13
1999	7.29	7.39	7.53	7.48	7.72	8.02
2000	8.33	8.29	8.37	8.40	8.90	8.48
2001	7.93	7.87	7.84	8.07	8.07	7.97
2002	7.87	7.89	8.11	8.03	8.09	7.95
2003	7.35	7.06	6.95	6.85	6.38	6.19
2004	6.44	6.27	6.11	6.46	6.75	6.78
2005	6.02	5.82	6.06	6.05	6.01	5.86
2006	6.24	6.27	6.41	6.68	6.75	6.78
2007	6.34	6.28	6.27	6.39	6.39	6.70
2008	6.54	6.82	6.89	6.97	6.93	7.07
2009	8.14	8.08	8.42	8.39	8.06	7.50
2010	6.25	6.34	6.27	6.25	6.05	6.23
2011	6.09	6.15	6.03	6.02	5.78	5.75
2012	5.23	5.14	5.23	5.19	5.07	5.02

* Source: Federal Reserve Bank of St. Louis, monthly data calculated as average of business days

MOODY'S SEASONED CORPORATE Baa* BOND YIELDS

JUL	AUG	SEP	OCT	NOV	DEC	
3.32	3.23	3.21	3.22	3.22	3.20	**1950**
3.53	3.50	3.46	3.50	3.56	3.61	**1951**
3.50	3.51	3.52	3.54	3.53	3.51	**1952**
3.86	3.85	3.88	3.82	3.75	3.74	**1953**
3.50	3.49	3.47	3.46	3.45	3.45	**1954**
3.52	3.56	3.59	3.59	3.58	3.62	**1955**
3.80	3.93	4.07	4.17	4.24	4.37	**1956**
4.73	4.82	4.93	4.99	5.09	5.03	**1957**
4.53	4.67	4.87	4.92	4.87	4.85	**1958**
5.08	5.09	5.18	5.28	5.26	5.28	**1959**
5.22	5.08	5.01	5.11	5.08	5.10	**1960**
5.09	5.11	5.12	5.13	5.11	5.10	**1961**
5.05	5.06	5.03	4.99	4.96	4.92	**1962**
4.84	4.83	4.84	4.83	4.84	4.85	**1963**
4.83	4.82	4.82	4.81	4.81	4.81	**1964**
4.88	4.88	4.91	4.93	4.95	5.02	**1965**
5.68	5.83	6.09	6.10	6.13	6.18	**1966**
6.26	6.33	6.40	6.52	6.72	6.93	**1967**
6.98	6.82	6.79	6.84	7.01	7.23	**1968**
7.84	7.86	8.05	8.22	8.25	8.65	**1969**
9.40	9.44	9.39	9.33	9.38	9.12	**1970**
8.76	8.76	8.59	8.48	8.38	8.38	**1971**
8.23	8.19	8.09	8.06	7.99	7.93	**1972**
8.24	8.53	8.63	8.41	8.42	8.48	**1973**
9.48	9.77	10.18	10.48	10.60	10.63	**1974**
10.55	10.59	10.61	10.62	10.56	10.56	**1975**
9.82	9.64	9.40	9.29	9.23	9.12	**1976**
8.87	8.82	8.80	8.89	8.95	8.99	**1977**
9.60	9.48	9.42	9.59	9.83	9.94	**1978**
10.29	10.35	10.54	11.40	11.99	12.06	**1979**
12.65	13.15	13.70	14.23	14.64	15.14	**1980**
16.17	16.34	16.92	17.11	16.39	16.55	**1981**
16.80	16.32	15.63	14.73	14.30	14.14	**1982**
13.39	13.64	13.55	13.46	13.61	13.75	**1983**
15.15	14.63	14.35	13.94	13.48	13.40	**1984**
12.43	12.50	12.48	12.36	11.99	11.58	**1985**
10.16	10.18	10.20	10.24	10.07	9.97	**1986**
10.61	10.80	11.31	11.62	11.23	11.29	**1987**
11.11	11.21	10.90	10.41	10.48	10.65	**1988**
9.87	9.88	9.91	9.81	9.81	9.82	**1989**
10.20	10.41	10.64	10.74	10.62	10.43	**1990**
9.89	9.65	9.51	9.49	9.45	9.26	**1991**
8.84	8.65	8.62	8.84	8.96	8.81	**1992**
7.93	7.60	7.34	7.31	7.66	7.69	**1993**
8.80	8.74	8.98	9.20	9.32	9.10	**1994**
8.04	8.19	7.93	7.75	7.68	7.49	**1995**
8.35	8.18	8.35	8.07	7.79	7.89	**1996**
7.75	7.82	7.70	7.57	7.42	7.32	**1997**
7.15	7.14	7.09	7.18	7.34	7.23	**1998**
7.95	8.15	8.20	8.38	8.15	8.19	**1999**
8.35	8.26	8.35	8.34	8.28	8.02	**2000**
7.97	7.85	8.03	7.91	7.81	8.05	**2001**
7.90	7.58	7.40	7.73	7.62	7.45	**2002**
6.62	7.01	6.79	6.73	6.66	6.60	**2003**
6.62	6.46	6.27	6.21	6.20	6.15	**2004**
5.95	5.96	6.03	6.30	6.39	6.32	**2005**
6.76	6.59	6.43	6.42	6.20	6.22	**2006**
6.65	6.65	6.59	6.48	6.40	6.65	**2007**
7.16	7.15	7.31	8.88	9.21	8.43	**2008**
7.09	6.58	6.31	6.29	6.32	6.37	**2009**
6.01	5.66	5.66	5.72	5.92	6.10	**2010**
5.76	5.36	5.27	5.37	5.14	5.25	**2011**
4.87	4.91	4.84	4.58	4.51	4.63	**2012**

COMMODITIES

COMMODITIES OIL - WEST TEXAS INTERMEDIATE CLOSING VALUES $ / bbl

	JAN	FEB	MAR	APR	MAY	JUN
1950	2.6	2.6	2.6	2.6	2.6	2.6
1951	2.6	2.6	2.6	2.6	2.6	2.6
1952	2.6	2.6	2.6	2.6	2.6	2.6
1953	2.6	2.6	2.6	2.6	2.6	2.8
1954	2.8	2.8	2.8	2.8	2.8	2.8
1955	2.8	2.8	2.8	2.8	2.8	2.8
1956	2.8	2.8	2.8	2.8	2.8	2.8
1957	2.8	3.1	3.1	3.1	3.1	3.1
1958	3.1	3.1	3.1	3.1	3.1	3.1
1959	3.0	3.0	3.0	3.0	3.0	3.0
1960	3.0	3.0	3.0	3.0	3.0	3.0
1961	3.0	3.0	3.0	3.0	3.0	3.0
1962	3.0	3.0	3.0	3.0	3.0	3.0
1963	3.0	3.0	3.0	3.0	3.0	3.0
1964	3.0	3.0	3.0	3.0	3.0	3.0
1965	2.9	2.9	2.9	2.9	2.9	2.9
1966	2.9	2.9	2.9	2.9	2.9	2.9
1967	3.0	3.0	3.0	3.0	3.0	3.0
1968	3.1	3.1	3.1	3.1	3.1	3.1
1969	3.1	3.1	3.3	3.4	3.4	3.4
1970	3.4	3.4	3.4	3.4	3.4	3.4
1971	3.6	3.6	3.6	3.6	3.6	3.6
1972	3.6	3.6	3.6	3.6	3.6	3.6
1973	3.6	3.6	3.6	3.6	3.6	3.6
1974	10.1	10.1	10.1	10.1	10.1	10.1
1975	11.2	11.2	11.2	11.2	11.2	11.2
1976	11.2	12.0	12.1	12.2	12.2	12.2
1977	13.9	13.9	13.9	13.9	13.9	13.9
1978	14.9	14.9	14.9	14.9	14.9	14.9
1979	14.9	15.9	15.9	15.9	18.1	19.1
1980	32.5	37.0	38.0	39.5	39.5	39.5
1981	38.0	38.0	38.0	38.0	38.0	36.0
1982	33.9	31.6	28.5	33.5	35.9	35.1
1983	31.2	29.0	28.8	30.6	30.0	31.0
1984	29.7	30.1	30.8	30.6	30.5	30.0
1985	25.6	27.3	28.2	28.8	27.6	27.1
1986	22.9	15.4	12.6	12.8	15.4	13.5
1987	18.7	17.7	18.3	18.6	19.4	20.0
1988	17.2	16.8	16.2	17.9	17.4	16.5
1989	18.0	17.8	19.4	21.0	20.0	20.0
1990	22.6	22.1	20.4	18.6	18.2	16.9
1991	25.0	20.5	19.9	20.8	21.2	20.2
1992	18.8	19.0	18.9	20.2	20.9	22.4
1993	19.1	20.1	20.3	20.3	19.9	19.1
1994	15.0	14.8	14.7	16.4	17.9	19.1
1995	18.0	18.5	18.6	19.9	19.7	18.4
1996	18.9	19.1	21.4	23.6	21.3	20.5
1997	25.2	22.2	21.0	19.7	20.8	19.2
1998	16.7	16.1	15.0	15.4	14.9	13.7
1999	12.5	12.0	14.7	17.3	17.8	17.9
2000	27.2	29.4	29.9	25.7	28.8	31.8
2001	29.6	29.6	27.2	27.4	28.6	27.6
2002	19.7	20.7	24.4	26.3	27.0	25.5
2003	32.9	35.9	33.6	28.3	28.1	30.7
2004	34.3	34.7	36.8	36.7	40.3	38.0
2005	46.8	48.0	54.3	53.0	49.8	56.3
2006	65.5	61.6	62.9	69.7	70.9	71.0
2007	54.6	59.3	60.6	64.0	63.5	67.5
2008	93.0	95.4	105.6	112.6	125.4	133.9
2009	41.7	39.2	48.0	49.8	59.2	69.7
2010	78.2	76.4	81.2	84.5	73.8	75.4
2011	89.4	89.6	102.9	110.0	101.3	96.3
2012	100.2	102.3	106.2	103.3	94.7	82.4

* Source: Federal Reserve

OIL - WEST TEXAS INTERMEDIATE CLOSING VALUES $ / bbl

COMMODITIES

JUL	AUG	SEP	OCT	NOV	DEC	
2.6	2.6	2.6	2.6	2.6	2.6	**1950**
2.6	2.6	2.6	2.6	2.6	2.6	**1951**
2.6	2.6	2.6	2.6	2.6	2.6	**1952**
2.8	2.8	2.8	2.8	2.8	2.8	**1953**
2.8	2.8	2.8	2.8	2.8	2.8	**1954**
2.8	2.8	2.8	2.8	2.8	2.8	**1955**
2.8	2.8	2.8	2.8	2.8	2.8	**1956**
3.1	3.1	3.1	3.1	3.1	3.0	**1957**
3.1	3.1	3.1	3.1	3.0	3.0	**1958**
3.0	3.0	3.0	3.0	3.0	3.0	**1959**
3.0	3.0	3.0	3.0	3.0	3.0	**1960**
3.0	3.0	3.0	3.0	3.0	3.0	**1961**
3.0	3.0	3.0	3.0	3.0	3.0	**1962**
3.0	3.0	3.0	3.0	3.0	3.0	**1963**
2.9	2.9	2.9	2.9	2.9	2.9	**1964**
2.9	2.9	2.9	2.9	2.9	2.9	**1965**
2.9	2.9	3.0	3.0	3.0	3.0	**1966**
3.0	3.1	3.1	3.1	3.1	3.1	**1967**
3.1	3.1	3.1	3.1	3.1	3.1	**1968**
3.4	3.4	3.4	3.4	3.4	3.4	**1969**
3.3	3.3	3.3	3.3	3.3	3.6	**1970**
3.6	3.6	3.6	3.6	3.6	3.6	**1971**
3.6	3.6	3.6	3.6	3.6	3.6	**1972**
3.6	4.3	4.3	4.3	4.3	4.3	**1973**
10.1	10.1	10.1	11.2	11.2	11.2	**1974**
11.2	11.2	11.2	11.2	11.2	11.2	**1975**
12.2	12.2	13.9	13.9	13.9	13.9	**1976**
13.9	14.9	14.9	14.9	14.9	14.9	**1977**
14.9	14.9	14.9	14.9	14.9	14.9	**1978**
21.8	26.5	28.5	29.0	31.0	32.5	**1979**
39.5	38.0	36.0	36.0	36.0	37.0	**1980**
36.0	36.0	36.0	35.0	36.0	35.0	**1981**
34.2	34.0	35.6	35.7	34.2	31.7	**1982**
31.7	31.9	31.1	30.4	29.8	29.2	**1983**
28.8	29.3	29.3	28.8	28.1	25.4	**1984**
27.3	27.8	28.3	29.5	30.8	27.2	**1985**
11.6	15.1	14.9	14.9	15.2	16.1	**1986**
21.4	20.3	19.5	19.8	18.9	17.2	**1987**
15.5	15.5	14.5	13.8	14.0	16.3	**1988**
19.6	18.5	19.6	20.1	19.8	21.1	**1989**
18.6	27.2	33.7	35.9	32.3	27.3	**1990**
21.4	21.7	21.9	23.2	22.5	19.5	**1991**
21.8	21.4	21.9	21.7	20.3	19.4	**1992**
17.9	18.0	17.5	18.1	16.7	14.5	**1993**
19.7	18.4	17.5	17.7	18.1	17.2	**1994**
17.3	18.0	18.2	17.4	18.0	19.0	**1995**
21.3	22.0	24.0	24.9	23.7	25.4	**1996**
19.6	19.9	19.8	21.3	20.2	18.3	**1997**
14.1	13.4	15.0	14.4	12.9	11.3	**1998**
20.1	21.3	23.9	22.6	25.0	26.1	**1999**
29.8	31.2	33.9	33.1	34.4	28.5	**2000**
26.5	27.5	25.9	22.2	19.7	19.3	**2001**
26.9	28.4	29.7	28.9	26.3	29.4	**2002**
30.8	31.6	28.3	30.3	31.1	32.2	**2003**
40.7	44.9	46.0	53.1	48.5	43.3	**2004**
58.7	65.0	65.6	62.4	58.3	59.4	**2005**
74.4	73.1	63.9	58.9	59.4	62.0	**2006**
74.2	72.4	79.9	86.2	94.6	91.7	**2007**
133.4	116.6	103.9	76.7	57.4	41.0	**2008**
64.1	71.1	69.5	75.6	78.1	74.3	**2009**
76.4	76.8	75.3	81.9	84.1	89.0	**2010**
97.2	86.3	85.6	86.4	97.2	98.6	**2011**
87.9	94.2	94.7	89.6	86.7	88.3	**2012**

GOLD $US/OZ LONDON PM MONTH CLOSE

	JAN	FEB	MAR	APR	MAY	JUN
1970	34.9	35.0	35.1	35.6	36.0	35.4
1971	37.9	38.7	38.9	39.0	40.5	40.1
1972	45.8	48.3	48.3	49.0	54.6	62.1
1973	65.1	74.2	84.4	90.5	102.0	120.1
1974	129.2	150.2	168.4	172.2	163.3	154.1
1975	175.8	181.8	178.2	167.0	167.0	166.3
1976	128.2	132.3	129.6	128.4	125.5	123.8
1977	132.3	142.8	148.9	147.3	143.0	143.0
1978	175.8	182.3	181.6	170.9	184.2	183.1
1979	233.7	251.3	240.1	245.3	274.6	277.5
1980	653.0	637.0	494.5	518.0	535.5	653.5
1981	506.5	489.0	513.8	482.8	479.3	426.0
1982	387.0	362.6	320.0	361.3	325.3	317.5
1983	499.5	408.5	414.8	429.3	437.5	416.0
1984	373.8	394.3	388.5	375.8	384.3	373.1
1985	306.7	287.8	329.3	321.4	314.0	317.8
1986	350.5	338.2	344.0	345.8	343.2	345.5
1987	400.5	405.9	405.9	453.3	451.0	447.3
1988	458.0	426.2	457.0	449.0	455.5	436.6
1989	394.0	387.0	383.2	377.6	361.8	373.0
1990	415.1	407.7	368.5	367.8	363.1	352.2
1991	366.0	362.7	355.7	357.8	360.4	368.4
1992	354.1	353.1	341.7	336.4	337.5	343.4
1993	330.5	327.6	337.8	354.3	374.8	378.5
1994	377.9	381.6	389.2	376.5	387.6	388.3
1995	374.9	376.4	392.0	389.8	384.3	387.1
1996	405.6	400.7	396.4	391.3	390.6	382.0
1997	345.5	358.6	348.2	340.2	345.6	334.6
1998	304.9	297.4	301.0	310.7	293.6	296.3
1999	285.4	287.1	279.5	286.6	268.6	261.0
2000	283.3	293.7	276.8	275.1	272.3	288.2
2001	264.5	266.7	257.7	263.2	267.5	270.6
2002	282.3	296.9	301.4	308.2	326.6	318.5
2003	367.5	347.5	334.9	336.8	361.4	346.0
2004	399.8	395.9	423.7	388.5	393.3	395.8
2005	422.2	435.5	427.5	435.7	414.5	437.1
2006	568.8	556.0	582.0	644.0	653.0	613.5
2007	650.5	664.2	661.8	677.0	659.1	650.5
2008	923.3	971.5	933.5	871.0	885.8	930.3
2009	919.5	952.0	916.5	883.3	975.5	934.5
2010	1078.5	1108.3	1115.5	1179.3	1207.5	1244.0
2011	1327.0	1411.0	1439.0	1535.5	1536.5	1505.5
2012	1744.0	1770.0	1662.5	1651.3	1558.0	1598.5

* Source: Bank of England

GOLD $US/OZ LONDON PM MONTH CLOSE

COMMODITIES

JUL	AUG	SEP	OCT	NOV	DEC	
35.3	35.4	36.2	37.5	37.4	37.4	**1970**
41.0	42.7	42.0	42.5	42.9	43.5	**1971**
65.7	67.0	65.5	64.9	62.9	63.9	**1972**
120.2	106.8	103.0	100.1	94.8	106.7	**1973**
143.0	154.6	151.8	158.8	181.7	183.9	**1974**
166.7	159.8	141.3	142.9	138.2	140.3	**1975**
112.5	104.0	116.0	123.2	130.3	134.5	**1976**
144.1	146.0	154.1	161.5	160.1	165.0	**1977**
200.3	208.7	217.1	242.6	193.4	226.0	**1978**
296.5	315.1	397.3	382.0	415.7	512.0	**1979**
614.3	631.3	666.8	629.0	619.8	589.8	**1980**
406.0	425.5	428.8	427.0	414.5	397.5	**1981**
342.9	411.5	397.0	423.3	436.0	456.9	**1982**
422.0	414.3	405.0	382.0	405.0	382.4	**1983**
342.4	348.3	343.8	333.5	329.0	309.0	**1984**
327.5	333.3	326.5	325.1	325.3	326.8	**1985**
357.5	384.7	423.2	401.0	383.5	388.8	**1986**
462.5	453.4	459.5	468.8	492.5	484.1	**1987**
436.8	427.8	397.7	412.4	422.6	410.3	**1988**
368.3	359.8	366.5	375.3	408.2	398.6	**1989**
372.3	387.8	408.4	379.5	384.9	386.2	**1990**
362.9	347.4	354.9	357.5	366.3	353.2	**1991**
357.9	340.0	349.0	339.3	334.2	332.9	**1992**
401.8	371.6	355.5	369.6	370.9	391.8	**1993**
384.0	385.8	394.9	383.9	383.1	383.3	**1994**
383.4	382.4	384.0	382.7	387.8	387.0	**1995**
385.3	386.5	379.0	379.5	371.3	369.3	**1996**
326.4	325.4	332.1	311.4	296.8	290.2	**1997**
288.9	273.4	293.9	292.3	294.7	287.8	**1998**
255.6	254.8	299.0	299.1	291.4	290.3	**1999**
276.8	277.0	273.7	264.5	269.1	274.5	**2000**
265.9	273.0	293.1	278.8	275.5	276.5	**2001**
304.7	312.8	323.7	316.9	319.1	347.2	**2002**
354.8	375.6	388.0	386.3	398.4	416.3	**2003**
391.4	407.3	415.7	425.6	453.4	435.6	**2004**
429.0	433.3	473.3	470.8	495.7	513.0	**2005**
632.5	623.5	599.3	603.8	646.7	632.0	**2006**
665.5	672.0	743.0	789.5	783.5	833.8	**2007**
918.0	833.0	884.5	730.8	814.5	869.8	**2008**
939.0	955.5	995.8	1040.0	1175.8	1087.5	**2009**
1169.0	1246.0	1307.0	1346.8	1383.5	1405.5	**2010**
1628.5	1813.5	1620.0	1722.0	1746.0	1531.0	**2011**
1622.0	1648.5	1776.0	1719.0	1726.0	1657.5	**2012**

FOREIGN EXCHANGE

FOREIGN EXCHANGE

US DOLLAR vs CDN DOLLAR MONTHLY AVG. VALUES*

	JAN		FEB		MAR		APR		MAY		JUN	
	US / CDN	CDN / US	US / CDN	CDN / US	US / CDN	CDN /US	US / CDN	CDN / US	US / CDN	CDN / US	US / CDN	CDN / US
1971	1.01	0.99	1.01	0.99	1.01	0.99	1.01	0.99	1.01	0.99	1.02	0.98
1972	1.01	0.99	1.00	1.00	1.00	1.00	1.00	1.00	0.99	1.01	0.98	1.02
1973	1.00	1.00	1.00	1.00	1.00	1.00	1.00	1.00	1.00	1.00	1.00	1.00
1974	0.99	1.01	0.98	1.02	0.97	1.03	0.97	1.03	0.96	1.04	0.97	1.03
1975	0.99	1.01	1.00	1.00	1.00	1.00	1.01	0.99	1.03	0.97	1.03	0.97
1976	1.01	0.99	0.99	1.01	0.99	1.01	0.98	1.02	0.98	1.02	0.97	1.03
1977	1.01	0.99	1.03	0.97	1.05	0.95	1.05	0.95	1.05	0.95	1.06	0.95
1978	1.10	0.91	1.11	0.90	1.13	0.89	1.14	0.88	1.12	0.89	1.12	0.89
1979	1.19	0.84	1.20	0.84	1.17	0.85	1.15	0.87	1.16	0.87	1.17	0.85
1980	1.16	0.86	1.16	0.87	1.17	0.85	1.19	0.84	1.17	0.85	1.15	0.87
1981	1.19	0.84	1.20	0.83	1.19	0.84	1.19	0.84	1.20	0.83	1.20	0.83
1982	1.19	0.84	1.21	0.82	1.22	0.82	1.23	0.82	1.23	0.81	1.28	0.78
1983	1.23	0.81	1.23	0.81	1.23	0.82	1.23	0.81	1.23	0.81	1.23	0.81
1984	1.25	0.80	1.25	0.80	1.27	0.79	1.28	0.78	1.29	0.77	1.30	0.77
1985	1.32	0.76	1.35	0.74	1.38	0.72	1.37	0.73	1.38	0.73	1.37	0.73
1986	1.41	0.71	1.40	0.71	1.40	0.71	1.39	0.72	1.38	0.73	1.39	0.72
1987	1.36	0.73	1.33	0.75	1.32	0.76	1.32	0.76	1.34	0.75	1.34	0.75
1988	1.29	0.78	1.27	0.79	1.25	0.80	1.24	0.81	1.24	0.81	1.22	0.82
1989	1.19	0.84	1.19	0.84	1.20	0.84	1.19	0.84	1.19	0.84	1.20	0.83
1990	1.17	0.85	1.20	0.84	1.18	0.85	1.16	0.86	1.17	0.85	1.17	0.85
1991	1.16	0.87	1.15	0.87	1.16	0.86	1.15	0.87	1.15	0.87	1.14	0.87
1992	1.16	0.86	1.18	0.85	1.19	0.84	1.19	0.84	1.20	0.83	1.20	0.84
1993	1.28	0.78	1.26	0.79	1.25	0.80	1.26	0.79	1.27	0.79	1.28	0.78
1994	1.32	0.76	1.34	0.74	1.36	0.73	1.38	0.72	1.38	0.72	1.38	0.72
1995	1.41	0.71	1.40	0.71	1.41	0.71	1.38	0.73	1.36	0.73	1.38	0.73
1996	1.37	0.73	1.38	0.73	1.37	0.73	1.36	0.74	1.37	0.73	1.37	0.73
1997	1.35	0.74	1.36	0.74	1.37	0.73	1.39	0.72	1.38	0.72	1.38	0.72
1998	1.44	0.69	1.43	0.70	1.42	0.71	1.43	0.70	1.45	0.69	1.47	0.68
1999	1.52	0.66	1.50	0.67	1.52	0.66	1.49	0.67	1.46	0.68	1.47	0.68
2000	1.45	0.69	1.45	0.69	1.46	0.68	1.47	0.68	1.50	0.67	1.48	0.68
2001	1.50	0.67	1.52	0.66	1.56	0.64	1.56	0.64	1.54	0.65	1.52	0.66
2002	1.60	0.63	1.60	0.63	1.59	0.63	1.58	0.63	1.55	0.65	1.53	0.65
2003	1.54	0.65	1.51	0.66	1.48	0.68	1.46	0.69	1.38	0.72	1.35	0.74
2004	1.30	0.77	1.33	0.75	1.33	0.75	1.34	0.75	1.38	0.73	1.36	0.74
2005	1.22	0.82	1.24	0.81	1.22	0.82	1.24	0.81	1.26	0.80	1.24	0.81
2006	1.16	0.86	1.15	0.87	1.16	0.86	1.14	0.87	1.11	0.90	1.11	0.90
2007	1.18	0.85	1.17	0.85	1.17	0.86	1.14	0.88	1.10	0.91	1.07	0.94
2008	1.01	0.99	1.00	1.00	1.00	1.00	1.01	0.99	1.00	1.00	1.02	0.98
2009	1.22	0.82	1.25	0.80	1.26	0.79	1.22	0.82	1.15	0.87	1.13	0.89
2010	1.04	0.96	1.06	0.95	1.02	0.98	1.01	0.99	1.04	0.96	1.04	0.96
2011	0.99	1.01	0.99	1.01	0.98	1.02	0.96	1.04	0.97	1.03	0.98	1.02
2012	1.01	0.99	1.00	1.00	0.99	1.01	0.99	1.01	1.01	0.99	1.03	0.97

Source: Federal Reserve: Avg of daily rates, noon buying rates in New York City for cable transfers payable in foreign currencies

US DOLLAR vs CDN DOLLAR MONTHLY AVG. VALUES

FOREIGN EXCHANGE

JUL		AUG		SEP		OCT		NOV		DEC		
US / CDN	CDN / US	US / CDN	CDN / US	US / CDN	CDN / US	US / CDN	CDN / US	US / CDN	CDN / US	US / CDN	CDN / US	
1.02	0.98	1.01	0.99	1.01	0.99	1.00	1.00	1.00	1.00	1.00	1.00	**1971**
0.98	1.02	0.98	1.02	0.98	1.02	0.98	1.02	0.99	1.01	1.00	1.00	**1972**
1.00	1.00	1.00	1.00	1.01	0.99	1.00	1.00	1.00	1.00	1.00	1.00	**1973**
0.98	1.02	0.98	1.02	0.99	1.01	0.98	1.02	0.99	1.01	0.99	1.01	**1974**
1.03	0.97	1.04	0.97	1.03	0.97	1.03	0.98	1.01	0.99	1.01	0.99	**1975**
0.97	1.03	0.99	1.01	0.98	1.03	0.97	1.03	0.99	1.01	1.02	0.98	**1976**
1.06	0.94	1.08	0.93	1.07	0.93	1.10	0.91	1.11	0.90	1.10	0.91	**1977**
1.12	0.89	1.14	0.88	1.17	0.86	1.18	0.85	1.17	0.85	1.18	0.85	**1978**
1.16	0.86	1.17	0.85	1.17	0.86	1.18	0.85	1.18	0.85	1.17	0.85	**1979**
1.15	0.87	1.16	0.86	1.16	0.86	1.17	0.86	1.19	0.84	1.20	0.84	**1980**
1.21	0.83	1.22	0.82	1.20	0.83	1.20	0.83	1.19	0.84	1.19	0.84	**1981**
1.27	0.79	1.25	0.80	1.23	0.81	1.23	0.81	1.23	0.82	1.24	0.81	**1982**
1.23	0.81	1.23	0.81	1.23	0.81	1.23	0.81	1.24	0.81	1.25	0.80	**1983**
1.32	0.76	1.30	0.77	1.31	0.76	1.32	0.76	1.32	0.76	1.32	0.76	**1984**
1.35	0.74	1.36	0.74	1.37	0.73	1.37	0.73	1.38	0.73	1.40	0.72	**1985**
1.38	0.72	1.39	0.72	1.39	0.72	1.39	0.72	1.39	0.72	1.38	0.72	**1986**
1.33	0.75	1.33	0.75	1.32	0.76	1.31	0.76	1.32	0.76	1.31	0.76	**1987**
1.21	0.83	1.22	0.82	1.23	0.82	1.21	0.83	1.22	0.82	1.20	0.84	**1988**
1.19	0.84	1.18	0.85	1.18	0.85	1.17	0.85	1.17	0.85	1.16	0.86	**1989**
1.16	0.86	1.14	0.87	1.16	0.86	1.16	0.86	1.16	0.86	1.16	0.86	**1990**
1.15	0.87	1.15	0.87	1.14	0.88	1.13	0.89	1.13	0.88	1.15	0.87	**1991**
1.19	0.84	1.19	0.84	1.22	0.82	1.25	0.80	1.27	0.79	1.27	0.79	**1992**
1.28	0.78	1.31	0.76	1.32	0.76	1.33	0.75	1.32	0.76	1.33	0.75	**1993**
1.38	0.72	1.38	0.73	1.35	0.74	1.35	0.74	1.36	0.73	1.39	0.72	**1994**
1.36	0.73	1.36	0.74	1.35	0.74	1.35	0.74	1.35	0.74	1.37	0.73	**1995**
1.37	0.73	1.37	0.73	1.37	0.73	1.35	0.74	1.34	0.75	1.36	0.73	**1996**
1.38	0.73	1.39	0.72	1.39	0.72	1.39	0.72	1.41	0.71	1.43	0.70	**1997**
1.49	0.67	1.53	0.65	1.52	0.66	1.55	0.65	1.54	0.65	1.54	0.65	**1998**
1.49	0.67	1.49	0.67	1.48	0.68	1.48	0.68	1.47	0.68	1.47	0.68	**1999**
1.48	0.68	1.48	0.67	1.49	0.67	1.51	0.66	1.54	0.65	1.52	0.66	**2000**
1.53	0.65	1.54	0.65	1.57	0.64	1.57	0.64	1.59	0.63	1.58	0.63	**2001**
1.55	0.65	1.57	0.64	1.58	0.63	1.58	0.63	1.57	0.64	1.56	0.64	**2002**
1.38	0.72	1.40	0.72	1.36	0.73	1.32	0.76	1.31	0.76	1.31	0.76	**2003**
1.32	0.76	1.31	0.76	1.29	0.78	1.25	0.80	1.20	0.84	1.22	0.82	**2004**
1.22	0.82	1.20	0.83	1.18	0.85	1.18	0.85	1.18	0.85	1.16	0.86	**2005**
1.13	0.89	1.12	0.89	1.12	0.90	1.13	0.89	1.14	0.88	1.15	0.87	**2006**
1.05	0.95	1.06	0.95	1.03	0.97	0.98	1.03	0.97	1.03	1.00	1.00	**2007**
1.01	0.99	1.05	0.95	1.06	0.95	1.18	0.84	1.22	0.82	1.23	0.81	**2008**
1.12	0.89	1.09	0.92	1.08	0.92	1.05	0.95	1.06	0.94	1.05	0.95	**2009**
1.04	0.96	1.04	0.96	1.03	0.97	1.02	0.98	1.01	0.99	1.01	0.99	**2010**
0.96	1.05	0.98	1.02	1.00	1.00	1.02	0.98	1.02	0.98	1.02	0.98	**2011**
1.01	0.99	0.99	1.01	.098	1.02	0.99	1.01	1.00	1.00	0.99	1.01	**2012**

FOREIGN EXCHANGE

U.S. DOLLAR vs EURO MONTHLY AVG. VALUES

	JAN		FEB		MAR		APR		MAY		JUN	
	EUR / US	US / EUR	EUR / US	US / EUR	EUR / US	US / EUR	EUR / US	US / EUR	EUR / US	US / EUR	EUR / US	US / EUR
1999	1.16	0.86	1.12	0.89	1.09	0.92	1.07	0.93	1.06	0.94	1.04	0.96
2000	1.01	0.99	0.98	1.02	0.96	1.04	0.94	1.06	0.91	1.10	0.95	1.05
2001	0.94	1.07	0.92	1.09	0.91	1.10	0.89	1.12	0.88	1.14	0.85	1.17
2002	0.88	1.13	0.87	1.15	0.88	1.14	0.89	1.13	0.92	1.09	0.96	1.05
2003	1.06	0.94	1.08	0.93	1.08	0.93	1.09	0.92	1.16	0.87	1.17	0.86
2004	1.26	0.79	1.26	0.79	1.23	0.82	1.20	0.83	1.20	0.83	1.21	0.82
2005	1.31	0.76	1.30	0.77	1.32	0.76	1.29	0.77	1.27	0.79	1.22	0.82
2006	1.21	0.82	1.19	0.84	1.20	0.83	1.23	0.81	1.28	0.78	1.27	0.79
2007	1.30	0.77	1.31	0.76	1.32	0.75	1.35	0.74	1.35	0.74	1.34	0.75
2008	1.47	0.68	1.48	0.68	1.55	0.64	1.58	0.63	1.56	0.64	1.56	0.64
2009	1.32	0.76	1.28	0.78	1.31	0.77	1.32	0.76	1.36	0.73	1.40	0.71
2010	1.43	0.70	1.37	0.73	1.36	0.74	1.34	0.75	1.26	0.80	1.22	0.82
2011	1.34	0.75	1.37	0.73	1.40	0.71	1.45	0.69	1.43	0.70	1.44	0.69
2012	1.29	0.77	1.32	0.76	1.32	0.76	1.32	0.76	1.28	0.78	1.25	0.80

Source: Federal Reserve: Avg of daily rates, noon buying rates in New York City for cable transfers payable in foreign currencies

US DOLLAR vs EURO MONTHLY AVG. VALUES

JUL		AUG		SEP		OCT		NOV		DEC		
EUR / US	US / EUR	EUR / US	US / EUR	EUR / US	US / EUR	EUR / US	US / EUR	EUR / US	US / EUR	EUR / US	US / EUR	
1.04	0.96	1.06	0.94	1.05	0.95	1.07	0.93	1.03	0.97	1.01	0.99	**1999**
0.94	1.07	0.90	1.11	0.87	1.15	0.85	1.17	0.86	1.17	0.90	1.11	**2000**
0.86	1.16	0.90	1.11	0.91	1.10	0.91	1.10	0.89	1.13	0.89	1.12	**2001**
0.99	1.01	0.98	1.02	0.98	1.02	0.98	1.02	1.00	1.00	1.02	0.98	**2002**
1.14	0.88	1.12	0.90	1.13	0.89	1.17	0.85	1.17	0.85	1.23	0.81	**2003**
1.23	0.82	1.22	0.82	1.22	0.82	1.25	0.80	1.30	0.77	1.34	0.75	**2004**
1.20	0.83	1.23	0.81	1.22	0.82	1.20	0.83	1.18	0.85	1.19	0.84	**2005**
1.27	0.79	1.28	0.78	1.27	0.79	1.26	0.79	1.29	0.78	1.32	0.76	**2006**
1.37	0.73	1.36	0.73	1.39	0.72	1.42	0.70	1.47	0.68	1.46	0.69	**2007**
1.58	0.63	1.50	0.67	1.43	0.70	1.33	0.75	1.27	0.78	1.35	0.74	**2008**
1.41	0.71	1.43	0.70	1.46	0.69	1.48	0.67	1.49	0.67	1.46	0.69	**2009**
1.28	0.78	1.29	0.78	1.31	0.76	1.39	0.72	1.37	0.73	1.32	0.76	**2010**
1.43	0.70	1.43	0.70	1.37	0.73	1.37	0.73	1.36	0.74	1.32	0.76	**2011**
1.23	0.81	1.24	0.81	1.29	0.78	1.30	0.77	1.28	0.78	1.31	0.76	**2012**